Praise for *The Marne*

"Herwig creates order out of overlapping events and makes vivid the full tragedy of the Marne set in motion." —*The Wall Street Journal*

"New sources allowed Herwig to write this important new book about the Battle of Marne, the first clash of World War One—then known as the Great War—a conflict that turned a page in military warfare. . . . Herwig paints a vivid portrait."
—Steve Goddard's History Wire

"Herwig excels at moving beyond the strategy sessions and onto the front line, painting vivid pictures of the sickening stench, chaos, and senseless violence of a war in which thousands of lives were sometimes lost within minutes." —*Shepherd Express*

"Holger H. Herwig adds new and enlightening information regarding the beginnings of WWI. . . . A must read for war historians."
—*The Paramus Post*

"As fine an addition to scholarly World War I literature as been seen in some time." —*Booklist*

"[An] engrossing narrative . . . Herwig combines colorful evocations of the horrors of fighting with a lucid operational history of the campaign." —*Publishers Weekly*

THE MARNE, 1914

RANDOM HOUSE TRADE PAPERBACKS

NEW YORK

The
MARNE,
1914

The Opening of

World War I and the Battle That

Changed the World

Holger H. Herwig

Published in the United States by Random House Trade Paperbacks,
an imprint of The Random House Publishing Group,
a division of Random House, Inc., New York.

RANDOM HOUSE TRADE PAPERBACKS and colophon are trademarks
of Random House, Inc.

Originally published in hardcover in the United States by Random House,
an imprint of The Random House Publishing Group,
a division of Random House, Inc., in 2009.

All photographs from the
George Grantham Bain Collection (Library of Congress)

LIBRARY OF CONGRESS CATALOGING-IN-PUBLICATION DATA
Herwig, Holger H.
The Marne, 1914: the opening of World War I and the
battle that changed the world / Holger H. Herwig.
p. cm.
Includes bibliographical information and index.
ISBN 978-0-8129-7829-2
1. Marne, first battle of the, France, 1914.   I. Title
D543.M3H477   2009   940.4'21—dc22   2009005687

Printed in the United States of America

www.atrandom.com

2 4 6 8 9 7 5 3

Book design by Barbara M. Bachman

For Jacob Linden Lawrence—my grandson

And in memory of Heinrich Herwig,
killed 22 March 1918 in Lorraine—my grandfather

Time connects our futures to our pasts

CONTENTS

———

LIST *of* MAPS

"A DRAMA NEVER SURPASSED"

———

Woe to him who sets Europe on fire,
who throws the match into the powder box!

—HELMUTH VON MOLTKE THE ELDER, MAY 1890

ON 2 AUGUST 1914, JUST A FEW HOURS BEFORE GERMAN TROOPS OC-cupied Luxembourg and thirty hours before war was declared between France and Germany, Lieutenant Albert Mayer of 5th Baden Mounted Jäger Regiment led a patrol of seven riders across a small ridge along the Allaine River near Joncherey, southeast of Belfort.[1] Suddenly, French guards of the 44th Infantry Regiment appeared. Mayer charged. He struck the first Frenchman over the head with his broadsword, causing him to roll into a roadside ditch. Another Jäger drove his lance into the chest of a second French soldier. A third Jäger shot Corporal Jules-André Peugeot, making him the first French casualty of the war. The remaining group of twenty French soldiers took cover in the ditch and opened fire on the German sharpshooters. Mayer tumbled out of the saddle, dead. In this unexpected manner, the twenty-two-year-old Jäger became the first German soldier killed in the war. And in this bizarre way, the first victim in what would collectively be called the Battle of the Marne.

THE MARNE WAS THE most significant land battle of the twentieth cen-tury. I made that claim nearly a decade ago in a special issue of *MHQ: The Quarterly Journal of Military History* dedicated to "Greatest Military Events of the Twentieth Century."[2] The research for this book has only reinforced that belief. In fact, I would argue that the Marne was the most decisive land battle since Waterloo (1815). First, the scale of the struggle was unheard of before 1914: France and Germany mobilized roughly two million men each, Britain some 130,000. During the momentous days between 5 and 11 September 1914, the two sides committed nearly two million men with six thousand guns to a desperate campaign along the Marne River on a front of just two hundred kilometers between the "horns of Verdun and Paris." Second, the technology of killing was unprecedented. Rapid small-arms fire, machine guns, hand grenades, 75mm and 77mm flat-trajectory guns, 150mm and 60-pounder heavy artillery, mammoth 305mm and 420mm howitzers, and even aircraft made the killing ground lethal. Third, the casualties ("wastage") suffered by both sides were unimaginable to prewar planners and civilian leaders alike: two hundred thousand men per side in the Battle of the Frontiers around the hills of Alsace-Lorraine and the Ardennes in August, followed by three hundred thousand along the chalky banks of the Marne in early September. No other year of the war compared to its first five months in terms of death. Fourth, the immediate impact of the draw on the Marne was spectacular: The great German assault on Paris had been halted, and the enemy driven behind the Aisne River. France was spared defeat and occupation. Germany was denied victory and hegemony over the Continent. Britain maintained its foothold on the Continent. Finally, the long-term repercussions of the Marne were tragic: It ushered in four more years of what the future German military historian Gerhard Ritter, a veteran of World War I, called the "monotonous mutual mass murder" of the trenches.[3] During that time, Britain and the empire sustained 3.5 million casualties, France 6 million, and Germany 7 million.* Without the Battle of the Marne, places such as Passchendaele, the Somme, Verdun, and Ypres would not resonate with us as they do. Without the Battle of the Marne, most likely no Hitler; no Horthy; no Lenin; no Stalin.

The Marne was high drama. The Germans gambled all on a brilliant operational concept devised by Chief of the General Staff Alfred von Schlieffen in 1905 and carried out (in revised form) by his successor, Helmuth von Moltke the Younger, in 1914: a lightning forty-day wheel through Belgium and northern France ending in a victorious

---

* Estimates by the U.S. War Department.

entry march into Paris, followed by a redeployment of German armies to the east to halt the Russian steamroller. It was a single roll of the dice. There was no fallback, no Plan B. Speed was critical; delay was death. Every available soldier, active or reserve, was deployed from the first day of mobilization. The sounds and sights of two million men trudging across Belgium and northeastern France with their kit, guns, and horses in sweltering thirty-degree-Celsius heat, stifling humidity, and suffocating dust was stunning, and frightening. Tens of thousands of soldiers fell by the wayside due to exhaustion, heatstroke, blisters, thirst, hunger, and typhus. Others collapsed with gastroenteritis after devouring the half-ripe fruits in the orchards they passed. Will Irwin, an American journalist observing the German "gray machine of death" marching across Belgium, reported on something he had never heard mentioned in any book on war—"the smell of a half-million un-bathed men. . . . That smell lay for days over every town."[4]

Still, hundreds of thousands pushed on, a ragged and emaciated gray mass buoyed by the "short-war illusion" that the decisive battle was just around the next bend in the road. The home front waited anx-iously for victory bulletins. Newspapers vied with one another for any scrap of news or rumor from the front. The atmosphere was electric—in Berlin, in Paris, and in London. Winston S. Churchill, looking back on 1914, opined: "No part of the Great War compares in interest with its opening." The "measured, silent drawing together of gigantic forces," the uncertainty of their deployment and engagement, and the fickle role of chance "made the first collision a drama never surpassed." Never again would battle be waged "on so grand a scale." Never again would the slaughter "be so swift or the stakes so high."[5] It is hard to argue with Churchill.

The Marne has lost none of its fascination. The famous "taxis of the Marne," the six hundred Renault cabs that rushed some three thousand men of French 7th Infantry Division to the Ourcq River in time to "save" Paris from Alexander von Kluck's First Army, remain dear to every tourist who has bravely ventured forth in a Parisian taxi-cab. Joseph Galliéni, the military governor of the Paris Entrenched Camp, whose idea it was to use the taxis, remains in the popular mind the brilliant strategist who appreciated the significance of Kluck's turn southeast before Paris, and who rallied the capital's forces as well as French Sixth Army to deprive the Germans of victory.

Books on the Marne abound. A keyword search of the catalog of the Library of Congress shows ten thousand titles. A similar perusal of the Google website brings up 174,000 hits. Most of these works are from the British and French perspective. They deal with virtually every aspect of the Battle of the Marne, from the company to the corps level, from the human to the material dimension. Bitter disputes still rage over "reputations"[6]—from those of French chief of staff Joseph Joffre to his British counterpart, Sir John French, and from General Charles Lanrezac of French Fifth Army to Sir Douglas Haig of British I Corps. No stone is left unturned in this never-ending war of ink.

This book is different. For the first time, the Battle of the Marne is analyzed from the perspective of those who initiated it: the seven German armies that invaded Belgium and France. There was no "German army" before August 1914. Thus, the story is told on the basis of what was a massive research effort in the archives of the various German federal contingents: Baden XIV Army Corps fighting in Alsace, Bavarian Sixth Army and Württemberg XIII Corps deployed in Lorraine, Saxon Third Army struggling in the Ardennes, and Prussian First, Second, and Fifth armies advancing in an arc from Antwerp to Verdun. The collapse of the German Democratic Republic in 1989–90 proved to be a boon for researchers: It gave me access to the records of Saxon Third Army at Dresden, and to roughly three thousand Prussian army files long thought destroyed by Allied air raids in 1945, but returned to Potsdam by the Soviet Union in 1988 and now housed at Freiburg. These allow a fresh and revealing look at the Marne.

This book raises a fundamental question: Was it truly the "Battle of the Marne"? The campaign in the west in 1914, as illustrated by Lieutenant Albert Mayer's death in the Vosges, was an extended series of battles that raged from the Swiss border to the Belgian coast. During its initial phase, commonly referred to as the Battle of the Frontiers, major operations took place in Alsace, Lorraine, Belgium, the Ardennes, and the Argonne. Each is an integral part of the larger Battle of the Marne. In many ways, what is generally called the First Battle of the Marne*—the bloody campaigns of German First, Second, and Third armies against French Fifth, Sixth, and Ninth armies and the

---

* There was to be a second in the early summer of 1918.

British Expeditionary Force (BEF) between Paris and Verdun from 5 to 11 September—was but the final act in this great drama. Even then, the critical, desperate battles of German First Army and French Sixth Army took place along the Ourcq River and not the Marne. Still, when it came time for the victor to name the battle, French chief of staff Joffre chose *Marne* mainly because most of the rivers in the region of decisive struggle—Ourcq, Grand Morin, Petit Morin, Saulz, and Ornain—all flowed into the Marne.[7]

The titanic clash of vast armies over an extended 480-kilometer front, then, was not one battle at all. Rather, in the words of Sewell Tyng, a distinguished historian of the Marne, it consisted of "a series of engagements fought simultaneously by army corps, divisions, brigades, and even battalions, for the most part independently of any central control and independently of the conduct of adjacent units."[8] Hence, the story is told from the perspective of individual units in separate theaters. These range from the cadets of France's Saint-Cyr Military Academy advancing on Altkirch, in Alsace, in full-dress uniform to the desperate struggle of German First Army's hundred thousand grimy and grisly warriors marching to the very outskirts of Paris.

The face of battle in each of these theaters is reconstructed on the basis of the diaries and letters of "common soldiers" on both sides, French *poilus* and German *Landser*. The much-neglected story of German atrocities committed in Belgium and Lorraine from fear of attack by enemy irregulars (francs-tireurs) likewise is rendered on the basis of the official reports, diaries, and letters of German unit commanders and soldiers in the field. The Bavarian archives reveal the horror of the atrocities at Nomeny, Gerbéviller, and Lunéville, while the Saxon archives help sort out the terrible days when Third Army stormed Dinant. In the process, many of the victims' reports as well as much of the Allied wartime propaganda are reevaluated.

Obviously, the Battle of the Marne did not end the war. Nor did it suddenly and irrevocably halt the war of maneuver envisioned by all sides before 1914. To be sure, many historians have argued that the Marne brought a formal end to maneuver warfare and that the military commanders thereafter callously accepted an inevitable and indeterminate war of attrition. This simply is a *post facto* construction. On the Allied side, General Joffre and Field Marshal French saw the Battle of the Marne first as a radical reversal of the Allies' "Great Retreat," and then as an opportunity to drive the Germans out of France and Belgium and to take the war into the heartland of the Second Reich. On the German side, Chief of the General Staff Helmuth von Moltke, First Army's Alexander von Kluck, Second Army's Karl von Bülow, and Lieutenant Colonel Richard Hentsch saw the withdrawal from the Marne as a temporary course correction, after which the drive on Paris would be renewed by refreshed and replenished armies. Only Wilhelm II, always prone to sudden mood swings, recognized the Marne as a defeat, as "*the* great turning point" in his life.[9]

Given its undisputed centrality in the history of World War I, the Battle of the Marne not surprisingly has raised many "what if?" questions and created myths and legends that have withstood almost a century of investigation. The greatest of these is the most obvious: What if the German operations plan had succeeded and Paris had fallen? The French government already had fled to Bordeaux. Civilians were rushing to train stations to evacuate the capital. And Kaiser Wilhelm II was not in a charitable mood. On the eve of the Battle of the Marne, when he learned that German Eighth Army had taken ninety-two thousand Russian prisoners of war during the Battle of Tannenberg, he suggested they be driven on to a barren peninsula at Courland along the Baltic shore and "starved to death."[10] The Marne, in fact, already was seen as a clash of civilizations, one pitting the German "ideas of 1914"—duty, order, justice—against the French "ideas of 1789"—liberty, fraternity, equality. Or, in Wilhelm II's simpler analogy, as a clash between "monarchy and democracy."[11]

On the basis of three decades of research on imperial Germany and World War I, I can state that the record on the implications of a German victory in 1914 is clear: The result would have been a German "condominium" over the Continent "for all imaginable time." The Low Countries would have become German vassal states, parts of northeastern France and its Channel coast would have come under Berlin's control, the countries between Scandinavia and Turkey would have been forced to join a German "economic union," and Russia would have been reduced to its borders under Peter the Great.[12] The British policy of the balance of power—that is, of not allowing any European hegemony to emerge—would have lain in tatters. The Battle of the Marne was consequential in blocking these developments. In the succinct words of General Jean-Jacques Senant, military commander of the French Army Archives at the Château de Vincennes, to an international gathering of scholars in 2004, "The Battle of the Marne saved France and the rest of Europe from German domination. . . . Indisputably, it is the first turning point of the war."[13]

As well, a host of lesser myths and legends enshrouded the Marne in Carl von Clausewitz's famous "fog of uncertainty" and refuse to disappear from the pages of contemporary accounts of the battle.[14] Some were simply propaganda designed for public consumption: the Kaiser's planned entry into Nancy sitting astride a white charger in the white dress uniform of the Guard Cuirassiers; the twenty-meter-long German flag specially made to fly from the top of the Eiffel Tower; the ten railroad cars loaded with commemorative medals for the fall of Paris that accompanied Kluck's First Army; and the twenty thousand Saxon soldiers who opted to be taken prisoner at the climax of the Battle of the Marne rather than to fight on. Others were the products of ambitious writers and mythmakers: General Édouard de Castelnau's alleged disobeying of Joffre's orders to abandon Nancy early in September (when the reverse was the case); General Ferdinand Foch's putative communiqué that while his position at the Saint-Gond Marshes was "impossible . . . I attack"; Joffre's reported command to his staff on the eve of the battle, accentuated by pounding his fist on the operations table, "Gentlemen, we shall fight it out on the Marne"; and General Maurice Sarrail's outrageous claim that he had refused Joffre's "order to abandon Verdun" and in the process assumed the title "Savior of Verdun."

Indeed, the Allies were not short on creating myths and legends of their own. On the British side of the ledger, there remains the legend that the BEF "discovered" the gap at the Marne between German First and Second armies; that it thereafter brilliantly "exploited" the gap; and that, in the process, it "saved" France. On the French side, there persists the myth of the putative *miracle de la Marne*.[15] For too long, this has served to obscure the fact that Joffre and his staff had not been the benefactors of a divine "miracle," but rather had brought about what Louis Muller, the chief of staff's orderly, called *"une victoire stratégique"* and *"un miracle mérite."*[16] This book will set the record straight.

Other myths were much more harmful, and again attest to the centrality of the Marne in the history of what was later called the Great War. Certainly, that of Richard Hentsch, a mere lieutenant colonel on the German General Staff, snatching victory from the hands of Generals von Kluck and von Bülow at the moment of certain triumph by ordering them to retreat behind the Marne was among the most damaging. It obscured for decades the truth behind the German retreat: a flawed command structure, an inadequate logistical system, an antiquated communications arm, and inept field commanders. In the verdict of the Germany official history of the war, *Der Weltkrieg 1914 bis 1918,* General von Bülow of Second Army had been hesitant and insecure; General von Kluck of First Army, overly aggressive and unwilling to adhere to commands; and Chief of Staff von Moltke, not up to the strains of command. "In the hour of decision over the future of the German people," the official historians concluded, "its leader on the field of battle completely broke down psychologically and physically."[17]

Perhaps most damaging, after the war numerous former commanders brought to the public the myth that the German armies had not been defeated in the field but rather denied victory by a "sinister conspiracy" on the part of Freemasons and Jews. Erich Ludendorff, the "victor" of the Battles of Tannenberg and the Masurian Lakes in 1914 and Germany's "silent dictator" from 1916 to 1918, championed this school. In postwar writings, such as *The Marne Drama,* he assured a defeated nation that the "secret forces of Freemasonry," the machinations of world Jewry, and the baleful influence of Rudolf Steiner's "occult" theosophy on General von Moltke's wife, Eliza, had combined forces against Germany.[18] Ludendorff's absurd claims, of course, helped to launch the infamous "stab-in-the-back" postwar legend. This book judges the performance of the German armies and their commanders at the Marne on the basis of official operational records rather than on mischievous mythmaking.

Fritz Fischer, arguably Germany's most famous historian of the latter half of the twentieth century, placed the Battle of the Marne squarely in the pantheon of that mythmaking. In 1974, he stated that in addition to the two best-known and most "highly explosive" German "moral-psychological complexes" arising from World War I—the "war-guilt question" of 1914 and the "stab-in-the-back legend" of 1918—there needed to be added a third: the Battle of the Marne. Or, better put, "the secret of the Marne," that is, the "defeat at the Marne 1914." From the moment that German troops stumbled back from the fateful river on 9 September, Fischer argues, first the government of Chancellor Theobald von Bethmann Hollweg and then the Army Supreme Command conspired "systematically to conceal" the enormity of the defeat from the public.[19] At the end of that twenty-year journey of deception and deceit lay another bid at redemption: World War II.

THE MARNE, 1914

CHAPTER ONE

WAR: "NOW OR NEVER"

War is . . . an act of force to compel our enemy to do our will.

—CARL VON CLAUSEWITZ

"SINCE I HAVE BEEN AT THE FOREIGN OFFICE," ARTHUR NICOLSON noted at Whitehall in May 1914, "I have not seen such calm waters."[1] Europe had, in fact, refused to tear itself to pieces over troubles in far-away lands: Morocco in 1905–06 and in 1911; Bosnia-Herzegovina in 1908–09; Libya in 1911–12; and the Balkans in 1912–13. The Anglo-German naval arms race had subsided, as had the fears about the Berlin-to-Baghdad Railway, since Berlin had run out of money for such gargantuan enterprises. Russia had overcome its war with Japan (1904–05), albeit at a heavy price in terms of men and ships lost and domestic discontent. Few desolate strips of African or Asian lands remained to be contested, and Berlin and London were preparing to negotiate a "settlement" of the Portuguese colonies. France and Germany had not been at war for forty-three years and Britain and Russia for fifty-eight.

Partition of the Continent by 1907 into two nearly equal camps— the Triple Alliance of Austria-Hungary, Germany, and Italy, and the Triple Entente of Britain, France, and Russia—seemed to militate against metropolitan Europe being dragged into petty wars on its periphery. Kurt Riezler, foreign-policy adviser to German chancellor Theobald von Bethmann Hollweg, cagily argued that given this model of great-power balance, future wars "would no longer be fought but calculated."[2] Guns would no longer fire, "but have a voice in the negotiations." In other words, no power would risk escalating minor con-

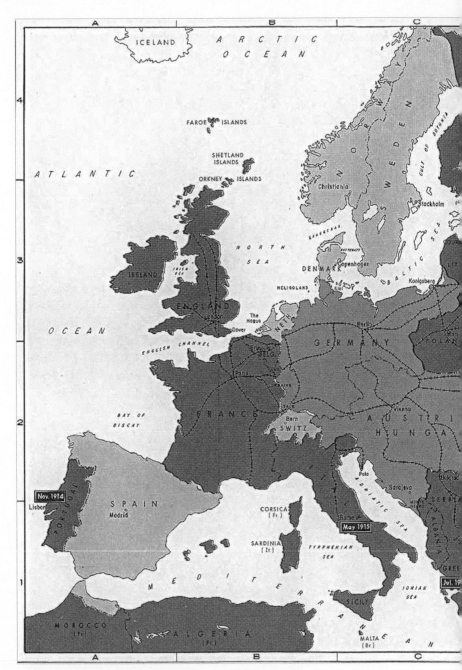

EUROPE, 1914, SHOWING MAJOR RAIL LINES

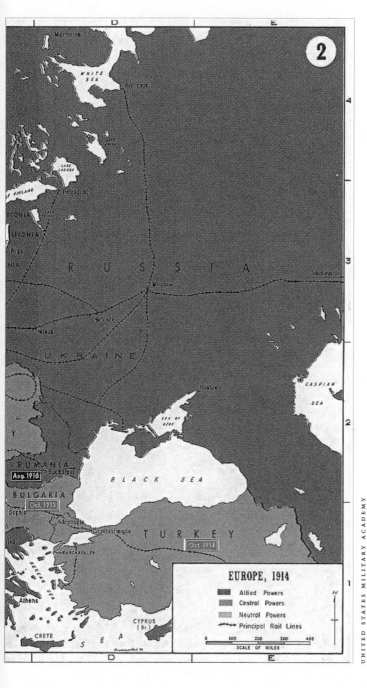

EUROPE, 1914

Allied Powers
Central Powers
Neutral Powers
Principal Rail Lines

SCALE OF MILES
0   100   200   300   400

flicts into a continental war; instead, each would "bluff" the adversary up the escalatory ladder, stopping just short of war in favor of diplomatic settlement. Peace seemed assured.

Domestically, for most well-off and law-abiding Europeans, the period prior to 1914 was a golden age of prosperity and decency. The "red specter" of Socialism had lost much of its threat. Real wages had shot up almost 50 percent between 1890 and 1913. Trade unions had largely won the right to collective bargaining, if not to striking, and their leaders sat in parliaments. Many workers had embraced social imperialism, believing that overseas trade and naval building translated into high-paying jobs at home. Germany had paved the path toward social welfare with state-sponsored health insurance, accident insurance, and old-age pensions. Others followed. Women were on the march for the vote. To be sure, there was trouble over Ireland, but then official London hardly viewed Ireland as a European matter.

Paris, as usual, was the exception. The capital had been seething with political excitement since January 1914, when Gaston Calmette, editor of *Le Figaro,* had launched a public campaign to discredit Finance Minister Joseph Caillaux—ostensibly over a new taxation bill.[3] When Calmette published several letters from Caillaux's personal correspondence, Henriette Caillaux became alarmed. First, that correspondence could make public her husband's pacifist stance vis-à-vis Germany during the Second Moroccan Crisis in 1911; second, she knew that it included love letters from her to Joseph that showed she had conducted an affair with him at a time when he was still married. The elegant Madame Caillaux took matters into her own hands: On 16 March she walked into Calmette's office, drew a revolver from her muff, and shot the editor four times at point-blank range. Her trial on charges of murder dominated Paris in the summer of 1914. Two shots fired by a Serbian youth at Sarajevo on 28 June paled in comparison.

Gavrilo Princip's murder of Archduke Franz Ferdinand, heir presumptive to the Habsburg throne, and his morganatic wife, Sophie Chotek, caused no immediate crisis in the major capitals. The dog days of summer were upon Europe. There ensued a mad rush to escape urban heat for cooler climes.[4] French president Raymond Poincaré and prime minister René Viviani were preparing to board the battleship *France* for a leisurely cruise through the Baltic Sea to meet Tsar Nicholas II at St. Petersburg. Kaiser Franz Joseph took the waters at Bad Ischl.

Wilhelm II was about to board the royal yacht *Hohenzollern* for his annual cruise of the Norwegian fjords. Chancellor Bethmann Hollweg was off to the family estate at Hohenfinow to play Beethoven on the grand piano and to read Plato (in the original Greek). Foreign Minister Gottlieb von Jagow saw no need to curtail his honeymoon at Lucerne.

Nor were military men much concerned. German chief of the General Staff Helmuth von Moltke struck out for Karlsbad, Bohemia, to meet his Austro-Hungarian counterpart, Franz Conrad von Hötzendorf. War Minister Erich von Falkenhayn was off to vacation in the East Frisian Islands. Navy Secretary Alfred von Tirpitz left Berlin for St. Blasien, in the Black Forest. Habsburg war minister Alexander von Krobatin took the cure at Bad Gastein.

Even the less prominent escaped the July heat. Sigmund and Martha Freud, like Moltke and Conrad, vacationed at Karlsbad. V. I. Lenin left Cracow to hike in the Tatra Mountains. Leon Trotsky took solace in a small apartment in the Vienna Woods. Adolf Hitler was back in Munich after a military court-martial at Salzburg had found the draft dodger unfit for military service ("too weak; incapable of bearing arms").[5]

But had the exodus of European leaders been all that innocent? Or had some deeper design lain at its root? The first move in what is popularly called the July Crisis rested with Vienna. Few in power lamented the passing of Franz Ferdinand. He was too Catholic; he detested the Czechs, Magyars, and Poles within the empire; and he distrusted the ally in Rome. But the spilling of royal blood demanded an official response.

FOR MORE THAN HALF a dozen years prior to 1914, Conrad von Hötzendorf had pressed war on his government as the only solution to the perceived decline of the multinational Austro-Hungarian Empire. Daily, the frail, thin, crew-cut chief of the General Staff had stood at his desk and drafted contingency war plans against "Austria's congenital foes" Italy and Serbia as well as against Albania, Montenegro, and Russia, or against combinations of these states. Each year, he had submitted them to Kaiser Franz Joseph and to Foreign Minister Aloys Lexa Count Aehrenthal. And each year, these two had steadfastly refused to act.

Why, then, was July 1914 different?[6] Conrad saw the murders at Sarajevo as a Serbian declaration of war. He cared little about the high

school lads who had carried out the plot and about the secret organization "Union or Death," or the "Black Hand," that had planned it; his
real enemy was Belgrade. He was determined not to let the last opportunity pass by "to settle accounts" with Serbia. He was haunted by the
empire's failure to use the annexationist crisis over Bosnia-Herzegovina
in 1908–09 to crush Serbian annexationist aspirations. There was also a
personal motive: He informed his mistress Virginie "Gina" von Rein-
inghaus that he was anxious to return from a war "crowned with success" so that he could "claim" her "as my dearest wife." Honor was at
stake as well. While the war might be a "hopeless struggle" against
overwhelming odds, Conrad informed Gina on the day of the Sarajevo
killings, it had to be fought "because such an ancient monarchy and
such an ancient army cannot perish ingloriously."[7] In a nutshell, Conrad's position in July 1914, in the words of the new foreign minister,
Leopold Count Berchtold, was simply: "War, war, war."[8]

By 1914, Franz Joseph shared Conrad's "war at any price" mind-set.
Serbian arrogance had to be rooted out, by force if necessary. The
kaiser was plagued by nightmares—of Solferino, where in 1859 he had
led Austrian armies to defeat at the hands of France and Piedmont-
Sardinia; and of Königgrätz, where in 1866 his forces had been routed
by those of King Wilhelm I of Prussia. Thus in July 1914, Franz Joseph
was prepared to draw the sword. Honor demanded no less. "If we must
go under," he confided to Conrad, "we better go under decently."[9]

That left the foreign minister. In the past, Berchtold, like Aehrenthal, had resisted Conrad's demands for war. But diplomacy had
brought no security. Thus, Berchtold, emboldened by the hard-line
stance of a small cohort of hawks at the Foreign Office, endorsed military measures. Just two days after the Sarajevo murders, he spoke of
the need for a *"final and fundamental reckoning"* with Serbia.[10] And he
worked out a set of assumptions to underpin his decision: Early and
decisive action by Berlin would deter possible Russian intervention
and "localize" the war in the Balkans.

But would Berlin play the role of gallant second? During past
Balkan crises, Wilhelm II and his advisers had refused to back Habsburg initiatives with military force. Would July 1914 confirm that pattern? Berchtold, knowing that he needed diplomatic and military
backing from Berlin, on 4 July dispatched Alexander Count Hoyos, his
chef de cabinet, to sound out what the German position would be in the

event that Vienna took actions to "eliminate" Serbia as a "political power factor in the Balkans."[11] It was a clever move, given the kaiser's well-known propensity for personal diplomacy. In meetings the next two days with Wilhelm II, Bethmann Hollweg, Falkenhayn, and Undersecretary of the Foreign Office Arthur Zimmermann, Hoyos and Habsburg ambassador László Count Szögyény-Marich obtained promises of "full German backing" for whatever action Vienna took against Belgrade. There was no time to lose. "The present situation," the kaiser noted, "is so favorable to us." Diplomats and soldiers "considered the question of Russian intervention and accepted the risk of a general war."[12] Austria-Hungary could count on "Germany's full support" even if "serious European complications"—war—resulted. And in the apparent interest of "localizing the war" in the Balkans, Berlin was ready to point to the soon-to-be-vacationing Wilhelm II, Moltke, and Falkenhayn as "evidence" that Germany would be "as surprised as the other powers" by any aggressive Austro-Hungarian action against Serbia.[13]

Having obtained what is often referred to as a blank check from Germany, Austria-Hungary was free to plot its actions. On 7 July, Berchtold convened a Common Council of Ministers at Vienna and apprised those present of Berlin's staunch support, "even though our operations against Serbia should bring about the great war."[14] War Minister von Krobatin favored war "now better than later." Austrian premier Karl Count Stürgkh demanded "a military reckoning with Serbia." Conrad von Hötzendorf as always was set on war. Only Hungarian premier István Tisza demurred. He desired no more Slavic subjects, given that his Magyars were already a minority within their half of the empire. And he feared that an attack on Serbia would bring on "the dreadful calamity of a European war." But within a week he joined the majority view—on condition that Belgrade be handed a stringent ultimatum that would allow Habsburg officials to enter Serbia to hunt down the assassins.

The final decision for war was made at a special Common Council of Ministers convened at Berchtold's residence on 19 July. It was quickly decided to hand the ultimatum, carefully crafted by the foreign minister's staff to assure rejection, to Belgrade on 23 July and to demand acceptance within forty-eight hours. The day after the Common Council, Berchtold advised Conrad and Krobatin to begin their planned summer holidays "to preserve the appearance that nothing is being planned."[15] Tisza's countryman István Count Burián laconically noted: "The wheel of history rolls."[16] Serbia rejected the ultimatum on 25 July. Sir Maurice de Bunsen, Britain's envoy to Vienna, informed Whitehall: "Vienna bursts into a frenzy of delight, vast crowds parading the streets and singing patriotic songs till the small hours of the morning."[17]

Berchtold visited Franz Joseph at Bad Ischl. He informed the kaiser that Serbian gunboats had fired on Habsburg troops near Temes-Kubin (Kovin). It was a lie, but it served its purpose. "Hollow eyed," the aged Franz Joseph signed the order for mobilization. His only recorded comment, delivered "in a muffled, choked voice," was *"Also, doch!"* ("So, after all!") Was it said in conviction? Or in relief? The next day, mobilization began and civil liberties were suspended. Vienna, in the words of historian Samuel R. Williamson Jr., "clearly initiated the violence in July 1914" and "plunged Europe into war."[18] It had set the tempo, defined the moves, and closed off all other options. In doing so, it was motivated by fear—of Pan-Slavic nationalism, of losing the military advantage to Serbia (and Russia), and of forfeiting Germany's promised support.

WHY WAR IN 1914? Why had Germany not drawn the sword during crises in 1905, 1908, 1911, 1912, or 1913? What made 1914 different? The answer lies in the seriousness of the Austro-Hungarian request for backing and in the changed mind-set at Berlin. First, a few myths need to be dispelled. Germany did not go to war in 1914 as part of a "grab for world power" as historian Fritz Fischer[19] argued in 1961, but rather to defend (and expand) the borders of 1871. Second, the decision for war was made in late July 1914 and not at a much-publicized "war council" at Potsdam on 8 December 1912.[20] Third, no one planned for a European war before 1914; the absence of financial or economic blueprints for such an eventuality speaks for itself. And Germany did not go to war with plans for continental hegemony; its infamous shopping list of war aims was not drawn up by Bethmann Hollweg[21] until 9 September, when French and German forces had squared off for their titanic encounter at the Marne River.

This having been said, Berlin issued Vienna the famous blank check on 5 July. Why? Neither treaty obligations nor military algebra demanded this offer. But civilian as well as military planners were dominated by a strike-now-better-than-later mentality. Time seemed to be running against them. Russia was launching its Big Program of rearmament, scheduled to be completed by 1917. Could one wait until then? Wilhelm II mused on the eve of the Sarajevo murders.[22] The Anglo-French-Russian Entente Cordiale encircled Germany with what it perceived to be an iron ring of enemies. More, there circulated in public and official circles dire prognostications of what Bethmann Hollweg summarized for the Reichstag in April 1913 as the "inevitable struggle" between Slavs and Teutons—what historian Wolfgang J. Mommsen called the classical rhetoric of "inevitable war."[23]

On 3 July, when Ambassador Heinrich von Tschirschky cabled Vienna's decision to avenge the Sarajevo killings, Wilhelm II noted "now or never" on the report.[24] Three days later, the kaiser promised Austria-Hungary "Germany's full support" even if "serious European complications" resulted from this—and advised Vienna not to "delay the action" against Belgrade. Pilloried in the press for having been too "timid" and for having postured like a "valiant chicken" during past crises, Wilhelm on 6 July three times assured his dinner guest, Gustav Krupp von Bohlen und Halbach, that this time he would not "cave in."

Bethmann Hollweg likewise adopted a belligerent stance.[25] Shortly after his meeting with the Austrians on 5 July, the chancellor informed Riezler that Russia "grows and grows and weighs on us like a nightmare." According to Hoyos, Bethmann Hollweg bluntly stated that "were war unavoidable, the present moment would be more advantageous than a later one." Two days later, the chancellor assured Vienna that he regarded a coup de main against Serbia to be the "best and most radical solution" to the Dual Monarchy's Balkan problems. For he had worked out a "calculated risk." If war came "from the east" and Germany entered it to preserve the Habsburg Empire, "then we have the prospect of winning it." If Russia remained idle, "then we have the prospect of having outmaneuvered the Entente in this matter." On 11 July, Bethmann Hollweg summarized his rationale for war: "A quick fait accompli and then friendly [stance] toward the Entente; then we can survive the shock." Whatever dark fate loomed over the Continent, the "Hamlet" of German politics was resigned to war. To have abandoned Austria-Hungary in July 1914, he wrote in his memoirs, would have been tantamount to "castration" on Germany's part.[26]

That left Moltke.[27] As early as 1911, he had informed the General Staff, "All are preparing themselves for the great war, which all sooner or later expect." One year later, he had pressed Wilhelm II for war with Russia, "and the sooner the better." During his meeting with Conrad von Hötzendorf at Karlsbad on 12 May 1914, Moltke had lectured his counterpart that "to wait any longer meant a diminishing of our chances." The "atmosphere was charged with a monstrous electrical tension," Moltke averred, and that "demanded to be discharged."[28] Two months before the Sarajevo tragedy, he had confided to Foreign Secretary von Jagow that "there was no alternative but to fight a preventive war so as to beat the enemy while we could still emerge fairly well from the struggle." To be sure, Moltke feared what he called a "horrible war," a "world war," one in which the "European cultural states" would "mutually tear themselves to pieces," and one "that will destroy civilization in almost all of Europe for decades to come."[29] But he saw no alternative. On 29 July, he counseled Wilhelm II that the Reich would "never hit it again so well as we do now with France's and Russia's expansion of their armies incomplete."

How was the decision for war reached? The gravity of the moment hit Berlin with full force after Vienna handed Belgrade its ultimatum on 23 July—and Prime Minister Nikola Pašić rejected it two days later. This greatly alarmed leaders in St. Petersburg, who felt that Austria-Hungary with this move was threatening Russia's standing as a great power and who believed that they needed to show solidarity with the "little Slavic brother," Serbia, to show resolve. On 29–30 July, Berlin learned first of Russia's partial mobilization and then of its general mobilization. War Minister von Falkenhayn truncated his holidays on 24 July and rushed back to the capital. Austria-Hungary, he quickly deduced, "simply wants the final reckoning" with Serbia. Moltke returned from Karlsbad two days later. Wilhelm II left the fjords of Norway and was back in Berlin by 27 July. He hastily convened an ad hoc war council. Falkenhayn tersely summed up its result: "It has now been decided to fight the matter through, regardless of the cost."[30]

What historian Stig Förster has described as the bureaucratic chaos of the imperial system of government[31] was fully in evidence in Berlin as the July Crisis entered its most critical stage. Bethmann Hollweg was in a panic to pass responsibility for the coming "European conflagration" on to Russia, and he drafted several telegrams for "Willy" to fire off to his cousin "Nicky," calling on Tsar Nicholas II to halt Russian mobilization—to no avail. Moltke and Falkenhayn raced in staff cars between Berlin and Potsdam. At times, they demanded that Wilhelm II and Bethmann Hollweg declare a state of "pre-mobilization"; at other times, they counseled against it. The chancellor conferred with the generals throughout 29 July. Moltke first lined up with the hawk Falkenhayn and pushed for the immediate declaration of a "threatening state of danger of war"; then he sided with Bethmann Hollweg and urged restraint. The chancellor sat on the fence, now supporting Falkenhayn, now Moltke, prevaricating on the issue of mobilization. At one point, he even dashed off a missive to Vienna asking its armies to "halt in Belgrade."

In fact, Bethmann Hollweg was waiting for the right moment to play his trump card. Shortly before midnight on 29 July, he called Ambassador Sir Edward Goschen to his residence and made him an offer: If Britain remained neutral in the coming war, Germany would offer London a neutrality pact, guarantee the independence of the Netherlands, and promise not to undertake "territorial gains at the expense of France."[32] Goschen was flabbergasted by what he called the chancellor's "astounding proposals"; a livid Sir Edward Grey, secretary of state for foreign affairs, called them "shameful." With that, Bethmann Hollweg ruefully informed the Prussian Ministry of State the next day that "the hope for England [was now] zero."[33]

Bethmann Hollweg withdrew behind a veil of fatalism. "All governments," he moaned, had "lost control" over the July Crisis. Europe was rushing headlong down the steep slope to war. "The stone has begun to roll."[34] The night of 30 July, at Moltke's insistence, the chancellor agreed to institute a state of emergency, the precondition for mobilization.

Around 2 PM on 31 July, Wilhelm II ordered the government to issue a decree stating that a "threatening state of danger of war" existed. Falkenhayn rushed to the palace through cheering crowds to sign the decree and to record the high drama. "Thereupon the Kaiser shook my hand for a long time; tears stood in both of our eyes."[35] The decision brought relief and joy to official Berlin.[36] The strain and stress of the past few days lay behind. At the Chancellery, Bethmann Hollweg, ever the pessimist, worried about what he termed a "leap into the dark," but concluded that it was his "solemn duty" to undertake it. At the Navy Cabinet, Admiral Georg Alexander von Müller crowed: "The mood is brilliant. The government has managed brilliantly to make us appear the attacked." At the General Staff, Moltke detected "an atmosphere of happiness." At the Prussian War Office, Bavarian military plenipotentiary Karl von Wenninger noted "beaming faces, shaking of hands in the corridors; one congratulates one's self for having taken the hurdle." Berlin was about "to begin the most serious, bloody business that the world has ever seen." Wenninger took "malicious delight" while riding in the Grunewald to note that "the army would soon expropriate the superb steeds of the city's wealthy Jews."[37]

Wilhelm II signed the order for general mobilization at 5 PM on 1 August—in the Star Chamber of the Neues Palais at Potsdam, on the desk made from the planking of Horatio Nelson's flagship HMS *Victory*, a present from his grandmother Queen-Empress Victoria. Cousins "Nicholas and Georgie," he informed his inner circle, "have played me false! If my grandmother had been alive, she would never have allowed it."[38] Champagne was served to celebrate the momentous moment.

But all had not gone as smoothly as the mere recitation of events would indicate. Late on the afternoon of 1 August, Moltke headed back to Berlin after the kaiser had signed the mobilization order. He was ordered to return to the Neues Palais at once. An important dispatch had arrived from Karl Prince von Lichnowsky in London: Grey had assured the ambassador that London would "assume the obligation" of keeping Paris out of the war if Germany did not attack France. "Jubilant mood," the chief of the General Staff noted.[39] An ecstatic Wilhelm II redirected Moltke, "Thus we simply assemble our entire army in the east!" Moltke was thunderstruck. The deployment of an army of millions could not simply be "improvised," he reminded the kaiser. The *Aufmarschplan* represented the labor of many years; radically overturning it at the last minute would result in the "ragged assembly" of a "wild heap of disorderly armed men" along the Russian frontier. In a highly agitated state, Wilhelm II shot back: "Your uncle [Moltke the Elder] would have given me a different answer."

The evening ended with a desultory debate as to whether 16th Infantry Division (ID), the first-day vanguard of the Schlieffen-Moltke assault in the west, should immediately cross into Luxembourg. Moltke insisted that it should to prevent the French from seizing Luxembourg's vital rail marshaling points. Bethmann Hollweg demanded that they be held back to give Lichnowsky time to seal the deal with Britain. Wilhelm II ordered the 16th to stand down. "Completely broken" by this open humiliation, Moltke feared that the kaiser was still clinging to hopes for peace. "I console Moltke," Falkenhayn devilishly wrote in his diary.[40] In fact, Moltke arrived home that night a "broken" man. His wife, Eliza, was shocked at his appearance, "blue and red in the face" and "unable to speak." "I want to conduct war against the French and the Russians," Moltke muttered, "but not against such a Kaiser." She believed that he suffered a "light stroke" that night. The tension of the day finally broke forth in a torrent of "tears of despair."[41] When Gerhard Tappen, chief of operations, presented him with the order to keep 16th ID on German soil, Moltke refused to sign the document.

Then another bolt out of the blue: At 11 PM, Moltke was ordered to return to Potsdam. The kaiser, already in a nightgown, informed him that King-Emperor George V had just cabled that he was unaware of the Lichnowsky-Grey discussion and that the matter rested on a misunderstanding. Wilhelm II dismissed Moltke. "Now you can do what you wish." Moltke ordered 16th ID to cross into Luxembourg.

It was an inauspicious start. The Younger Moltke had never wanted to measure himself against his great-uncle, the architect of Otto von Bismarck's wars of unification. The kaiser's acid comment concerning the Elder Moltke's possible "different answer" had unnerved him. One can only wonder if, on that 1 August 1914, his mind did not wander back to Königgrätz, where on 3 July 1866, during a critical part of the battle, Bismarck had held out a box of cigars to the Elder Moltke to test his nerves: Helmuth Karl Bernhard von Moltke had passed the test by picking the Iron Chancellor's best Cuban.

FRENCH DECISIONS MADE DURING the July Crisis, in the words of historian Eugenia C. Kiesling, "mattered rather little." For whatever course Paris took, "France would be dragged into an unwanted war."[42] In the face of the frenetic diplomatic actions at Vienna, Berlin, and St. Petersburg, French policy makers in July 1914 were content to make no decision at all. Most were interested merely in making sure that Paris was not seen as pursuing an aggressive policy, one that could possibly encourage war. In President Poincaré's well-chosen words, "It is better to have war declared on us."[43]

But this does not mean that France was without a policy in 1914. France had sketched out a secret military alliance with Russia in 1892. Formally signed by Nicholas II two years later, it called on each side to assist the other "immediately and simultaneously" if attacked by Germany—France with 1.3 million and Russia with 800,000 men.[44] Thus, even to discuss the matter of support for Russia during the July Crisis risked arousing suspicions concerning French reliability. If Paris as much as hinted that it had a "free hand" in shaping its course of action, then this would imply the same for St. Petersburg. Neither side, of course, was willing to jeopardize Europe's only firm military alliance.

The main issue concerns the French diplomatic mission to Russia. At 5 AM on 16 July, President Poincaré, Premier Viviani, and Pierre de Margerie, political director of the French Foreign Ministry, boarded the battleship *France* at Dunkirk. They shaped a course for the Baltic Sea to conduct state visits to Russia and to the Scandinavian countries. Was it "design" or "accident"?[45] Was it sheer lack of responsibility, given the escalating crisis over the murders at Sarajevo and the certain but still undetermined Austro-Hungarian response? Was it a gross miscalculation, given that radio transmission was still in its infancy? And just what did French leaders hope to accomplish in St. Petersburg? Whatever the case, they had intentionally isolated themselves from the decision-making process.

It was an uneasy voyage. Poincaré, shocked at the degree of naïveté exhibited by his premier concerning foreign policy, spent the days at sea lecturing Viviani on European statecraft. Viviani, for his part, was preoccupied by what bombshells might be revealed at the Caillaux trial—and by the whereabouts of his mistress from the Comédie française. On 20 July, the French delegation boarded the imperial yacht *Alexandria* in Kronstadt Harbor and set off for discussions at the Peterhof. The talks continued at the Winter Palace, in the capital, where massive strikes reminded the French visitors of the fragility of the tsar's empire. No formal record of the discussions has ever been found.

Through interception and decryption of Austro-Hungarian diplomatic telegrams by the Russian Foreign Ministry's code breakers, French and Russian leaders became aware that Vienna was planning a major action against Serbia. But they hardly needed such clandestine information: On 21 July, the Habsburg ambassador to Russia, Friedrich Count Szápáry, informed the French president that Austria-

Hungary was planning "action" against Belgrade. Poincaré's blunt warning that Serbia "has some very warm friends in the Russian people," that Russia "has an ally France," and that "plenty of complications" were to be "feared" from any unilateral Austrian action against Serbia[46] apparently fell on deaf ears. For on 23 July, after having made sure that the French had departed Kronstadt, Vienna delivered its ultimatum to Belgrade.

Poincaré received word of the ultimatum on board the *France* the next day. From Stockholm, he set course for Copenhagen, where on 27 July he received several cables urging him to return to Paris at once. He complied—after sending off a telegram to Russian foreign minister Sergei Sazonov assuring him that France was "ready in the interests of the general peace wholeheartedly to second the action of the Imperial Government."[47] French ambassador Maurice Paléologue unofficially assured Sazonov of "the complete readiness of France to fulfill her obligations as an ally in case of necessity."[48]

Poincaré, Viviani, and Margerie landed at Dunkirk on Wednesday, 29 July. The president, fearing what he termed Viviani's "hesitant and pusillanimous" character, at once assumed control of foreign affairs. But by then, events had already spun out of his control. On 28 July, Austria-Hungary had declared war on Serbia, and the next day its river monitors shelled Belgrade. Two days later, Russia posted red mobilization notices (*ukases*) in St. Petersburg. Poincaré called a meeting of the Council of Ministers for the morning of 30 July to assess the situation. While no minutes of the meeting were kept, Abel Ferry, undersecretary of state for foreign affairs, committed the main points of the "impressive cabinet" to his diary. "For the sake of public opinion, let the Germans put themselves in the wrong." There was no panic among the group of "solemn" ministers. "Cabinet calm, serious, ordered." For the time being, there was little to be done. "Do not stop Russian mobilization," Ferry summed up. "Mobilize, but do not concentrate."[49] At the army's insistence, War Minister Adolphe Messimy agreed to establish the *couverture,* or frontier-covering force, but demanded that it be kept ten kilometers from the frontier to avoid any unintentional contact with the Germans.

On 31 July, Germany declared a state of "imminent danger of war" to exist, and at 6 PM the next day declared war on Russia. On 2 August, as previously noted, Lieutenant Albert Mayer's Jäger regiment violated

French territory at Joncherey. Under the pretext that French airplanes had bombed railways at Karlsruhe and Nürnberg—a claim that the Prussian ambassador at Munich, Georg von Treutler, immediately informed Berlin could not be substantiated—Germany declared war on France at 6:45 PM on 3 August. To Poincaré's great relief, Rome had announced on 31 July that it considered Vienna's attack on Serbia to be an act of aggression and hence did not bind it to act on behalf of the Triple Alliance.

Poincaré, who as a child had witnessed the German occupation of Bar-le-Duc, in Lorraine, carried France through the July Crisis with "firmness, resolve and confidence."[50] France appeared to the world as the victim of German aggression. Domestic unity had been maintained. The Russian alliance had been honored. Despite the eternal cry of *la patrie en danger* and the sporadic looting of German shops in Paris, the president demanded calm and maintained control. On 2 August, he signed the proclamation that a state of emergency existed. The next evening, he again spelled out to his cabinet his "satisfaction" that Germany, and not France, had made the move toward war. "It had been indispensable," he stated, "that Germany should be led into publicly confessing her intentions." He allowed himself only one misstep—"at last we could release the cry, until now smothered in our breasts: *Vive l'Alsace Lorraine*"*—but at the urging of several ministers omitted that xenophobic phrase from his message to Parliament two days later.[51]

The German declaration of war against France on 3 August spared the Senate and the Chamber of Deputies from having to debate—and much less to approve—a formal declaration of war. That left War Minister Messimy free to compile a "wish list" of war aims: Germany was to lose Alsace-Lorraine, the Saar, and the west bank of the Rhine, thereby greatly reducing its territory. France thus defined its war-aims program a month before Bethmann Hollweg did likewise for Germany.

Poincaré next proclaimed a *union sacrée* ("No, there are no more parties"); it met with near-universal acceptance. The famous declaration of a newfound "sacred union" was in fact read by Minister of Justice Jean-Baptiste Bienvenu-Martin in the Senate and by Prime Minister Viviani in the Chamber of Deputies, since the president did not have

---

* A reference to the two provinces of Alsace and Lorraine, hotly disputed between France and Germany.

the right to address those bodies directly. Then Poincaré silenced critics who feared that Britain would remain aloof from the continental madness about to take place. London, he assured his colleagues, would join the war. "The English are slow to decide, methodical, reflective, but they know where they are going."[52]

BRITAIN'S LEADERS WERE CONCERNED first and foremost with the security of the empire. Continental Europe was far removed from their innermost concerns. In early July 1914, Whitehall was busily redrafting terms of the entente with Russia. Britain's security lay in the power of the Royal Navy and in its geographical separation from the Continent. Its army was small and trained to deploy "east of Suez." London was beset by what historian Paul Kennedy has famously called "imperial overstretch,"[53] that is, with mustering the power required to maintain the greatest empire since the days of Rome—and concurrently to meet the industrial and naval challenges of up-and-comers such as Germany, Japan, and the United States. As well, the Liberal government of Prime Minister Herbert Henry Asquith had come to power to undertake a sweeping program of social reforms, and it faced daunting challenges at home with regard to Irish Home Rule, labor unrest, and women's suffrage. Not surprisingly, then, the double murders at Sarajevo initially hardly registered at Whitehall. Surely, Europe could survive a possible third Balkan war.

State Secretary Grey was slow to appreciate the potential danger of the Balkan situation. His mind was on his upcoming vacation, to flyfish for stippled trout in the river Itchen. His critics later charged him with failing to avoid a European war owing to his timidity, his studied aloofness, and his failure to inform Berlin that London would not allow it to invade France unpunished.[54] David Lloyd George after the war spoke of Grey in the July Crisis as "a pilot whose hand trembled in the palsy of apprehension, unable to grip the levers and manipulate them with a firm and clear purpose."[55] At the Foreign Office, Sir Eyre Crowe simply called Grey "a futile useless weak fool."[56]

He was none of these. He appreciated the Austro-German threat. He was determined to stand by France and Russia. Belgium's "perpetual" neutrality, guaranteed by the great powers by 1839, was to Grey neither a "legal" nor a "contractual" matter, but rather a power-political calculation. He played for time. He urged caution on the involved parties. He offered four-power mediation. Above all, he was uncertain of how the cabinet would react to war over Sarajevo.

Three events rudely interrupted Grey's insouciance—the tenor of the Austro-Hungarian ultimatum ("the most formidable document I have ever seen addressed by one state to another that was independent") delivered at Belgrade on 23 July; Berlin's rejection of his offer of mediation by the less interested powers on 28 July; and Russia's partial mobilization of the military districts of Odessa, Kiev, Moscow, and Kazan the following day. Still, when Grey on 29 July suggested to the cabinet that defense of Belgium and France lay in Britain's vital interest, the majority rejected this view and, in president of the Board of Trade John Burns's famous words, "decided not to decide."[57]

Although the cabinet kept no formal records of its minutes and votes, historian Keith Wilson has argued that its nineteen members by 1 August fell into three unequal groups: The largest, led by Asquith, was undecided; a smaller middle group of about five demanded an immediate declaration of British neutrality; and only Grey and First Lord of the Admiralty Winston S. Churchill ("the naval war will be cheap") favored intervention on the Continent.[58] Grey was thus in a weak position. A good deal of it was due to his secretiveness. For years, he had studiously avoided formal discussion of whether a German attack on France would involve Britain's vital security interests. In what historian Elie Halévy has called "an ignorance whose true name was connivance,"[59] he had declined even a cursory mention in cabinet of the fact that in 1911 he had, quite on his own, authorized "military conversations" with the French General Staff.

Nor was Asquith more forthcoming. Foreign policy, after all, was Grey's bailiwick. While the prime minister feared that Vienna's ultimatum to Belgrade might lead to war between France and Germany and/or between Austria-Hungary and Russia—"a real Armageddon"—he nevertheless saw "no reason why we should be more than spectators." Ten days later, he shared with the socialite Venetia Stanley his firm conviction that Britain had "no obligations of any kind either to France or Russia to give them military or naval help," and that it was "out of the question" at this time (2 August) to "dispatch" any "Expeditionary Forces" to France.[60] An astute politician, Asquith had taken stock of the deep divisions within the cabinet over the issue of a "continental commitment." As late as 2 August, he estimated that "a good 3/4 of our own

[Liberal] party in the H[ouse] of Commons are for absolute non-interference at any price."[61]

But Asquith was also plagued by fear of German domination of the Continent. France was a "long-standing and intimate" friend. Belgium counted on Britain to "prevent her being utilized and absorbed by Germany." In terms of naked realpolitik, Britain could not "allow Germany to use the Channel as a hostile base." It was not in the nation's "interests that France should be wiped out as a Great Power."[62] And how would the country react to a Liberal government that jettisoned the hallowed principle of the balance of power, whereby Britain since the days of Louis XIV had formed coalitions to deny all hegemonic aspirations on the Continent? Yet if he opted for military deployment in Europe, would the substantial stubborn group of ministers that refused to countenance intervention in France bring down his government? And how would even a *perceived* refusal as part of the Triple Entente to stand up against Germany play in Paris? French ambassador Paul Cambon reported the British conundrum to his government, wondering whether the word *honor* had been "struck out of the English vocabulary."[63] Finally, if Asquith did not back Grey, would the state secretary's certain resignation bring down the government? "No more distressing moment can ever face a British government," historian Barbara Tuchman cheekily remarked, "than that which requires it to come to a hard and fast and specific decision."[64]

Germany saved Grey and Asquith from their dilemma. During the evening of Sunday, 1 August, news arrived in London that Germany had declared war on Russia and that Germany and France had begun to mobilize their armies. Obviously, whatever war was in the offing could no longer be "localized" in the Balkans. On the morning of 3 August, Belgium rejected the German ultimatum of the previous day to permit its troops unfettered passage through the country. "Poor little Belgium" was later given out as the decisive "moral issue" on which Grey and Asquith rallied the country. Put differently, German violation of Belgian neutrality spared the cabinet what promised to be an unpleasant debate: whether war on the side of France was in Britain's vital interests. But according to historian Wilson, "poor little Belgium" hardly figured in most of Asquith's and Grey's deliberations.

The cabinet in London "never did make a decision for war." The only decisions taken by Asquith's ministers were "either to resign (two), or to resign and retract (two) or to remain in office (the rest)."[65] The Unionist opposition, led by Andrew Bonar Law and Lord Lansdowne, let it be known that it would support a policy of intervention on behalf of France and Russia—unqualified by any reference to Belgium. Thus emboldened, Grey put his cards on the table at two cabinet meetings on 2 August. "Outraged" that Berlin had spurned his offer of mediation and "marched steadily towards war,"[66] he demanded that the country come to the aid of Belgium and France. He declined to inform the ministers that Ambassador von Lichnowsky that morning had assured him that Germany would not invade France if Britain remained neutral.

The confusion that still gripped much of official London as late as 2 August can be gleaned from a telephone call that Field Marshal Sir John French made to Chancellor of the Exchequer Lloyd George and Sir George Riddell of the Newspaper Proprietors' Association as they dined with Labour Party leader Ramsay MacDonald. "Can you tell me, old chap," French queried Riddell, "whether we are going to be in this war? If so, are we going to put an army on the Continent, and, if we are, who is going to command it?"[67] Resolution came after Riddell conferred with Lloyd George. Britain would be in the war; it would send an army to the Continent; and French would command it.

Grey carried his case in the cabinet, largely it seems, through intervention from an unlikely source: Herbert Samuel, president of the Local Government Board, who argued that the cabinet needed to hold together in the face of the German threat.[68] When news arrived that evening that Germany had invaded Luxembourg, the dice were cast: Grey was instructed to inform the House of Commons the next day that a German invasion of Belgium would constitute the casus belli. An antiwar demonstration that day in Trafalgar Square drew only a thin crowd. The bankers in The City alone were opposed to war, fearing that a European war would cause the collapse of the foreign exchange.

At 3 PM on 3 August, Grey, "pale, haggard and worn," addressed a packed House of Commons. He asked its members to ponder whether it would be in the nation's interests for France to be "in a struggle of life and death, beaten to her knees . . . subordinate to the power of one greater than herself?" The "whole of the West of Europe," he went on, could fall "under the domination of a single Power." Britain's "moral position," if it stood by and allowed Germany to subjugate Belgium and France, would be "such as have lost us all respect."[69] The House accorded him enthusiastic applause.

The next day, the cabinet learned that Germany had invaded Belgium. A British ultimatum that Berlin withdraw its troops at once, set to expire at midnight German time, went without reply. As Big Ben struck 11 PM, Britain declared war on Germany. While Grey is best remembered for his memorable comment that "the lamps" were "going out all over Europe" and that "we shall not see them lit again in our life-time,"[70] more revealing for his rationale in urging war was his comment that Britain would suffer hardly more if it went to war with Germany than if it stayed out. For Grey had adopted the conviction of fellow interventionist Churchill that what was about to come would only be a "short, cleansing thunderstorm," after which it would be "business as usual."

If any further moral position was required, it was provided by Bethmann Hollweg's comment that the 1839 accord, which guaranteed Belgium's neutrality, was but "a scrap of paper," and by his Machiavellian pronouncement in the Reichstag on 4 August that "necessity knows no law."[71] Apparently, no one in Berlin remembered Bismarck's dire warning that a German invasion of Belgium or the Low Countries would constitute "complete idiocy," as it would immediately bring Britain into such a war.[72]

In the end, historian Wilson has argued,[73] the decision for war resulted from a combination of factors: Grey's determination to resign if Britain did not opt for war; Asquith's "determination to follow Grey"; Samuel's ability to rally the cabinet behind Grey and Asquith; Bonar Law's and Lord Lansdowne's timely support for intervention; and the slowness and dysfunction of the noninterventionists in making their case stick. As well, fear of German domination of the Continent, and with it France's Channel and Atlantic ports, played its role in convincing the Asquith government that it lay in its best interests to uphold the territorial integrity of Belgium and France.

To sum up, decision-making coteries in Vienna, St. Petersburg, Berlin, Paris, and London carefully assessed their situations, weighed their options, calculated the risks, and then decided that war lay in the national interests. These coteries saw their states to be in decline or at least to be seriously threatened. To check that perceived decline and threat, they felt the recourse to arms to be imperative. There was no "unexpected slide" into "the boiling cauldron of war," as David Lloyd George would later famously claim. The major powers had not simply "glided, or rather staggered and stumbled" into the conflict, had not "slithered over the brink into the boiling cauldron of war without any trace of apprehension or dismay."[74] Instead, strategic considerations had been paramount in their deliberations.

BRITISH POET RUPERT BROOKE's words about "a world grown old and cold and weary" in many ways summarize the much-debated "spirit of 1914." For, whatever their arguments about the level and the location of war "enthusiasm" in 1914, historians largely agree that the generation of 1914 had grown "cold and weary" of their flaccid times. The "foul peace" (Conrad von Hötzendorf) that Bismarck had imposed on Europe with his *pax Germanica* was much resented.[75] The young in Germany especially were bored by the endless palaver of their fathers and grandfathers at beer halls and wine taverns about their glorious deeds in the wars of 1866 and 1870. Many had taken refuge in youth groups, where they retreated into a mystical past replete with hikes, campfires, guitars, chansons, and medieval castles. July 1914 offered action, chivalry, dash, and daring—in short, relief from boredom and a chance to create their own legends and myths.

The war would be short. Statesmen such as Churchill in Britain, Poincaré in France, and Ottokar Count Czernin in Austria-Hungary used the image of a "thunderstorm" to convey the prevailing mood. Somewhere in northeast France or Russian Poland, there would take place the decisive Armageddon. Few cared for the past dire warnings of outsiders such as the Polish financier Ivan S. Bloch and the German Socialist Friedrich Engels that future wars would be "world wars" that could easily last three or four years. Engels had predicted that armies of "eight to ten million soldiers" would be engaged in such a "world war," and that they would "decimate Europe as no swarm of locusts ever did," ending with "famine, pestilence, and the general barbarization of both armies and peoples."[76]

Thus, the young volunteered for war. While German published estimates of between 1.3 and 2 million volunteers were grossly exaggerated, military lists revealed a total of 185,000 accepted in 1914.[77] Unfortunately, we know little about their motivation. Fortunately, Paul Plaut of the Institute for Applied Psychology at Potsdam realized a research opportunity and sent his staff out into the streets to canvass the volunteers.[78] Most allowed that they saw the war as a chance for adventure and action, as an escape from the dreariness of everyday life. Many stated that they were fulfilling their civic "duty"; or defending home and hearth (*Heimat*) against the foreign threat; or wanting just to be "part of it," not to miss what they vaguely perceived to be a great historical moment. Some joined up to prove their "patriotism," others their "manliness." Only a few offered hatred of the enemy (except "perfidious Albion") as a reason for enlisting. The minute it got wind of Plaut's activities, the Prussian army ended the polling.

The literary elite, as always, left their impressions for future generations.[79] In Germany, the novelist Thomas Mann, "tired, sick and tired" of Bismarck's uninspiring peace, saw the war as "a purification, a liberation, an enormous hope." His colleague Hermann Hesse was delighted that his countrymen would finally be "torn out of a capitalistic peace" and uplifted by war to a "higher" moral value. The sociologist Max Weber opined that "*regardless* of the outcome—this war is great and wonderful." The economist Johann Plenge contrasted the German "ideas of 1914"—duty, order, justice—with the French "ideas of 1789"—liberty, fraternity, equality. Gertrud Bäumer of the Federation of German Women's Associations called on her sisters to put their demands for greater equality aside during the war: "We are the *Volk*." Perhaps best remembered by the next generation was the reaction to the news of war by Adolf Hitler, who volunteered for the Bavarian army. "The war liberated me from the painful feelings of my youth," he later wrote in *Mein Kampf*. "I fell down on my knees and thanked heaven with an overflowing heart for granting me the good fortune to be alive at this time."[80] Another Habsburg citizen, Franz Kafka, was of a more sober mind-set: The war, he noted, had above all been "caused by a tremendous lack of imagination."[81]

Nor was war enthusiasm absent in France.[82] On 28 July, the capital was rocked by the sensational news that Madame Caillaux had been acquitted of the murder of Gaston Calmette. Many of France's best-selling newspapers, such as *Le Temps, Le Petit Parisien,* and *L'Echo de Paris,* devoted twice the coverage to the Caillaux trial as they did to the mounting European crisis. Yet when Poincaré and Viviani returned to the capital, they were received by ecstatic crowds chanting, *"Vive la France."* Soon those chants changed to *"Vive l'armée."*

Britain, in fact, became the first country in which the coming of the war was cheered in the streets even before the cabinet had decided on a "continental commitment." The third of August was the traditional Bank Holiday Monday. It was a delightfully sunny day. There was drink and entertainment. The next afternoon, as the ministers drove to Parliament to deliver the declaration of war against Germany, they were hailed lustily by what the prime minister called "cheering crowds of loafers & holiday makers."[83] General Sir William Birdwood, secretary to the government of India in the Army Department, no doubt spoke for many when, a few months into the war, he recalled: "What a real piece of luck this war has been as regards Ireland—just averted a Civil War and when it is over we may all be tired of fighting."[84]

In a country without a tradition of conscription, young men rallied to the colors: 8,193 British men in the first week of August, 43,354 in the second, and 49,982 in the third.[85] Most came from the commercial and professional classes, far fewer from the agricultural sector. "Urban civic pride" came to the fore as 224 so-called Pals battalions—made up of friends linked mainly by educational, professional, and recreational ties—were raised locally. Few had any idea of the realities of modern warfare.

Historians have questioned the war euphoria of August 1914.[86] Unsurprisingly, Germans and Frenchmen alike viewed the coming of war not as a monolithic, robotic, nationalist bloc, but rather on the basis of their age, class, gender, and locale.[87] By and large, war enthusiasm was a product of the educated and professional classes in urban centers. It was driven primarily by students and clerks—and by army and government officials. There were few workers among these crowds. There were more males than females. The enthusiasm came slowly. At first, the crowds that gathered at the Quai d'Orsay in Paris and the Wilhelmstrasse in Berlin numbered only in the hundreds, rarely in the thousands. Even at the height of the putative euphoria, the crowd in Berlin reached only thirty thousand, less than 1 percent of the capital's population. Beyond Berlin, the crowds in cities such as Cologne, Frankfurt, Hamburg, Leipzig, Munich, and Nürnberg were perhaps a thousand each.

Observers noted the prevalence of drink among students and a carnival-like atmosphere. But after Austria-Hungary's declaration of war against Serbia on 28 July, the public mood became somber, then fatalistic, and finally fearful. Hoarding of food and other essential items became commonplace. Small middle-class investors, mostly women, made a run on the banks, afraid that their savings would soon disappear. Employment levels in major cities plummeted anywhere between 24 and 70 percent as Europe began to retool from consumer to war materials production.[88] Stories of spies caused near panic. Prussian soldiers in "strange" army uniforms were mistakenly arrested in Nürnberg; Bavarians with "strange accents" in Cologne. In Munich, news reverberated that "several Slavs" had been captured and shot while trying to blow up the army's ammunition dump at Schleißheim; spies "dressed as nuns" had supposedly tried to dynamite railway bridges; and Russians "dressed up as ladies" apparently had been arrested at the main train station.[89] There were also reports of French bombs falling on Nürnberg, flour and water wells poisoned in Strasbourg, Russian spies in Berlin disguised as doctors and nurses, and eighty million francs bound for Russia seized at Stuttgart.[90] Especially, rumors of spies in automobiles laden with gold refused to go away. In London, the Metropolitan Police had received almost nine thousand reports of enemy aliens at work; Frederick Lord Roberts estimated their number at eighty thousand.

Not all crowds marched for war. Antiwar demonstrations, in fact, outnumbered those demanding defense of the *Vaterland* or *la patrie*. On the day Vienna declared war on Belgrade, the Social Democratic Party (SPD) in Berlin turned out a hundred thousand antiwar protesters. By 31 July, there had taken place 288 antiwar demonstrations throughout Germany, involving some 750,000 people in 183 cities and villages.[91] In Paris, Socialists and Syndicalists mounted seventy-nine demonstrations against the war. But in the end, all 110 SPD Reichstag deputies voted for war credits, as did all 98 Socialist deputies in Paris. Party solidarity and patriotism counted for more than Socialist rhetoric.

The countryside by and large remained calm. The July Crisis found the agricultural sector at a critical stage. Grain and legume fields were maturing, as were fruit orchards and vineyards. Soon, armies of farm laborers would hasten to bring in the produce before the sudden arrival of fall rains. War would mean the conscription of young male labor needed in the villages; the loss of secure urban markets; the requisitioning by the army of hundreds of thousands of horses and wagons; and the likely imposition of price controls. For France, historian Jean-Jacques Becker's analysis of six rural departments showed that 16 percent of the population received news of mobilization favorably, 23 percent with nonchalance, and 61 percent with reserve.[92]

The military in France and Germany established control of the domestic agenda. In France, a decree concerning the "state of siege" was signed on 2 August. It gave the military sweeping powers to appoint judges and subprefects, and to control the press and the telephone system. Anxious to keep politicians from interfering in military operations, the newly constituted Grand quartier général (French military headquarters) also denied the government access to the war fronts. Parliament was prorogued on 3 August. In Germany, Wilhelm II on 1 August declared from the balcony of the City Castle in Berlin, "I no longer know parties, or confessions; today we are all German brothers, and only German brothers."[93] This so-called *Burgfrieden* did not, however, prevent the resurrection of the Prussian Law of Siege of June 1851. It gave the deputy commanding generals of the Reich's twenty-five military corps districts powers over recruitment, labor distribution, and the food supply, as well as dissemination of news and information.

It is perhaps safe to say that once mobilization was declared, most people felt a sense of pride and patriotism, exuberance and curiosity, fear and desperation. The war, so long predicted, was finally at hand. Reservists, who had some inkling of what was to come, largely were apprehensive. Wilhelm Schulin, with 29th ID in Württemberg, on 1 August recorded "incredible tension" among the people of his native Öhringen, which quickly turned to "something horribly heavy, dark, a depressing burden" as the troop transports headed for the front.[94] Martin Nestler at Chemnitz noted that the reservists of Saxon 12th Jäger "wept" as they reported for duty.[95] Still, adventure was in the offing. Sergeant Marc Bloch of French 272d Regiment arrived at Paris's Gare de Lyon in the "oppressive dog-day heat" of early August full of hope and of pride. "Behold the dawn of the month of August 1914!"[96] Within days, he would rue the "terrible and hidden meaning" of those joyous words.

Military leaders took a more philosophical stance once mobilization had been announced. General Hubert Lyautey, a future war minister, saw a brighter future for France "because the politicians have shut up." Some of his colleagues were delighted that "the Whore," the republic, would now have to yield to the dictates of "military secrecy." Others crowed that "the prefects are finished, the deputies don't matter, the generals can feed on civilian flesh." Abel Ferry at the Foreign Office detected a sense of restoration of the Old France afoot. "Clericalism has donned uniform," he wrote, "to make war on the Republic."[97]

In Berlin, General von Moltke was pleased that the strain and stress of recent days were a thing of the past. "There was . . . an atmosphere of happiness." Crown Prince Wilhelm, the designated commander of Fifth Army, looked forward to a "fresh and jolly" (*frisch und fröhlich*) campaign. Lieutenant Colonel Wilhelm Groener, the mastermind of the Reich's railway mobilization, cheerily wrote his wife that the time had come to deal "not only with the French" but also with Chancellor von Bethmann Hollweg and "the rubbish at the Foreign Office."[98] War Minister von Falkenhayn perhaps best summed up the feelings of many senior commanders in Berlin in his diary on 1 August: "Even if we go under as a result of this, still it was beautiful."[99]

CHAPTER TWO

"LET SLIP THE DOGS OF WAR"

When you mobilize the army and form strategic plans,
you must be unfathomable.

—SUN-TZU

NO WAR PLAN BROUGHT ABOUT WHAT THE DIPLOMAT GEORGE F. Kennan called *"the* great seminal catastrophe" of the twentieth century.[1] No war plan had been formally adopted by any government, and no war plans (except for France and Russia) had been coordinated. No government in reaching its decision to "let slip the dogs of war" in 1914 referred even in passing to an inexorable timetable drafted by military leaders that demanded a *decision* for war. Instead, as argued in the previous chapter, civilian leaders weighed their options, assessed their chances, considered the alternatives, and then opted for war. Only thereafter did deployment plans take center stage. In short, no "military doomsday machine," as Henry Kissinger once put it, drove Europe's leaders "into the vortex" in 1914.[2]

And yet, the German deployment plan of 1914—named after Alfred Count von Schlieffen, chief of the General Staff from 1891 to 1905—remains the one plan most people are likely to recall when asked about military planning. For the "Schlieffen Plan" has become synonymous with militarism run amok, with operational considerations trumping statecraft, and with the rote mechanics of war replacing the art of war. Since Germany went to war in 1914 with the (revised) Schlieffen Plan, and since much of the debate about the Battle of the Marne revolves around whether the plan, if properly carried out, could have brought Germany victory as prescribed by Schlieffen, both the man and his plan deserve attention.

ALFRED VON SCHLIEFFEN WAS born at Berlin on 28 February 1833 into the junior branch of a family that had settled at Kolberg, in Pomerania, in the fourteenth century. His father's side had a long tradition of military service. His mother's side was devoutly Hutterian Pietist, believing in the Godhead of the Father, the Son, and the Holy Spirit; in trine baptism (hence their popular name, Dunkers); and in the infallibility of the New Testament. Thus, the boy's upbringing was a mixture of traditional Prussian virtues such as austerity, discipline, duty, and order, and Hutterian values including dignity, modesty, respect, and a firm belief in the presence of God in history.[3] After a brief stint studying law, Alfred opted for a career with the cavalry. He attended the War Academy from 1858 to 1861, and then along with his three brothers saw action during the decisive Battle of Königgrätz in the Austro-Prussian War (1866), followed by combat in the Franco-Prussian War (1870–71) at Toul and Soissons as well as during the winter campaign along the Loire River. After the Wars of German Unification, Schlieffen served as commander of the prestigious 1st Guard Ulan Regiment at Potsdam from 1876 until 1884, when he was appointed to the institution he would serve until retirement—the Great General Staff in Berlin.

Schlieffen arrived at the General Staff at a time of uncertainty. The Elder Helmuth von Moltke, architect of Prussia's wars with Austria and France, increasingly became alarmed about the newfound Reich's geographical position, wedged in between two "wing powers," France and Russia. The prospect of a two-front war in Central Europe caused Moltke to reassess the utility of using military power to resolve great-power tensions. "Germany dare not hope to free itself in a short time from the one enemy by a quick and successful offensive in the west," he ominously concluded, "in order thereafter to turn against another [enemy in the east]."[4] Put differently, Moltke came to believe that war was no longer an option for the Reich. He best expressed this view in his last speech in Parliament in May 1890: "The age of cabinet wars is behind us—now we have only peoples' wars." Industrial Europe, armed as never before, was capable of conducting wars "whose duration and ending cannot be gauged." He predicted future "Seven Years'

Wars, even Thirty Years' Wars." He ended his farewell address with a dire warning. "Woe to him who sets Europe on fire, who throws the match into the powder box!"[5]

Under Moltke, Schlieffen headed the crucial French Department within the Third Section of the General Staff. France remained the "hereditary enemy." From the perspective of Berlin, French statesmen and soldiers from Cardinal Richelieu to Louis XIV, from Napoleon I to Napoleon III, had used Central Europe as venue for the sport of kings—war. Louis XIV had "raped" the Rhenish Palatinate and annexed Alsace and Lorraine. Napoleon I had defeated and then occupied the 365 German states and forced many of them to join his war with Russia in 1812. Napoleon III had been determined in the 1860s to establish the Rhine as France's eastern border. After 1871, France repaid its reparations (imposed on a per-capita basis for what Napoleon I had extracted from Prussia after 1806) much faster than anticipated, and cries of "revenge" for 1870–71 reverberated in right-wing military, political, and public circles. From the perspective of Paris, German unification had destroyed the European "concert" established at Vienna in 1815, and had eroded France's preeminent great-power status. The Reich's rapidly expanding industrial output (double that of France) and its bourgeoning population base (twenty million more than France) threatened to create a continental hegemony.

Little love was lost between France and Germany. Each created what historian Michael E. Nolan has called an "inverted mirror" of the other, and in the process mythologized the "hereditary enemy." Each saw the other side not as individuals but rather as members of the opposite and hostile nation, "imbued with an elaborate baggage of history and heredity in the form of preconceived character traits representing a strange inversion of the observer's own perceived qualities."[6] This "inverted" mirror imaging did not escape the literati. Jules Verne caught the Franco-German antagonism already in 1877 in his popular novel *The 500 Millions of the Bégum*. Therein, the fictitious French Dr. François Sarrasin and the German professor Schultze agreed to use a massive fortune bequeathed by a deceased Bégum of India, each to plan a new city. Sarrasin decided to build a model community, France-Ville, on the Oregon coast near Coos Bay. It was based on "freedom from inequality, peace with its neighbors, good administration, wisdom among its inhabitants, and bountiful prosperity"—in short, on the

French ideals of liberty, equality, and fraternity. Schultze, on the other hand, opted to establish a counterutopia: a formidable factory, Steel City (Stahlstadt), an "industrial and technological nightmare" with a Krupp-like leader directing his laborers from a "base tower." While we have to assume that the residents of France-Ville dined on pâté, grilled meats, and fresh fish, washed down with *grand cru* wines, those of Stahlstadt had to make do with the German fare of "withered vegetables, mounds of plain cheese, quarters of smoked sausage meat, and canned foods," all consumed amid "sacks of iron."[7] Verne's novel, while obviously grossly exaggerated, nevertheless captured the public image of the two countries and showed that popular culture was not out of step with military thinking.

More specifically, Schlieffen had carefully monitored the construction under General Raymond Séré de Rivière of a massive French belt of 166 forts in two major lines running from Verdun to Toul and from Épinal to Belfort between 1874 and 1885, and the expansion of Paris's old ring of 14 inner forts (that had withstood the German siege of 1870–71) with an outer ring of 25 forts by 1890. When Kaiser Wilhelm II as one of his first acts after the dismissal of Chancellor Otto von Bismarck in 1890 allowed the Reinsurance Treaty with Russia, wherein both parties agreed to remain neutral in a war waged by the other, to lapse, and when Paris at once leaped at the chance in August 1891 to begin negotiations of a military agreement with St. Petersburg (formalized in 1892), the time had come to reevaluate the Reich's tenuous strategic situation in the center of the Continent.

In fact, Bismarck's dismissal, Wilhelm II's cancellation of the tie to Russia, and the kaiser's desire to be his "own General Staff chief" brought about a radical shift toward a "New Course" of global expansion and fleet building as well as a reorientation of the Reich's land strategy. In August 1888, Alfred von Waldersee succeeded Moltke as chief of the General Staff. Schlieffen briefly served as head of the Third Section (foreign armies) and in 1889 became Waldersee's deputy chief of staff. Waldersee transformed Moltke's cautionary military strategy into simultaneous offensive operations against France and Russia. During good weather, he would mount an offensive into Russian Poland with five to seven corps, while thirteen to fifteen corps would first hold the line of the Rhine River, then counterattack, envelop, and annihilate the French army before it could retreat to its fortress line Belfort-Verdun.

In inclement weather, he would hold in the east and launch seventeen corps as well as all of his horse-drawn artillery against the French forts. An increasingly dense and sophisticated German railroad system as well as the assumed superiority of the German army, corps for corps, encouraged this offensive design. But Waldersee was too impetuous and undisciplined, much like his Supreme War Lord, and indulged in frequent political intrigues. On 7 February 1891, Wilhelm II appointed Schlieffen to head the General Staff. Sarcastic, prone to ridicule, nearly unapproachable, and an inveterate workaholic, Schlieffen for the next fourteen years put his personal stamp on the General Staff—and on German war planning. Since the Reich never developed a national coordinating body akin to the French Conseil supérieur de la défense nationale or the British Committee of Imperial Defence, it fell on Schlieffen to draft plans for national defense.

Schlieffen set about his task with several deep-rooted assumptions.[8] First, France remained the primary adversary. Second, given France's military alliance with Russia, he had to prepare for a future two-front war. Third, well aware that France had by far the better railway network and that it could ill afford to trade space for time, he decided as early as August 1892 to concentrate the greater part of his forces in the west before wheeling them around to face the more slowly developing Russian steamroller in the east. After his staff convinced him that the massive French fortifications in Lorraine could not simply be stormed by infantry, Schlieffen in August 1897 considered bypassing them by way of a grand march through neutral Belgium, Luxembourg, and the Netherlands. That *Westaufmarsch* was painstakingly detailed from the first day of mobilization (M+1) on, thereby ignoring the Elder Moltke's sage counsel that no operations plan survived the initial engagement with enemy forces. Fourth, since France and Russia could bring greater initial forces as well as subsequent reserves into the field, Schlieffen argued that Germany had to avoid a protracted war. A strategy that cost "billions" in Reichsmark and "millions" in soldiers' lives, he warned, would serve only the enemy. Thus, fifth, speed was of the essence. "The French army," he stressed time and again, "must be annihilated." The attack could never be allowed "to come to a standstill"; it was to be driven forward at all cost.[9] "Normal victories" would not do. "A series of rapidly fought brilliant victories would not suffice," General Bernhard Rothe, Schlieffen's deputy (1896–99), wrote: "instead we must deal the enemy such a defeat early on that it will be impossible for him to continue the war."[10]

Schlieffen used selective military history to buttress his radical concept. Napoleon I's dramatic march through neutral Prussian Franconia en route to destroying an Austrian army at Ulm in 1805 served as a model for his planned violation of Belgian neutrality. Around 1900, he read an account of the famous Battle of Cannae (216 BC). There Hannibal's Carthaginian army, outnumbered almost two to one, had destroyed an entire Roman army under Consuls Gaius Terentius Varro and Lucius Aemilius Paullus by offering a weak infantry center while cavalry and light infantry moved around the flanks and into the Romans' rear.[11] This was the key for Schlieffen. Hannibal's double-envelopment tactic with six thousand African cavalry at each of the flanks had guaranteed not just victory, but rather annihilation of the Roman legions. An estimated sixty thousand bloody and mutilated Roman corpses attested to the brilliance of Hannibal's tactical feat. The idea of a gigantic battle of encirclement and annihilation (*Kesselschlacht*) against French forces now became an idée fixe with Schlieffen. Over time, it became less a historical event and more a philosophical construct. In the process, he raised tactics to the level of operations, and subordinated considerations of statecraft to purely operational concepts. As well, Schlieffen chose to ignore the fact that Rome, rather than Carthage, eventually won the Punic Wars, and that it did so largely on the basis of an element absent in Schlieffen's grand design—sea power. General Hans von Seeckt, architect of the Reichswehr in the 1920s, in retrospect lamented Schlieffen's obsession with it. "Cannae: no slogan became so destructive for us as this one."[12]

On 28 December 1905, after fourteen years of tinkering on his strategic blueprint, Schlieffen committed his final thoughts on a future war with France and Russia to the famous memorandum that bears his name.[13] The keys to victory lay in rapid mobilization and numerical superiority at the decisive point. In its final form, the Schlieffen Plan ordered roughly 15 percent of German forces (two weak armies of five corps) along with Italian Third Army (three corps), transported to the Rhine through Austria-Hungary, to anchor the front on the Upper Rhine. The bulk of the German armies would quick-march west through the Low Countries; drive around the French left (or northern) flank; and, sweeping the English Channel with their "sleeves," wheel into the Seine basin southwest of Fortress Paris, where they would destroy the main French armies. This "hammer" would then pound any remaining enemy units against the German "anvil" in Lorraine, or against the Swiss border. Depending on the pace of the fighting in the south, Schlieffen was even prepared to detach two army corps from Lorraine and rush them north to reinforce the right wing (which would then constitute 91 percent of his forces). Six Ersatz divisions (surplus trained reserves) would follow up the initial assault and mop up or besiege Belgian and French forces and fortresses. In the meantime, a single army, using the lake- and swamp-studded terrain of East Prussia to advantage, would hold off the Russians.

Schlieffen meticulously crafted his grand design. The first twenty days of mobilization were laid out down to the minute for 20,800 trains of fifty cars each that were to transport 2.07 million men, 118,000 horses, and 400,000 tons of war materials to the fronts.[14] Each active army corps was assigned 140 trains, each reserve corps 85, and each cavalry division 31. Thirteen major rail lines were secured for the *Westaufmarsch* alone, and 660 trains per day were to run along each line. Major operations, Schlieffen lectured the General Staff, needed to be calculated down to the last detail. "It must be the same as it is at battalion-level exercises."[15] The campaign against France was to be over in forty days, after which the armies would race across Germany to deal with the slowly mobilizing Russian armies. Schlieffen had decided on a high-risk offensive between Thionville (Diedenhofen) and the Dutch border with all available forces (five armies of seventeen active corps) for political reasons: Russia's poor performance in its war against Japan that year convinced him that the French would stand on the defensive for years to come.[16]

In his last "General Staff Tour West 1905," Schlieffen twice had his operations staff game three scenarios (Steuben, Kuhl, Freytag) for a campaign against France. In each case, he led the German (blue) side, which defeated his adversary (red). The most interesting for our purposes is Case Freytag II, in which Schlieffen pursued the retreating French armies across the Marne, cut them off from Paris by turning south before he reached the capital, "pursued the French east of Paris," drove southeast, and finally broke them against the Swiss border by the fifty-sixth day of mobilization.[17]

It was an all-or-nothing throw of the dice, a high-risk operation born of hubris and bordering on recklessness. It was coordinated with neither the Chancellery, the Navy Office, the Foreign Office, the Finance Ministry, the War Ministry, nor the Austro-Hungarian ally. It disregarded Carl von Clausewitz's concepts of interaction, friction, escalation, reassessment, the "genius of war," and the "fog of uncertainty." It violated the neutrality of Belgium and the Netherlands, thus making Britain's entry into the war more probable. It was crafted without regard for existing German troop strengths. The final memorandum failed to mention that Germany was eight corps shy of Schlieffen's original prescription. And while it envisaged first the siege and then the battering of Fortress Paris by seven or eight corps, none of these as yet existed even on paper.[18]

Moreover, the Schlieffen Plan was based on a number of fragile assumptions: that the Russians would take at least forty days to mobilize; that the Dutch and Belgian railroad systems would assure his speed of advance; that the element of surprise would throw the French (and British) off their guard; and that the German railroad system would be able expeditiously to transfer the bulk of the armies from west to east in time to stall the Russian steamroller. And Schlieffen's 1905 blueprint was riddled with hedge words such as *if, when, perhaps,* and *hopefully.* It was a classic best-case scenario, an "audacious, yes, overly audacious gamble, whose success depended on many strokes of luck."[19]

Schlieffen was not without his critics.[20] Senior commanders questioned his "miraculous" strategy. Karl von Einem-Rothmaler pointed out that whereas the Elder Moltke in 1870–71 had led a Prussian army of 462,000 soldiers, Schlieffen proposed directing one of 2 million. Colmar von der Goltz questioned the concept of a forty-day *Blitz* through Belgium and France. Gottlieb von Haeseler argued that one could not expect to capture a great power such as France "like a cat in a sack." Martin Köpke, Rothe's predecessor as deputy chief of staff, as early as August 1895 had warned his chief against such an all-or-nothing strategy. France's numerical superiority in troop strength and its vast network of fortresses along its eastern border with Germany precluded another quick victory such as that scored by the Prussians against Napoleon III at Sedan in 1870. "We cannot expect quick, decisive

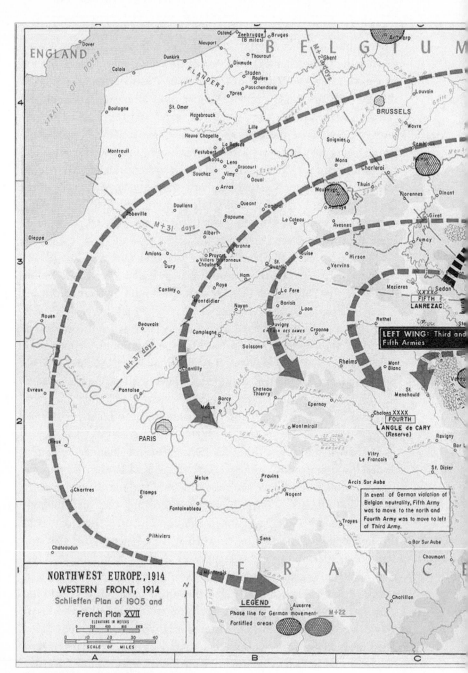

ENGLAND

Dover
Calais
Boulogne
Montreuil
Dieppe
Rouen
Evreux
Dreux
Chartres
Chateaudun

FLANDERS
Dunkirk
Ostend Zeebrugge Bruges
(8 miles)
Nieuport Thourout
Dixmude
Staden
Roulers
Ypres Passchendaele
St. Omer
Hazebrouck
Lille
Neuve Chapelle
Festubert La Bassée
Loos Lens Drocourt
Souchez Vimy Douai
Arras
Doullens Queant Cambrai
Bapaume Le Cateau
Albert Peronne
Amiens
Bury Proyart St.
Villers Bretonneux Quentin
Chaulnes
Roye Ham
Cantigny Montdidier Noyon Barisis Laon
Juvigny Craonne
Beauvais CHEMIN DES DAMES
Compiègne
Soissons
Pontoise Chantilly
Senlis
PARIS
Meaux Barcy
Chateau
Thierry
Melun Montmirail
Etampes
Fontainebleau
Pithiviers
Montereau

BELGIUM
Antwerp
Ghent Mt. Kemmel
BRUSSELS
Wavre
Louvain
Soignies
Mons Charleroi
Thuin
Maubeuge Florennes Dinant
Aulnoye Givet
Avesnes
Hirson Fumay
Guise Vervins Mezieres Sedan
La Fère
Rethel
Rheims Mont
Blanc
Epernay St.
Menehould
Chalons XXXX
FOURTH
L'ANGLE de CARY
(Reserve)
Vitry
Le Francois
Provins
Nogent
Sens
Troyes
Arcis Sur Aube
Bar Sur Aube
Chaumont
Chatillon

XXXXX
FIFTH
LANREZAC

LEFT WING: Third and
Fifth Armies

Revigny Bar L
St. Dizier

In event of German violation of
Belgian neutrality, Fifth Army
was to move to the north and
Fourth Army was to move to left
of Third Army.

M + 31 days
M + 37 days

Auxerre M + 22

FRANCE

NORTHWEST EUROPE, 1914
WESTERN FRONT, 1914
Schlieffen Plan of 1905 and
French Plan XVII
ELEVATIONS IN METERS
200 400 600 OVER
0 10 20 30 40
SCALE OF MILES

N

LEGEND
Phase line for German movement
Fortified areas

A   B   C

SCHLIEFFEN PLAN 1905 AND FRENCH PLAN XVII

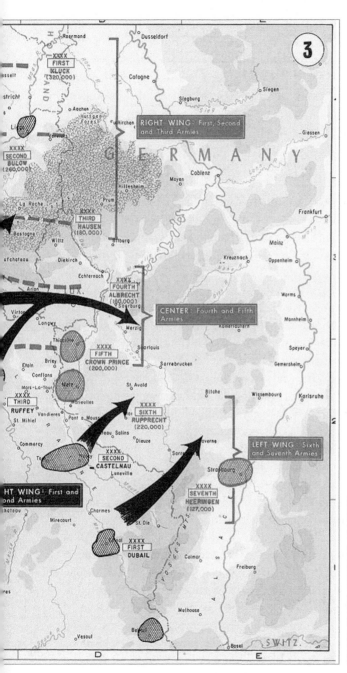

victories," he cautioned, as even "the most offensive spirit" could achieve little more than "a tough, patient and stout-hearted crawling forward step-by-step." Foreshadowing what was to come twenty years later, Köpke argued that Schlieffen's plan, if enacted, would degenerate into "siege-style" warfare.[21] The "storm of steel" that dominated the modern battlefield by 1905 was lethal: Prussian troops suffered 68 percent casualties at Mars-la-Tour in 1870, whereas the Japanese Nambu Brigade incurred 90 percent losses during the Russo-Japanese War of 1904–05. What nation would accept that loss rate for an army of two million young men?

Schlieffen apparently accepted Köpke's critique—and continued with his operational planning. For his critics offered no viable alternative. Germany could not fight a protracted war against a superior hostile coalition either in terms of men and money, or without endangering domestic stability (the "red specter," as Schlieffen put it). It could not divide its armies equally between the west and the east and hope to stay on the defensive indefinitely. Above all, the General Staff could not simply admit that war was no longer a viable option for Germany without calling into question its very existence. It was a Hobbesian choice.

ALTHOUGH SOME REVISIONISTS HAVE argued, "There never was a 'Schlieffen plan,' "[22] Germany's senior military leaders had no doubt as to its existence well before 1914. As early as 1907, Moltke had Karl von Fasbender, chief of the Bavarian General Staff, game various aspects of it. In 1912, Wilhelm II asked his senior military planners whether they were prepared to execute the Schlieffen Plan. Two years later, Moltke confirmed that he had inherited a copy of Germany's "one" operations plan from Schlieffen. Throughout the march to the Marne ("the basic idea of the Schlieffen operation"), Lieutenant Colonel Wilhelm Groener of the Prussian army's railroad section wrote his wife praising "the late Schlieffen" as "the man who thought up all the ideas we are carrying out."[23] Crown Prince Rupprecht of Bavaria, commander of Sixth Army, throughout August and September 1914 compared every operation mounted by Moltke to "the Old Schlieffen" or to "the Schlieffen Plan."[24] Moltke's successor, Erich von Falkenhayn, cryptically noted on taking command of the General Staff in mid-September 1914: "Schlieffen's notes are at an end and therewith also Moltke's wits."[25] Colonel Wilhelm Müller-Loebnitz of the General Staff (and later official army historian) knew of the existence of the plan well before 1914 and participated in many of the maneuvers designed to test it. Moreover, Schlieffen had frequently and "thoroughly discussed" the plan with Müller-Loebnitz as far back as 1905.[26] And the editors who produced the fourteen-volume official history of the war (*Der Weltkrieg 1914 bis 1918*) had no problem identifying that operations plan to have been Schlieffen's.

In fact, there existed no formal German war plan. Only Wilhelm II in his function as Supreme War Lord could exercise "the power to command."[27] As is well known, the kaiser was utterly unable to carry out such a demanding role. Thus, war planning fell by default to the chief of the General Staff, Moltke, even though he commanded not a single soldier, battalion, regiment, division, or corps. He could issue no formal orders, purchase no equipment, and authorize no war plan. His position was not embedded in the Constitution of 1871. And until a state of war was decreed by the kaiser and his chancellor (with the approval of the Bundesrath, or Upper House) and the various federal armies united into one German army in August 1914, the chief of the General Staff remained a purely *Prussian* official, one without formal command over the other federal armies.

THE YOUNGER MOLTKE LITERALLY inherited the Schlieffen Plan in January 1906, for Schlieffen upon retirement had "purposefully" left the memorandum of 28 December 1905 in the General Staff's iron safe.[28] Who was this man, who later would march 2.147 million men into battle?[29] Helmuth Johannes Ludwig von Moltke was all things to all people. To his friends, he was decent, honest, earnest, and cultured. To his detractors, he was dour, pessimistic, insecure, and an "occultist." For he had learned what one German prince called "wretched faith-healing"[30] from his wife, Eliza, and her spiritual mentor, the Austrian theosophist Rudolf Steiner.* Friends and foes alike agreed that Moltke was a complex figure, and one without the sharp Napoleonic eye for the main prize (*coup d'oeil*) or the necessary ambition and drive (*feu sacré*).

Born on 25 May 1848, Moltke saw action during the Franco-Prussian War in the Vosges, at Sedan, and during the siege of Paris. He rose quickly in rank to become Wilhelm II's personal adjutant. He dabbled in

---

* Theosophy (the name comes from a Greek word meaning "wisdom of the divine") professed to achieve knowledge of God by "spiritual ecstasy, direct intuition, or special individual revelation." Steiner is best known for the pedagogic theories taught in his worldwide Waldorf (or Steiner) schools.

music and painting. He was a tall, corpulent man. He aspired to command an army corps, but his famous name eventually placed him at the head of the General Staff. He neither sought nor desired the position, fearing not only the kaiser's well-known penchant for meddling in military affairs but also the "difficult inheritance" of becoming Schlieffen's successor.[31] He was appointed to the post on 1 January 1906, just before turning fifty-eight. While senior army commanders were shocked by the appointment, Wilhelm II crowed that Moltke was just the right man because he, the kaiser, did "not require a General Staff."[32]

Moltke quickly adopted Schlieffen's blueprint. He shared it with only a few members of his planning staff and cut off all communications with Schlieffen, obviously intent on establishing his own credentials independent of the "master." He maintained most of Schlieffen's blueprint, but eventually changed some of its bolder force concentration. As a result, Germany went to war on 4 August with a "modified Schlieffen Plan with similar goals."[33]

The basic similarities are glaring.[34] Both men believed that Germany was "encircled" by hostile powers, and that only military action could "break" the iron ring. Both accepted that Germany would be numerically inferior in a future war; hence, it had to dictate the timing and pace of that conflict. This led to a third common constant, namely, that the main thrust of the offensive had to fall on France. In 1909, as the annexation crisis over Bosnia-Herzegovina evoked a possible Austro-Russian war, Wilhelm II revealed that he knew the Schlieffen Plan. "In order to be able to march against Moscow," he noted, "Paris must be taken first."[35] That same year, Moltke reminded his Austro-Hungarian counterpart, Franz Conrad von Hötzendorf, that in case of a two-front war, he would advise the kaiser "to deploy the main mass of German forces initially against France," leaving only a minimum number of troops "to guard our eastern provinces" against Russia. He gamely promised Conrad that the German army would redeploy in the east "3–4 weeks + 9–10 days transport" after the start of hostilities in the west.[36]

In December 1912, Moltke went out of his way to make certain that both the chancellor and the Prussian war minister were aware of the German plan in the event of war. He informed Theobald von Bethmann Hollweg and Josias von Heeringen in writing that "given its central location," Germany needed a thin screen against one enemy in order to hurl its main forces against the other. "That side always can only be France." More, "in order to take the offensive against France, it will be necessary to violate Belgian neutrality."[37] Therewith, all pretense at innocence by the Reich's political elite regarding the Schlieffen Plan was destroyed. After the war, Wilhelm von Dommes of the General Staff recalled that Moltke had confided in him that he had discussed the basic contours of the Schlieffen Plan already with Bethmann Hollweg's predecessor, Bernhard von Bülow.[38] During the critical first week of August 1914, Moltke assured the Bavarians that he remained true to Schlieffen's concept: Germany's strategy was to "advance upon Paris with all our might via Belgium in order to settle accounts quickly with France."[39]

The basic differences are also important.[40] First, Moltke feared the impact of a British naval blockade on the German food and raw materials supply. Hence, he canceled Schlieffen's march through the Maastricht Appendix in southern Holland, for that country would have to remain "the last windpipe, through which we can breathe."[41] Put differently, Germany planned to import strategic materials "under cover of the [neutral] American flag" through neutral Holland in time of war. Moltke's decision, while politically advantageous, brought to the surface new "technical problems." To wit, the six hundred thousand men of First and Second armies as well as their horses and trains would now have to break into Belgium (and then France) through a twenty-kilometer defile between the Ardennes Forest and the Maastricht Appendix. In the way stood one of Europe's most formidable fortresses—Liège (Lüttich),* guarded by a belt of twelve massive steel and concrete forts with four hundred guns and a garrison of perhaps thirty thousand men. Schlieffen had planned to bypass it by marching through southern Holland. Moltke in his "Deployment Plan 1909/10" decided to take Liège by way of a bold strike (*Handstreich*) with five infantry brigades by the fourth or fifth day of mobilization.[42] But if this failed, he, like Schlieffen, was more than ready to advance through the Netherlands.[43] The assault on Liège was one of the General Staff's "best-guarded secrets," hidden especially from the gossipy kaiser.

Second, Moltke developed doubts concerning Russia's predicted slow mobilization. In retirement, Schlieffen assured staff officers that the Russian armies marching against Germany would not reach even

* Sites in Belgium and Alsace-Lorraine are given their more customary French names, with their 1914 German names in parentheses. Spelling of French city names was taken from www.viamichelin.com.

Galicia in Russian Poland "before the dice were cast in the west." Austria-Hungary's "fate," he stated, would be decided "not along the Bug but rather the Seine" River.[44] Moltke was not so sure. With a massive infusion of capital from France, Russia had expanded and modernized the railway system leading to its western border with Germany. In 1912, Moltke noted his concerns about the expected pace of Russian mobilization in the margins of Schlieffen's draft, concluding that his predecessor had underestimated the strength of the Franco-Russian military alliance.[45] Still, Moltke could not bring himself to abandon Schlieffen's blueprint. He expanded the Prussian army by 9,000 men in March 1911 and by 117,000 in March 1913; in February 1913 he canceled the General Staff's only operations plan in the east.

Third, Moltke grew increasingly nervous about concentrating seven-eighths of his forces on the right wing, which would form the eventual hammer to swing around Paris. It seemed too great a gamble. It "made no sense," he lectured his future deputy chief of staff,★ Hermann von Stein, to advance with the bulk of the army into a region (Belgium) where the enemy likely would not concentrate its forces.[46] Already in 1905, Moltke noted on Schlieffen's great memorandum that the French would not oblige Germany and simply stand on the defensive. The "inherent offensive spirit" of the French and their desire to regain the "lost provinces" of Alsace and Lorraine pointed toward a French offensive the day war was declared.[47] Thus, whereas Schlieffen had hoped for a major French drive across the Vosges Mountains to make his sweep through Belgium and northern France that much swifter and more effective, Moltke began to worry about the understrength of the German left flank facing France in the south, with its vital industries in the Saar. In his "Deployment Plan 1908/09," Moltke for the first time assigned an entire army corps to defend Upper Alsace; thereafter, in "Deployment Plan 1913/14," he increased the southern flank to include Seventh Army (two active and one reserve corps) to defend Alsace and the Rhine, and Sixth Army (four active corps) to hold southern Lorraine. In the process, he reduced the relative strength of the right wing from Schlieffen's 7:1 to a mere 3:1.[48]

Perhaps Moltke was emboldened to undertake this critical shift of forces by what has been called "one of the greatest [coups] in the his-

---

★ I have used this familiar Anglo-Saxon term rather than the German quartermaster-general.

tory of espionage." Berlin's man in Paris, officially designated "Agent 17," was in fact an Austrian national, August Baron Schluga von Rastenfeld. Working in a shroud of mystery—Schluga refused to inform Berlin of any of his sources, which were mainly open-source materials and conversations at cocktail parties—Agent 17 shortly before the outbreak of war in 1914 had provided the General Staff with a document showing that the French would deploy their forces in the center of their main line of advance on the fifth day of mobilization.[49] The German sweep through the Low Countries would thus evade the French offensive through the Ardennes.

In talks with his Italian counterpart, Alberto Pollio, in 1912, 1913, and 1914 as well as with the newly appointed commander of Italian Third Army, Luigi Zuccari, in April 1914, Moltke received assurances that Rome would dispatch Third Army to the Upper Rhine by M+17 "as soon as the *casus foederis* was established."[50] But there was widespread doubt in Berlin whether the Italian promise would eventuate, and thus by 1914 Moltke committed no fewer than eight German corps to his left flank, both to tie down French forces opposing them and to deny their being shunted north to face the great wheel through Belgium and northern France.[51] His critics never forgave him for this "dilution" of the critical right wing.

Still puzzling to scholars is the fact that in light of his concerns with the Schlieffen Plan, Moltke in the first six years of his tenure at the General Staff failed to create the forces required to execute the grand design, or to acquire desperately needed modern war materials (such as aircraft and communications systems), instead channeling funding to the three main branches: artillery, infantry, and cavalry.[52] Nor did he manage sufficiently to expand the reserves—while lamenting as late as May 1914 that thirty-eight thousand qualified young men annually evaded the draft owing to a shortage of funds. This is especially puzzling given Moltke's growing fears that the British might undertake amphibious assaults on Danish Jutland or on Schleswig-Holstein at the onset of a continental war. Whereas Schlieffen in 1905 had cavalierly decreed that the British were of no concern to him since the decision in the war would come in France,[53] Moltke recognized correctly the British threat and decided to base IX Reserve Corps (roughly twenty thousand men) in Schleswig-Holstein for what he feared could be a three-front war.

In August 1914, Moltke had a formidable force at his disposal: 880,000 active soldiers, including the regular army of 794,310 men, the Imperial Navy of 79,000, and the colonial forces of 7,000. With the addition of the Landwehr I (reserves aged twenty-eight to thirty-three) and the Landwehr II (aged thirty-three to thirty-nine), the total ballooned to 2.147 million men organized into eighty-seven and a half infantry divisions and fifty-five cavalry brigades. Almost one million Ersatz reserves—men who had escaped the draft and at age twenty committed to twelve years of service—stood as a last manpower reservoir.[54] Seventy infantry divisions were to march west at the outbreak of war; facing them would likely be ninety-two enemy divisions.

German forces in the west in 1914 were organized into seven field armies, each consisting of about four army corps. There were as yet no "army groups." A corps resembled a small village armed and on the move. Each peacetime corps, consisting of roughly twenty thousand men, upon mobilization was brought up to a wartime cohort of fifteen hundred officers and forty thousand noncommissioned officers and men, fourteen thousand horses and twenty-four hundred ammunition and supply wagons for its twenty-five battalions; fully mobilized, it covered fifty kilometers of road. A corps consumed about 130 tons of food and fodder per day. Its artillery consisted of twenty-four field batteries, each of six 135mm guns, and of four heavy artillery batteries, each of four guns. Of special note was a battalion of sixteen superb 150mm howitzers. Each corps had eight regiments of cavalry. Each had a squadron of six mainly Gotha and Albatros biplanes for reconnaissance, as did each corps headquarters. The aircraft had a flight endurance of two to three hours, mounted two 25cm cameras for surveillance, and carried a single Mauser pistol as "armament." Bomb capacity was restricted to several five- and ten-kilogram missiles that the pilot could "freely throw" over the side of the craft.[55]

In terms of organization, the army was arranged by twos: two divisions to a corps, two brigades to a division, and two regiments to a brigade. The heart of the German army was its combat division.[56] It consisted of four regiments, each of 3,000 soldiers; each regiment contained three battalions of 1,000; and each battalion, four companies of 250. The divisional commander had at his disposal an artillery brigade of seventy-two guns, fifty-four of which were flat-trajectory 77mm pieces. Moltke had added to each infantry division an additional company with six 1908 Maxim water-cooled machine guns as well as a battalion of eighteen 105mm howitzers.

Infantry remained the "queen of battle." The German Field Regulations of May 1906 identified it as "the primary weapon . . . its fire will batter the enemy. It alone breaks his last resistance. It carries the brunt of combat and makes the greatest sacrifices." Above all, "infantry must nurture its intrinsic drive to attack aggressively. Its actions must be dominated by one thought: Forward against the enemy, cost what it may!"[57] Each soldier was provided with a sturdy 7.9mm bolt-action Mauser Rifle 98, a bayonet, a knapsack of twenty-three kilograms, an entrenching tool, a haversack, a mess kit, six ammunition pouches, and a small metal disk with his name on it. While infantry still wore the leather spiked helmet (*Pickelhaube*), its colorful tunics had yielded to standard field gray, a color that blended well with smoke, mud, and autumn foliage. Each soldier carried a leather greatcoat looped outside his backpack; each marched in stiff, nailed boots (*Blücher*). While the Field Regulations of 1909 raised the possibility that infantry advance in columns of thin lines and that it adopt "swarming" skirmish tactics, infantry, in fact, continued to be drilled to advance in thick marching columns. Charles Repington, military correspondent for *The Times* of London, in October 1911 concluded from German maneuvers: "No other modern army displays such profound contempt for the effect of modern fire."[58]

Cavalry had been greatly reduced since the Franco-Prussian War of 1870–71. Whereas the Elder Moltke's army of 462,000 soldiers had included 56,800 "sabers," his nephew's army of 2 million in 1914 had but 90,000 cavalry. The Younger Moltke had done much to upgrade the firepower of the cavalry, with the result that every brigade of 680 riders had with it three batteries each of four guns as well as a company of six machine guns. Still, what one German scholar called a "true chivalrous mounted mentality" reigned among the cavalry: "lance against lance, saber against saber."[59] Its role remained reconnaissance and shock. In early August 1914, the slick stone pavements of Belgian towns and villages caused many a cavalry charge to come to grief, with riders at times skewering one another on their steel-tube lances.[60]

There was one glaring area of neglect: electronic communications. Year after year, Schlieffen and Moltke had been content to conduct annual maneuvers and staff rides by each night handing out detailed plans and directives for the next day's assignments. But would this suffice for the modern, lethal battlefield?[61] By 1914, plans had been finalized to provide each army corps with a company and its headquarters with a battalion of telephone specialists as well as a company of wireless operators. Thus, the number of telephone companies had increased from twenty in 1912 to forty by the following year. The outbreak of war in August 1914, however, found these units still being created. The army's stock of twenty-one thousand carrier pigeons was to offset this deficit.

To Moltke's credit, he brilliantly supervised the mobilization of Germany's armed forces in 1914. For two decades, the General Staff's best and brightest had labored day and night to shave minutes off the Military Travel Plan, the critical stage five of mobilization. They sprang into action after noon on 31 July, when Wilhelm II declared a "threatening state of danger of war"—which effectively amounted to a declaration of war—to exist.[62] Gerhard Tappen, chief of operations, unlocked the great steel safe and took out the most recent "Deployment Plan 1914/15." "It was a peculiar feeling," he noted in his diary.[63] Thereupon, the Military Telegraph Section instructed two hundred thousand telegraph employees and one hundred thousand telephone operators at Berlin's major post offices to send out news of the state of *Kriegsgefahr* to the 106 infantry brigades scattered throughout the Reich. The Railroad Section and its twenty-three directorates outside the capital began to requisition thirty thousand locomotives as well as sixty-five thousand passenger and eight hundred thousand freight cars needed to assemble twenty-five active corps. Mobilization formally began on 2 August.

Germany's declaration of war (under Article 68 of the Constitution of 1871) against Russia on 1 August and against France two days later put the mobilization process into high gear. In 312 hours, roughly eleven thousand trains shuttled 119,754 officers, 2.1 million men, and six hundred thousand horses to the various marshaling areas under stage seven ("attack march") of the Military Travel Plan. The 1.6 million soldiers of the west army—950 infantry battalions and 498 cavalry squadrons—rolled across the Rhine River bridges at the rate of 560 trains, each of fifty-four cars, per day at an average speed of thirty kilometers per hour. The Hohenzollern Bridge at Cologne alone witnessed 2,150 trains thundering over it in ten-minute intervals between 2 and 8 August.[64] The Germans, Evelyn Princess Blücher noted in Berlin, "take to war as a duck takes to water."[65] There was no disorder and no opposition to mobilization, with the result that Chancellor von Bethmann Hollweg shelved prewar plans to arrest "unpatriotic" Socialists. In fact, on 3 August, the Social Democratic Party caucus voted 78 to 14 to grant war credits; the next day, it closed ranks and unanimously approved 2.27 billion Reichsmark for the first thirty days of mobilization, followed by an immediate supplementary grant of 5 billion.[66]

Mobilization was executed equally flawlessly in Germany's second largest federal state, the Kingdom of Bavaria. News of the "threatening state of danger of war" arrived by telegram from Berlin at 2 PM on 31 July, and by next morning Munich's post offices sent out forty-seven thousand telegrams to district commands, barracks, and depots. In the Bavarian lands east of the Rhine River the General Staff mobilized three thousand trains; in the Bavarian Palatinate, twenty-five hundred. In eight to twelve days, the active army (*Feldheer*) of 6,699 officers, 269,000 noncommissioned officers and ranks, 222 heavy artillery pieces, and 76,000 thousand horses, as well as the reserve army (*Besatzungsheer*) of 2,671 officers, 136,834 noncommissioned officers and ranks, 104 heavy artillery guns, and 9,000 horses, were mobilized and pointed for the front in Lorraine.[67]

Similarly smooth mobilizations also took place in the other federal states. Archduke Friedrich II of Baden's forces were close to the French border, and hence there was no need for extensive railway transport.[68] Baden XIV Army Corps under Ernst von Hoiningen-Huene consisted of thirty battalions of infantry, eight squadrons of cavalry, and twenty-four batteries of field artillery. Its task was to guard the east bank of the Rhine between Breisach and Lörrach, and then to march toward Thann, at the base of the Vosges Mountains.[69] Richard von Schubert's XIV Reserve Corps, a hodgepodge of twelve infantry battalions and Prussian as well as Württemberg Landwehr units, assembled farther north between Lahr and Breisach with orders to proceed to Neuenburg and Mulhouse. All units were issued the new field-gray uniforms. Grateful villagers, noted Sergeant Otto Breinlinger, 10th Company, 111th Reserve Infantry Regiment, stood in awe and showered the men with "bread, coffee, wine, lemonade, apples, raspberry juice, pears & cigars."[70] On 1 August, Hoiningen-Huene had rallied his men with a bristling Order of the Day: "Our enemies have forced the sword into our hands—forced to use it, we will, even should the waves of the Rhine turn red."[71]

Around midnight on 7–8 August, Baden's soldiers marched off to war in rain and storm. They came under the command of Prussian general Josias von Heeringen, whose Seventh Army was responsible for securing the extreme left wing of the German line.

King Friedrich August III of Saxony entrusted Third Army to Max von Hausen, at age sixty-eight war minister and peacetime commander of XII Army Corps in Dresden. Mobilization orders arrived from Berlin in the afternoon of 1 August. Hausen spent the next week assembling Third Army: 101 active and reserve infantry battalions, 30 squadrons of cavalry, and 99 artillery batteries. Third Army entrained at Dresden-Neustadt late in the evening of 7 August, en route to the Eiffel Mountains near the French border.[72] It was assigned to the central front, its right wing attached to Second Army and its left wing to Fourth Army. Hausen's orders were to advance against the line of the Meuse (Maas) River between Namur and Givet.

Finally, the childless King Wilhelm II of Württemberg turned XIII Army Corps over to Max von Fabeck as part of Crown Prince Wilhelm of Prussia's Fifth Army at Thionville. Then, to assuage royal sensibilities, Kaiser Wilhelm II gave Duke Albrecht, head of the Catholic branch of the House of Württemberg, command of Fourth Army. Its 123 infantry battalions—an amalgam of German federal units—were the heart of the central front, facing the formidable Ardennes Forest as far down as Luxembourg.[73] In historian Sewell Tyng's apt description, Fourth Army was the "hub of the wheel," of which Hausen's Third Army and Karl von Bülow's Second Army were the "spoke," and Alexander von Kluck's First Army the "outer rim."[74] Albrecht's corps were in position by 12 August, reserve corps two days later, and Ersatz draft divisions by 18 August.

Moltke assembled his forces according to the Revised Deployment Plan.[75] In the south, Heeringen's Seventh Army (125,000 men) took up position east of the Rhine from Strasbourg (Straßburg) down to the Swiss border; just north of him, Crown Prince Rupprecht of Bavaria's Sixth Army (220,000) advanced between Saargemünd and Saarburg. The two armies were to "fix" French forces in the Reichsland and to "prevent their transportation to the French left wing." The giant Schwenkungsflügel (pivot wing) of First to Fifth Armies was to be anchored on Thionville-Metz. The German center consisted of three armies: Crown Prince Wilhelm of Prussia's Fifth Army (200,000) was to drive west between Thionville, Metz, and Saarbrücken in the direction of Florinville and Verdun; north of him, Duke Albrecht's Fourth Army (200,000) was to march through Trier, Luxembourg, and the Ardennes Forest toward Sedan and Semois; and north of Albrecht, Hausen's Third Army (180,000) was to head through the Ardennes Forest toward Dinant, Fumay, and Givet.

The hammer of the German advance, of course, consisted of Kluck's First Army (320,000 men) and Bülow's Second Army (260,000). In the early-morning hours of 3 August, Georg von der Marwitz's II Cavalry Corps stormed the Belgian border near Gemmenich; Kluck's and Bülow's six hundred thousand gray-clad formations crossed the Meuse River the next day. First Army headed for Brussels and Antwerp, Second Army for Namur. Directly ahead of them lay Liège. Moltke had detailed Otto von Emmich's X Army Corps to storm the fortress with six infantry brigades and three cavalry divisions. On its success rested Kluck's and Bülow's rapid advance through a twenty-kilometer-wide funnel into the heart of Belgium—and beyond.

Moltke in the spring of 1914 had undertaken a cursory evaluation of his likely counterpart. The word from the German military attaché in Paris was that Chief of the General Staff Joseph Joffre was "renowned" for "his sense of responsibility, his work ethic and his common sense." But he was also suspected to be phlegmatic, "incapable of making hard and fast decisions." How would he hold up under the pressure of war? The final verdict, italicized for emphasis, was: *"In any case, one can not assess him as a ruthless, energetic leader capable of doing whatever the situation demands."*[76]

FRANCE'S NATIONAL POLICY AND its military strategy were clear in 1914: to "push" its allies "into the fight" and to assure St. Petersburg of "unequivocal" support in case of war. As stated previously, Paris's goal in 1914 "was to avoid making decisions."[77] With President Raymond Poincaré and Prime Minister René Viviani en route to St. Petersburg after 16 July and with the Senate as well as the Chamber of Deputies (which had to approve a declaration of war) in summer recess from 15 July through 4 August, it proved no great task to "avoid making decisions."

Of course, the military stood on alert after the assassinations at Sarajevo on 28 June. How would the Russian ally react to any Austro-Hungarian action against Serbia? This was a pivotal question, for in 1914 France and Russia had the only firm military alliance in Europe. Under its terms, in the case of a German attack, France would field 1.3 million men and Russia 800,000.[78] Formal staff talks held every year after 1900 reaffirmed the original pledge to wage war against Germany from the first day of its mobilization. At the last peacetime meeting in August 1913, Russia promised to mount an offensive into the "heart" of Germany by the fourteenth day of mobilization; France, to concentrate "nearly all its forces" along its northeastern frontier by the fifteenth day.[79] Both General Staffs expected the brunt of a German offensive to fall in the west, with only light forces defending East Prussia.

After Austria-Hungary's declaration of war against Serbia one month after the double murders at Sarajevo France entrusted mobilizing her armies to Joseph Césaire Joffre, chief of the General Staff since July 1911. Joffre had not been the obvious choice for the post. War Minister Adolphe Messimy's top candidate, General Joseph Galliéni, had turned down the post in part because he was close to retirement age. Galliéni had then recommended two men: Paul-Marie Pau and Joseph Joffre. But Pau was a devout Catholic and demanded upon appointment the right (reserved for the war minister) to select commanding generals. Thus, Joffre got the post by default.

Joffre was born on 12 January 1852 at Riversaltes, in the eastern Pyrenees. He came from "modest blood," an artisan family of coopers. He graduated not from the Military College at Saint-Cyr, but rather from the École Polytechnique, and with a mediocre school record at that. He commanded an artillery battery during the siege of Paris in 1870–71 and then, as an engineer, served in Indo-China, West Africa, and Madagascar. Upon returning to France, he commanded an artillery group and then became director of Engineers and director of Support Services at the War Ministry, where he acquired an intimate appreciation for logistics and railway transportation. In 1907, he took command of 6th Infantry Division and the following year of II Army Corps at Amiens. Unlike his European counterparts, he had not made a name for himself either by publishing treatises on strategy or by distinguishing himself at army maneuvers. His main claim to fame in 1911 rested on the fact that he was a competent fortifications engineer and a decorated colonial soldier.

In terms of character, to his detractors, Joffre was unimaginative and feckless, lacking grand gestures, almost featureless. He was known to be stubborn, almost to the point of stolidity and obstinacy. His baggy clothes—black tunic and red breeches—hardly inspired dash and daring. To his supporters, Joffre was known for his forthrightness, honesty, consideration for subordinates—he retained throughout his life his boyhood nickname *le père Joffre,* Papa Joffre—and imperturbable calm under stress. To politicians in Paris, he offered what they valued most—an utter lack of ambition and deviousness. His physical appearance—stout, white hair, with a full round face accentuated by pale blue eyes and a long white mustache—tended to efface any impression of distinction or drive. His strict daily regimen of work, rest, sleep, and meals—usually ending with a heaping serving of his favorite leg of lamb (*gigot à la Bretonne,*)—further seemed to indicate a placid (and even dull) personality.

His career as chief of the General Staff would prove otherwise. Although he later claimed that he detested staff work, Joffre was a master of details and a bureaucratic micromanager. He carefully read every major study and, if it supported his policies and decisions, initialed it to show approval. If it did not, he pondered his choices carefully and then edited the study to bring it into line with his own position. During the war, he flooded his field commanders—from army to division level—with telegrams, telephone calls, and a host of staff officers to make certain that they adhered to his strategy. He took to the roads by day and night to maintain a short leash on those commanders. He was not above visiting army headquarters and sitting there for hours to see that his will was being carried out. He had no patience for incompetent or failed commanders. He fired and promoted at will, the former often accompanied by fits of towering rage. But there were limits to his power, and he was careful for the most part to keep the war ministers whom he served informed of his actions and designs. And he showed the patience of Job in dealing with the testy British, fully recognizing that a breach in the Anglo-French relationship could jeopardize the war effort, and even the Entente.

Soon after his appointment to the army's highest post, Joffre revealed his iron hand as he reshaped the French army. Along with his aristocratic and devout Catholic deputy, Édouard de Castelnau, Joffre was the architect of the French deployment plan in 1914. The so-called Plan XVII, historian Robert Doughty has argued, was "Joffre's own."*

In 1911, Joffre inherited a wealth of information from his intelligence branch, the Deuxième Bureau, pointing to a likely German thrust through southeastern Belgium and the Ardennes. This assumption had stemmed from British, French, and Russian observers at German maneuvers; from seemingly reliable espionage reports; and from recent German railway construction to its western border. Most spectacularly, in 1903 and 1904 French intelligence agents had received the so-called Vengeur documents—presumably purchased from a disgruntled German staff officer—that provided them with a rough outline of what less than two years later would be the Schlieffen Plan. Close examination especially in 1907 and 1913 of German railway building in and around Aachen led the Deuxième Bureau to the conclusion that the Germans likely would invade north of Liège in the direction of Brussels.[80] Joffre's operations branch, the Troisième Bureau, for its part argued that from the days of Frederick the Great to Helmuth von Moltke, German doctrine had favored massive envelopments. Still, there was always room for misinterpretation—but none for error.

Joffre had also inherited an operations plan and a political-strategic nightmare. Plan XVI, crafted by Henri de Lacroix and approved by the Superior Council of War in March 1909, addressed the expected German envelopment strategy.[81] Believing that the enemy would seek to turn the French line of fortifications in Lorraine by sending one army through the Ardennes at Verdun and another through Sedan, and knowing the political objections to marshaling forces along the Belgian frontier, Lacroix created a flexible defensive-offensive strategy. He proposed placing a new Sixth Army at Châlons-sur-Marne,† west of Verdun, ready to deploy toward Toul-Épinal on the right, Verdun on the left, or Sedan-Mézières on the far left of the French line. The nature of the German invasion would determine the eventual choice.

The political-strategic nightmare had been brought about by Lacroix's successor, Victor Michel. Much concerned about a German

---

* Neither the French government nor Joffre had a formal name for the *Plan de renseignements*, popularly referred to as Plan XVII.

† In 1998, the city reverted to its prerevolutionary name, Châlons-en-Champagne.

thrust through "the very heart of Belgium," Michel in July 1911 proposed defending on the right from Belfort to Mézières while simultaneously launching a "vigorous offensive" on the left toward Antwerp, Brussels, and Namur.[82] Since France lacked the regular forces for such a massive deployment, Michel suggested that it revive the "demi-brigade" of the French Revolution, one that featured three combined-arms battalions, including reservists. The Superior Council unanimously rejected his reorganization—and with it his strategy. Generals close to Minister of War Messimy referred to Michel as a "loony"[83] and to his plan as *"une insanité."* Michel resigned within two days of this rebuff.

Whom to choose as successor? Messimy, as previously stated, decided on youth: Joseph Joffre was a mere fifty-nine years of age, a moderate republican, and an experienced administrator. As well, Messimy reformed the army's splintered system of High Command, Superior Council, and General Staff by placing the High Command "completely and without reserve" under Joffre.

Six weeks into the job, Joffre began work on what was to become France's deployment plan in 1914. He rejected Michel's notion of defending along the frontier with Belgium and shifted the center of gravity for the mass of French armies to the line Paris-Metz, assigning only reserve units to the Belgian border. His staff was convinced that the Germans would hold in Alsace-Lorraine and advance through Belgium, but in January 1912 the Superior Council of National Defense again made it clear that the French army was not to advance into Belgium until the Germans did so.[84]

Joffre kept the Belgian option to himself. He informed neither the politicians at Paris nor his corps commanders that he preferred to attack into southern Belgium against what he believed would be the "weak" German center. He later confided in his memoirs: "I preferred to say nothing [about the Belgian option] in an operations plan."[85] At most, he spoke of an advance "in the general direction of the northeast as soon as all French forces were assembled." Clear as mud.

On 18 April 1913, Joffre shared with the Superior Council of War the basic contours of his *Plan de renseignements*. It was accepted on 2 May. His staff put the final touches on it in February 1914, and the ponderous annexes to the plan were completed on 1 May.[86] France would concentrate five armies in the northeast. On the right of the French line, First Army was to drive toward Sarrebourg and Second

Army against Saarbrücken; at the center, Third Army was to attack Metz-Thionville; and on the left, Fifth Army was to advance into Luxembourg toward Belgium. If the Germans came through Belgium, Joffre was given the green light to "penetrate the territory of Belgium at the first news of the violation of that territory by the German army."[87] In a secret annex, Joffre would have the British deploy on the left of Fifth Army west of Mézières. But in no case would he allow their action (or inaction) to affect his overall deployment.

Joffre's army closely paralleled that of Moltke's in terms of organization.[88] The typical army corps consisted of about forty thousand men organized into two divisions. Each corps had as well a brigade of reserves, divided into two regiments of two battalions each, and a cavalry regiment of four squadrons. Its artillery consisted of 120 superb flat-trajectory 75mm (soixante-quinze) guns—nine four-gun batteries for each of its infantry divisions as well as twelve four-gun batteries as special corps artillery. Industrial output was set at about 13,600 rounds per day. Since the French army expected and prepared for a series of highly mobile battles, it saw little need to burden the corps with slow and ponderous heavy artillery. The concept of preliminary bombardment to "soften" the enemy line was rejected by most staff planners. Moreover, the army's technical services objected to introducing additional calibers that would only multiply supply problems. And although the War Ministry had ordered 220 105mm howitzers (range twelve kilometers) on the eve of the war, similar objections from the technical services prompted it to reduce the order to 36. As a result, France entered the war in 1914 with a plethora of heavy artillery pieces—mostly 105mm and 120mm as well as elderly Rimailho 155mm guns.

Each French infantry division had two brigades of two regiments each; each regiment, in turn, had three battalions, including a machine-gun section of two guns. The divisional commander had at his disposal three groups of 75mm mobile field artillery pieces. Cavalry divisions (ten in 1914) were made up of three brigades each of two regiments (four squadrons), a total of about forty-five hundred "sabers." Two four-gun, horse-drawn batteries of 75mm guns and a bicycle detachment of 324 men accompanied a cavalry division into battle. Each brigade had a machine-gun section with Model 1907 Saint-Étienne guns. The proverbial arme blanche carried lances, sabers, and antiquated single-action 1890 Lebel carbines (without bayonet). Cuirassiers and dragoons were resplendent in their steel breastplates, heavy cavalry in their brass helmets streaming long horsehair plumes. Cavalry's major role was to scout enemy positions and to assist the infantry during attack.

Aviation was still in its infancy. The French Armée de l'air of some 140 operational aircraft organized into squadrons of 5 or 6 planes in 1914 was designed to track enemy movements and to fight its opposite numbers for control of the air. Range and bomb loads were limited. There were as yet no separate fighter and bomber squadrons. On 14 August, several French Voisin pusher biplanes bombed German Zeppelin hangars at Metz-Frescaty, thereby showing the way toward the future of military aviation.

Joffre was an ardent admirer of the all-out offensive, *l'offensive à outrance*. He vowed never again to allow a French army to be encircled as at Sedan on 1 September or to surrender under siege as at Metz on 27 October 1870. "The French Army, returning to its traditions," he wrote in regulations in 1913, "accepts no law in the conduct of operations other than the offensive."[89] His forces, the proverbial *furia française,* would advance en masse with drums and bugles sounding the attack. *Cran* (guts) and *élan vital* (spirit) would carry the day. "Battles are above all moral contests. Defeat is inevitable when hope for victory ceases." Victory would come "to the one whose will is the steadiest and whose morale is the most highly tempered." Defeat of the German armies, Joffre trumpeted, "remains, no matter what the circumstances, the first and principle [sic] objective."[90] He offered no further details on his intentions, other than to drive into the "heart" of Germany. There was no overall strategic goal. After all, by the time the French armies arrived in central Germany, the Russians would surely be in Berlin! And even if "beaten," the French army would have "opened the way for the Russian offensive" and thus assured "final success."[91]

The "will to win" also shaped French artillery doctrine. Whereas the 1895 regulations had stressed that the artillery was decisive in battle from start to finish, those of December 1913 rejected this postulate: "The artillery does not prepare attacks; it supports them."[92] Artillery was not to pulverize enemy positions before an attack was launched, but to limit its role to supporting the attack, once under way. In a war of maneuver, the legendary French 75mm rapid-firing field gun—deadly accurate and firing twice as fast (twenty to thirty rounds per

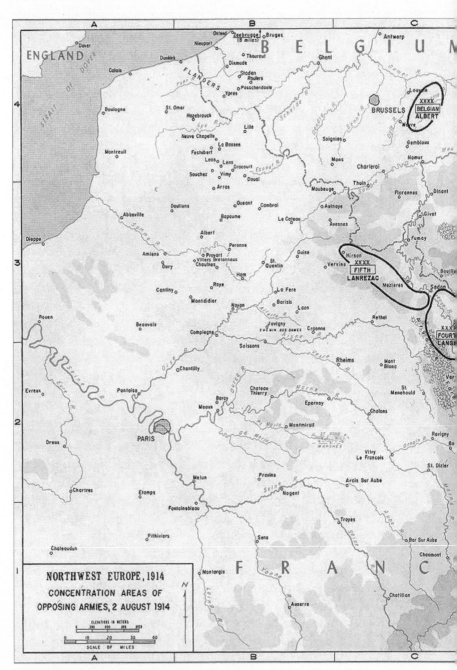

CONCENTRATION AREAS OF OPPOSING ARMIES, 2 AUGUST 1914

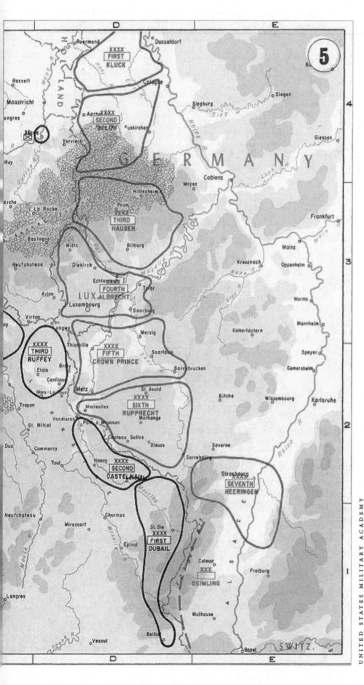

minute) as the German 77mm or the British 13-pounder guns—alone could keep up with the advancing infantry; less mobile heavy artillery would only slow the advance.

Infantrymen in their heavy wool blue coats, red trousers, blue cap with red top (képi), nailed boots (*brodequins*), and carrying twenty-five kilograms of kit (poncho, entrenching tool, ammunition, mess gear, water bottle, as well as a pack with spare socks, shirt, and field dressing) would storm entrenched positions, led by their officers and drum-and-bugle corps. The combination of a withering hail of bullets from mainly single-shot 1886 Lebel 8mm rifles and 75mm cannon shells would turn the tide. Once among the enemy, the *poilus* would fix bayonets—*la Rosalie,* the thin, triangular "supreme weapon" according to the Infantry Regulations of April 1914—and finish off remaining defenders.[93] "*À la baionette! En avant!*"* rang lustily through the woods of Alsace-Lorraine, the Ardennes, and the Argonne in August 1914. Few staff officers appreciated that the French corps with 120 75mm guns might be outmatched if a slugfest ensued against German corps with 108 77mm, 36 105mm, and 16 150mm guns.

Also not fully resolved by summer 1914 was the role that the reserves would play in a future war. In October 1913, British or Russian intelligence sources passed on to the French army a report on the state of the German army, in which one conclusion stood out: Moltke planned to use his first-line reserve formations "at the same time as the active army."[94] But what precisely did this mean? French military intelligence did not place a high value on Germany's reserves and hence were convinced that the Landwehr would not be integrated with active units. Most likely, this precluded a drive across Belgium, as German regular forces would be insufficient to storm Belgium and France as well as Russian Poland.

With regard to his own reserves, Joffre was adamant that France, with a stagnant population of twenty million less than Germany, not only would have to draft all eligible males (in fact, 84 percent as opposed to 53 percent in Germany), but also to deploy its reserves from the outset of a war. His guiding planning principle, he later wrote, was "to wage war with all my forces."[95] Thus, he stood in the forefront (with President Poincaré) of those who in 1913 called for the extension

* "Plant bayonets! Forward!"

of the term of conscripts' service from two to three years. While this has generally been interpreted as preparation for a prolonged industrial war, it was in fact nothing more than Joffre's conviction that the republic needed to have as many well-trained men under arms as Germany and to deploy them in an opening campaign. Under the terms of the *loi troisième* of August 1913, France increased the size of its "come-as-you-are" army to 884,000 men (against Germany's 880,000 after its army increases of 1912 and 1913).[96] Given that Germany would have to deploy one army to delay the anticipated Russian onslaught in the east, that Charles Mangin's *force noire* would arrive from Africa, and that the British might deploy on the French left, the Allied armies would outnumber the Germans.

Last but not least, Joffre's fixation with the "cult of the offensive" ruled out a prolonged war. While he warned the Superior Council of National Defense in February 1912 that a struggle with Germany might last for an "indefinite period"—at least six months just to reach the Rhine River after victorious opening battles—he did little to prepare either army or nation for that eventuality. That the war had to be short became an article of faith not to be assailed. The Field Regulations of October 1913 squared the circle: "The nature of war, the size of forces involved, the difficulties of resupplying them, the interruption of social and economic life of the country, all encourage the search for a decision in the shortest possible time in order to terminate the fighting quickly."[97] Alfred von Schlieffen could not have put it better.

On 31 July 1914, Joffre warned the cabinet that time was of the essence. Every twenty-four-hour delay in mobilization translated into a fifteen- to twenty-kilometer loss of territory.[98] The Council of Ministers authorized mobilization on 1 August, when Germany declared war on Russia; 2 August was the first day of mobilization. Unlike 1870, mobilization proceeded smoothly. Between 2 and 18 August, fourteen major railway lines shuttled 4,278 trains, on average 56 per day, to garrisons and depots near the front at Sedan, Montmédy, Toul, Nancy, and Belfort. Only 20 were late. The peacetime home army of 884,000 absorbed 621,000 reservists into its forty-five infantry divisions; a further 655,000 men formed the twenty-five reserve divisions; and another 184,000 were organized into twelve territorial divisions. Last but not least, about one million men remained at their depots, awaiting deployment.[99] The French navy escorted Louis Comby's Constantine 37th and

Paul Muteau's Alger 38th colonial divisions as well as fourteen hundred men and horses of African 3d and 4th chasseurs from Algeria and Tunisia to France. Slowly, a vast force of 1.6 million infantrymen moved to the front at twenty-five to thirty kilometers per day.

There were far fewer deserters than the anticipated 10 to 13 percent: A mere 1.2 percent of the 1914 cohort of conscripts failed to report for duty, and many of these were classified as mentally handicapped, itinerants, or Bretons (who could not read French). Roughly 350,000 volunteers flooded recruiting depots and 3,000 peacetime deserters returned to serve.[100] In fact, the response was so patriotic that Minister of the Interior Louis Malvy on 1 August shelved the infamous *Carnet B,* the government's secret list of roughly twenty-five hundred known agitators, anarchists, pacifists, and spies to be arrested in case of mobilization as they posed a "national threat."[101] Not even the assassination of the supposed "pro-German Socialist traitor" Jean Jaurès by a radical nationalist on the day before mobilization sparked an outcry against the war.

Lieutenant Henri Desagneaux of the Railway Transport Service on 4 August recorded the intense enthusiasm of the slogans painted on the transports as the *poilus* departed for the front: DEATH TO THE KAISER. STRING THE KAISER UP. DEATH TO THE BOCHES.* And everywhere he noted the same caricatures: "pigs' heads in pointed helmets." The civilian population was equally stirred. "Bouquets, garlands, flags."[102]

The pressing question for the General Staff was where the main German blow would fall. Joffre spent the first week of August poring over intelligence reports, hoping that they would confirm the calculus behind his concentration plan. It was still "too early," he later put it, "to announce formally my intention to operate in [central] Belgium."[103] Germany's declaration of war on France on 3 August and on Belgium one day later relieved him of that quandary. On 8 August, Joffre issued his General Instruction No. 1, finally revealing his strategy.[104] The goal remained nothing less than the "destruction" of the entire German army. To that effect, he ordered a double blow: In the south, Yvon Dubail's First Army and Édouard de Castelnau's Second Army were to attack in Lorraine, south of the German fortifications at Metz-Thionville; in the center, Pierre Ruffey's Third Army and Fernand de Langle de Cary's Fourth Army were to drive into eastern

---

* *Boche* is a disparaging term for a German, likely from the French dialectical *caboche* (cabbage, blockhead).

Belgium, north of the enemy line at Metz-Thionville. Joffre held Charles Lanrezac's Fifth Army back at Rethel-Mézières as a reserve to repel what he took to be the main German drive through central Belgium.

Joffre believed that he had the right men in the right places. Castelnau, a devout Catholic in a largely anticlerical army, was known as the "fighting friar." He was broad and short, and sported imperial-period whiskers. He had worked with Joffre on "all studies for Plan XVII" and was one of its "principal authors," just the man to storm the Vosges and take Metz. Dubail, tall, slender, and solemn, was a "faithful, solid soldier, great disciplinarian, and conscientious." Lanrezac, the "swarthy" native of Guadeloupe, was France's most feared teacher of strategy at Saint-Cyr, the veritable "lion of the French army." Ruffey had a stellar reputation as an artillery expert with a "brilliant and imaginative mind." Langle de Cary was "a disciplinarian, full of authority, and animated to a very high degree by a sense of his responsibility."[105] It was Joffre's plan, and these were his handpicked commanders. The offensives would start on 14 August. It was up to the Germans to deploy as Joffre expected.

"WHAT WOULD YOU SAY was the smallest British military force that would be of any practical assistance to you?" Sir Henry Wilson, the tall, bony, energetic Ulsterman who, after three times failing to gain admission to the Royal Military College at Sandhurst, headed the Camberley Staff College, asked his French counterpart, Ferdinand Foch. The head of the École supérieure de la guerre, a proud and erect man with a bushy handlebar mustache and a boxer's nose, did not blink for a moment. "One single private soldier—and we would take good care that he was killed."[106]

Foch's bon mot captured the essence of the Anglo-French military-strategic relationship before 1914. France was the driver, Britain the passenger. France decided on the nature of the British involvement in World War I and the deployment of the British Expeditionary Force (BEF). Foch and Wilson exchanged sensitive operational intelligence. They studied maps of Belgium on which Wilson in heavy black ink marked every major road. They agreed that Britain would send the BEF to France the minute that Germany crossed the Belgian or French border. They concurred that the onus for provoking a conflict in Europe had to rest with Germany. They concealed the intimate nature of their discussions from politicians, both in Paris and in London.

For those politicians did not share the concepts concocted by the two military academy heads. French leaders such as Caillaux and Poincaré had steadfastly rejected plans that called for an early French deployment into Belgium, before clear evidence of a "positive menace of German invasion."[107] British leaders remained wedded to imperial defense—read, India—and were reluctant about what historian Michael Howard has called a "continental commitment."[108] Most preferred a maritime strategy: The Royal Navy would serve as a barrier to invasion and guarantor of British command of the sea. The army, in the cheeky words of First Sea Lord John A. Fisher, was but a "missile" to be "fired" by the navy. And even some army commanders feared that Henry Wilson, who would soon become widely known throughout the army as "the Intriguer," was "more French than the French!!"[109]

Britain in 1914 did not possess a war plan. Rather, its admirals and generals individually had drafted a series of contingency plans to address a plethora of possible conflicts that London might face around the globe. To be sure, one of these concerned the possibility of German expansion on the Continent. After its less-than-stellar performance against the Boers in South Africa (1899–1902), the British army in 1906 had created a General Staff to further the professionalization of its officers. John Grierson, the first director of military operations in the General Staff, had served as military attaché in Berlin. Convinced of the bellicose nature of the Berlin regime, Grierson drafted plans for sending an expeditionary force to the Continent to assist France. Secretary of State for Foreign Affairs Sir Edward Grey gave Grierson the green light—provided that talks with the French proceeded "unofficially and in a non-committal way."[110]

This they did—in 1906, 1907, and 1908. Under Grierson's successor, Wilson, the plans matured into the dispatch of a BEF consisting of four infantry divisions and one cavalry division—to be augmented by an additional two infantry divisions once the Territorial Forces were deemed fit to stand up an effective home defense. The BEF was to deploy on the left wing of the French army near Le Cateau-Maubeuge-Hirson. While Wilson viewed its five divisions as "fifty too few,"[111] he nevertheless set the wheels in motion for a formal British "continental commitment." And he upset the Admiralty, where Their

Lordships favored amphibious operations in the North and Baltic seas.

The army-navy antagonism over strategy came to a head on 23 August 1911 at a critical meeting of a subcommittee of the Committee of Imperial Defence (CID)—created in 1902 as a forum where Foreign Office, Admiralty, War Office, and Treasury could discuss national security policy. Prime Minister Herbert Henry Asquith was in the chair that day. The meeting has taken on almost mythical proportions in the debate over British war planning prior to 1914, with historian Niall Ferguson going so far as to argue that it "set the course for a military confrontation between Britain and Germany."[112]

Asquith's purpose in calling the meeting was to tackle a broad question: How could Britain, if asked, provide "armed support" to France in the event of a German attack? Wilson and Sir William Nicholson, chief of the Imperial General Staff, presented the army's case first. Six infantry divisions and one cavalry division would be sent to the Continent at once, to be deployed on the left wing of the French army. The two officers viewed this as critical, since otherwise the Germans might well overrun France and leave Britain with a naval struggle "that could be measured in years."[113] Wilson, having bought into French intelligence estimates, expected the enemy advance to come between Verdun and Maubeuge. Since there were but thirteen major roads in this corridor, he projected no more than forty German infantry divisions in the area, which would be defended by a similar number of French infantry divisions. Hence, the BEF could prove to be the decisive "tipping point" in the campaign.

Asquith next called on Britain's admirals to state their case.[114] Sir Arthur Wilson, the new first sea lord, called for a close blockade of the German North Sea coast, augmented by tip-and-run operations against enemy ports, at first in the North Sea and later also in the nearly landlocked Baltic Sea. Had he left it at that, Wilson might well have escaped unscathed. But as head of the Senior Service, he could not resist taking jabs at the army's presentation. The dispatch of almost all British forces to France would cause a collapse in public morale, he argued, and it would leave no regular troops at home to defend the island. Worse yet, it left no troops for the Royal Navy to "launch" onto German soil. Almost as an afterthought, Wilson opined that the Royal Navy was not prepared even to cover the transport of the BEF across the English Channel.

It was a disastrous misstep. Home Secretary Winston S. Churchill and Chancellor of the Exchequer David Lloyd George at once pounced on the fact that Wilson had, in fact, stated in writing in 1908–09 that the fleet could escort the BEF across the Channel, and that it could protect the island against German invasion. Churchill viciously queried Wilson as to how under his scheme a German invasion fleet could get past the entire Royal Navy blockading Germany's North Sea ports! The cabinet concluded that the Royal Navy had no war plan worthy of the name. Admiral Wilson was removed from his post within two months of the meeting. "Continental intervention," in the words of historian Samuel R. Williamson Jr., "had become the accepted dogma."[115]

But how to transform this "dogma" into reality? Where were the troops to be landed? How would they be deployed? Who would command? Above all, how was the cabinet to be brought onside? Prime Minister Asquith let it be known within three months of that CID meeting that "all questions of policy have been & must be reserved for the decision of the Cabinet, & that it is quite outside the function of military or naval officers to prejudge such questions."[116] This was clear political language, even for Henry Wilson.

The real test came only after Britain had declared war on Germany on 4 August—without ever having debated its "war plan." Over the next two days, Asquith convened meetings of his top military and naval advisers at 10 Downing Street. The most important of these took place in late afternoon of 5 August.[117] Chaired by Prime Minister Asquith, it included, among others, cabinet ministers Churchill and Lloyd George, First Sea Lord Prince Louis of Battenberg, Field Marshals Sir John French and Horatio Herbert Lord Kitchener, and Generals Henry Wilson and Douglas Haig. Kitchener confounded the group by stating that the war would last three years, and that Britain would have to raise million-man armies to fight it. Haig likewise raised hackles by suggesting that the BEF ought to be held back in Britain for a while (perhaps "2 or 3 months"), while the full resources of the empire were marshaled. "Johnnie" French, the newly appointed commander in chief, a paunchy, bulldog-like, white-haired cavalry officer who, in the words of historian Hew Strachan, had "made one reputation in South Africa and another in ladies' bedrooms,"[118] crossed Wilson by stating that since Britain's mobilization was already three days behind that of France, the BEF ought to be disembarked at Antwerp rather than at a French Channel port. Wilson thought that a "ridiculous proposal." Foreign Secretary Grey chimed in that this would violate Dutch (!) territory. French, along with Churchill and Lloyd George, argued that the Germans likely would debouch north of Maubeuge and the Meuse River, and thus called for further landings at Zeebrugge and Ostend (Oostende).

On the contentious issue of the BEF's deployment on the Continent, Kitchener, who would be appointed the secretary of state for war the next day, opted for Amiens, well behind the French front. Sir John French then suggested that after landing at Antwerp, the BEF operate on the German right flank—and thus along both banks of the Scheldt River, which were in neutral Holland. After what Wilson derisively called "desultory strategy" and "idiocy,"[119] the cabinet on 6 August decided to dispatch four infantry divisions and one cavalry division to the Continent; 4th Infantry Division was kept on the coast to defend against possible German landings, while 6th Infantry Division remained in Ireland to guard against unrest. They would be sent to France as soon as conditions warranted. The octogenarian field marshal Frederick Lord Roberts carried the day by suggesting that British deployment be left for the French to decide. And decide they did—for Maubeuge, where, in Foch's words, it was certain that "a single British soldier" would in fact be quickly "killed."

The British Expeditionary Force of 1914, in the words of the official history of the war, "was incomparably the best trained, best organized, and best equipped British Army which ever went forth to war."[120] This certainly was true with regard to the ranks and to materials. The regular army, or First Line, consisted of six mixed-arms divisions and one cavalry division. Each infantry division of eighteen thousand soldiers comprised three brigades (each of four battalions) with artillery, engineers, mounted troops, signal service, and supply and transport train. Service dress included a thick woolen tunic dyed khaki green, a stiffened peak cap, hobnailed boots, puttees around the ankles, and webbing as well as a small haversack that held thirty-two kilograms of ammunition, entrenching tool, personal items, knife, washing and shaving kit, water bottle, daily rations, and a knife, fork, and spoon set. The British soldier in 1914 carried a superb rifle, the Short Magazine Lee-Enfield .303-inch caliber weapon, capable of firing fifteen aimed rounds per minute and mounting a seventeen-inch

Wilkinson Sword bayonet. It was every bit as good as, and perhaps even better than, the German Mauser.

In terms of firepower,[121] each division of four thousand artificers commanded fifty-four 18-pounder guns, eighteen 4.5-inch (114mm) light howitzers, and four 60-pounder (127mm) guns. The 18-pounder (which later became the American 75mm Model 1917) was the Royal Field Artillery's mainstay. It could fire as many as thirty 8.6kg shells per minute, with maximum range of 5,960 meters. Its only drawback was the meager allotment of one thousand to thirteen hundred shells per gun, which translated into only four to five hours of sustained fire support. The 4.5-inch howitzer was a simple and robust weapon with a rate of fire of four rounds per minute and maximum range of 6,680 meters. The British failure to produce modern heavy field howitzers— like the 152mm and 203mm pieces of the latter part of the war— limited offensive operations in 1914. The 60-pounder was the main heavy artillery gun of the BEF. It could fire two 27kg shells per minute to a maximum range of 11,250 meters—roughly 4,000 meters shorter than the German 135mm piece. It required a crew of ten to operate the weapon and a team of eight horses to tow its 4.4 tons. Only the how-itzers and the 60-pounders had high-explosive shells. Finally, each di-vision was given twenty-four Vickers Model 1912 water-cooled machine guns that could fire at a rate of 450 bullets per minute.

The BEF's reinforced cavalry division comprised five brigades each of three regiments, in all some nine thousand sabers as well as about four thousand supporting artillery and auxiliary troops. The division had thirty Vickers machine guns and two brigades of horse-drawn artillery, or a total of twenty-four 13-pounders. The latter were de-signed as rapid-fire field guns for the Royal Horse Artillery in maneu-ver warfare, and had a range of 5,390 meters. Unfortunately, they were much too light against entrenched enemy positions. Fourteen di-visions (three hundred thousand men) of the Territorial Forces, raised by county lieutenancies, were the last reserve. They had but thirty-five guns per division and were not expected to be combat-ready in less than six months after mobilization.[122]

Finally, the recently organized Royal Flying Corps consisted of sixty operational airplanes of various types and makes.[123] Four self-contained squadrons went to France in 1914. Each squadron consisted of three flights, each with four airplanes. Their primary mission was operational reconnaissance. By October 1914, however, the mission had been extended to include air-to-air combat and some aerial bombardment.

British military doctrine on the eve of World War I was in transition, an amalgam of lessons learned from the Boer War and the Russo-Japanese War as well as observation of what mainly the French practiced.[124] Its tactics of fire and maneuver to close with the enemy, followed by the decisive final shock assault, were the key to solving the problem of infantry attack in an age of modern rifles, smokeless powder, rapid-fire artillery, and the machine gun. They were tailored to its long-service regulars. The 1911 manual *Infantry Training* stressed attack, defense, and security. Fire, maneuver, and interarms cooperation were critical to success. The days of swarming lines of infantry, solid massed columns advancing, and inspired bayonet charges with trumpets blaring and colors flying seemingly belonged to the past. Direct artillery fire remained the primary mode of supporting infantry in the assault. Indirect fire still lacked the technology to relay information quickly and accurately while on the move. There was little liaison between artillery and infantry. Cavalry doctrine emphasized the rifle as the primary weapon for dismounted riders, but Sir John French insisted that the *arme blanche* was not obsolete in modern war; hence he retained the sword and reintroduced the lance for the hallowed cavalry charge.

The verdict on the British High Command remains mixed. The General Staff, established only in 1906, still lacked the experience and professional expertise of the French or German staffs. It was hardly prepared to conduct a war on the continental scale. Neither the 1913 maneuvers nor the winter 1913–14 General Staff war game, both resulting in "total confusion" and inept command and control, had installed confidence in the British staff system. While most scholars have long rejected the simplistic notion of the army as "lions led by donkeys," historian Tim Travers maintains that its upper echelons were dominated by men who were openly "class conscious" and "anti-intellectual," who rejected theory and doctrine as "bookish," and who preferred "traditional Victorian" values such as experience, common sense, good breeding, and classical education.[125] They stressed character: human qualities such as bravery and self-control. While aware of the impact of modern technology and firepower on the battlefield and the need to prepare the nation to accept high casualties ("wastage"), they still defined battle as a structured and ordered phenomenon based on preparation, assault, and exploitation. War remained essentially the triumph of will. Although it might be too strong to state that the British were as animated by the cult of the offensive as the major continental armies, the concept nevertheless remained strong, especially with leaders such as French and Haig.

British mobilization—down to collecting 120,000 horses in twelve days—proceeded much more efficiently than it had fifteen years earlier for the war in South Africa. Southampton was the major port of troop embarkation; Le Havre, the major port of disembarkation. The Royal Navy closed both ends of the English Channel against enemy raids.[126] There were to be neither convoys nor escorts. The security of the BEF's transport to France was left to Fifth, Seventh, and Eighth battle squadrons of the Channel Fleet under Vice Admiral Sir Cecil Burney. French destroyers and submarines of the Boulogne Squadron would guard the Straits of Dover. The Grand Fleet was kept at sea to intercept any attempt by the German High Seas Fleet to attack the transports.

Over the five most intensive days of transport, eighteen hundred trains were mobilized in Britain and Ireland.[127] On the busiest day of the enterprise, eighty trains arrived at Southampton Docks. From there, the troops proceeded to France, in single ships or in pairs, by day and by night. At the peak in shipping, more than 137 simultaneous passages ferried 130,000 soldiers across the Channel. On 14 August, Field Marshal French and his staff arrived at Amiens. They deployed the BEF in a pear-shaped area measuring forty by sixteen kilometers between Maubeuge and Le Cateau, and ordered it to advance northeast on the left of French Fifth Army in the direction of Nivelle. Sir Douglas Haig took command of I Corps and "Jimmy" Grierson of II Corps; upon Grierson's sudden and unexpected death due to a heart attack, Sir Horace Smith-Dorrien was given II Corps. Kluck's First Army and Bülow's Second Army lurked on Belgium's eastern border.

OF ALL THE EUROPEAN states, Belgium was in the most unenviable position. For centuries, it had been the playground of the great captains: Julius Caesar, Charles the Bold, Philip II, Louis XI, Louis XIV, the Duke of Marlborough, Napoleon I, and the Duke of Wellington. In 1830, after an uprising against the Dutch ruler Willem I, the European powers had declared it to be an "Independent and perpetually Neutral State." In international accords signed in 1831 and 1839, they had recognized Leopold of Saxe-Coburg-Gotha as King of the Belgians.[128] For seven decades, Belgium hung in a precarious state of scrupulous neutrality, aware that its continued existence depended on the goodwill of the great powers.

To give the new kingdom a chance to defend itself (at least initially) in case of hostile incursion by any of its neighbors, the great powers had insisted that Belgium "uphold" its territorial integrity. Thus, between 1878 and 1906 Brussels set about creating a system of ten fortresses—the major ones being at Antwerp, Namur, and Liège. By 1914, *la position fortifée de Liège* had received an additional eleven forts and twelve field works, equally divided along both banks of the Maas, making it one of Europe's most formidable fortresses. The regular army consisted of 117,000 men, divided into six light infantry divisions and one cavalry division.

Under the leadership of Prime Minister Charles de Brocqueville, Brussels in May 1913 introduced universal male conscription and increased the annual intake of recruits from 13,300 to 33,000.[129] The grand design was to stand up an army of roughly 340,000 soldiers by 1918. The regular field army was to consist of 180,000 men, organized into six army corps, each of three or four light infantry divisions. The new king, Albert, the last of the European warrior-kings, was prepared to use these assets against any and all potential invaders; he regarded no power as a potential ally. Thus, in historian Strachan's words, Brussels boxed itself into a policy of "international political purity" but "strategic and military absurdity."[130]

Belgium's precarious position of "perpetual" neutrality suffered a rude shock in 1913. In his last peacetime "Deployment Plan 1913/14," Moltke demanded that on the first day of mobilization, the Belgian government be handed an "ultimatum of short duration" in which it openly declared itself "to be Germany's ally or adversary," and that it "open" the fortresses of Liège, Namur, and Huy to a German advance across its territory.[131] During a state visit to Berlin in November, Wilhelm II and Moltke warned Albert that "small countries, such as Belgium, would be well advised to rally to the side of the strong if they wished to retain their independence."[132] It was at best an insensitive comment; at worst a direct threat to a king who stemmed from an ancient and noble German house, whose mother was a Hohenzollern princess, and who had married a Bavarian duchess, Elisabeth of Wittelsbach. Above all, both Wilhelm II and Moltke badly misjudged Albert's temperament.

How to deploy Belgium's army? King Albert and his military reached general agreement that, depending on the nature of an external threat, the army would concentrate along a west-east axis running from Aat to Namur to Liège, ready to face either France or Germany. But in May 1913, Chief of the General Staff Antonin Selliers de Moranville ordered a refinement of these plans as it became evident that Germany would be the likely adversary. Since Germany could mobilize and deploy its forces faster than Belgium, Deputy Chief of Staff Colonel Louis de Rijckel (Ryckel), with King Albert's approval, decided to deploy his entire force along the line of the Maas. The plan made sense. The army could thus be anchored on Fortress Liège and its four hundred guns, with its front protected by the "formidable wet ditch" of the Maas; its left wing rested against the Dutch border, and its right wing sheltered behind the Maas and Fortress Namur.[133] Of course, such a massive overhaul of the Belgian war plan required the one thing that Brussels did not have in 1913—time.

How well prepared was Liège for war? When General Gérard Leman took command of 3d Infantry Division at Liège at the beginning of 1913, he was shocked by its "deplorable state."[134] The "lamentable slackness" of the troops "greatly distressed" him: By and large, they were "dirty and untidy," avoided officers so as not to have to salute, carried no arms, and in public "slouched, hand across stomachs or behind backs, humped up, chins on chests and feet dragging." A forced refresher course at Beverloo in May did little to address the sad state of the forces. Fully one-third of the division's officers, Leman lamented, "knew nothing of fire control or maneuver." The infantry "were very poor marksmen." The artillery "had not the equipment to communicate with its own infantry." The only bright spot was that by the end of their training, at least the young recruits "showed willingness and endurance in marching" and generally "gave the impression of having personal courage."

On 3 August, King Albert rejected Berlin's ultimatum of the previous evening calling on Brussels to grant German armies free passage with the terse comment, "It is war."[135] The theoretical planning of the last years was now hard reality. Under Article 68 of the Constitution, King Albert became commander in chief of the Belgian army. And since no plans existed as yet for Rijckel's redeployment of the bulk of his forces on the line of the Maas, Albert had no alternative but to marshal 3d Infantry Division at Liège, 4th Infantry Division at Namur, and the remainder of his troops at Tirlemont, Perwez, and Leuven (Louvain), between the Gette (Gete) and Dyle (Dijle) rivers. Leuven was to serve as army headquarters.

The Belgian army called up 200,000 men, followed by 18,500 volunteers and 18,000 conscripts. In fact, the field army, excluding fortress troops, amounted to but 117,000 regulars and 37,600 horses. Each of the six corps comprised between twenty-five thousand and thirty thousand men; the cavalry division, forty-five hundred sabers. Each infantry division was subdivided into three or four brigades of two regiments each, with one artillery regiment of a dozen 75mm guns and a second with a plethora of 36mm, 75mm, and 150mm guns. There existed no heavy artillery and a mere 102 machine guns, with the result that Brussels in August hastily purchased twelve heavy howitzers and one hundred machine guns from France.[136] About two hundred thousand soldiers manned the country's ten major fortresses. Behind them stood a last reserve, the Garde civique, weekend warriors garbed in semimilitary uniforms. Still caught up in the midst of Brocqueville's expansion plans, much of Belgium's army in 1914 consisted of what Émile Galet of its École militaire called "phantom battalions and skeleton companies."[137] The full force of the German assault would soon fall on this army at Liège.

CHAPTER THREE

DEATH IN THE VOSGES

———

*A single error in the original assembly of the armies can
hardly ever be rectified during the entire course of the campaign.*

—HELMUTH VON MOLTKE THE ELDER

TWO ARMIES CLOSED ON EACH OTHER ON THE PLAIN OF ALSACE in the heat of early September. One had advanced out of the west through the Belfort Gap, a broad swath of land where the Vosges Mountains of France fail to meet the Jura Mountains of Switzerland; the other, out of the northeast and across the Rhine. They met somewhere between Cernay (Sennheim) and Mulhouse (Mülhausen) along the edge of the southern Vosges Mountains. One took up an attacking position on "a large plain" west of the Rhine; the other debouched on "a rising ground of considerable height" in the Vosges. Both "fell to work with their spades" and built strong entrenchments. Both were about fifty thousand men strong.[1] One was commanded by Julius Caesar, the other by the German chieftain Ariovistus.

Precisely 1,972 years later, such a battle was repeated. The troops pouring out of the Belfort Gap in 1914 were French and those out of the northeast, German. French forces consisted of VII Army Corps and 8th Cavalry Division (CD) of Yvon Dubail's First Army; German forces, of Baden XIV and XV army corps as well as XIV Army Reserve Corps of Josias von Heeringen's Seventh Army. Both were rushing headlong toward the villages of Altkirch and Thann as well as Mulhouse, a textile town known as "the city of a hundred flues," some of which belonged to the family of Alfred Dreyfus. Upper Alsace was devoid of major fortifications, for it had no pride of place in either side's concentration plan.

WITH THE POSSIBLE EXCEPTION of the Rhenish Palatinate—the left bank of the river Rhine bordered by France to the west and Baden to the south—no area of the historic wars between France and Germany so agitated the public as the two ancient lands of Alsace and Lorraine. They had been part of the Holy Roman Empire of the Germanic Nation since the Treaty of Meersen in 870, but eight hundred years later, in the words of the Elder Helmuth von Moltke, Louis XIV "severed" them "like a sound limb from the living body of Germany."[2] That same Moltke brought the "Old Reichsland" back into Germany in 1871. He was moved in doing so not only by national passion but also by military necessity: The two provinces formed a triangle with the apex, formed by the confluence of the Ill and Rhine rivers, a veritable dagger pointing at the heart of Germany; and the Vosges Mountains and the Plain of Alsace accorded France a perfect sallying point for a future revenge attack on the new Reich.

Annexation brought with it a return to old Germanic names. Alsace reverted to Elsaß, Lorraine to Lothringen, Sarrebourg to Saarburg, Strasbourg to Straßburg, and Thionville to Diedenhofen. The Vosges were once more the Vogesen. Many villages exchanged the French endings of *-vihr* and *-viler* for the ancient German *-weier* and *-weiler,* respectively. Lorraine remained French culturally and linguistically, while Alsace retained its Aleman roots. Many French Alsatians migrated to France. Villages were torn apart by the new border. Roads were studded with sentry gates; the ridge of the Vosges, with border posts. The German administration—Prussian military—impressed the local population with neither its charm nor its grace. In the petty bickering leading up to the Treaty of Frankfurt in 1871, two decisions were made that were to impact the course of events in 1914: Fortress and Territoire de Belfort remained with France (in exchange for a German victory parade through Paris), and the new Franco-German border was drawn along the crest of the Vosges rather than farther west at the eastern edge of the Plateau of Lorraine. Belfort in 1914 would anchor the French extreme right flank; the Vosges heights would provide France access to the major passes through the mountains.

—

ON 7 AUGUST, THE French landed the first blow in the south. Chief of the General Staff Joseph Joffre's General Instruction No. 1 of 8 August, as detailed in the previous chapter, had made clear that he primarily wanted to "jab" in Alsace with his First Army, to "fix" the German left wing, and, if possible, to draw enemy units to the south while he delivered the main blow against the German center via a two-pronged offensive on each side of the Metz-Thionville defenses.[3] But Joffre could not resist the temptation to arouse the nation's passion for war by an early coup de théâtre in Alsace. He selected Louis Bonneau, Alsatian-born, to lead French forces against Mulhouse, destroy the Rhine bridges, and then march north against Colmar and Strasbourg. A cautious man, Bonneau's one claim to fame was that at a general maneuver, he had delivered a blistering public attack on a divisional commander—Ferdinand Foch.[4] At 5 AM* on 7 August, Bonneau led VII Corps out of the Belfort Gap on what he termed a "delicate and hazardous" undertaking.[5] He directed Louis Curé's 14th Infantry Division (ID) to attack Altkirch and Paul Superbie's 41st ID, Thann—two villages close to the Swiss border. The infantrymen were conspicuous in their bright blue jackets, shining red trousers, and képi, led by officers in white gloves clutching drawn swords. Louis Aubier's flanking 8th CD was resplendent in dark blue jackets, red breeches with blue seams, and brass helmets streaming long back plumes.[6] Cadets from the Saint-Cyr Military Academy deployed in full-dress uniforms with white plumed casoar. Bonneau's troops advanced haltingly against virtually no opposition. Then in a spirited bayonet charge, they drove the small German garrison out of Altkirch. Bonneau sent news of the victory to Paris, where it evoked wild celebrations.

Joffre, while pleased with the public fervor over the seizure of Altkirch, was infuriated by Bonneau's failure to quickly follow up the initial victory. He ordered VII Corps to move at once against Mulhouse.[7] It did so slowly. The city fell to Bonneau without opposition at 3 PM on 8 August, the covering German 58th Infantry Brigade (IB) having withdrawn. Bonneau paraded his troops through Mulhouse's main square for two hours, displaying the German border posts they

* Actions in German Alsace are given in German General Time (DGZ); in French Lorraine, in Greenwich Mean Time (GMT), one hour earlier.

had ripped out of the ground the previous morning. Joffre now hailed the soldiers of VII Corps as "pioneers in the great work of revenge."[8] French Alsatians welcomed the troops with cheers of *"Vive la France!"* and hearty renditions of "La Marseillaise" as well as the "Sambre et Meuse."* They also took advantage of the opportunity to turn against their German brothers. The latter responded by passing on French troop formations and strengths to General von Heeringen at Strasbourg.

Within twenty-four hours of Bonneau's strike on Mulhouse, Heeringen overthrew his entire deployment plan and moved to dislodge the French from Mulhouse. He ordered Bertold von Deimling's XV Corps at Strasbourg and Ernst von Hoiningen-Huene's XIV Corps at Breisach to retake the city; Richard von Schubert's XIV Reserve Corps was to continue to mobilize along the Rhine bridges. To assure success, Heeringen secured the temporary addition of Oskar von Xylander's Bavarian I Army Corps for the operation. His plan was to turn the French left flank and to throw Bonneau's VII Army Corps against the Swiss border. XIV Corps, fifty-eight battalions strong, straddled the Rhine River. Due to their close proximity to Mulhouse, Hoiningen-Huene's corps forwent rail transport and instead headed on foot across the Rhine Valley.[9] For forty hours, the troops marched over fields of clover and grain, past vineyards and orchards, through hawthorn hedges and forests under a blazing forty-degree-Celsius sun.[10] En route, they sharpened bayonets. Most adhered to Hoiningen-Huene's orders to restrict their beer intake and not to purchase hard liquor.

Debouching from the mosquito-infested bogs of the Forest of Harth at 3 PM on 9 August, Hoiningen-Huene's units attacked French positions around Mulhouse. The orderly advance quickly disintegrated into a series of bloody frontal assaults. The fighting in heavily wooded and vineyard-studded terrain was bitter and at close quarters. Heat, exhaustion, and lack of water took their toll. Men dropped off to rest in roadside ditches. Others had to be carried forward on trucks and carts. Infantry companies straggled. Field kitchens ("goulash cannons") fell behind. By nightfall, vicious street fighting ensued at the small village of Rixheim, just east of Mulhouse. In their baptism of

---

* A patriotic military march arranged by Joseph François Rauski in 1879, after the Franco-Prussian War.

fire, many companies blindly fired off ten to sixteen thousand rounds. In the darkness, soldiers mistakenly fired on one another. A semblance of order was finally restored by having the men sing the patriotic song "Die Wacht am Rhein," as a means of identification. In the melee, 112th Infantry Regiment (IR) suffered 41 dead, 163 wounded, and 223 missing.[11]

The fighting at Mulhouse was even more disorderly and just as deadly. At Napoleon Island on the Rhône-Rhine Canal, the French fired at the Baden Landwehr (reserves) from raised platforms across ripe grain fields, inflicting "severe losses." Confusion reigned at battalion and regimental levels. Orders were either not received or ignored. To avoid the withering French machine-gun fire, the men of 2d Battalion, 169th IR, took refuge in a gravel pit. When the battalion commander, Major Otto Teschner, ordered a frontal attack, only his officers and "a few men" obeyed; the rest beat a hasty retreat to the shelter of the pit— and beyond. Teschner stemmed the flood back to the canal only by threatening to shoot shirkers and by striking at least one on the head with his dagger.[12]

There were similar scenes of disorderly retreat elsewhere. When Major Maas, commanding 1st Battalion, 169th IR, dispatched Lother Hauger to reconnoiter Banzenheim, the officer encountered several companies streaming back from the front. "They told me that they had been beaten and wanted to [go back] across the Rhine." The nineteen-year-old Hauger rose to the occasion. "I took the next available horse, had the Rhine bridge closed and gave the order not to let anyone across."[13] He received a regimental citation for valor and later the Iron Cross, Second Class.[14]

The German losses may have been severe, but Bonneau was shaken by the massive enemy response to his invasion and ordered a general retreat later that night. He did not stop until VII Corps was safely under the shelter of Belfort's guns. War Minister Adolphe Messimy threatened to court-martial and execute any commander found to be lacking the requisite offensive spirit.[15] By 13 August, Mulhouse and the surrounding area were back in German hands. It was now the turn of the returning German Alsatians to take revenge on their French brothers. *"Deutschland, Deutschland über alles!"* was sung well into the night. Martial law was proclaimed, and residents suspected of having aided the French were evicted. But worse was to come. Numerous commanders—at the company, battalion, and regimental levels—reported that their men had been fired on by civilians. The nightmarish specter of 1870, when French irregulars had taken up arms against the invading German troops, had raised its ugly head: francs-tireurs!* Although all Baden formations had been read the "rules of war" on 4 August, a General Corps Order of 11 August stated: "Soldiers or civilians offering even the least resistance are to be shot at once." At Baldersheim, armed civilians operating out of houses flying the Red Cross flag were hanged.[16] At Didenheim and Niedermorschweier, Hoiningen-Huene's units took mayors and priests hostage and threatened to execute armed civilians and burn down the homes of those who sheltered them.[17]

The persistent encounter with suspected or real francs-tireurs prompted General Hans Gaede, deputy commander of XIV Corps, to issue a special decree defining just who constituted a franc-tireur. The decree was as sweeping as it was draconian. Any citizens of "France, England, Belgium, Russia and Japan" not in uniform and who in any way disrupted German military operations, communications, or supply were to be regarded as *Franktireure*. If caught in the act, they were "to be killed at once, naturally in self-defense." If not caught redhanded, they were still to be executed, but only by emergency courtsmartial requiring one officer. Residents of the "Reichsland" who were caught with arms were to be summarily executed; those merely suspected of such actions, handed over to formal courts-martial.[18] Without question, the war in the west had turned ugly in its first days.

The first of four engagements in the so-called Battle of the Frontiers had not gone well for France.† Joffre, who had earlier heralded Bonneau's seizure of Mulhouse, now allowed no news of its recapture by the Germans or of the number of casualties to be released. He relieved Bonneau, the hero of yesterday, of command—the first of many so-called *limogés,* so named because War Minister Messimy assigned them to rear duty at the army depot of Limoges, some four hundred kilometers away from the political nerve center of Paris. Within a week, Joffre would also sack Louis Aubier, commanding 8th CD in Alsace.

The Battle of Mulhouse had been fought for the wrong reason—national prestige—and at the wrong place—the southernmost flank of

* In today's terminology, "partisans" to one side and "terrorists" to the other.
† The others were the Ardennes, Sambre-et-Meuse (Battle of Charleroi), and Mons.

both armies. Joffre's General Instruction No. 1 had made clear that he simply wanted to tie down enemy units to the south while he delivered his main blow against the Germans around the Metz-Thionville defenses. His German counterpart, Helmuth von Moltke, likewise had instructed the commanders on his left flank merely to "attract and to tie down" as many French forces "as possible" in the area between the Upper Moselle and Meurthe rivers to prevent the French from transporting them to their left wing, where the main German attack would be delivered through Belgium. Beyond that, they were to secure Alsace and Baden against invasion.[19]

But as Carl von Clausewitz made abundantly clear in *Vom Kriege,* "war is the realm of uncertainty." A host of "intangibles" such as interaction, friction, moral factors, and the "fog of uncertainty" at all times interacted with what he called "primordial violence" or "slaughter" and the "passions of the people" to prolong war, to escalate conflict, and to bedevil the best-laid plans of staff officers. Thus it was with regard to Alsace-Lorraine in 1914.

BAVARIAN CROWN PRINCE RUPPRECHT and the staff of German Sixth Army departed Munich-Laim by train at 9:50 PM on 7 August and arrived at their headquarters at Saint-Avold, a dreary industrial hamlet some forty kilometers east of Metz, at precisely 7:47 AM on 9 August.[20] It was hot, the air sullen. Sixth Army was composed of I Corps (Oskar von Xylander), II Corps (Karl von Martini), III Corps (Ludwig von Gebsattel), and I Reserve Corps (Karl von Fasbender)—183 infantry battalions, 28 cavalry squadrons, and 81 artillery batteries; roughly 220,000 men in all. The next night, Rupprecht, at age forty-five, also assumed command of Heeringen's Seventh Army and Rudolf von Frommel's III Cavalry Corps. Prewar plans for his forces to be augmented by Italian Third Army—two cavalry divisions at Strasbourg and three infantry corps on the Upper Rhine, possibly to storm Belfort by the seventeenth day of mobilization (M+17)—had died when Italy declared its neutrality on 2 August. Sixth Army was thus thinly spread out: about 2,960 men per kilometer of front as opposed to 11,100 for First Army, on the right wing. According to the operational plan ("Thoughts About the Operations of Sixth and Seventh Armies") that Moltke had submitted to Sixth Army and that Rupprecht's chief of staff, Konrad Krafft von Dellmensingen, had refined on 6 August before leaving Munich, the Bavari-

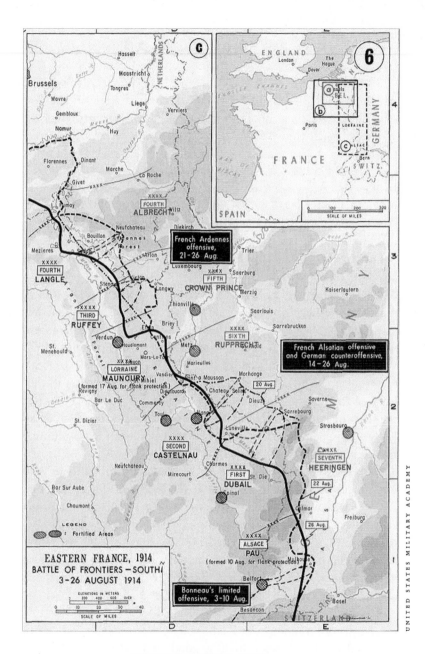

EASTERN FRANCE, 1914
BATTLE OF FRONTIERS — SOUTH
3-26 AUGUST 1914

ELEVATIONS IN METERS
200   400   600   OVER

0   10   20   30   40
SCALE OF MILES

LEGEND
: Fortified Areas

French Ardennes offensive, 21-26 Aug.

French Alsatian offensive and German counteroffensive, 14-26 Aug.

Bonneau's limited offensive, 3-10 Aug.

XXXX FOURTH ALBRECHT
XXXX FOURTH LANGLE
XXXX FIFTH CROWN PRINCE
XXXX THIRD RUFFEY
XXXX SIXTH RUPPRECHT
XX LORRAINE MAUNOURY (formed 17 Aug. for flank protection)
XXXX SECOND CASTELNAU
XXXX FIRST DUBAIL
XXXX SEVENTH HEERINGEN
XXXX ALSACE PAU (formed 10 Aug. for flank protection)

20 Aug
22 Aug
26 Aug

Brussels, Hasselt, Maastricht, Tongres, Wavre, Gembloux, Liege, Verviers, Namur, Huy, Florennes, Dinant, Marche, La Roche, Givet, Mezieres, Bouillon, Neufchateau, Ardennes Forest, Arlon, Diekirch, Trier, Luxembourg, Saarburg, Longwy, Merzig, Kaiserlautern, Thionville, Saarlouis, Sarrebrucken, Verdun, Briey, Metz, St. Menehould, Mars-La-Tour, Marieulles, St. Mihiel, Vandier, Pont-a-Mousson, Morhange, Saverne, Bar Le Duc, Commercy, Toul, Nancy, Chateau Salins, Dieuze, Sarrebourg, Strasbourg, Luneville, St. Dizier, Neufchateau, Charmes, Mirecourt, St. Die, Bar Sur Aube, Chaumont, Colmar, Freiburg, Mulhouse, Belfort, Basel, Besancon, SWITZERLAND

ENGLAND, London, The Hague, Dover, Paris, BEL., LORRAINE, ALSAC, Bern, FRANCE, SPAIN, GERMANY, SWITZ.

6

100   200   300
SCALE OF MILES

ARDENNES AND LORRAINE, AUGUST 1914

ans were to tie down French forces in Lorraine and thereby "gain time" for the war to be decided on the right flank of the German advance.[21]

Rupprecht was born to King Ludwig III of Bavaria (crowned 1913) in Munich on 18 May 1869. He studied law and attended the War Academy. Most contemporaries described him as being regal, even handsome, with kind eyes and a smart mustache, but hardly martial. Once having chosen a military career, he advanced quickly: command of a regiment in 1899, of a brigade the following year, and of a division in 1903. He was given I Army Corps in 1906 and six years later, Fourth Army Inspectorate. Under the German federal system, it was natural that as head of the second most important kingdom in the empire he would command Bavarian forces in the war. Constituted as Sixth Army, Rupprecht's men fought as a unified Bavarian force for the first (and last) time in Lorraine.

The Bavarian units, tired by the long rail journey from Munich, took advantage of their role as occupiers in what soon became a familiar pattern. At Blâmont, east of Lunéville, on 10 August, Captain Otto von Berchem, a staff officer of Xylander's I Corps, reported that troops of 3d IB had looted local wine cellars. "The result was a most unpleasant drunken matins." Fueled by the free red wine, the Bavarians shot off their rifles throughout the town, and in the bacchanalia also turned the guns on one another. Berchem's observations were seconded by Sergeant Joseph Müller of 4th Chevauleger Regiment, who admitted having taken part in the "liberation" of the wine cellars.[22] The Bavarians also reported countless incidents of civilians firing at them with hunting pieces. Lieutenant Colonel Eugen von Frauenholz, the future Bavarian military historian, noted some residents of Blâmont shooting at soldiers and horses from treetops and church steeples as they marched through the town.[23] The 3d IB reacted to similar occurrences at Nonhigny and Montreux that same day by burning down both villages.[24] It was a new and unexpected type of warfare, Frauenholz conceded.

Confusion reigned at Rupprecht's headquarters. Bonneau's theatrical charge into Mulhouse, in Krafft von Dellmensingen's acid words, "had indeed drawn onto itself a good deal—the entire Seventh Army!"[25] Both Sixth and Seventh armies scrambled furiously to get back on their original deployment schedules. Moreover, the overall situation remained unclear. Frommel's cavalry had not managed to penetrate the French forward screen, and aerial reconnaissance had detected little fresh enemy movement. During a skirmish among elements of Bavarian 59th IB and 65th IB and French 15th ID and 16th ID as well as 2d CD of Joseph de Castelli's VIII Corps at Lagarde (Gerden) along the Marne-Rhine Canal on 11 August, the Germans discovered a valuable document on the body of a fallen French general: A report from Édouard de Castelnau's Second Army staff that six French army corps were being concentrated in the sixty-kilometer-wide Trouée de Charmes between Toul and Épinal.[26] Krafft von Dellmensingen quickly calculated that this meant that the enemy had placed nine of its twenty-one active army corps (43 percent) on the southern flank.[27] Sixth and Seventh armies were more than fulfilling the role of tying down as many French units as possible in the south accorded them in Moltke's *Westaufmarsch*. Still, French intentions remained unclear.

Papa Joffre would soon provide clarity. From the Grand quartier général (GQG), situated in a schoolhouse at Vitry-le-François, a sleepy little town on the Marne River halfway between Paris and Nancy, Joffre on 11 August decided to launch a major offensive into Alsace-Lorraine north of the Vosges three days later in accordance with his Instruction générale No. 1.[28] He anchored the extreme right wing on a new Army of Alsace, composed of Frédéric Vautier's VII Corps, Albert Soyer's 44th ID from the Army of the Alps, four reserve divisions, Aubier's 8th CD, and five battalions of Chasseurs alpins from First Army—three army corps in all under Paul-Marie Pau, a veteran of 1870 brought out of retirement.[29] Pau was charged with defending the vast stretch of frontier from the Swiss border north to the Col de la Schlucht, west of Munster (Münster) on the Fecht River. North of Pau, Joffre ordered Dubail's First Army and de Castelnau's Second Army to advance out of the Charmes Gap just south of the major German fortifications between Metz and Thionville. Dubail's four corps would spearhead the attack. First, they would storm several valleys in the Vosges south of Mount Donon; thereafter, they were to seize Sarrebourg (Saarburg), sixty kilometers east of Nancy, and then hurl the enemy eastward into Lower Alsace and the region around Strasbourg. Three corps of Castelnau's Second Army were to screen Dubail's attack by advancing toward Dieuze (Duß) and Château-Salins, with two corps on First Army's left moving against Morhange

(Mörchingen), some forty-five kilometers northeast of Nancy. Joffre placed the rest of Castelnau's forces on the left to guard against a possible German counterattack from Fortress Metz. Most importantly, the Army of Alsace was to secure the eastern flank of the attack by marching north without delay.

Joffre was, in fact, playing straight into Moltke's hands. He continued to believe that the main German offensive by regular army corps was being launched into Lorraine against his own center, and hence he moved to counter this threat. All the while, he ignored evidence from his own intelligence branch, the Deuxième Bureau, that significant German units were advancing into Belgium.

Simple in conception, Joffre's attack[30] was fraught with danger—quite apart from the still-unconfirmed German thrust into central Belgium. The farther French forces advanced out of the Vosges passes and the Trouée de Charmes, the broader their fronts became: eventually, eighty kilometers for First Army and seventy for Second Army. Dubail's dual objectives of Sarrebourg and Donon necessitated splitting his forces and thus exposing his flanks to German counterattack. Finally, the terrain was rugged, studded with hills, valleys, rivers, and ravines.

Joffre's second invasion of Alsace-Lorraine was based on the wishful thinking inherent in his deployment plan. Accordingly, the strong German defensive line between Metz and Thionville—the so-called *Moselstellung*—simply *had* to be a screen for Moltke's major troop concentration in the Ardennes and in German Lorraine. In fact, only five regular divisions manned the *Moselstellung,* giving the French a three-to-one advantage in the region. But in Alsace-Lorraine, where Joffre suspected no more than six German corps facing the twenty divisions of his own First and Second armies, Crown Prince Rupprecht in fact commanded eight army corps of twenty-four divisions.

General de Castelnau, a cultured nobleman and able strategist, already before the war had feared a possible German concentration in Lorraine and advised Joffre against an offensive into the area.[31] He preferred instead to stand on the defensive in well-prepared positions in front of Nancy. He repeated his concerns in August 1914. Joffre brusquely rejected this defensive mentality. No major enemy formations, he assured Castelnau, faced Second Army.[32] And when news arrived from St. Petersburg on 13 August that the Russian steamroller would move into East Prussia the next day, Joffre gave the order to attack. "I count on you absolutely for the success of this operation," he admonished Dubail and First Army. "It must succeed and you must devote all your energy to it."[33]

At Saint-Avold, Rupprecht and Krafft von Dellmensingen, like Joffre, were chomping at the bit to go on the offensive. Both feared that the purely defensive role assigned to them by the Army Supreme Command (Oberste-Heeresleitung, or OHL) would negatively affect the morale of their troops; any form of retreat would be disastrous. Hence, they began to toy with options. Krafft's first plan was to advance to the line of the Upper Moselle and Meurthe rivers and thereby threaten the flank of the French center. On 11 August, he had dispatched Major Rudolf von Xylander of his staff to Seventh Army to urge greater speed on Heeringen and the two corps of Sixth Army that still had not reached Strasbourg from Mulhouse. Xylander found Heeringen's General Headquarters to be in a state of "panic" due to the hurried shift up north, and because the former Prussian war minister had given Krafft's plan the "cold shoulder."[34] One day later, Rupprecht received his first official instructions from the OHL: It was not "interested" in a joint advance by Sixth and Seventh armies *"across"* the Upper Moselle and the Meurthe; at best, it would sanction an advance *"against"* the two rivers under favorable conditions.[35] As a sop to the Bavarians, the OHL agreed that they could reduce Fort Manonviller in French Lorraine.

Frustrated in his offensive design, Krafft von Dellmensingen turned to a second option: If the Bavarians had to remain on the defensive and if Joffre truly had ranged substantial forces against them, then why not entice the French into advancing into an artificially created "sack" somewhere between Metz and Strasbourg? In other words, show the French that the Bavarians were withdrawing in the face of superior forces, lure them into the sack, and then cut them to pieces from three sides—Fifth Army and Fortress Metz from the west, Sixth Army from the east, and Seventh Army from the south.[36] A "small Cannae" (the German obsession) might thus be achieved at an unexpected sector of the front.

As if on cue, the German military attaché at Bern, Switzerland, reported that Joffre had indeed amassed "12–15" or even "15–18 army corps" against Rupprecht's two armies—that is, perhaps as much as two-thirds of the French army![37] Option two was now on the table. Moltke's deputy chief of staff, Hermann von Stein, was enthusiastic and ordered Sixth Army to withdraw behind the Saar River north of Saarbrücken. To Rupprecht, the plan seemed too "artificial," an obvious pandering to what he called the southern defensive posture of the "Old Schlieffen" Plan of 1905.[38] Still, it was now up to Joffre to take the bait, charge into the sack, and place his head into its noose.

On 13 August, French ambassador to Russia Maurice Paléologue informed Paris that the Russians would launch their much-anticipated offensive against the Germans in East Prussia at dawn the next morning. It was the news Joffre had been waiting for. On the morning of the fourteenth, he sent the armies on the right wing—roughly four hundred battalions and sixteen hundred guns, almost one-third of the chief of staff's effective strength—into Germany. Bands struck up "La Marseillaise." Soldiers in the lead formations tore down the striped posts that marked the Reichsland's boundary with France.[39] Ahead of them lay lush green fields of alfalfa and golden strips of cereal crops— and beyond that the industrial Saar region and eventually the Rhine Valley. On the left flank of First Army, César Alix's XIII Corps headed for Cirey and Castelli's VIII Corps, for Blâmont. On Dubail's left, Castelnau directed Louis Taverna's XVI Corps to advance from Lunéville to Elfringen, Louis Espinasse's XV Corps from Serres to Monhofen, and Ferdinand Foch's XX Corps from Lunéville to Kambrich. Overall, the French force formed a gigantic wedge aimed straight at Sarrebourg and the left wing of Rupprecht's Sixth Army.

Progress was good. For four days, Joffre's troops advanced methodically.[40] German Sixth Army relied mainly on long-range artillery fire from its 1,068 guns and on brief but violent rearguard actions to slow the French advance. Frédéric Bourdériat's 13th ID of Émile-Edmond Legrand-Girarde's XXI Corps seized Mount Donon while Alix's XIII Corps and Castelli's VIII Corps drove Xylander's Bavarian I Corps behind the Marne-Rhine Canal, advancing to within twelve kilometers of Sarrebourg. The Germans everywhere were withdrawing, burning villages as they abandoned them. Only an ill-conceived attack on Cirey by Gustave Silhol's 26th ID just before 7 PM sounded a sour note. As the 26th swept across a flat field, German artillery and machine guns cut it to ribbons.[41] Joffre formed a new cavalry corps under General Louis Conneau by combining Dubail's 6th CD with Castelnau's

10th CD in hopes of breaking through the German positions the next day.

The attack resumed on 15 August. It quickly turned into a bloody slogging match as the first rain* of the campaign soaked the fields and turned the Lorraine clay into beige-gray ooze. By 9 AM, Castelnau's Second Army reported a thousand casualties. Classic infantry charges with flags unfurled, bugles blaring, and drums beating, the caustic commander of Second Army lectured Joffre, had to be supported by "heavy firing by artillery" prior to the attack. Thereafter, the troops needed to establish step-by-step field defenses such as "extensive trenches, shelter against shrapnel, helmets for riflemen, etc." Both infantry and artillery, Castelnau tartly noted, "have been sorely tested."[42] German heavy artillery kept the lighter French 75s out of range, and the infantry dug in. At General von Stein's urging, Moltke rushed six Ersatz divisions originally assigned to the right wing in Belgium to Alsace-Lorraine. Superstitious Alsatian peasants noted that thirty storks had prematurely headed south out of the Rhine Valley—a bad omen.

Still, the French advance continued over the next two days in dreary cloud and rain. The Germans poured lethal artillery fire into the advancing French forces in the Seille lowland from their commanding positions on the Côte de Delme and from their double fortresses of Morhange-Dieuze. They used forest cover to conceal the whereabouts of their machine-gun nests. The result was slaughter for the French. Charles de Gaulle, a lieutenant in 1914, later acknowledged that "on a tactical plane," German firepower had "made nonsense" of Joffre's theories of the *offensive à outrance*. "Morally, the illusions behind which the soldiers had taken refuge were swept away in a trice."[43] Yet at this early stage in the war, Joffre was unwilling to concede that French tactical doctrine and the inadequacy of its artillery had become apparent.[44]

But Joffre was no fool. He kept a tight rein on the advance, limiting it to roughly five kilometers per day. He refused to take the German bait—that is, to stick his head into the sack prepared for the French between Metz and Strasbourg. He constantly admonished Dubail and Castelnau to maintain contact on their flanks.[45] He urged Pau's Army of Alsace, fronted by only German reserve and Landwehr units around

---

* Weather descriptions were taken from a special compilation, *Das Wetter,* in the German official history, *Der Weltkrieg,* vol. 1, p. 893, and were cross-checked against army and corps war diaries (KTB) as well as soldiers' letters from the front.

Colmar, to march north at greater speed. On 17 August, Foch's XX Corps, strengthened by long-service white Troupes Coloniales, advanced from the Donnelay-Juvelize ridge and took Château-Salins; the next day, Espinasse's XV Corps occupied Dieuze. That same day, Louis de Maud'huy's 16th ID of Castelli's VIII Corps, having beaten back Ludwig von Hetzel's Bavarian 2d Division, moved into an abandoned Sarrebourg, while Foch's XX Corps advanced against Martini's Bavarian II Corps on the fortified heights of Morhange. But Conneau's cavalry corps could not get across the Saar River due to heavy enemy artillery fire. Rupprecht's Sixth Army continued to retreat in an easterly direction, leaving behind guns, wagons, field kitchens, knapsacks, and rifles as well as its dead and wounded. It also left behind a burning Sarrebourg, having doused its stores of ammunition and supplies with gasoline and set them on fire.

As an interesting footnote in history, the war diary of 2d Battalion, Baden 112th IR, recorded on 18 August: "Lt. Goering 8C brings in 3 prisoners of [French] IR 85."[46] The twenty-one-year-old Hermann Goering of 8th Company, future head of the German Luftwaffe and successor-designate to Adolf Hitler, received the Iron Cross, Second Class, for his frontline service in Lorraine.[47]

Joffre, no doubt buoyed by his successes, but also fearing that the enemy was preparing a trap for his armies east of Sarrebourg, ordered Second Army to shift the direction of its attack to the north, up the valley of the Saar River.[48] As a result, the two French armies lost contact with each other. Pau's Army of Alsace continued to cling to the security of the Vosges Mountains between Mulhouse and Colmar. Unknown to the Germans, on 16 August, Joffre withheld African XIX Corps from Dubail's First Army and transferred Arthur Poline's XVII Corps to Charles Lanrezac's Fifth Army north at Rethel-Mézières. Two days later, he sent Pierre Dubois's IX Corps to Fernand de Langle de Cary's Fourth Army at Sainte-Menehould. Obviously, a French withdrawal of forces to the north had begun. Moltke, for his part, made no move to shift forces from his left to his right wing. On 20 August, Joffre informed War Minister Messimy, "Overall, the situation appears to me to be favorable."[49]

German hopes of trapping the French in a sack east of the Metz-Nancy line died just as quickly as they had been raised. Already on 16 August, Lieutenant Colonel Gerhard Tappen, chief of operations of the OHL, informed Rupprecht that the Bern reports concerning French heavy concentrations in the Charmes Gap had been grossly overstated and that the German withdrawal accordingly was advancing at far too fast a pace.[50] Moreover, the stiff resistance mounted against Dubail and Castelnau by Sixth Army undoubtedly had frustrated the overall sack design. While the Bavarian crown prince had been more than willing to let the French storm across the Rhine into the Black Forest in order to surround and annihilate them elsewhere,[51] Moltke's headquarters refused to concede German soil for a theoretical small Cannae.

In the south, Vautier's VII Corps had advanced on Mulhouse almost as slowly as it had earlier under Bonneau. Once again, the fighting was vicious and the losses severe. Once again, there had been little or no reconnaissance, with the result that the two opposing armies unexpectedly ran head-on into each other. The so-called Second Battle of Mulhouse was in full swing by 10 AM on 19 August. It was at its most ferocious in the suburb of Dornach. The French commanded the heights and mercilessly poured machine-gun fire into the massed German infantry columns, cutting the *Landser* down "like a scythe does stalks of grain." Panic quickly set in. Poorly trained Baden Landwehr units yet again fired wildly—thirty-five thousand rounds by one company alone—and occasionally at Württemberg troops, whose blue pants they mistook for French blue capes in the smoke and confusion of battle. Colonel Koch, commanding the hard-hit 40th IR, spent much of his time trying to stanch the flow of Landwehr companies streaming back to the Rhône-Rhine Canal.[52] Three times he rallied his men; three times their charge was bloodily repelled.

Communications from the company to the regimental level totally broke down. Major Leist, commanding 1st Battalion, 40th IR, recorded: "There can be no talk of a connection with the Regiment; not a single regimental order was passed down during the entire battle."[53] Thus, the general order to retire to the Eichenwald at 4 PM did not reach all units, and more than five hundred German soldiers had no choice but to surrender to the French. Sergeant Otto Breinlinger, 11th Reserve Infantry Regiment (RIR), sadly wrote home that after Mulhouse and Dornach, his 10th Company had shrunk from 250 to 16 men.[54] Dominik Richert, a German-Alsatian farmer, was appalled at the sight of the battlefields. "Some of the dead looked horrible. Some lay on their faces, others on their backs. Blood, claw-like hands, glazed over eyes, distorted faces. Many grotesquely clutched rifles in their hands, others had their hands full of dirt and grass which they had torn out in their death pangs."[55] For most men of Hoiningen-Huene's Baden XIV Corps, there was but one thought: back to the Rhine.

Paul Gläser, a noncommissioned officer with 2d Company, 40th IR, informed his parents that his vocabulary simply was inadequate to describe the brutal street fighting at Dornach. The regiment was fired on from countless windows as it withdrew. "Certainly, more than 100 bullets whistled about my head, from behind, from left and from right of me." Storming one house in search of francs-tireurs, Gläser found four French soldiers in civilian clothes and a "young wench" who loaded rifles for them. "We finished them off with a triple salvo."[56] At a higher level in the chain of command, General Gaede informed Grand Duke Friedrich II of Baden that civilians had yet again fired on his men "in vile and despicable fashion." Revenge would be swift. "If we get Dornach back, not a single house must be allowed to stand."[57]

At their new headquarters in a "miserable school house" at Hellimer, Rupprecht and Krafft turned their thoughts to mounting a powerful counterattack.[58] The latest intelligence reports suggested that Joffre had marshaled seven and one-half corps as well as three cavalry divisions against Sixth Army and XV and XIV corps of Seventh Army, which had finally marched up from their ill-conceived detour to Mulhouse and linked up with Rupprecht's left flank. Krafft suggested launching the counterattack on 18 August, the anniversary of the Battle of Gravelotte in 1870.[59] He dispatched Major von Xylander on a "diplomatic mission" to Heeringen's Seventh Army to garner support for the plan. Once again, the Prussian turned a "cold shoulder" to the Bavarian initiative. Krafft was livid. "The great Heeringen, the former *Prussian* War Minister, will accommodate the *Bavarian* Crown Prince only grudgingly."[60] And when the crown prince and his chief of staff relayed their decision to the OHL, Moltke and his staff reacted with what the Bavarians sarcastically called "a most oracle-like"[61] directive: Stick to the original *Aufmarschplan*. To mollify Bavarian royal feelings, Moltke dispatched Lieutenant Colonel Wilhelm von Dommes, chief of the Political Section of the General Staff, to Hellimer.

Dommes's mission was the first of several such confusing encounters over the ensuing days. He had come, Dommes informed the Bavarians, not with specific directives but only with general talking points. Moltke and Tappen by now had dropped the idea of luring the French into the vaunted sack between the Saar and Nied rivers. They also had ruled out any major offensive against the Trouée de Charmes. On the basis of this apparent return to the original deployment plan, Dommes suggested that Sixth and Seventh armies fall back to defensive positions between Metz and the Lower Nied River to prevent Joffre's First and Second armies from attacking the flank of German Fifth Army near Verdun. "6. and 7. Armies should not engage in adventures. Stand firm! Task: secure the army's left flank."[62] But neither Rupprecht nor Krafft von Dellmensingen was willing to accept a prolonged passive stance by the Bavarian army on the Nied, as this would seriously impair its "offensive spirit" and cause the men to lose faith in their leaders.[63] Krafft pressed his case for the offensive, "the first great battle of the war." It would be risky, "*but it must be attempted.*" He closed the meeting on a harsh note. "One either lets me do as I want or one gives me concrete orders."[64] Dommes possessed no such orders from Moltke. Rupprecht noted that Dommes was so "nervous" during the talks that he left "helmet and sword" behind upon departing Hellimer.[65]

Just to be on the safe side, Krafft on 18 August telephoned the OHL to make known his intentions to attack. Deputy Chief of Staff von Stein cagily replied: "No, I will not prevent you from doing this by ordering a stop to it. You will have to bear the responsibility. Make your decision as your conscience dictates." Krafft did not hesitate for a moment. "It has been made."[66] Both he and Rupprecht would later be accused of having placed Bavarian dynastic interests above German national strategy.

The charge does not sit well. For, while refusing to issue Rupprecht direct orders, the OHL continued to second-guess his intentions. "One assumes here," Bavarian military plenipotentiary Karl von Wenninger reported from the OHL, "that the Crown Pr[ince] will solve his task offensively, but at the same time one hopes—albeit in silence—that [his] commander's nerves will allow him to draw the enemy onto Saarburg in order then to crush him between two fronts."[67] The Younger Moltke's copying of his great-uncle's loose command style was beginning to show cracks. While it had been relatively easy for the Elder Moltke to decentralize command and to have divisions and even corps "march to the sound of the guns" (*Auftragstaktik*) over relatively narrow fronts in 1870, the Younger Moltke was beginning to realize that this was not the case with what amounted to small army groups of four to five hundred thousand men extended over more than a hundred kilometers of front.

Dawn on 20 August broke gray and foggy, prohibiting aerial reconnaissance by either side. At 4:30 AM, a blood-red sun—"the sun of Austerlitz,"* Rupprecht and Krafft giddily noted—broke through the mist. For a sixth day, Joffre's armies in Lorraine renewed the attack. Conneau's cavalry corps debouched into the rear of German Sixth Army to roll up its flank. On this day, however, the French were met by a withering hail of artillery fire—and by a spirited counterattack.[68] In fact, like the classical charges of Athenians and Spartans, Romans and Carthaginians, the two forces, quite unaware of the fact, had each mounted separate attacks that morning and crashed head-on along a hundred-kilometer-wide front.

The men of Bavarian Sixth Army had leaped out of their defensive positions at 3:30 AM "with flags unfurled" and pressed their concentrated attack all along the line. The battle almost immediately disintegrated into a series of isolated and uncoordinated engagements. Clumps of soldiers rushed wildly across the hills and valleys of the Vosges, and through the fences and hedges of its quaint villages. Foch's XX Corps alone made progress at Morhange. At one point, his forces stormed two lines of German trenches—only to discover that they were being "held" by field-gray straw figures.[69] Foch had undertaken this deep penetration of the enemy lines against Castelnau's express orders, and in the process had exposed the left flank of Second Army's two center corps. Bavarian Sixth Army counterattacked that exposed flank of Castelli's VIII Corps with wave after wave of infantry supported by heavy artillery. Enfilading machine-gun fire from Gebsattel's III Corps caused what Foch called "gruesome" losses for his XX Corps. In the heated melee, it was often difficult to distinguish friend from foe. Near Bisping, for example, Bavarian 1st IB was nearly annihilated by a withering barrage of artillery shells from its own 9th Field Artillery Regiment.[70] "Unfortunately," Krafft noted in his diary, he had not been able "to move" Heeringen's Seventh Army "to attack

---

* On 2 December 1805, Napoleon I with a "lion leap" charged the Austrian and Russian right flank at the Battle of Austerlitz through a thick morning fog; at 7:45 AM, the sun rose over the battlefield.

before 11 AM."[71] In Paris, President Raymond Poincaré quietly marked his fifty-fourth birthday.

In fact, Carl von Clausewitz's "fog of uncertainty" had bedeviled the French at Morhange. On the evening of 19 August, two contradictory orders were issued: While Castelnau instructed Foch to hold the line where he stood, Foch ordered his troops to renew the attack the next morning. Foch informed Castelnau of his decision forty-five minutes before that attack, set for 6 AM on 20 August, and the commander of Second Army replied by repeating his earlier order to stand pat and to guard against a possible German counteroffensive—by telephone as well as by sending a staff officer to XX Corps. Foch in his memoirs claimed that he received no instruction on the night of the nineteenth and that Castelnau's order to halt on the morning of the twentieth reached him too late, for the Germans had preempted his own attack by launching their offensive around 5 AM (French time). Joffre was content to note in his report to Paris only that XX Corps had "advanced perhaps a little too quickly."[72] He was not about to cashier one of his most energetic corps commanders.

A disaster ensued for the French—despite the fact that they had captured the war diary of a fallen German officer detailing Rupprecht's plan of attack. German heavy artillery arrayed on the Morhange Ridge and ranged by means of preselected aiming points decimated first French artillery and then the enemy infantry marching through the valleys below it. By late afternoon, as the broiling heat of the first two weeks of the campaign returned, Castelnau had lost not only his son in battle but much of his field artillery as well. Espinasse's XV Corps and Taverna's XVI Corps were in full retreat. French 68th ID and 70th ID had been severely mauled. Foch's XX Corps had taken a bad knock. In the words of one officer, "a sublime chaos, infantrymen, gunners with their clumsy wagons, combat supplies, regimental stores, brilliant motor cars of our brilliant staffs all meeting, criss-crossing, not knowing what to do or where to go."[73] Still seething over Foch's unauthorized advance, Castelnau had no choice but to order a retreat to the original starting line of the offensive on 14 August—the Meurthe River and the Grand Couronné de Nancy, the long chain of fortified ridges that shielded the city against attack. Believing the situation to be "very grave" and his army desperately in need of at least forty-eight hours' rest, he entertained thoughts of further withdrawals behind the

Upper Moselle and perhaps as far as Toul and Épinal. Joffre refused even to consider the suggestion. "Speak no more of retiring beyond the Moselle."[74] Instead, he rushed 64th RID and 74th RID to buttress Second Army and halted the shunting of Dubois's IX Corps to the north, already in progress. And he sent a number of "defensive-minded" brigade and division commanders into "retirement" at Limoges.

Castelnau's retreat also sealed the fate of Dubail's advance. Initially, and without contacting Castelnau, the fiery Dubail was determined to continue the attack. General de Maud'huy's 16th ID was engaged in bitter house-to-house fighting in Sarrebourg. A relief attempt by Léon Bajolle's 15th ID was repulsed with heavy losses by Xylander's Bavarian I Corps. Maud'huy had no choice but to abandon Sarrebourg. He did so with a defiant last gesture: Amid a storm of shrapnel, he and his staff stood at attention at the southern end of the city while 16th Division's massed bands played the "Marche Lorraine" as the troops marched out of Sarrebourg.[75]

It was heroic, but it was not war. Late in the day, a telephone call from Joffre apprised Dubail that Second Army's retreat threatened to turn into a rout. Foch's XX Corps alone remained combat-effective and was doing its best to cover the hasty withdrawal of Espinasse's XV Corps and Taverna's XVI Corps. Still, its 39th ID and 11th ID took a terrible pounding and were driven back from one defensive position to another. Dubail was left no option but to withdraw VIII and XIII corps to cover Castelnau's exposed flanks. Pau's Army of Alsace still was nowhere in sight.

French losses on 20 August were appalling: Bavarian III Corps registered thirteen hundred enemy prisoners of war; Bavarian II Corps, eight hundred; and Bavarian I Corps, nineteen hundred. Special burial details took care of twelve hundred dead *poilus*.[76] The Great Retreat in the south was in full swing by the evening of 20 August. The French army admitted five thousand casualties; historians have put that figure at ten thousand. Friedrich von Graevenitz, Württemberg's plenipotentiary to the OHL, reported "total victory" against "at least nine active corps," and the capture of fourteen thousand prisoners of war and thirteen artillery batteries.[77] Kaiser Wilhelm II, who had been roused from bed by his senior military entourage to receive the news, celebrated "the greatest victory in the history of warfare."[78]

At daybreak on 21 August, the gunners of Sixth Army showered Castelnau's battered formations with another withering artillery barrage. As the early-morning mists evaporated, Foch's 39th ID was hurled back north of Château-Salins, and his 11th ID likewise was forced to retreat. As Rupprecht's Bavarians began a sweep around Castelnau's Second Army, the previously shattered XV Corps and XVI Corps disintegrated. By 10 AM, the little "monk in boots" ordered the first general retreat of the day. As his officers in vain tried to rally the troops to defend scattered hills and ridges, the German pursuit continued. Some four thousand shells pulverized the small town of Sainte-Geneviève over seventy-five hours. Castelnau's men, morally and physically shaken, abandoned carts and wagons, guns and horses. At 6 PM, the commander ordered another general retreat—under cover of darkness. Dubail's First Army, with its western flank left in the air by Castelnau's precipitous retreat, was forced to fall back to the line of the Meurthe River. He never forgave Castelnau.

Despite Joffre's attempts to isolate the *zone des armées* from the home front, word of the disaster that had befallen Espinasse's XV Corps at Morhange spread fast. The endless wagons filled with the wounded bore witness to what had taken place. On 24 August, *Le Matin* at Paris reported:

> Companies, battalions passed in indescribable disorder. Mixed in with the soldiers were women carrying children on their arms . . . girls in their Sunday best, old people, carrying or dragging a bizarre mixture of objects. Entire regiments were falling back in disorder. One had the impression that discipline had completely collapsed.[79]

At the front near Rambervillers, northeast of Épinal, Lieutenant Henri Desagneaux was amazed by the seemingly endless columns of French refugees: "the peasant carrying his little bundle; the worker with a few old clothes; small farmers, shopkeepers and their cases, finally the bourgeois, dragging along a dog or a trunk." He was shocked by what came next: "whole trains" bringing back the two thousand wounded at Rambervillers. "Their limbs shot off, their heads a pulpy mess; all these bandages, spattered with blood mingle with the civilian population."[80] Marcel Papillon with 356th RIR wrote home of the "awful weather—cold with a fine rain" that plagued the men for four days as they fell back to the Grand Couronné de Nancy. "War is sad," he allowed, especially on the local population living amid the mounds of gray corpses (*des grises*). "I saw villages burned up by bombardments. It is cruel. The infantry of French XX Corps has suffered *very heavy* losses."[81] Not even the canteens offering *vin ordinaire* at the exorbitant rate of three francs per bottle offered relief.

Through it all, Joffre at Vitry-le-François maintained his clockwork regimen of eating regularly and well, sleeping undisturbed and long, and weeding out what he considered to be "weak" or "defensive" commanders. Minister of War Messimy tried to put the best spin on the debacle in the Vosges: "The day before yesterday, a success; today, a defeat. *C'est la guerre.*" Joffre dismissed the comment as "lapidary."[82]

THE VIOLENT ENGAGEMENT AROUND Sarrebourg shocked even its victor in terms of the human toll.[83] Annual staff rides and field maneuvers had not prepared commanders for the true face of battle. On 21 August, Crown Prince Rupprecht inspected the previous days' battlefields. In Serres Forest and in the region around Château-Brehain, he noted, the enemy had "left behind masses of dead and wounded." But his own troops had also suffered grievously: At Eschen, one of the battalions of 9th Regiment, 4th ID, had been nearly annihilated and henceforward could only be deployed as a single company. Elsewhere, 18th IR had sustained 45 percent casualties; 70th IR had lost twelve hundred men. Especially the cavalry had suffered from both the heat and the steep climbs up the slopes of the Vosges. It had been forced to race back and forth on reconnaissance missions and then to deploy dismounted. One cavalry division had lost 213 riders over seventeen days of continuous patrol, and many of its mounts had no shoes; another reported that its horses were utterly worn out, and that seventy had died of exhaustion.

As Rupprecht rode toward his new headquarters at Dieuze, he came across more scenes of carnage. At Conthil, the fields were studded with mass graves, for both men and horses. Houses were burned out, shot to pieces by the artillery. Cows not milked for days, their udders nearly bursting, roamed about "bellowing in pain." At Morhange, artillery shells had hit the gasworks, and fires ravaged the city. On a nearby hillside, where an enemy unit had been caught in the flank,

French dead, recognizable by their red pants, "lay in rows and looked like a field of poppies." The corpses presented an eerie sight. "They lie man to man. Some still hold their rifles at the ready. Due to the intense heat, most of the men's faces have already turned a bluish black." Yet again, the crown prince witnessed the effects of "friendly fire": Bavarian artillery had mistakenly fired on its own advancing infantry.

Next, Rupprecht made his way through the Forest of Dieuze. Shirts, boots, hats, rifles, and knapsacks had been hastily abandoned. In the city itself—"a typical French town: ugly and dirty"—the scene of abandonment was even greater. Where earlier the citizenry had thrown a ball for the approaching French forces, automobiles now lay overturned in ditches, knapsacks and uniforms scattered about, and rifles with smashed butts littered the streets. The barracks attested to the "flight" of two French divisions. "An indescribable filth. Bones and pieces of meat from butchered animals lay in the courtyard and torn pieces of uniforms inside the rooms." Rupprecht estimated recent enemy losses at thirty thousand dead and wounded.

Ominously, reports again began to filter in to Sixth Army headquarters from company to regimental levels that the fighting had not been restricted to the battlefield or to regular forces. Countless commanders stated that armed civilians had shot at their troops with hunting pieces from windows and rooftops as they entered a town. Francs-tireurs! Word about French civilians firing on German troops spread like wildfire. Reprisals were swift. Already on the first day of the Bavarian offensive, 20 August, at Nomeny, a small town on the Meuse River between Metz and Nancy,[84] men of French 277th IR at a bridge over the Seille River had held up the advancing Bavarian 2d IR and 4th IR; when the Germans finally took the bridge, French enfilading fire from a nearby field inflicted heavy casualties. Karl von Riedl's 8th IB and Viktor Bausch's 33d RID were convinced that the *poilus* of the French 277th had been assisted by civilians, who also had sheltered sharpshooters after the battle. That night 3d Battalion, 8th IR, burned much of the village; the next day, its inhabitants were expelled. Fifty-five residents of Nomeny died on 20–21 August; of those, forty-six had been shot.

At Gerbéviller, southeast of Nancy, a similar scenario had developed.[85] Soldiers of French 2d Battalion and 19th Dragoons as well as some chasseurs had stiffly defended a bridge over the Mortagne River against units of Bavarian 60th IR and 166th IR. Frustrated by this rear-guard action and seeing French civilians firing on them, the Germans between 24 and 27 August pillaged and burned the city. Albert von Berrer, commanding 31st ID, ordered Gerbéviller destroyed. Sixty civilians reportedly died in the process.

At Lunéville, southeast of Nancy, savage "reprisals" took place on 25 August.[86] For three days, Friedrich Kress von Kressenstein's 5th RID and Maximilian von Höhn's 6th ID had taken heavy losses—25,003 casualties—attempting to breach General de Castelnau's defensive line before Nancy.[87] Demoralized by failure, the men returned to Lunéville in a foul mood. They found the city clogged with columns of supply wagons and carts full of the wounded. They were sure that armed civilians on rooftops were firing at them, at supply columns, and at field hospitals. They shot wildly into homes and shops, at anything that moved. Several civilians were caught carrying cartridges to fellow shooters. "Mindless fear," in the words of the Bavarian semi-official history, "was the reaction. Vehicles rushed in every direction, while guards returned the fire without plan or purpose." As darkness fell, seventy homes had been burned and nineteen civilians killed. For the soldiers, it was "a horribly beautiful, wild scene, one which deepened and reinforced their impression of this bloody and fateful day."[88] Major von Xylander of Rupprecht's staff wrote in his war diary: "In Lunéville, murder and slaughter. Fires. Panic among our rear-guard formations. Wild rumors." The young officer found it simply "unbelievable" how an army victorious in the Battle of the Saar* just three days earlier "in such a short time" could have degraded "to such a state." He blamed it on the "overly excited nerves" of troops engaged in almost daily combat.[89] A larger massacre was avoided by the swift action of Major Berthold Schenk von Stauffenberg of XXI Corps, who ordered his troops to stop plundering and who took sixty civilians hostage as a human shield to end the shooting. Crown Prince Rupprecht denounced the "foolish" torching of villages, which held up his train and denied the soldiers quarters.[90]

Fritz Nieser, the Grand Duchy of Baden's acting plenipotentiary at Munich, reported that the capital was decked with flags to celebrate

---

* I follow the established practice of letting the victor name the battle. Allied historians usually refer to the Battle of the Saar as the Battle of Sarrebourg-Morhange.

Rupprecht's victory in the Battle of the Saar, and that King Ludwig III had received enthusiastic public ovations. The French army "obviously had been totally defeated in the west."[91]

THE BATTLE OF THE Saar had not fulfilled Rupprecht's dream of a great flanking movement primarily because Heeringen's Seventh Army, although augmented by Bavarian I Corps, had not been able to make sufficient progress north of the Marne-Rhine Canal. By attacking more than six hours later than Rupprecht, Heeringen had surrendered the element of surprise. Moreover, his Landwehr brigades had become bogged down in the Vosges in countless encounters with crack French Alpine troops.[92] Unlike the French, the Germans had neither specially trained Alpine troops nor high-angle-fire mountain artillery. The going was nearly impossible. Dense fog not only inhibited accurate fire but also turned the battlefields into semidarkness. Combat was close and personal, in most cases ending with bloodcurdling bayonet charges. The small creeks of the Vosges at times ran red. The din was unbearable. The woods rang with the screams of wounded soldiers rolling on the ground. Drums and bugles sounded advance and retreat, alternately. Men accidentally shot their own. And even in the mountains, there was little relief from the broiling heat.

Adolf Hartner, a Bavarian telegraph specialist, noted that the artillery reduced the great trees of the Vosges to matchsticks and enemy soldiers to grotesque heaps of body parts. "Here a torn off foot, there an arm, a leg, then another body torn apart to the point of nonrecognition; one was missing half his face & both hands; truly horrible." At Lucy, Hartner almost became sick at the sight of a pitiful French corporal.

> A grenade had ripped open his body & he now attempted to push back into it the intestines that had spilled out of it—until death took mercy on him. Thus he lay there with distorted eyes & a snarl on his teeth. I believe that none of us could resist a mild shudder.[93]

Karl Gruber, an architect from Freiburg in charge of an infantry company, noted in his diary that the war enthusiasm of the first days of August quickly wilted in the heat and savagery of mountain warfare.

More and more, his Baden soldiers badgered him with questions such as: "Lieutenant, will we be in Paris soon?" and "Lieutenant, won't the murdering soon stop?"[94]

The Bavarian semiofficial history of the war reproduced the travails of two battalions of 15th RIR and 30th RID in the area around Markirch in Upper Alsace on 24 August. What today is a charming resort known for its Munster cheese and Gewürztraminer wine was in 1914 a tough textile town of twelve thousand people. The countryside was still studded with open pits and slag heaps from earlier days of lead and silver mining. Bavarian infantry ran up against a natural fortress. "Everywhere, felled trees, barricades made with branches, barbed-wire entanglements, and tripwires impeded progress." Enemy sharpshooters hid behind "bushes, boulders, rock walls," in "holes and trenches," as well as "in tree tops."[95] The battle raged all day across the face of the 772-meter-high Col de Sainte-Marie and the Robinot and Lièpvrette rivers. At Brifosse, the advance of 5th RIR over a bridge crossing the Robinot was halted by French machine gunners. Panic ensued.

> The troops, seized by fear, run for their lives down the southern hillside . . . to seek safety in Brifosse. The horses, hit by the bullets, roll on the ground and wildly flay their legs into the harnesses. The wagons, wheels inter-locked, crash into one another; are pulled to the side; then pushed over the edge. Dead and wounded men and horses lie about everywhere. There was neither any going "forward" nor any going "backward."[96]

The arrival of the 5th in Markirch later that night brought no relief. A rumor circulated that a French infantry brigade from 58th RID of Paul Pouradier-Duteil's XIV Corps was attacking the regiment's artillery en route to Lièpvre (Leberau). The supply wagons took off down the single, narrow road—only to run headlong into their own artillery. "A wicked chaos ensued. The wagons bump each other and collide. Shafts splinter. Horses spook and collapse. Oaths and agitated cries ring out into the darkness. One artillery piece even falls into the stream alongside the road." Suddenly, shots rang out. "Now the disaster is complete. Whoever has a rifle or can lay their hands on one begins to shoot about wildly."[97] It took several hours to restore order. The French infantry brigade never appeared. The source of the rumor was never uncovered. In fact, the occupying units of French 71st RID from Épinal had withdrawn from Markirch during the night of 23 August. From 7 AM until 2 PM the next day, German reserves drove the remaining French up and across the strategic Sainte-Marie Pass.[98]

Bloody engagements, whether in open fields or along mountain slopes, brought Seventh Army's reserve troops greater losses in August 1914 than their forefathers had encountered in the entire Franco-Prussian War (1870–71).[99] At Lagarde, 2d Jäger Battalion lost 161 men and the Kaiser-Ulanen-Regiment, 158 riders and 149 mounts. At Badonviller, the King's Own Infantry Regiment sustained losses of 97 dead, 322 wounded, and 17 missing. At Diespach, 15th RIR lost 408 men. And the closer the troops came to the French border, the lustier became the civilian cries, "Beat the Prussian filth."* In many instances, the reply of the "Prussian filth" was to burn down hostile villages and remove their inhabitants.

Nor were conditions much better on the Plain of Alsace. There, the heat was abominable, the roads dry and dusty, and the still-unripe fruit fuel for intestinal disorders. In the region where, almost two millennia before, Caesar had clashed with Ariovistus, French and German troops engaged each other in ancient combat.[100] By and large without artillery, they resorted to savage bayonet charges and hand-to-hand fighting. The steep, terraced vineyards of the eastern slopes of the Vosges around Colmar, Turckheim (Türkheim), Kaysersberg, Riquewihr (Reichenweier), and Ribeauvillé (Rappoltsweiler) were easily turned into miniature fortresses by interweaving felled trees with chest-high grapevines and barbed wire. Bavarian 1st and 2nd Landwehr regiments each lost 150 to 200 men in the first few days of fighting alone—as did French 13th and 30th chasseur brigades ranged against them.

THE BAVARIAN ARMY ALSO experienced a new logistical impediment to maneuver warfare—mail. Whereas in the Franco-Prussian War, the postal services of Prussia, Baden, and Württemberg daily had to move 500,000 letters and packets, that figure in 1914 shot up to 9.9 million pieces to the front and 6.8 million back home *per day*. Roughly eight thousand postal employees handled the increasing flood of mail.[101] In part, the explosive expansion was due to the fact that German authorities

---

* *"Il faut battre les sales Prussiens!"*

allowed these mailings postage-free. For the government saw a potential for patriotic uplifting at home by publishing many of the letters in local newspapers and in special book editions—sixty in 1914 alone.

Apart from sheer volume, a second problem lay in the nature of many of the packets sent to the front. Especially after the death of Pope Pius X on the day of Rupprecht's offensive in Lorraine—20 August—these took on a macabre composition. Officers reported a host of "forbidden" items reaching their men: amulets rubbed with herbs, playing cards, engagement or wedding rings, vials of wine mixed with gunpowder, creams to ward off bullets, identification cards, chain letters, Bible verses, curses, and "hexes" of all manner and form.[102] For their part, soldiers reported sighting the Madonna smiling down on them through the black powder smoke.

Furthermore, relations between the "Old Reichsland" and German military authorities rapidly deteriorated. General Gaede, head of a special Army Detachment Gaede on the Vosges front, so distrusted the indigenous population that he literally fenced in the front in Upper Alsace with three Landsturm battalions and hundreds of kilometers of barbed wire. "A *fluidum* of betrayal," he reminded his officers, "runs throughout the entire population."[103] He arrested 574 civilians for "anti-German utterances" and 913 for "anti-German sentiments." He deported 752 Alsatians and ordered summary executions for 6. Finally, he called up 15,000 Alsatian reservists, transferred them to the right bank of the Rhine, and with the consent of the Prussian War Ministry distributed them in groups of 100 throughout the Reich. "A very severe but also very necessary and salutary measure," he informed Grand Duke Friedrich II of Baden.[104]

TO JOSEPH JOFFRE'S PLEASANT surprise, the Bavarians, equally exhausted by the Battle of the Saar, took three days to pursue Dubail and Castelnau. At times, they lagged twenty kilometers behind the beaten foe. Especially French Second Army used these precious seventy-two hours to regroup, resupply, refresh, and reinforce Nancy's defensive belt along the line Gerbéviller-Lunéville-Amance. Joffre created a new Army of Lorraine under Michel-Joseph Maunoury and ordered it not only to hold Lorraine but to "fix" as many German units as possible in the south while he launched his great assault across the Ardennes.[105] Still, Lunéville fell to the Bavarians on 23 August and Saint-Dié shortly thereafter.

Given that Pau had done little to be of help at Sarrebourg and had lingered in the Alsatian vineyards for six days since 20 August, Joffre dissolved the Army of Alsace on 26 August. He left a single division to guard the Col de la Schlucht and transferred the rest of Pau's units into Vautier's VII Corps, which he then sent to reinforce Fortress Paris—a major reshuffle that required 110 to 120 trains and five to six days of travel. Four days later, German 55th Landwehr Brigade retook luckless Mulhouse.

In fact, the Bavarian army had been temporarily derailed by the Army Supreme Command to deal with a nagging problem: Fort Manonviller, perhaps the strongest French fortress, which commanded the strategically important Paris-Nancy-Strasbourg rail line.[106] General Karl Ritter von Brug, chief of the Bavarian Corps of Engineers, was given an enhanced brigade of I Corps to take the fort. At 10:30 AM on 25 August, the 300mm and 210mm howitzers opened fire on the giant fortress. They were joined at 2 PM by Krupp 420mm howitzers and at 6 PM by 150mm coastal howitzers. By dusk the next day, the fort "looked like a hill spouting fire." It surrendered at 5:30 PM on 27 August. The Germans over fifty-two hours had fired about sixteen hundred artillery rounds at Manonviller, including two hundred shells, 922kg each, from the mammoth Krupp "Big Berthas" that had been hauled to Manonviller by Daimler Benz tractors and sited at Elfringen, 14.5 kilometers from the fort.[107] Deputy Officer Fritz Burger of 1st Foot Artillery Regiment was shocked at the "unbelievable devastation" caused by the Krupp howitzers. Manonviller looked like a "rooted-up molehill."[108] There had been just 2 fatalities among the 820 officers and men inside the well-protected fortress, but its defenders had been physically and psychologically shaken by the terrible pounding. A direct hit on Manonviller's ventilation plant had greatly accelerated the decision to surrender. In an act of "chivalry," General von Brug had requested that the French garrison be allowed to withdraw "with honor." Rupprecht vetoed the suggestion. The French had been "less than chivalrous" at Lunéville, he countered, firing on German medics and wounded.[109] It was a new, "hard" war.

Kaiser Wilhelm II was "simply ecstatic" over the battlefield success of a fellow royal and on 27 August bestowed the Iron Cross, First and Second Class, on Crown Prince Rupprecht. Moltke, in the words of a Bavarian staff officer, had been "moved to tears" by the gesture. But their Prussian paladins were less charitable. Rupprecht's failure to dispatch his "tired" cavalry to cut the defeated French Second Army to pieces after the Battle of the Saar, War Minister Erich von Falkenhayn testily recalled on the eve of the Battle of the Marne, meant that the Bavarians had missed a "golden moment" to decide the war on the southern flank, the so-called *Südflügel*. Prussian cavalry, unlike its Bavarian counterpart, he savagely noted, was never "too tired" to pursue a beaten foe![110]

With Fort Manonviller taken and the French driven to the line of the Meurthe River, Rupprecht and Krafft began preparations to send a major portion of their forces north to assist Fifth Army in and around Verdun. This had been "Case 3" of the modified Schlieffen Plan that Moltke had distributed on 6 August as the Bavarian part in the great *Westaufmarsch*. They awaited new instructions from the OHL. Eventually, Lieutenant Colonel Tappen informed them that since the German rail net in the southwest only ran as far north as Aachen—after which the troops would face a very long march to the front—they would arrive much too late to assist in the envelopment of Paris.[111] The Bavarians were left alone to plot their future course of action.

CHAPTER FOUR

THE BLOODY ROAD WEST: LIÈGE TO LOUVAIN

———

*No plan of operations survives with any certainty beyond
the first encounter with the enemy's major forces.*

—HELMUTH VON MOLTKE THE ELDER

THE CITY OF LIÈGE WAS NOT ONE OF EUROPE'S DESIRED TOURIST destinations before 1914. In fact, it was a grimy industrial city of about 168,000 inhabitants that straddled the Meuse (Maas) River in northeastern Belgium—thirty kilometers from the German border to the east and fifteen from the Dutch border to the north. But it did get the occasional visitor. Among these in 1911 was a foreboding German dressed in a nondescript business suit. He was conspicuous not so much by his large round head with its receding hairline, jowled red face, piercing blue eyes, drooping bushy mustache, or barrel chest, but rather by a face that never smiled and a demeanor that never showed a hint of kindness or compassion. Humor was beyond his range.

The German visitor parked his open-top automobile on a promontory southeast of what to him was Lüttich, above the Maas Valley.[1] One hundred meters below him spread the sights of Liège: the curve of the river, the gleaming steel bands of the Belgian railway, and the spires of the Cathedral de Liège, the Église Saint-Barthélemy, and the Église Saint-Jacques. He neatly unfolded a map on the hood of the car. On his right, the river flowed through a deep ravine in the center of the city and then disappeared off to the north; on his left, wooded hills stretched to the Ardennes Plateau, off to the southeast. But mostly, the visitor took careful note of a sixteen-kilometer-wide passageway, the Liège Gap,

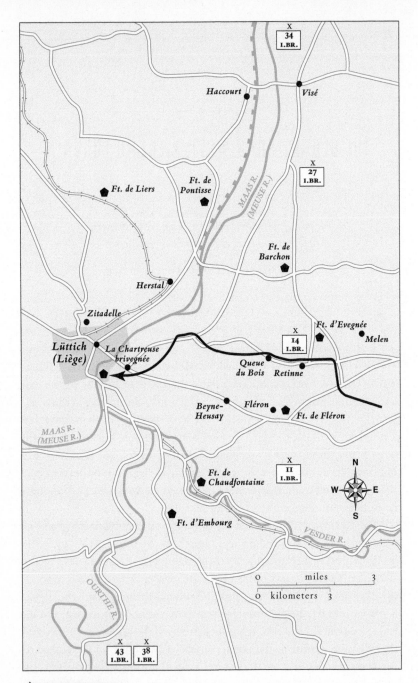

LIÈGE, EVENING OF 6 AUGUST 1914

which ran through the city and stretched between the Netherlands and the Ardennes; beyond lay the rolling plains of the Hesbaye region. As well, he studied the city's outer belt of a dozen fortresses. For Colonel Erich Ludendorff, chief of the Mobilization and Deployment Section of the German General Staff, was in charge of drafting plans for the *Handstreich* (bold strike) against Liège that would kick off the Schlieffen-Moltke deployment plan in a future war.

LIÈGE WAS FOUNDED IN 558 when Saint Monulph, bishop of Tongres, built a chapel at the confluence of the Meuse and Legia rivers. It saw its share of Europe's violent past. In 1467 and again in 1468, when the Liègois foolishly declared war on the Duchy of Burgundy, Charles the Bold razed the walls of the city. In 1703, the Duke of Marlborough stormed Liège's two forts, the Citadel and La Chartreuse, preparatory to his invasion of the German states the next year. In 1794, French Revolutionary armies sacked the city and destroyed the great cathedral of Saint-Lambert. Napoleon I occupied Liège for the duration of his rule.

But Liège survived—and prospered. The high-grade coal of the Meuse Valley between Seraing and Herstal fueled Liège's factories, and the city quickly developed into Belgium's chief manufacturing center—the fabled "Birmingham of Belgium." The faubourg of Herstal became world-renowned as a producer of fine arms—to the point that Ludwig Loewe of Berlin, manufacturer of the famous Mauser small arms, in 1896 seized a controlling interest in the giant Fabrique nationale d'armes de guerre. The railway brought further wealth and prominence, and Liège became a major hub on the main rail line leading from Berlin to Brussels—and on to Paris.

All this strategic wealth demanded protection. Beginning in 1888, Henri Alexis Brialmont, a military engineer who had built Bucharest's belt of defenses, began work on what over time became a fifty-two-kilometer ring of twelve forts some six to seven kilometers from Liège's center. From north to south, there were six on the right bank of the Meuse (Barchon, Evegnée, Fléron, Chaudfontaine, Embourg, and Boncelles), and another six on the river's left bank (Pontisse, Liers, Lantin, Loncin, Hollogne, and Flémalle). The average distance between the forts was nineteen hundred meters, with the largest gap seven thousand meters. Friedrich Krupp of Essen had won the contract to modernize the forts' four hundred guns, with the result that by 1914 a new mix of

modern 120mm, 150mm, and 210mm heavy guns, mortars, and howitzers overlapped one another's zones of fire.

Brialmont built well. All the forts were constructed with concrete
casemates. The turtle-shaped steel cupolas that housed the heavy guns
could be elevated automatically to fire and then to retract. A clear field
of fire was assured by sloping the cleared terrain down and away from
the guns. Brialmont studded this glacis with barbed-wire entanglements. Underground tunnels connected the forts, each of which
was self-contained with its own ammunition chambers, storerooms,
kitchens, water cisterns, power generators, latrines, and laundry facili-
ties. A ventilation system assured fresh air for each fort's peacetime
complement of eighty defenders.

General Gérard Mathieu Leman, an officer of engineers and a long-
time instructor at the Belgian War College, had been selected as governor of Liège only a few months before the outbreak of the war. He had
under his command twenty-five thousand regular troops of 3d Infantry Division (ID) as well as 15th Infantry Brigade (IB) of the field
army, forty-five hundred garrison troops, and about twelve thousand
soldiers of the reserves and the Garde civique (militia). His handwritten orders from King Albert on 4 August 1914 were simple: "I charge
you to hold to the end with your division the position which you have
been entrusted to defend."[2]

DURING THE NIGHT OF 1–2 August, advance elements of German 29th
and 69th regiments, 16th ID, crossed into the Grand Duchy of Luxembourg on bicycles, in armored cars and automobiles, and by train.[3] They
met no resistance and no sabotage. They secured the duchy's bridges,
railways, and roads, and occupied its capital on the morning of 2 August.
The next day, Germany declared war on France and Belgium.

Horsemen from 2d, 4th, and 9th cavalry divisions (CD) smartly
moved westward out of Aachen and into Belgium. Their mission was
to scout the thirty kilometers of terrain that lay between Aachen and
Liège. They encountered no resistance. Late in the morning of 3 August, they entered the small village of Battice, about ten kilometers
east of Liège. They assumed that the "neutral" Belgians would put up
only token resistance. Several shots rang out from one of the houses.
Three or four riders tumbled out of their saddles onto the cobbled
street. Francs-tireurs! For four decades, German soldiers had been fed

stories of how French "irregulars" had ambushed, mutilated, and poisoned German forces during the Franco-Prussian War (1870–71). In short order, the cavalrymen executed three Belgian civilians, drove the rest out of their homes, and set Battice on fire.[4]

Still farther north, Georg von der Marwitz advanced with the remainder of II Cavalry Corps and 34th IB against Visé, on the Meuse River just south of the Dutch border. At Warsage, his uhlans took fire from several houses.[5] Marwitz's troopers seized and then executed six hostages. At Visé, Marwitz discovered that the Meuse bridges had been destroyed. For a third time that day, his horsemen came under fire from civilians. He ordered suspected houses burned to the ground and 627 hostages rounded up and eventually deported to Germany. Heavy fire from Liège's northernmost fort (Pontisse) prevented the uhlans from crossing the river on 4 August. But at four o'clock* the next morning, units of Otto von Garnier's 4th CD managed to ford the Meuse at Lixhe, hard against the Dutch frontier. They strapped together numerous steel boats, laid boards across them, and thus assisted 34th IB across the river.[6] Marwitz's riders then pushed on toward Tongeren, northwest of Liège.

The noose around Liège was beginning to tighten. Allied fliers at dusk on 4 August had caught brief glimpses of an awe-inspiring sight: six gray-clad, reinforced infantry brigades and an entire cavalry corps—twenty-five thousand soldiers, eight thousand horsemen, and 124 guns—advancing in five mighty columns out of the east along a forty-kilometer front from Aachen to Malmédy. They were part of Otto von Emmich's X Army Corps, Second Army. While the latter's commander, Karl von Bülow, was leisurely making his way west from Hanover, his deputy chief of staff was already on the scene. Erich Ludendorff instantly became one of the few staff planners in history ever to draft and then take part in the execution of his own operations plan.

The *Handstreich* prepared for Liège by Ludendorff in 1911 was based on a garrison force of six thousand regulars, augmented by three thousand militiamen.[7] This proved to be a gross miscalculation. As noted earlier, Leman in early August 1914 had under his command about

---

* Belgian/French time (Greenwich Mean Time). German army records give German General Time (DGZ), one hour ahead.

thirty thousand soldiers of 3d ID, 15th IB, the garrison force, and the Garde civique. But it was a motley collection, as if imported directly from the stage of a Franz Lehár operetta: the regular infantry in blue-and-white uniforms, the *chasseurs à pied* in green and yellow with flowing capes and peaked caps, and the Civic Guard in high round hats and red facings. Flemish milk-cart dogs pulled the machine guns (*mitrailleuses*) only recently begged from France. How would this ragtag rabble, led by a quiet academic from the Belgian War College, stand up against the approaching *furor teutonicus*?

The answer was not long in coming. On the afternoon of 4 August, the defenders of Barchon bloodily repulsed an attack by units of 53d Infantry Regiment (IR) as it charged the glacis leading up to the fort's walls. The next day, 34th IB lost 30 officers and 1,150 men at Visé. On 6 August, 14th IB, attacking the center line of Liège, sustained more than 50 percent casualties.* In the south, the Belgians warded off all attempts by 9th CD to cross the Meuse between Liège and Huy. Not even a spectacular night bombing attack on Liège by Zeppelin VI out of Cologne intimidated Leman; while its thirteen small bombs killed nine civilians and in the process launched a new form of warfare, the military effect was negligible. Moreover, the airship leaked gas on the way home and had to crash-land at Bonn.[8] And when Emmich sent an emissary under a white flag to demand Leman's surrender, the plucky professor, who had earlier barely escaped an attempt by the Germans to take him prisoner, replied, "Force your way through the gap."[9]

Leman's valiant defenders had caused five of the six German attacking brigades to beat a hasty retreat. Headlines in Brussels papers screamed out the news: *"Grande Victoire Belge!"* Those in London and Paris spoke of a major "rout" of no fewer than 125,000 German troops, and of at least 20,000 enemy casualties. The French republic bestowed the Grand Cross of the Legion of Honor on Liège and the Military Medal on King Albert. However, Chief of the General Staff Joseph Joffre adamantly re-

---

* Casualty figures are notoriously inexact. Armies tend to understate their own and to overstate those of the enemy. Moreover, the records are incomplete: Many were not kept in the heat of battle and others were lost in subsequent actions. And there is little consistency in counting: The Germans only tallied wounded who were evacuated to field hospitals; the British included even those returned to duty after immediate, cursory treatment. I have used the term *casualties* to apply to men killed, wounded, captured, or missing in battle, but not to those affected by disease, mental trauma, psychiatric shock, neuralgia, or battle fatigue. See the entry "casualties" in Richard Holmes, ed., *The Oxford Companion to Military History* (Oxford: Oxford University Press, 2001), 182–85.

fused to divert French troops from his concentration plan to assist the beleaguered Belgians. Firmly convinced that the main German thrust would not come across the Meuse, he only reluctantly dispatched Louis Franchet d'Espèrey's I Corps to secure the Meuse bridges between Givet and Namur and Jean-François Sordet's I Cavalry Corps to scout southern Belgium.[10] For almost ten days, Sordet managed mainly to exhaust both men and horses.

What had happened to the German assault? Carl von Clausewitz's proverbial "fog of uncertainty" ruled the battlefield. Already during the advance, units lost their way in the dark. Officers were separated from their horses. Maps could not be located. Field kitchens were left behind. Soldiers panicked and shot at one another. Suspected fire from civilians added to the chaos. German units stopped to shoot and burn. Moreover, war in its primordial form, as Clausewitz stated, was "slaughter" (*Schlacht*). German infantry assaults in close formation were a target-rich environment even for Leman's half-trained soldiers. The *mitrailleuses* spat out a steady stream of death at 150 rounds every sixty seconds. A withering artillery fire swept the massed German infantry columns before the forts' walls.

Still, the Hanoverians and Westphalians of Emmich's X Corps continued to advance. They made their way over a veritable wall of dead—only to be gunned down in turn. A letter by an anonymous Belgian officer told the story well:

> As line after line of German infantry advanced, we simply mowed them down. . . . They made no attempt at deploying, but came on, line after line, almost shoulder to shoulder, until, as we shot them down, the fallen were heaped one on top of the other, in an awful barricade of dead and wounded men that threatened to mask our guns and cause us trouble.[11]

Perhaps some of the veterans on the German General Staff remembered that in 1895, Martin Köpke had warned Alfred von Schlieffen against expecting "quick, decisive victories," as even "the most offensive spirit" could achieve little more than "a tough, patient and stouthearted crawling forward step-by-step." Liège in 1914 confirmed Köpke's dire prediction. The campaign in Belgium, to use the general's words, had degenerated into "siege-style" warfare.[12] Only the means had changed, with monstrous howitzers, still to be brought up, becoming the modern trebuchet.

Numerous German commanders lamented that there had not been sufficient prewar nighttime training, that neither war games nor staff rides had prepared the army for the lethality of the modern battlefield, and that commanders from the company level on up had sought to overcome firepower with dash and daring. The results had been staggering casualty rates, especially among infantry officers. With regard to nighttime fighting, many units adopted special white armbands as well as common passwords, and officers ordered the men to advance with unloaded rifles to cut down on the devastating occurrences of friendly fire.[13]

Not surprisingly, the Germans were furious that the Belgians had refused them free passage through what they considered a neutral country. They denied the legitimacy of Belgian military resistance. The result was predictable: a veritable orgy of shooting and burning. By 8 August, almost 850 civilians had been killed and thirteen hundred buildings burned down in such nondescript places as Micheroux, Retinne, Soumagne, and Melen, among others.[14] Whereas Schlieffen had believed that Liège could be invested by a single division, and Ludendorff that it could be stormed by thirty-nine thousand men, the reality was that by 8 August, the Belgians had beaten back all attempts by X Corps to storm the forts—at the cost in blood of fifty-three hundred casualties. The corpses bloated in the broiling sun.

Still, the German attack threatened to cut Liège off from the rest of the country. Faced with this possibility, General Leman on 6 August released 3d ID and 15th IB to withdraw to the line of the Gette (Gete) River and fight another day. But he was determined to hold the twelve forts with their skeletal complements for as long as possible in accordance with the instructions he had received from King Albert.

The one bright note in the otherwise disastrous German assault was the plan's architect, Ludendorff. As deputy chief of Second Army, he was not scheduled to play an active role in the campaign. But fate intervened. While waiting for Bülow to make his way to Belgium, Ludendorff found himself caught up in the maelstrom of the battle for Liège. He followed Emmich into the outskirts of the city. At Retinne, just north of Fort Fléron, he stumbled across 14th IB, whose commander, Friedrich von Wussow, had recently been killed. Ludendorff did not hesitate for even a moment. He took command of the brigade and in house-to-house fighting made his way through the Queue-de-Bois, up out of the Meuse Valley, and onto the heights near the old Carthusian monastery of La Chartreuse. After overnighting there, Ludendorff at around noon on 7 August spied a white flag flying from the Citadel. Surrender? He sent an officer to investigate. No such luck. At 6 PM, the officer returned to report that General Leman had informed him that the white flag had been raised against his will.

By then, Ludendorff and 14th IB found themselves in a precarious position—short of ammunition and food, down to a strength of only fifteen hundred men, burdened with a thousand Belgian prisoners of war, isolated within the iron ring of Leman's forts, and cut off from the rest of their forces. The men were nervous. "I shall never forget the night of August 6/7," Ludendorff later wrote. "It was cold. . . . I listened feverishly for the sound of fighting. I still hoped that at least one brigade or another had broken through the line of forts."[15] None had.

Undaunted, Ludendorff pushed on into the city the next morning. He dispatched an advance guard under Colonel Burghardt von Oven to take the Citadel. Then he commandeered an automobile and with his adjutant drove up to the Citadel. There was not a German sentry to be seen, only Belgian soldiers. In a piece of audacious cheek, Ludendorff straightened himself up, dusted off his uniform, clenched the monocle into his right eye socket, strode up to the Citadel's gates, and rapped on them with the pommel of his sword. The gates opened. The courtyard was filled with startled Belgian troops. One of the truly great "what if?" scenarios of modern history was at hand. What if a Belgian soldier had shot the general? What if he had been arrested and turned over to the French? Modern German history may well have taken a different course.* "The few hundred Belgians [inside the Citadel]," Ludendorff later triumphantly recorded, "surrendered at my summons."[16] For some reason, Colonel von Oven had opted to bypass the Citadel and to head for Fort Loncin.

---

* Ludendorff was assigned chief of staff of Eighth Army in East Prussia and, together with Paul von Hindenburg, defeated two Russian armies at Tannenberg and the Masurian Lakes. From 1916 to 1918, the two men exercised a "silent dictatorship" over Germany. In 1918, they helped invent the infamous "stab-in-the-back" lie, according to which Germany had never been defeated militarily but rather "stabbed in the back" by its domestic enemies—Jews, Socialists, and Communists. In November 1923, Ludendorff took part in Adolf Hitler's so-called Beer Hall Putsch in Munich, hoping to use Bavaria as a springboard to topple the democratic and republican government in Berlin.

A grateful Kaiser Wilhelm II "smothered" Helmuth von Moltke, chief of the General Staff, with kisses.[17] Next, he awarded the war's first prestigious Pour le Mérite medal to Ludendorff.* Then, remembering that Emmich was the field commander of X Corps, he bestowed the decoration on that officer as well.

News of the coup de main at the Citadel hit the newspapers in Germany immediately. Joyous celebrations erupted in many cities. Bülow's staff—without a direct connection to the troops besieging Liège, since X Corps had not been provided with a communications detachment—had intercepted Emmich's terse private telegram to his wife: "Hurrah, at Liège." A more formal epistle informed Second Army that Emmich had entered the city at 7:45 AM on 7 August. "The Governor in Flight. The Bishop a prisoner. Liège evacuated by Belgian troops. Citadel of Liège occupied by our troops. As yet not known which forts have been taken."[18] The last sentence raised eyebrows at Bülow's headquarters—as did the fact that thereafter a deafening silence ensued. For almost two days, no word came out of Liège. Wild rumors circulated at once: The entire 14th IB had been taken prisoner by the Belgians; Ludendorff had been killed in action; Bülow had been shot by his sentry; losses on both sides had been horrendous; and all the forts had surrendered.

The delay at Liège caused near panic on the morning of 8 August at Army Supreme Command (Oberste-Heeresleitung, or OHL) in Berlin as well as at Bülow's temporary headquarters at Aachen. In Berlin, Wilhelm II maliciously accused Moltke of having "brought the English down about my ears for nothing" with his invasion of neutral Belgium. For a second time since 1 August, when the kaiser had brutally rebuked Moltke for his refusal to concentrate solely against Russia after Ambassador Karl von Lichnowsky had sent word that London would keep Paris out of the war if Germany did not attack France, the chief of the General Staff collapsed psychologically. His deputy, Hermann von Stein, witnessed "a most serious nervous breakdown," a "cascade of tears," and eventual "utter apathy" on the part of Moltke. The latter "never forgot those words"; they "weighed heavily on him" in subsequent days. Moltke eventually recovered and put on a brave

---

* Ludendorff never received a patent of nobility for his services, mainly because Kaiser Wilhelm II disliked his gruff nature.

front. "Gentlemen, you have seen me weak and agitated," he informed his staff. "The struggles before mobilization and the Kaiser's words had made me brittle. I have now overcome that and you shall witness a different me."[19]

At Aachen, Bülow's staff also became anxious. First and Second armies, roughly six hundred thousand soldiers and a quarter million horses, had to squeeze through the narrow corridors first of Aachen and then of Liège before they could debouch on the Hesbaye Plateau. Martial law had been declared at Aachen and the streets cleared for the troops; it would take five days to march them through its narrow medieval lanes. Their equipment had been routed through Düsseldorf to ease the congestion. Each army corps occupied thirty kilometers of road, each division fifteen, and each corps' munitions trains twenty. If Liège held out much longer, First and Second armies would have to march through the Netherlands—and thus violate another neutral nation.

Bülow took charge. On 8 August, with Moltke's consent, he augmented Emmich's original force of thirty-three thousand infantry and cavalry with a new siege army of sixty thousand (IX and VII corps) commanded by Karl von Einem-Rothmaler. A former Prussian war minister, Einem had won the Iron Cross as a lieutenant in the Franco-Prussian War and in 1914 commanded VII Corps at Münster. He took his time. He put an end to the senseless slaughter of massed infantry charges at the Liège forts and waited for the heavy siege artillery—developed in peacetime by Ludendorff for just this purpose—to arrive on the scene.

As soon as he set foot on Belgian territory, Einem confessed to his wife that he deeply "regretted" the "brutal nature" of the conflict. "Unfortunately," he wrote on 8 August, "the [Belgian] populace takes part in the war." Men and women from concealed positions fired on the troops, especially under the cover of darkness. "I have ordered that the villages be burned down and everyone [seized] shot." Two days later, he repeated his outrage at "the insidious, detestable blood thirstiness of the Belgians." He maintained a hard stance. "Unfortunately, we had to singe and burn a lot and many inhabitants forfeited their lives." The burned-out villages between Battice and Herve, he noted, "defy description. This is what the ruins of Pompey . . . must look like." He lamented that many soldiers in their eagerness to get at the enemy had fired on their fellow warriors.[20]

While he waited for the heavy artillery to arrive, Einem took stock of the situation. Not a single fort had fallen. Their garrisons had held tough. General von Emmich was in the "remarkable position" of having forced his way into the city between Forts Fléron and Evegnée—only to "find himself in a mousetrap." Military history, Einem wryly noted, had been "enriched by a new, paradoxical example" at this "damned fortress": "Emmich inside and we outside."[21] The men were hungry, thirsty, and tired. What remained of Marwitz's eight thousand cavalry mounts were dangerously short on oats. The heat continued unabated. The only good news was that on 8 August, 14th IB finally managed to break out of the Belgian steel ring that encircled them and to take Fort Barchon. Fort d'Evegnée fell on the night of 11 August.

In the afternoon of 12 August, Einem spied a welcome sight: the monstrous black heavy siege guns. First came the 305mm Austrian Škoda howitzers. Moved in three sections, they could be assembled in forty minutes. Instead of tires, they crept forward on what their crews called "iron feet"—that is, steel tracks. Next came the four 420mm Krupp monsters. Each had a crew of two hundred. Each took six hours to emplace. Each could fire a shell with 150 kilograms of explosives a distance of fourteen kilometers. Each was fired electrically from a distance of three hundred meters by a gun crew wearing protective head padding. Célestin Demblon, a deputy of Liège, marveled at the Krupp piece.

> The monster advanced in two parts, pulled by 36 horses. The pavement trembled. . . . Hannibal's elephants could not have astonished the Romans more! The soldiers who accompanied it marched stiffly with an almost religious solemnity. It was the Belial* of cannons![22]

Both the Škodas and the Krupp "Big Berthas"† fired armor-piercing shells with delayed fuses that allowed them to penetrate their targets before exploding.

The issue was never in doubt. Within forty-eight hours, Leman's forts were pulverized into submission: first Pontisse, then Chaudfontaine and Embourg, next Liers and Fléron and Evegnée east of the

---

* Biblical name for the devil or one of his associates.
† The nickname referred to the somewhat corpulent F. A. Krupp heiress, Bertha Krupp von Bohlen und Halbach; she was not amused.

Meuse; thereafter, Boncelles, Lantin, and Loncin west of the river. The last two, Hollogne and Flémalle, lowered the Belgian tricolor on 16 August.[23] Each fort took about thirty heavy shells. Ludendorff had arrived at Fort Loncin just in time to see a single shell from a Big Bertha rip through the concrete roof, blow up its magazine, and cause the entire structure to collapse.

Dazed and blackened Belgian soldiers, accompanied by some Germans who had been taken prisoner on the night of August 5/6, crawled out of the ruins. Bleeding, with their hands up, they came toward us. *"Ne pas tuer, ne pas tuer."*★ . . . We were no Huns. Our men brought water to refresh our enemies.[24]

Loncin held a surprise for the Germans: Under its broken concrete slabs and twisted girders they found General Leman, unconscious and nearly asphyxiated by poisonous fumes. Emmich was at the scene. He had met Leman at peacetime military maneuvers and congratulated the Belgian on the tenacity of his defense. Leman's one concern was that it be recorded that he had carried out King Albert's orders to the letter. "Put in your dispatches that I was unconscious." He then offered Emmich his sword. In the war's first (and perhaps last) act of true chivalry, the German declined to take it. "No, keep your sword. To have crossed swords with you has been an honor."[25] Leman had lost twenty thousand men at Liège.[26]

As soon as the debris could be cleared from the roads, German First and Second armies filed through and around the city and headed for the Liège Gap. Lieutenant Colonel Wilhelm Groener's Field Railway Service of twenty-six thousand men had restored the lines between Aachen and (now) Lüttich, and only the great tunnel at Nasproué remained blocked, for the Belgians had rammed seventeen locomotives at full speed into one another inside the tunnel.[27] Leman's gallant defense of Liège had cost the Germans perhaps two days on the Schlieffen-Moltke master timetable.[28]

MILITARY WISDOM NOW SUGGESTED that King Albert concentrate his remaining units at Namur, Belgium's second great fortress on the Meuse,

★ "Don't kill, don't kill!"

and there force the Germans into another bloody siege. But Albert was determined to maintain his army on Belgian soil—the only escape from Namur would have been south or west into France—and to keep open his line of retreat to Fortress Antwerp. Hence, he regrouped his formations along the line of the Gette River. At the little village of Haelen, Leon de Witte's cavalry division, fighting as dismounted riflemen, on 12 August gallantly blunted the saber and lance charges of six regiments of Marwitz's II Cavalry Corps as it attempted to storm the river crossings.[29] Known as the Battle of the Silver Helmets in Belgian folklore, Haelen was the first cavalry battle (and the first Allied victory) of the war. Still, Namur, to the southwest of Liège, and Louvain (Leuven), to the northwest, lay squarely in the path of the German advance.

On 17 August, Moltke issued new orders for the main German thrust into Belgium by sixteen army corps and two cavalry corps, three-quarters of them the pride of the Prussian army. The three northernmost armies were to converge on the Sambre River; First and Second armies were to cut off any Belgian attempt to withdraw to Antwerp; and Third Army was to attack the line of the Meuse between Namur and Givet. Speed was of the essence. First and Second armies had to pass through a dangerous eighty-kilometer-wide corridor between the fortresses of Namur and Antwerp, all the while securing their left flanks against suspected French forces south of the Sambre.

Unlike the armies in the German center and south, these were commanded not by royal princes but rather by professional soldiers with the special rank of *Generaloberst* (literally, colonel general, or a "four-star"). At the extreme right wing, Alexander von Kluck's First Army consisted of 120 battalions and 748 guns. Schlieffen had assigned this formation the role of "hammer" in his plan: First Army was to march some seven hundred kilometers through Belgium, across northern France, and along the English Channel before descending on Paris from the northwest and driving the French armies against the "anvil" of the German forces holding in Lorraine. Its commander in 1914 was a rarity in the highest echelons of Prussian field commanders: a self-made man, non-noble and non-Prussian. Kluck was born at Münster, in Westphalia, on 20 May 1846 and saw service with the Prussian army against both Austria (1866) and France (1870–71). Thereafter, he rose rapidly through the ranks on the basis of merit: command of a division by 1902, of V Corps in 1906, of I Corps one year later, and then of

Eighth Army Inspectorate at Berlin in 1913. Kluck was rewarded for his military career with a patent of nobility in 1909. His service had been primarily commanding troops rather than staff work. He was fierce-looking and self-assured, almost to the point of arrogance.

South of First Army ranged Karl von Bülow's Second Army of 137 battalions and 820 guns. Its primary task, along with First Army, was to deliver the decisive blow against the French forces in and around Paris. Bülow was a striking contrast with Kluck: Born at Berlin on 24 March 1846 into an ancient Mecklenburg noble clan, he had a plethora of career paths open to him. He chose the military. His brother Bernhard opted instead for the diplomatic corps and then served as chancellor from 1900 to 1909. Like Kluck, Bülow had fought in the Austro-Prussian and the Franco-Prussian Wars. Thereafter, he had enjoyed a notable rise: commander of the prestigious 4th Foot Guards, department head at the Prussian War Ministry, and in 1902 deputy chief of the General Staff under Schlieffen. The following year, he received III Corps and in 1909 Third Army Inspectorate at Hanover. In 1914, Bülow was given Second Army and would soon be entrusted also with command over Kluck's First Army. With white hair and mustache and a puffy face, he looked more the genial uncle than the fierce warrior. Much of the campaign in the fall of 1914 would depend on how closely these two vastly different personalities cooperated.

South of Second Army was Max von Hausen's Third Army—the third formation of the pivot wing, the so-called *Schwenkungsflügel*. At 101 battalions and 596 guns, it was the smallest of the German armies. And it was Saxon. Hausen was born in Dresden on 17 December 1846. During the Austro-Prussian War of 1866, Saxony sided with the Austrian Empire, and as a result Hausen had fought against Berlin.[30] After German unification, he taught at the Military Academy from 1871 to 1874, and then transferred to the General Staff (1875–87). He commanded XII Corps from 1900 to 1902, and then served as Saxon war minister until 1914. During his tenure, Hausen worked diligently to uphold and even to expand the Prusso-Saxon Military Convention of 1867.* He resisted all attempts from within the army to reassert Saxon

* In 1866 the Saxon army had not invaded Prussia, but had stood alongside the Austrians in Bohemia; thus, it was spared the fate of the Kingdom of Hanover, annexation. Under the Military Convention of 7 February 1867, Saxony was allowed to maintain its own War Ministry, army corps (XII), and cadet corps, but it had to undergo "Prussianization" in terms of organization and weaponry.

particularism. In May 1914, Hausen retired after a brilliant career that had spanned half a century. But given that King Friedrich August III had no military interest and that Crown Prince Friedrich August Georg was but twenty-one years old, Wilhelm II on 1 August reactivated Hausen's commission and entrusted him with Third Army. Hausen's was a difficult role: to cross the Meuse River near Dinant and, as the situation demanded, offer assistance either to Bülow's Second Army on his right flank or to Duke Albrecht of Württemberg's Fourth Army on his left. His relationship with the senior Bülow would be critical to the execution of his mission.

THE ADVANCE ON PARIS by three German armies of 358 battalions of infantry and 2,164 guns required tight command and control. It received neither. Instead, Imperial Headquarters—the Großes Hauptquartier (GHQ), of which the OHL was but one, albeit major, part—consisted of what one scholar has called "a middle thing between a supreme military council and an imperial court."[31] It, in fact, was a mammoth, unwieldy conglomeration consisting of the kaiser, the chief of the General Staff and his deputy, the chief of the Admiralty Staff, the Prussian war minister, the chiefs of the Civil, Military, and Navy cabinets, the chancellor, the state secretary of the Foreign Office, the military plenipotentiaries of the German federal states, the military representative of the Austro-Hungarian ally, and the kaiser's host of adjutants and personal staff. Master of ceremonies for this vast camp was an imperial favorite, General Hans von Plessen.

Imperial Headquarters remained in Berlin during the period of mobilization and concentration. Then, at 7:55 AM on Sunday, 16 August, it departed for the front—or at least Koblenz, eight hundred kilometers southwest at the confluence of the Rhine and Mosel rivers—in eleven trains. Karl von Wenninger, the Bavarian military plenipotentiary, captured the enormity of the operation in his war diary.[32] "Wonderful express-train cars; a separate compartment for every 2 gentlemen. I even saw a dining car." The sign on one compartment startled him: " 'Her Excellency v. Moltke with lady's-maid.' So, we are even being mothered." The chief of the General Staff had insisted that his wife accompany him into battle. There were no cheering crowds to see them off in Berlin. Just out of the station, Wenninger stood in amazement as the "gigantic royal train of H[is] M[ajesty] glided by." The chefs were already at their stations, perspiring profusely as they prepared the midday meal. The trains avoided major routes and slowly rolled toward Koblenz on stretches of rail well off the beaten track. Guards had been posted at every crossing. Before noon, a major from the General Staff distributed seating lists for the dining car: "12 o'clock breakfast, 7 o'clock dinner." Within minutes, he returned with the list of sleeping car assignments. "Now, are we truly warriors," General von Wenninger caustically wondered, "or sybarites?" Whatever the case, the minute his train entered the Kingdom of Bavaria near Ritschenhausen, he had a hundred-liter keg of beer meet it.

Precisely according to plan—this was, after all, the German General Staff—the trains pulled into Koblenz station at eight o'clock the next morning. "Patches of fog enveloped castles and vineyards," Wenninger noted. Wilhelm II established his headquarters at Koblenz Castle; the General Staff, at the Hotel Union; the rest of the retinue, at the Parkhotel Koblenzer Hof. That afternoon, the kaiser took his military paladins on an automobile outing to Bad Ems, where on 13 July 1870 the fateful interview that helped launch the Franco-Prussian War had taken place,* and he planted a small oak beside the memorial stone. "I wonder," Wenninger mused, "whether the little oak will become a mighty tree?"

It was pure theater. The kaiser's place was in Berlin, supervising the war effort, directing the machinery of government, and offering encouragement to the home front. His pretense of conducting military operations from Koblenz, where he ostentatiously dined on the silver field service of Frederick the Great, fooled no one. An anecdote perhaps best caught the Supreme War Lord's true role. During a walk in one of the local parks with Admiral Georg Alexander von Müller, chief of the Navy Cabinet, and General Moriz von Lyncker, chief of the Military Cabinet, Wilhelm II sat on a bench to rest. The two officers, not wishing to disturb the kaiser and concerned that the short bench might not hold three stout, middle-aged flag officers, pulled up a second bench. "Am I already such a figure of contempt," Wilhelm II churlishly inquired, "that no one wants to sit next to me?"[33]

---

* French foreign minister Antoine de Gramont had instructed his ambassador to Prussia, Vincent de Benedetti, to seek out King Wilhelm I, then taking the cure at Bad Ems, to gain assurances that no member of the Hohenzollern family would ever seek the throne of Spain. Prussian prime minister Otto von Bismarck fueled the flames of war by editing out all conciliatory phrases from Wilhelm's report of this discussion and then publishing it in the newspapers.

Moltke insisted on remaining at Koblenz partly to keep a close eye on the volatile kaiser, and partly to be equidistant from the Eastern Front. He resisted several pleas from Lieutenant Colonel Gerhard Tappen, his chief of operations, to move at least the OHL closer to the front in Belgium, perhaps somewhere north of Namur, with the argument that this "insurrectionist" land had not yet been pacified.[34] Incredibly, Moltke directed General William Balcke, his chief of field telegraphy, to take up headquarters at Bad Ems, well hidden in a small valley east of the General Staff nerve center at Koblenz. And in sharp contrast with his French counterpart, Joffre—who used his private chauffeur, Georges Bouillot, winner of the French Grand Prix in 1912 and 1913, to rush him to the various army commands—Moltke left execution of his war plans to the individual army commanders. He remained firm in the belief that peacetime staff rides and war games had sufficiently honed their skills at interaction and cooperation, and that the "intentions" of the General Staff could best be relayed "orally through the sending of an officer of the High Command." Most especially, he placed his trust in the sixty-eight-year-old Bülow, whom he considered to be Germany's "most competent" army commander.[35]

BY 18 AUGUST, THE second Battle of the Frontiers (also known as Sambre-et-Meuse, or Charleroi) was about to begin. The northern German armies were driving west across the undulating plains of Brabant into Hainaut Province—Kluck just south of Brussels, and Bülow along the Wavre-Namur axis. The right wing of Hausen's Third Army as well as elements of the left wing of Bülow's Second Army were closing on Namur, at the junction of the Sambre and Meuse rivers. At Andenne and Seilles, where Bülow's men crossed the Meuse, and at Aarschot, where Kluck's troops drove the Belgian army behind the Gette, the pattern established at Battice and Visé repeated itself. German soldiers were convinced that civilians had fired on them and, worse, mutilated the bodies of their fallen comrades. *"Man hat geschossen!"* ("We have been shot at!") became the battle cry. Reprisals were swift and harsh: Suspected shooters were rounded up and executed, homes of suspected armed civilians burned to the ground, priests as well as burgomasters taken hostage, and hundreds of Belgians deported to Germany in cattle cars.[36]

General Ludwig von Sieger, chief of field munitions and recently returned from Liège, regaled Imperial Headquarters with gruesome stories of the "bestiality" of Belgian civilians in the path of war. Many had "clawed out the eyes and cut the throats" of wounded German soldiers. Despite the constant prewar reminders of francs-tireurs in 1870–71, Moltke's warriors simply had been unprepared for this form of irregular warfare. "But now we are finally moving against [Belgian] residents with utmost severity," Sieger was happy to report. "They have been executed en masse, their villages razed." He concluded that such "ruthless severity" had not been "without effect."[37]

At other places in Belgium, the German advance was more orderly and less brutal. After Liège, General von Einem's VII Corps, part of Bülow's Second Army, pointed west toward Wavre. The plains of Brabant were a welcome relief from the concrete forts of Liège. "The land has been cultivated just like it is at home," Einem noted in his diary. "It is very pretty, stretching well off to the distance; a great region to do battle." By 20–21 August, VII Corps had passed Wavre and approached Waterloo. "99 years ago all those people who today are our enemies defeated Napoleon and his Frenchmen there," he ruefully noted. "We are now on historic ground and today will advance along the same roads that took [Field Marshal Gebhard von] Blücher and his victorious formations to Waterloo or Belle Alliance."[38] Einem, the graduate of the Prussian Military Academy, had fulfilled one of his youthful dreams. He could not repress his feelings. "On the basis of [my] studies, I knew the configurations of the land so well that nothing surprised me"—except the British Lion Mound of 1826, a conical heap with 226 steps leading up to a great stone lion. A century ago the battle had been fought in rain; in 1914, a blazing sun scorched the fields.

The Belgian army, its brief heroics at Haelen notwithstanding, was in danger of being cut off from Antwerp by German First and Second armies along the line of the Gette. King Albert appealed to Joffre for French forces to come north across the Sambre to strike the enemy armies driving toward Antwerp in the flank. Joffre coldly replied that German formations west of the Meuse were but a "screen" for the main German drive around Sedan.[39] The truth of the matter is that Joffre continued to ignore warnings from both his intelligence staff and his field commanders that as many as eight German army corps and four cavalry divisions were already in Belgium, and instead clung to his firm belief that the Germans would not cross the Meuse in force but concentrate their efforts in the center, through the Ardennes. Obstinacy and stolidity, two of his main character traits, hampered early reassessment.

On 18 August, Moltke repeated his earlier placement of German Sixth and Seventh armies in Alsace-Lorraine under a single command—that of Crown Prince Rupprecht of Bavaria—and "subordinated" Kluck to Bülow in Belgium.[40] It was an ill-advised move. Bülow at once used his new authority to order Kluck to release Alexander von Linsingen's II Corps to execute a flank attack left from north of Diest against the retreating Belgian forces in hopes of encircling them before they reached Antwerp, while First and Second armies, each with three corps, advanced on the Gette from the east. Kluck was furious. He believed that his command authority had been infringed upon, that the new orders to II Corps only meant needless further marching and fatigue, and that Bülow's action would force him to cover the advance of II Corps, thereby slowing his advance toward the west. His anger was at full tide when he discovered the same day that King Albert had refused to make a stand on the Gette and instead had ordered a withdrawal behind the Dijle River to Fortress Antwerp. He found little consolation in the fact that Ferdinand von Quast's IX Corps had inflicted severe losses (1,639 officers and men) on the Belgians' left at Tirlemont.[41]

King Albert reached Antwerp on 20 August, only to be met by a sharp protest concerning the "retreat before a mere cavalry screen" from Colonel Jacques Aldebert of the French Military Mission. Aldebert, obviously briefed by Joffre, still insisted that the Germans would not advance beyond the Meuse in force. Had King Albert done the right thing? Or should he have withdrawn to the southwest to link forces with the British?[42] As King of the Belgians, he refused to abandon his country. By falling back on Antwerp—which Moltke had hoped to prevent—he forced Kluck to detach Hans von Beseler's III Reserve Corps (and later also IX Reserve Corps) to cover Antwerp and its garrison of sixty thousand men, thereby substantially weakening First Army.

Albert's decision to abandon his capital was militarily unimportant. Brussels was not a fortress. It had no strategic arteries. It had not figured in prewar military planning. When foreign diplomats discovered that the Garde civique was digging trenches and mustering companies in the city's parks, they pleaded (successfully) with Burgomaster Adolphe Max to end the foolishness, to declare Brussels an "open city" and thus

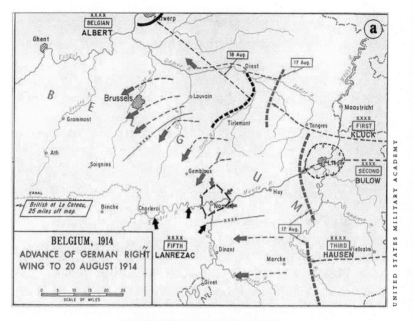

THE ADVANCE TO LOUVAIN AND ANTWERP

spare it the fate of Liège. At 3:30 PM on 20 August, Friedrich Sixt von Arnim's IV Corps entered the city with divisional bands playing the patriotic march "Die Wacht am Rhein"; the troops paraded for hours before their commander. American ambassador Brand Whitlock likened the German entry by a "mighty grey, grim horde" to a "thing of steel that came thundering on with shrill fifes and throbbing drums."[43] The Germans imposed an indemnity of 50 million francs on Brussels and 450 million on Brabant Province, to be paid within ten days. News of the fall of the Belgian capital evoked "fierce joy in Berlin." Church bells rang well into the night and people embraced one another, "frantic with delight."[44] Brussels had been spared destruction.

Not so Louvain (Leuven). When troops of First Army approached the city on 19 August, its forty-two thousand inhabitants—mainly educated, genteel people such as priests, nuns, professors, and wealthy retirees—sensibly declared it to be an "open city." Kluck thought it sufficiently secure to establish his headquarters there for the next four days. An uneasy truce held for almost a week under the cover of martial law in what the Germans called Löwen. Then, as First Army moved out toward the French border, fears mounted at the OHL that King Albert's forces might see this as the moment to sally out from Antwerp and hit Kluck's overextended supplies and communications network. Elements of Belgian 2d ID and its cavalry detachment in fact did so on 25–26 August, driving some German units back as far as Malines (Mechelen) and Louvain. By the afternoon of 25 August, about ten thousand German troops—many just arrived from the siege of Liège—bivouacked in Louvain.

Suddenly, an alarm sounded.[45] Eyewitnesses could not agree whether it was at 5:30, or 6:30 PM. Both sides did agree that sporadic shooting broke out by 8 PM. It soon spread through the city's main streets and squares. The *tac-tac* of machine guns then joined in. The whistles of emergency workers pierced the dusk that by now had enveloped Louvain. The cry of "We have been shot at!" was taken up by countless German soldiers—fueled by fear, panic, hunger, exhaustion, and drink. The few Belgian civilians who dared venture out saw a heavy red glow and gray smoke swirl down the Boulevard de Tirlemont and across the Place de la Station and the Place du Peuple. The flames spread to the Palais de Justice, the Church of Saint-Pierre, the university, and the Clothworkers' Hall with its library of 230,000 volumes, including more than 1,000 incunabula* and 750 medieval manuscripts. Dead horses littered the streets. Corpses were collected and piled up at the Place de la Station. Priests and members of the Garde civique were singled out for abuse.

For three days, Louvain lived in terror. On 27 August, the Germans announced that they were about to bombard the city and expelled 10,000 civilians. The bombardment was never carried out. When the fires finally died down, 248 citizens had been killed, perhaps as many as 40,000 deported to Germany, and twenty-one hundred buildings destroyed. Hugh Gibson, secretary of the American legation in Brussels, visited Louvain on 28 August.[46] "The road was black with frightened civilians carrying away small bundles from the ruins of their homes. Ahead was a great column of dull gray smoke which completely hid the city. We could hear the muffled sound of firing ahead." A small boy joyously cried out, *"Les Américains sont arrivés! Les Américains sont arrivés!"* After assuring the lad that the Americans had not arrived in Belgium, Gibson penetrated deeper into Louvain. He was confronted by burning houses and cinders so thick that he had to put on his motoring goggles. Many of the city's former stately homes were little more than "blackened walls with smouldering timbers inside." The streets were littered with wreckage: "hats and wooden shoes, German helmets, swords and saddles, bottles and all sorts of bundles which had been dropped and abandoned when the trouble began." Telegraph and trolley wires were down. Dead men and horses littered every square. Countless houses were still burning. The Boulevard de Tirlemont "looked as though it had been swept by a cyclone." Everywhere, the looting and shooting continued unabated. "It was all most businesslike."

The story of what occurred at Louvain during those terrible three days in August quickly made its way around the world and has remained a topic of debate ever since. For the Germans, the looting, burning, and shooting were "justified reprisals" for armed civilians inserting themselves into a military battle. There is a great deal of comment in German unit histories about the soldiers being tired, hungry, thirsty, and drunk from "liberated" wine stocks. But there is equal insistence on having witnessed Belgian civilians firing from windows

---

* Books printed before 1501.

and rooftops. General von Kluck in his memoirs conceded that "tough and inexorable reprisals" including "summary shooting of individuals" and "punitive burning of houses" had been applied by "local commanders on the spot."[47] The German official history of the war merely acknowledged that 27th Landwehr Brigade stood in and around Louvain on 27–28 August and that Belgian soldiers and Civic Guardsmen had discarded their uniforms and shot at German regulars "from behind bushes and houses."[48] Not a word more.

For the Allies, *Louvain* became synonymous with German "barbarism." Hundreds of lurid posters showing the Germans as modern-day "Huns" and Wilhelm II as "the modern Attila" or as "King of the Vandals" circulated almost immediately. Undoubtedly, the most famous was produced in the United States. It showed a giant gorilla, wearing a German spiked helmet with the word MILITARISM inscribed on it and sporting a Kaiser Wilhelm–like upturned mustache, emerging from the sea against the background of a burned-out European city. In his right hand he held a bloody club labeled KULTUR; in the other, a bare-bosomed damsel obviously in distress.[49] American journalists from *Collier's Weekly, The Saturday Evening Post,* and the *Chicago Tribune,* among others, fed their readers a steady diet of despondent Belgian refugees, burned-out cities, rotting animal and human corpses, and taunting "Huns." In their exhaustive study, *German Atrocities 1914,* historians John Horne and Alan Kramer conclude that while there "is no serious evidence that the German actions in Louvain were premeditated,"[50] the "reprisals" of arson, executions, expulsions, and deportations were part of a systematic policy of intimidation and terror. They record a total of 4,421 Belgian civilians killed.[51]

THERE REMAINED NAMUR, THE last of the great eastern Belgian fortresses not yet taken. It not only was an important commercial center at the confluence of the Meuse and Sambre rivers, but also a potential rallying and sallying point for Franco-Belgian formations.[52] By 18 August, the three infantry divisions of Max von Gallwitz's Guard Reserve Corps were advancing on Namur. The next morning, Moltke's staff sent Gallwitz a detailed siege plan prepared already in peacetime.[53] It contained data on the size of the fortress, the number of defenders, the caliber and placement of guns, and even a step-by-step plan of attack. Gallwitz ignored it. The front was fluid, and he was not about to halt the advance to conduct a leisurely, medieval siege. Instead, he persuaded Bülow to send him XI Corps—of Hausen's Saxon Third Army—as reinforcement. It was the first of many such encroachments to come. Hausen raised no objection, although he would have preferred to detach XII Reserve Corps instead in order to keep his regulars in the line of advance.[54]

The Romans had built a fortified outlook post on a rocky ledge overlooking Namur and the Meuse Valley in the third and fourth centuries; Emperor Charles V had constructed a citadel, La Médiane, on the very spot between 1542 and 1555; and Sebastien de Vauban had greatly expanded the citadel into a stone fortress for Louis XIV of France. Napoleon I had demolished large parts of the citadel since he saw no need for it as he had expanded his empire far to the east. But the new Kingdom of Belgium saw merit in the old ruins as part of its planned east-west line of defense, and thus hired Brialmont to fortify Namur between 1888 and 1892. He sited a ring of nine forts some eight kilometers from the center of the city and linked them (as at Liège) with an elaborate system of trenches and barbed-wire entanglements. In August 1914, *la position fortifiée de Namur* was defended by thirty-five thousand soldiers, mostly of Augustin Michel's Belgian 4th ID as well as four regiments of fortress infantry. At the last moment, the garrison had been augmented by Belgian 8th Infantry Brigade—which, finding itself isolated at Huy, had blown up the bridges over the Meuse there and fallen back on Namur. King Albert's orders again were straightforward: "Resist to the last."[55] Carrier pigeons maintained contact between Namur and the Belgian field army.

On 20 August, Gallwitz, an artillery specialist, began to test Namur's defenses by randomly shelling one of its forts, Marchovellette. But he was not about to repeat the senseless massed infantry assaults with which Emmich had shattered a good part of his X Corps at Liège. Instead, he methodically concentrated his forces—Guard Reserve Corps to the north and Saxon XI Corps to the southeast of Namur. Then he brought up the heavy siege guns released by the surrender of Liège: four batteries of Austrian Škoda howitzers and one battery of the Krupp Big Berthas. Finally, he convinced Bülow to attack the French at Charleroi to tie down Charles Lanrezac's French Fifth Army and so prevent it from lifting the siege at Namur.

Gallwitz got serious on 21 August, pulverizing Namur's forts relentlessly with his heavy siege guns.[56] Two forts were reduced within forty-eight hours. Two counterattacks by Michel's men were easily beaten back. By 23 August, the entire northern and eastern fronts of *la position fortifiée de Namur* had been reduced and five of its nine forts put out of commission. In all, the Germans fired 126 Krupp 420mm shells, 573 Škoda 305mm shells, and 6,763 coastal artillery 210mm shells at Namur.[57] Only 45th and 148th regiments, 45th IB, from Augustin Gérard's II Corps of French Fifth Army managed to approach Namur. They arrived just in time for the vanguard to be swept up in the German assault. On the evening of 23 August, the Prussians and Saxons stormed Namur. Gallwitz took sixty-seven hundred Belgian and French prisoners of war, captured twelve field guns as well as the forts' defensive artillery, and added vast stores of ammunition, food, and wagons to his corps. German losses were but nine hundred, of which one-third were fatal. Overall Belgian losses were set at fifteen thousand men, two-thirds of whom had belonged to 4th ID.[58]

The capture of Namur yet again was accompanied by acts of terror on the part of the occupiers. As before, the cry "We have been shot at!" sufficed to stampede German commanders into severe "retaliation." Upon receiving reports that nineteen armed civilians had fired on his men, Hans von Kirchbach, commanding XII Reserve Corps, reacted swiftly. "We burned down the houses from which the shots had come."[59] Saxon soldiers sent countless letters home confirming the "reprisals." Arthur Prausch, with 139th IR advancing on Namur, wrote his brother that civilians had fired on his unit and that he had seen comrades "with their throats slit" lying in the streets.[60] Villages where such "despicable acts" purportedly occurred were immediately burned to the ground. "In one village we shot 35 men as well as several women, including two priests. . . . They all lie heaped in a pile." Max Basta, 65th IR, Württemberg 16th Reserve Infantry Division (RID), likewise wrote home his impressions of the brutal nature of the war south of Namur. "All Belgian villages have been leveled to the ground; we marched through smoldering ruins." He most remembered the smell of destruction. "The swirling smoke caused by burning human and animal corpses forced our eyes to tear." It had become a harsh war. "Whoever fired on our troops or in any way appeared suspicious was gunned down."[61] Namur's inhabitants were gathered up to witness the public executions, and then released.

Inside Namur, isolated shots fired by civilians during the night of

24 August also brought instant "reprisals"—thirty civilians were executed and 110 buildings (including the City Hall and much of the Grand'Place) torched. "Our soldiers have been fired on," one German officer barked at a group of four hundred hostages. "We are going to act as we did at Andenne.★ . . . More than 500 shot." Charges that Belgian civilians "have also cut off our soldiers' noses, ears, eyes and fingers" threatened to escalate the reprisals into an orgy of murder and burning.[62] This was prevented at the last moment—and the hostages released—by the joint efforts of Bishop Thomas-Louis Heylen and the new city commandant, General Fritz von Below of XXI Corps.

General Michel had managed to march roughly fifty-six hundred soldiers of Belgian 4th ID out of the ruins just before Gallwitz's forces stormed Namur in hopes of eventually joining King Albert at Antwerp. It was not to be. Near Bioul, 4th Infantry Division was intercepted by Saxon 23d RID and virtually its entire complement taken prisoner without a struggle.[63] With the capture of Namur, the Germans had removed a vital corner post of the Allied front on the Meuse and the Sambre. Bülow's Second Army was now free to march westward along the Sambre River.

★ On 20–21 August, units of the Guard Reserve Corps, believing that they had been fired upon by francs-tireurs at Andenne, Belgium, killed 130 civilians in the town and an equal number in the outlying areas.

CHAPTER FIVE

DEADLY DEADLOCK: THE ARDENNES

———

A leader has the right to be beaten, but never the right to be surprised.

—NAPOLEON BONAPARTE

A<small>T MIDMORNING ON 22 AUGUST 1914, KARL VON BÜLOW AND HIS</small> staff motored to the heights above Fleurus, northeast of Charleroi. It was a sun-drenched autumn day. The countryside was equally delightful—a bountiful land with numerous small settlements unscarred by stone quarries, coal pits, or factories. "Large grain, potato and beet fields covered the land and grand, majestic rows of trees that lined both sides of the roads gave the countryside its particular character," the general noted. "Individual manor houses and castles with large, often magnificent parks were scattered throughout the region."[1] It must have reminded him of the family's hereditary estates in Mecklenburg. But when he reached the crest of the ridge at Fleurus, Bülow's thoughts returned to more mundane matters. From where he stood, a gentle slope fell away to the deep ravines of the Sambre Valley, while the northeastern side of the industrial town of Charleroi consisted of a "threatening steep wall" of rock. The entire stretch of the river was covered for several hundred meters on both banks with a jarring jumble of slag heaps, small factories, warehouses, homes, and cobblestone streets—the so-called *borinage*.* It was not a good place to attack.

On the basis of the latest reports from Chief of the General Staff

———

* *Le borinage* refers to the coal-mining district of Hainaut Province in southwest Belgium extending to the French border. The term came from *borin* or *borain*, pejorative French names for "buddy."

Helmuth von Moltke, which suggested that the French had marshaled seven or eight army corps south of the Sambre and that no British formations had yet arrived on the French left, Bülow made his operational decision. He ordered the 137 battalions and 820 guns of Second Army—from left to right, Karl von Plettenberg's Guard Corps, Otto von Emmich's X Corps, Guenther von Kirchbach's X Reserve Corps, and Karl von Einem's VII Corps—to advance to the Sambre against Charles Lanrezac's French Fifth Army of 193 battalions and 692 guns coming up from the south. With no enemy apparently in front of First Army, Bülow ordered Alexander von Kluck to alter his line of advance from southwest to due south so as to bring First Army into alignment with Second Army and to secure the latter's flank as it turned against French Fifth Army. Both Kluck and his chief of staff, Hermann von Kuhl, vigorously protested the order. A turn to the south would expose First Army's flanks to a possible attack by British forces, which they, unlike Moltke, believed had already landed at Ostend, Calais, and Dunkirk. They wanted to continue on a course north of Mons (Bergen) in order to turn the Allied flank.[2] Bülow, fearing that this would create a gap between First and Second armies, overruled them.

SECOND ARMY'S ARRIVAL NORTH of the Sambre River finally forced French chief of the General Staff Joseph Joffre to question his deployment plan. Until that point, Joffre, like almost no other senior commander in modern times, had lived in a world of denial, oblivious to all intelligence reports—French, British, and Belgian alike. At a time like this, his dominant characteristics—imperturbableness and stubbornness, if not downright pigheadedness—ill served the French army. For Joffre's fixation on carrying out Plan XVII regardless of what the enemy did blinded him to the grave danger developing in Belgium. As late as 5 August, he still believed that the main German thrust into France was coming via Sedan rather than farther north by way of Namur, Dinant, and Givet, and that the Ardennes remained the least defended pathway into Germany. Put differently, he did not appreciate that the Ardennes constituted the hub of the German wheel through Belgium.

For two weeks, Joffre stubbornly insisted that his deployment plan be executed. From 8 to 14 August, he ignored intelligence reports from his Deuxième Bureau and from the Belgians that the Germans had at least six army corps heading for Liège. He grudgingly moved

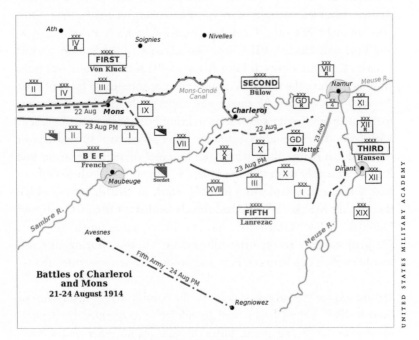

Battles of Charleroi and Mons, 21-24 August 1914

Louis Franchet d'Espèrey's I Corps to Dinant, but in his Instruction particulière No. 6 insisted that the rest of Fifth Army be ready to storm the Ardennes; hence, he augmented it with 37th and 38th infantry divisions (ID) of African XIX Corps.[3] Reports from Jean-François Sordet's cavalry corps, in fact, suggested no major German buildup in Belgium. Sordet had taken his horsemen on a mad three-day, 180-kilometer dash through southern Belgium, the Ardennes, and west of the Meuse River as far as Charleroi. Nowhere had they spotted significant enemy formations. Thus, the information Sordet sent to Joffre reinforced the generalissimo's preconception of German intentions.

On 14 August, the day on which he launched the great offensive by First and Second armies in Lorraine (to coincide with the Russian offensive into East Prussia), Joffre had two distinguished visitors at the Grand quartier général (GQG) in Vitry-le-François.[4] The first was Charles Louis Marie Lanrezac. Born on 31 July 1852 in the French colony of Guadeloupe, Lanrezac fought in the Franco-Prussian War and thereafter established his reputation at the Saint-Cyr Military Academy as a brilliant teacher and gifted theoretician. In 1906, he served under Joffre with 6th ID and became the general's protégé. In 1911, Joffre briefly considered the "lion of the French army" for the post of deputy chief. Instead, Lanrezac was made divisional commander that year and corps commander in 1912. In the spring of 1914, he reached what might well have been the pinnacle of a stellar career when he was selected for the Supreme War Council and appointed commander-designate for Fifth Army in the event of war. Historian Sewell Tyng suggested that Lanrezac was "endowed with the gift of Cassandra,"* and that he "lacked confidence in himself, in his superiors and . . . in the men under his orders."[5] He also lacked faith in Joffre's operations plan. When he was handed the details of the wartime mission for Fifth Army in May 1914, Lanrezac expressed grave concern about a design that discounted a German drive west of the Meuse River.[6]

By August, that concern bordered on panic. Lanrezac informed Joffre that the known German force in Belgium was equal to his Fifth Army *plus* the British Expeditionary Force (BEF), in all eight army corps and four cavalry divisions. He strongly suggested that Fifth Army

---

* When Apollo, the Greek god of sunlight and son of Zeus, granted Cassandra the gift of prophecy and she did not return his love, Apollo placed a curse on her so that no one would ever believe her predictions.

not face northeast for the charge through the Ardennes but rather north to deploy along the line of the Sambre River; failure to do so would allow Bülow to envelop Fifth Army's flank as it marched toward the east. More, Lanrezac begged GQG not to proceed with its main offensive, and especially not to send Pierre Ruffey's Third Army and Fernand de Langle de Cary's Fourth Army into "that death-trap of the Ardennes."[7] In short, to cast aside the French deployment plan. Joffre would have none of this. "We are of the opinion that the Germans have not deployed there."[8]

Joffre's second visitor was even more formidable. Joseph-Simon Galliéni was France's most distinguished soldier. Of Corsican stock, Galliéni was born at Saint-Béat, in southwestern France, on 24 April 1849. After serving in the Franco-Prussian War, he spent the next three decades in the colonies: Senegal, French Sudan, Indo-China, and Madagascar, where Joffre served under him. In 1905, Galliéni returned to France as commander of XIV Corps at Lyon; five years later, he was considered for the post of chief of the General Staff, but he declined. He retired in April 1914 but was reactivated in August to organize the defense of Paris.

Galliéni's physical appearance alone commanded respect: Straight as an arrow and always immaculate in full-dress uniform, he had a rugged, chiseled face with piercing eyes, a white droopy mustache, and a pince-nez clamped on the bridge of his nose. Already rumored to be Joffre's successor, he was unsurprisingly kept at arm's length by the chief of the General Staff in a small office at Paris and denied forces with which to defend the capital. On 14 August, Joffre granted Galliéni a cursory few minutes of his time and then passed him off to Deputy Chief of Staff Henri Berthelot, a corpulent man stripped down to blouse and slippers to alleviate the torrid August heat. Joffre and Berthelot had as little time for Galliéni's "alarmist" warnings of a German advance west of the Meuse as they had shown for Lanrezac's concerns.

But the Grand quartier général planned without the Germans. The next day, 15 August, reports poured in that ten thousand enemy riders had crossed the Meuse at Huy and that Franchet d'Espèrey's I Corps, recently detached from Lanrezac's Fifth Army, was engaged in a fight with strong German troop formations around Dinant. These reports troubled Joffre: Could it be possible that Lanrezac and Galliéni were right in their assessments? Might the Germans really be trying to pull off a "grand Cannae," suckering the main French advance into the Ardennes while two southern armies were driving through the Trouée de Charmes north to Sedan, and two (or three) armies were advancing through the Namur-Brussels gap south across the Sambre River? If this was the case, the entire French army might be swept up in a giant battle of encirclement west of the Ardennes.

These were trying days at Vitry-le-François. Raymond Poincaré's cabinet was on the verge of dissolution. The Chamber of Deputies was demanding War Minister Adolphe Messimy's resignation due to his inability to exert civilian control over Joffre and GQG. Georges Clemenceau was screaming for the president's head. Poincaré, in turn, was incensed that Joffre refused to allow him to visit the front. The Belgians were accusing the French of having "abandoned" them to their fate. Lanrezac and Galliéni were badgering the General Staff with their "alarmist" assessments of German troop strength in Belgium. And the British remained as diffident as ever.

The German advances toward Huy and Dinant forced Joffre and Berthelot grudgingly to come to grips with the fact that the enemy might already be dictating the flow of battle. At 3:30 PM[*] on 15 August, Joffre sprang into action and issued the first of three major "instructions." As a precautionary measure, Instruction particulière No. 10 ordered Lanrezac to move Fifth Army up into the right angle of the Meuse and Sambre rivers—that is, to face the approaching German Second Army around Charleroi and Third Army at Dinant. This necessitated a march of 120 kilometers in five days. As well, Joffre subordinated Sordet's cavalry corps to Fifth Army. But still, the preconceived notions of German intentions and the fixation on the original concentration plan remained. While Special Instruction No. 10 acknowledged that the enemy seemed to be making "his principal effort by his right wing north of Givet," it nevertheless ordered Lanrezac to spread his corps out in the direction of Mariembourg and Philippeville "in concert with the BEF and Belgian forces." As stated earlier, it also forced him to surrender Joseph Eydoux's XI Corps to Langle de Cary's concurrently ordered attack "in the general direction of Neufchâteau"—that is, the heart of the Ardennes.[9] Incredibly, Joffre informed Field Marshal Sir John French

---

[*] All actions on French soil are given in French (GMT) time.

that apart from the forces around Liège, the Germans had only cavalry in Belgium. Lanrezac was convinced that Fifth Army alone stood between the Germans and defeat.

To be sure, the German buildup in Belgium could no longer be ignored. Thus, on 18 August, Joffre issued his second order (Instruction particulière No. 13) to the three armies on the French left.[10] It was based in part on his latest assessment of the enemy's strength and position "around Thionville, in Luxembourg and in Belgium." Above all, the shift to the left was dictated by the fact that the French the day before had captured the order of battle of Bülow's Second Army. Still, Joffre put the best spin on the captured document: He interpreted it to mean that the German center was weak because of Moltke's concentration on both flanks, in Lorraine and in Belgium. Thus, Plan XVII was still on the table. But the Deuxième Bureau now estimated that there were thirteen to fifteen German corps between Liège and Thionville (Diedenhofen), divided into two "principal groups": a northern wing of seven or eight corps and four cavalry divisions between Liège and Bastogne, and a southern wing of six or seven corps and two to three cavalry divisions between Bastogne and Thionville. Joffre compromised, in his own way. He decided to strike what he mistakenly insisted on calling the enemy's "northern group" with his Third and Fourth armies around Sedan and Montmédy. Third Army was to advance toward Beuveille and Fourth Army toward Nives. Once they had defeated the German forces between Liège and Bastogne, Ruffey and Langle de Cary were to sweep west and roll up the flank and rear of the German northern armies. Intelligence reports from his cavalry still insisted that the enemy had not yet crossed the Meuse between Huy and Givet. Secrecy and surprise were the keys to Joffre's design. "I draw your attention," he lectured Langle de Cary, "to the necessity of not revealing our maneuver prior to the moment when it is unleashed."[11] In short, Joffre's cherished offensive design seemed back on track.

With regard to Fifth Army, Joffre laid out two possible scenarios. If the German right wing marched on both banks of the Meuse in an attempt to pass the corridor between Givet and Brussels, Lanrezac "in complete liaison with the British and Belgian Armies" was to oppose this movement by outflanking the Germans from the north. But if the enemy deployed "only a fraction of his right wing" on the left bank of

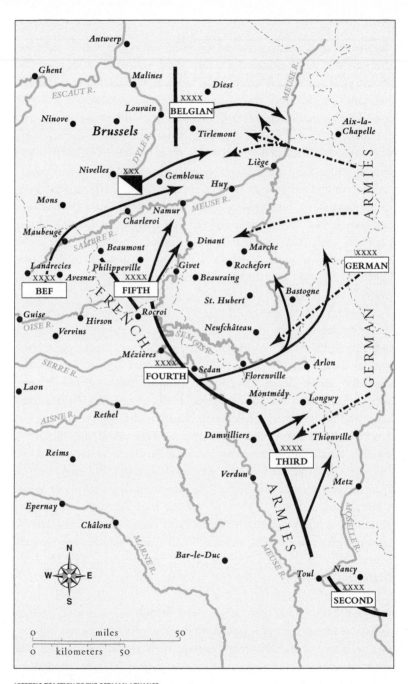

JOFFRE'S REACTION TO THE GERMAN ADVANCE

the Meuse, then Lanrezac was to wheel his forces east to help the drive through the Ardennes planned for Third and Fourth armies. The British and the Belgians would be left to deal with the German units in Belgium. For an army consisting of three corps and seven divisions spread over a front nearly fifty kilometers wide and on the move up to the Sambre, Special Instruction No. 13 was impossible. Lanrezac ignored it and continued his drive north, drums beating, bugles blowing, flags flying, and the men lustily singing the march "Sambre-et-Meuse."

Mercifully for Lanrezac, at 5 PM on 21 August, Joffre, appreciating his commander's "impatience," sent out his third order (Instruction particulière No. 15).[12] It canceled the first option previously laid out for Fifth Army. The time had come to mount the offensive that Joffre had planned for years: Ruffey's Third Army, now divided in two (Third Army and a new Army of Lorraine under Michel-Joseph Maunoury), was to charge toward Arlon in Belgium; Langle de Cary's Fourth Army was to cross the Semois River and drive on Neufchâteau. From Verdun to Charleroi, the decisive moment for the great French offensive by nine corps of 361,000 men was at hand. At the same time, Special Order No. 15 gave Lanrezac the green light to attack "the northern enemy group," specifically, Bülow's Second Army, in concert with whatever British and Belgian forces were on his left. The precise "line of demarcation" between British and French units was left for Field Marshal French and General Lanrezac to decide. Berthelot cheerily informed Lanrezac that since the French were about to drive through the Ardennes on their way into Germany, the more enemy troops committed to Belgium, "the easier it will be for us to break through their center." It was one of those typical orders from Berthelot that, in the words of historian Hew Strachan, "did not always accord with reality or with realism."[13] Still, Joffre was downright optimistic. "The moment of decisive action," he informed War Minister Messimy, "is near."[14]

JOFFRE'S THROWAWAY COMMENT THAT French and Lanrezac were to decide on the manner of cooperation between their forces was ingenuous, at best. For the first two meetings between the two British and French field commanders had not gone well. The arrogant, combative, and mercurial John French had left Vitry-le-François on Sunday, 16 August, less than impressed with Joffre and his staff. "*Au fond,* they are a low lot," he informed London, "and one always has to remember the class these French generals mostly come from."[15] Apparently, the noble squire from Kent had not found a suitable *confrère* in the humble artisan from the Pyrenees. When Sir John incredibly asked GQG to place Sordet's cavalry corps as well as two French infantry divisions under his command, Joffre was not amused. He brusquely refused.[16]

The next day's meeting between French and Lanrezac at Rethel had been equally disastrous. Lanrezac's chief of staff, Alexis Hély d'Oissel, met the British contingent with a tart, "At last you're here; it's not a moment too soon. If we are beaten we will owe it all to you!"[17] From there, the meeting went downhill. When Lanrezac informed Sir John that the Germans were at the Meuse near Huy, the field marshal in halting French twice inquired what they were doing there and what they were going to do. Lanrezac, who knew no English, allowed his acerbic bile to pour forth. *"Pourqoui sont-ils arrivés?"* he snapped at French. *"Mais pour pêcher dans la rivière!"*★ Henry Wilson, deputy chief of the British General Staff, impeccably translated that for Sir John: "He says they're going to cross the river, sir."[18] Tit-for-tat, when Lanrezac asked French for his fresh cavalry division to supplement Sordet's weary cavalry corps, the field marshal declined. Finally, Sir John stated that the BEF could not be ready for action until 24 August.[19] It would then deploy left of Lanrezac's Fifth Army on the Sambre. The French must have wondered about the value of British intervention on the Continent.

What to Joffre and Lanrezac could only have seemed haughty behavior on the part of Field Marshal French was, in fact, rooted in British tradition and in "Johnnie" French's orders. Horatio Herbert Lord Kitchener, Britain's most famous colonial soldier and in 1914 secretary of state for war, had sent Sir John off to France with the specific instruction "that your command is an entirely independent one, and that you will in no case come in any sense under the orders of any Allied General."[20] As well, Kitchener—soon nicknamed "the Great Poster" for the famous recruiting poster in which his blazing eyes, martial mustache, and pointing finger loomed over the message YOUR COUNTRY NEEDS YOU—had warned the field marshal to exercise "the greatest care . . . towards a minimum of losses and wastage." Knowing

★ "Why have they come here? But, to fish in the river!"

the French military's penchant for the all-out offensive (*l'offensive à outrance*), Kitchener had further admonished his field commander to give "the gravest consideration" to likely French attempts to deploy the BEF offensively "where large bodies of French troops are not engaged, and where your Force may be unduly exposed to attack." Sir John meant fully to adhere to those instructions.*

IN THE REAL WAR, Lanrezac's weary soldiers moved into position on the afternoon of 20 August. In essence, Fifth Army formed a giant inverted V in the Sambre-Meuse triangle pointing toward the northeast, with German Second Army to the north and Third Army to the east. Franchet d'Espèrey's I Corps remained on the Meuse, guarding Lanrezac's right flank, while Gilbert Defforges's X Corps (with African 37th ID) held the left flank. In the center, Henri Sauret's III Corps (with African 38th ID) and Eydoux's XI Corps advanced along the Sambre River between Namur and Charleroi. This vanguard spied the first units of Bülow's Second Army at 3 PM on 20 August. Later that night, as previously noted, Joffre ordered Third and Fourth armies to storm the Ardennes, the heart and soul of his grand design, and Lanrezac to attack the enemy on the Sambre around Charleroi. As well, he "requested" Field Marshal French "to co-operate in this action" on the left of French Fifth Army by advancing across the Mons-Condé Canal "in the general direction of Soignies."[21] Henry Wilson was ecstatic. All the years of planning for British formations to be deployed alongside the French on the Continent were finally coming to fruition. "To-day we start our forward march, and the whole line from here [Le Cateau] to Verdun set out," he wrote home on 21 August. "It is at once a glorious and an awful thought, and by this day [next] week the greatest action that the world has ever heard of will have been fought."[22]

General Wilson's burst of enthusiasm was ill founded. The British, Lanrezac furiously informed Joffre, reported that they would not be ready to advance on his left flank for another two days. Around noon on 21 August, Lanrezac demanded precise instructions from Joffre. While he awaited a reply, Lanrezac mulled over his options.[23] Should he cross the Sambre and deny Bülow the heights on the northern side?

---

* The extent to which the troops adhered to Kitchener's instruction to keep on guard against "excesses" and "temptations, both in wine and women," cannot be accurately determined.

Or should he entrench his forces on the southern bank and await the arrival of the British on his left flank—as well as the start of the advance into the Ardennes by Third and Fourth armies? In no case was he willing to fight in the Valley of the Sambre, the coal pits and slag heaps of *le borinage*. The "keen intellect" of Saint-Cyr many times had posed similar problems to his students; now he prevaricated and kept his corps commanders in the dark for forty-eight hours.

Joffre let Lanrezac stew. "I leave it entirely to you to judge the opportune moment for you to decide when to commence offensive operations."[24] But then GQG instructed Fifth Army to advance without the British. Precious time had been squandered. Already on the morning of 20 August, Bülow's advance guard of cavalry and bicycle units had found two bridges unguarded between Namur and Charleroi. Numerous German cavalry formations in their field-gray uniforms had been mistaken by the local Walloon population as being "English" and showered with food and gifts.

At noon on 21 August, 2d ID of Plettenberg's Guard Corps had reached the north shore of the Sambre. But Bülow proved to be as cautious as Lanrezac. Neither his cavalry scouts nor his aerial reconnaissance could confirm whether an entire French army was south of the Sambre. Moreover, he wanted at all cost to maintain contact with his left wing (Max von Hausen's Third Army) and his right wing (Kluck's First Army) during the advance. Yet his corps commanders were chomping at the bit. After some indecision concerning Bülow's intentions, Arnold von Winckler decided to storm the bridges at Auvelais and Jemeppe-sur-Sambre with his 2d Guard Division (GD). Farther to the west, Max Hofmann's 19th ID of Emmich's X Corps likewise took the bridges at Tergné. With two bridgeheads secured against repeated French counterattacks, the Germans were ready to advance against Lanrezac's main force the next day.

General von Bülow hurled three corps against French Fifth Army on 22 August—only to discover that the French had preempted him with an attack of their own. At his headquarters at Chimay, thirty kilometers from the front, Lanrezac at first had become incapacitated, mulling over his options. He neither approved nor disapproved a suggestion from the commanders of III and X corps to counterattack and retake the lost bridges. Without orders, Sauret and Defforges charged the German positions in the early-hour mists of 22 August, flags unfurled, bugles blaring, bayonets fixed—and without artillery support. Both attacks were brutally beaten back around Arsimont with "staggering losses." Tenth Corps' desperate bayonet charges were mowed down by the machine guns of the Prussian Guard; those of III Corps ran headlong into a fierce assault by Emmich's X Corps.[25] The fields were littered with six thousand French dead and wounded; the roads soon clogged with thousands of Belgian civilians fleeing the deadly mayhem.

In fact, a bloody and confused melee (what military theorists call a "battle of encounter") quickly developed in *le borinage*. All along the Sambre, a ragged, unplanned series of battles ensued. By late afternoon, Lanrezac's center had collapsed, with two corps retreating at great loss of life; by nightfall, nine divisions of French III and X corps had been driven ten kilometers back from the Sambre at Charleroi by a mere three divisions of German X Corps and Guard Corps. The entire center and right of French Fifth Army seemed on the point of collapse. On the French left near Fontaine, two divisions of Einem's VII Corps hurled Sordet's cavalry corps back across the Sambre, exposing the right flank of the late-arriving BEF at Mons. At 8:30 PM, Lanrezac informed Joffre of the day's "violent" events. "Defforges' X Corps suffered badly. . . . Large numbers of officers *hors de combat*. 3rd Corps and its 5th Division heavily engaged before Chatelet. . . . The Cavalry Corps, extremely fatigued, no longer in contact with l'armée W[ilson]"[26]—that is, with the British.

That night, Lanrezac again considered his options. He decided to resume the offensive on 23 August. Perhaps he could strike Bülow's Second Army in the flank from the east. Thus, he shifted Franchet d'Espèrey's I Corps on the right north toward Namur and ordered Fourth Army to advance on the Meuse. But before Lanrezac could mount his offensive with Fifth Army, a series of disastrous reports from the fronts arrived at Chimay: Fortress Namur had capitulated; French Third and Fourth armies were heavily engaged in the Ardennes and could not come to his rescue; the BEF had been forced to retreat at Mons; and lead elements of German Third Army had crossed the Meuse at Givet. Lanrezac at once grasped the gravity of the situation. He now faced the dire prospect of Bülow's ponderous advance from the north being augmented by a flanking attack on both his right rear (German Third Army) and his left front (German First Army). Still, his troops fought valiantly, grudgingly yielding ground. General von

Kirchbach reported late on 23 August that his X Reserve Corps had been shattered and would not be able to resume the attack the next day. He need not have worried: At 9:30 PM, Lanrezac, appreciating that he had suffered a major defeat, ordered a general retreat to the line Givet-Maubeuge, to begin at three o'clock the next morning.[27] Joffre spied therein a decided lack of "offensive spirit," but Lanrezac's action likely saved Fifth Army from annihilation.

AS THE FIGHTING LEFT the broken landscape of slag heaps and pitheads, it entered a gentler, more open, agricultural countryside. At this point, there were no physical obstacles to slow down the German advance—or the French retreat. The situation was ripe with choice.

Charles Lanrezac had good reason to fear for his Fifth Army. The immediate, mortal danger lay on his right flank facing east. The Grand quartier général remained blissfully ignorant of the danger. Joffre continued to insist that Moltke had deployed but six corps in the "weak" center of the German line, where he had in fact marshaled eight. Moreover, he was certain that the Germans would not fight in the rugged terrain of the Ardennes but instead make their stand just east of the forest. He had a point. The Ardennes was wooded, hilly, and irregular, oftentimes shrouded in fog and rain, traversed by muddy paths and roads, and cut by countless streams and ravines. Julius Caesar in 57 BC had taken ten days to cross "the forest of Arden." The woods had been "full of defiles and hidden ways." The enemy had been elusive and clever. "Wherever a cave, or a thicket, or a morass offered them shelter," he recorded, "thither they retired." Only what today are called "small-group tactics" had allowed Caesar eventually to "extirpate this race of perfidious men."[28]

On 21 August, Joffre ordered his armies to attack the enemy "wherever encountered" throughout the Ardennes—the centerpiece of his deployment plan.[29] Once across the forest between Liège and Bastogne, the French armies were to turn west and deliver a fatal right hook to the left flanks of German First, Second, and Third armies racing through Belgium. To maintain the element of surprise, no supply columns were attached to the French armies. The campaign began at six o'clock on a chilly morning shrouded by gray fog and rain; it ended late at night in dense mist following a heavy rain. Surprise and chaos were the order of the day. Few of Joffre's commanders had bothered to study the terrain. Some of the more optimistic had maps of the Rhineland; of the Ardennes, only a very few had tourist maps or crude maps torn out of railway timetables.[30]

General Ruffey commanded Third Army at Verdun. An apostle of heavy artillery—which had earned him the sobriquet *"le poète du canon"*—Ruffey had made many enemies in the French army for seemingly slighting the famous 75s and for championing what Ferdinand Foch in 1910 had satirized as the "sport" of airpower. On 21 August, Ruffey moved his headquarters up to Marville to lead IV, V, and VI corps against Arlon. On his left, Fourth Army under Langle de Cary at Stenay pointed toward Neufchâteau. Already past the mandatory retirement age (sixty-four) in 1914, the energetic, bantam-like Langle de Cary had been entrusted by Joffre with breaking the back of the German offensive. In addition to his own three corps and Jules Lefèvre's colonial corps, Fourth Army had been augmented by Franchet d'Espèrey's I Corps (Fifth Army) and Pierre Dubois's IX Corps (Second Army), giving it a fighting strength of about 160,000 men. To guard against a possible German thrust from Fortress Metz against the flank and rear of Third Army, Joffre had created the Army of Lorraine, composed entirely of reserve divisions, under General Maunoury. The three French armies numbered 377 battalions with 1,540 guns. They were to attack along a forty-kilometer front and to penetrate the Ardennes Forest to a depth of at least a dozen kilometers. Unfortunately, Ruffey was never informed of the creation or the mission of the Army of Lorraine. But it seemed to matter little at the time. Neither Sordet's riders nor French aviators had spied any major German troop concentrations. "No serious opposition need be anticipated on the day of August 22nd," GQG cheerily informed Ruffey and Langle de Cary.[31]

Joffre had entrusted Ruffey and Maunoury not only to carry out the centerpiece of his famous Plan XVII, but also to secure France's vital iron-mining and steel-producing region, with an annual output of five million tons in 1913. German forces advancing from Metz-Thionville had already occupied or were threatening the great steel plants at Fraisans, Hayange, Longwy, and Briey. Other vital steel producers needed to be secured at Saint-Étienne, Fourchambault, Anzin, and Denain, among other places. France's industrial war effort hung in the balance.

On that dismal morning of 22 August, Third and Fourth armies did not encounter the anticipated light German screen in the Ardennes, but rather the full weight of ten army corps. The southern Ardennes region around Metz-Thionville was held by Crown Prince Wilhelm of Prussia's Fifth Army; it was advancing against the French fortress belt of Longwy and Montmédy—and eventually Verdun. To Wilhelm's immediate right in the central and northern Ardennes around Luxembourg was Duke Albrecht of Württemberg's Fourth Army; it was advancing against Neufchâteau. As the hub of the German wheel, the two armies (236 battalions with 1,320 guns)[32] could afford to move at a relatively leisurely pace—much like the inside of a line of marchers in a band making a ninety-degree right turn—while waiting for the outer-rim armies of the pivot wing, or *Schwenkungsflügel,* to quick-march across Belgium and on to Paris.

But Crown Prince Wilhelm and his chief of staff, Konstantin Schmidt von Knobelsdorf, were anxious for battle honors. On 21 August, they decided on their own initiative to mount an offensive against the French fortified cities of Longwy and Montmédy and "ruthlessly defeat everything that stood [in] between" at Longuyon, in the angle of the Chiers and Crusnes rivers. When Moltke reminded them that according to the concentration plan, "defense by Fifth Army imperative, not attack," they simply ignored him.[33] Visions of his own Cannae danced through the crown prince's head.[34] Despite the fact that Fifth Army's offensive in the direction of Virton would create a twenty-kilometer-wide gap between Wilhelm's army and that of Duke Albrecht, Moltke did not press his case. Thus, by 21 August, after Liège and Brussels had fallen, German Fourth and Fifth armies were advancing on a southwesterly course, while French Third and Fourth armies were moving up to the Ardennes on a northeasterly trajectory. A head-on collision was inevitable.

French historians refer to the events beginning on 21–22 August as the Battle of the Ardennes; German scholars as the twin Battles of Longwy and Neufchâteau. Neither is entirely correct. What developed, in the words of historian Sewell Tyng, was "a series of engagements, fought simultaneously by army corps, divisions, brigades and even battalions, for the most part independently of any central control and independently of the conduct of adjacent units."[35] German reconnaissance had detected the French advance and, accordingly, most of the troops of Fourth and Fifth armies were well dug in and supported by heavy artillery. Fog and rain helped their concealment. Moreover, the French deployed in a peculiar echelon formation: One officer has depicted it as being akin to a flight of stairs, descending from left to right, with each "stair" consisting of an army corps facing north. While this theoretically would allow each corps to attack either north or east, as the situation demanded, it also meant that the right flank of each corps depended fully on the advance of its neighbor on the right. Failure of one corps to do so not only imperiled the flank of the neighbor on the left, but also threatened to collapse the entire set of "stairs."[36]

The latter case set in by the second day of the battle. Between 5 and 6 AM on 22 August, Ruffey's Third Army advanced through heavy fog. Charles Brochin's V Corps was in the center of the line.[37] Moving on Longwy and its steel furnaces, V Corps immediately stumbled into the well-prepared German defensive positions of Max von Fabeck's XIII Corps. Brutal hand-to-hand combat ensued, with neither side able to make out friend from foe. Ruffey had placed his mobile *soixante-quinzes* up front so as to better sweep the German "screen" from the woods. But soon after the initial contact, the fog lifted, allowing the German 105mm and 150mm heavy howitzers' high-angle fire to decimate Brochin's 75s.[38] Heroic French bayonet attacks foundered against well-hidden machine-gun positions. Panic ensued. One division broke and fled, leaving a huge gap in the middle of Third Army's line. The next day, Joffre relieved Brochin of command of V Corps and replaced him with Frédéric Micheler.

Of Ruffey's other two army corps, Victor-René Boëlle's IV Corps fared no better: Its advance on Virton ran head-on into Hermann von Strantz's V Corps; one of its infantry divisions also broke and ran.[39] Maurice Sarrail's VI Corps, beefed up with the addition of a third infantry division, stood its ground alone on the right side against Konrad von Goßler's VI Reserve Corps. The German artillery fire, a French officer recalled, was lethal. "Thousands of dead were still standing, supported as if by a flying buttress made of bodies lying in rows on top of each other in an ascending arc from the horizontal to an angle of 60°." A French sergeant likewise commented on the horror of the slaughter. "Heaps of corpses, French and German, are lying every which way, rifles in hand. Rain is falling, shells are screaming and bursting . . . we hear the wounded crying from all over the woods."[40] A corporal with

French 31st Infantry Regiment (IR) recalled his comrades jumping from tree trunk to tree trunk in the dense forest, seeking shelter in ditches and potholes, "dazed by the thunderous explosions that followed them from clearing to clearing."[41] In the small villages, women and children dressed in their Sunday best were swept up in the carnage and tried to flee, carrying whatever goods they could on their shoulders. Eventually, the panic of the other two corps forced Sarrail's VI Corps also to retreat to avoid a flanking movement by two German corps.

Ruffey, finally apprised of the existence of the Army of Lorraine at Verdun, at 1:30 PM on 22 August contacted General Maunoury and pleaded for help for his embattled right wing. Maunoury responded at once.[42] He ordered Jules Chailley's 54th Reserve Infantry Division (RID) to advance to the line Ollières-Domprix, and Henry Marabail's 67th RID to take up positions around Senon and Amel.[43] But delays in relaying the general's orders resulted in neither formation arriving in time to turn the tide of battle.

Ruffey's offensive had collapsed. The "staircase" effect noted previously now set in for Langle de Cary's neighboring Fourth Army advancing on Neufchâteau. Augustin Gérard's II Corps, Fifth Army, on the extreme right was stopped dead in its tracks around 8 AM, first by a massive artillery barrage and then by murderous machine-gun fire from Kurt von Pritzelwitz's VI Corps (Fourth Army). On its left, Lefèvre's colonial corps, veterans of France's wars in Africa and Indo-China, nevertheless pushed on between the Forest of Chiny and Neufchâteau.[44] The early-morning fog and rain had turned into searing heat and enervating humidity. Georges Goullet's 5th Colonial Brigade and Arthur Poline's XVII Corps were surprised in the thick woods near Bertrix, initially by German uhlans fighting dismounted and then by Kuno von Steuben's XVII Reserve Corps and Dedo von Schenck's XVIII Corps. Desperate, violent combat ensued.[45] When Otto von Plüskow's XI Corps of Saxon Third Army appeared from the north, the German iron ring around Bertrix was virtually complete. Without an escape route, Poline's XVII Corps panicked, abandoned its artillery, and fled, leaving a breach in the front of Langle de Cary's Fourth Army similar to that left by V Corps in the front of Ruffey's Third Army.

A *poilu,* Désiré Renault of 88th IR with Poline's XVII Corps, on 22

August wrote home of the frightful slaughter. "The fighting has ended, all my buddies are beaten into retreat, and we, the wounded, have been left abandoned without care, dying of thirst. What a terrible night!" The coming dawn brought only more misery. "A new torture has added itself to the others: since the sun rose, the flies, drawn by the smell of blood, go after me fiercely."[46] Utterly exhausted and seriously wounded in the bludgeoning in the Ardennes, Renault was spared death or capture by two Red Cross nurses who carried him to a field hospital at Longwy.

Worse was yet to come at the small village of Rossignol, north of the Semois River and fifteen kilometers south of Neufchâteau. There, 3d Colonial Division ran hard up against 12th ID of Pritzelwitz's VI Army Corps. In short order, it sent five battalions of *pantalon rouges* in waves against the Germans on a front roughly six hundred meters wide. One furious frontal bayonet charge after another, accompanied by lusty cries of *"En avant!,"** was mowed down by murderous artillery and machine-gun fire. As darkness fell, 3d Colonial Division had ceased to exist: Eleven thousand of its fifteen thousand soldiers had been killed or wounded; its commander, General Léon Raffenel, had been shot; and its last remnants gallantly buried the regimental colors.

Rossignol for France constituted the deadliest campaign of the Battle of the Frontiers. Langle de Cary in classic understatement reported to Joffre from his headquarters at Stenay: "On the whole results hardly satisfactory."[47] He ignored the generalissimo's demand that he resume the offensive the next day and instead ordered a retreat behind the Meuse and Chiers rivers near Sedan. Ruffey, furious that his infantry charges had not been supported by artillery, fell back on Verdun. Lanrezac's hard-pressed Fifth Army at the Sambre could expect no help from either Third or Fourth armies. Maunoury's unbloodied Army of Lorraine limped off to the safety of Amiens.

More than eleven thousand *poilus* paid the butcher's bill. At Virton, 8th ID lost 5,500 of its 16,000 men. At Ethe, 7th ID was so badly mauled that it was depicted as having been "stomped." At Ochamps, 20th IR lost almost half (1,300) of its soldiers; the neighboring 11th IR, 2,700 out of 3,300 men. Goullet's 5th Colonial Brigade had entered the Ar-

* "Forward!"

dennes with 6,600 effectives; it left with only 3,400.[48] Langle de Cary reported to Joffre that of one of his corps (40,000 men), roughly 15,000 remained combat-ready; more than 15,000 had been killed or wounded. The survivors were evacuated to Vouziers between 23 and 31 August.[49]

But the Germans had not escaped unscathed. Duke Albrecht's Fourth Army suffered 7,540 men dead or missing and 11,678 wounded between 21 and 31 August, with Schenck's XVIII Corps and Pritzelwitz's VI Corps each sustaining about 6,000 casualties. Crown Prince Wilhelm's Fifth Army in the same period lost 7,488 men dead and missing and 11,529 wounded.[50] Still, a delirious Wilhelm II awarded his son the Iron Cross, First and Second Class—as he had earlier to Crown Prince Rupprecht of Bavaria.

AS THE TWO OPPOSING sides battled each other into bloody exhaustion in the Ardennes, the final drama of the Battle of Charleroi unfolded south of the Sambre River. Once Bülow realized that his corps commanders had attacked an entire French army across the wide Sambre front, he quickly appreciated that he needed help to secure both his flanks and victory. A discussion with Otto von Lauenstein, his chief of staff, on the night of 23 August confirmed the tension at Bülow's headquarters at Walcourt. "There were critical hours yesterday and during the night," Lauenstein noted, "in which the worry whether all would go according to plan almost gained the upper hand. Our operation had undoubtedly been most audacious."[51] There existed only one option: to renew the attack on Lanrezac the next morning, 24 August, and to call on the two flanking armies to lend support.

Bülow had already contacted Hausen's Third Army earlier that day to press across the Meuse at Dinant; he repeated that plea on 24 August. At noon welcome (if deceptive) news arrived from Third Army. "Sector seized; French gone; our right wing [at] Florennes-Philippeville." Bülow was ecstatic. The battle was almost won. Around 3 PM, he triumphantly cabled Moltke. "Enemy's right flank decisively defeated by 2 Army. 3 Army across the Maas toward Philippeville. To be passed on to the Kaiser. All [armies] continue the attack."[52]

Still, Bülow worried that he had received no news from Kluck or his chief of staff, Kuhl. First Army seemed to be continuing its march southwest, ignoring Bülow's repeated requests that it turn onto a more southerly course and thereby maintain contact with Second Army's right flank. Lauenstein shared his commander's anxiety. "If my friend and my right neighbor Kuhl now deals with the English as we have dealt with the French, then the first phase of the campaign in the western theater will have been decided in our favor."[53] It was time for Bülow to issue a direct order to First Army: "IX Army Corps is to advance immediately west of Maubeuge in order to carry out an enveloping attack against the enemy's left wing. III Army Corps is to join it in echelon formation."[54]

But whereas Bülow was able to intimidate Hausen and his chief of staff, Ernst von Hoeppner, the same was not the case with Kluck and Kuhl. First Army's duumvirate appreciated that they were the hammer that was to smash the Allied armies around Paris, and they were not about to let Bülow interfere with that goal. "Hour after hour went by," in the words of the German official history, without a reply from First Army. Bülow and Lauenstein seethed with anger. Moltke had, after all, put First Army under Bülow's command. By late afternoon, Bülow had lost all patience. "Where II and IV Army Corps today?" he testily demanded to know from Kluck. "How does the battle stand today?" Finally, he issued a barely concealed reminder of their command relationship. "Request daily to be notified accordingly."[55] Moltke at Koblenz chose not to pull his field commanders into line.

FIRST ARMY WAS ABOUT to make contact with the British Expeditionary Force. On 19 August, Wilhelm II reportedly* had "commanded" Kluck to "exterminate the treacherous English" and to roll over Field Marshal French's "contemptible little army."[56] First Army stood west of Lanrezac's Fifth Army. It had marched nearly 250 kilometers in eleven days, much of it in excruciating heat and suffocating dust. Information gathered from local villagers suggested to Kluck that seventy thousand British troops were moving on Mons. But communications with Second Army remained nonexistent, and no orders had been received from Moltke. Nor had anyone thought of sending out liaison

---

* No record of this order was ever found in the German archives, and Wilhelm II after the war vehemently denied having issued such a command. The British press made a meal of the quote—apparently "invented" by Frederick Maurice in the British War Office. The soldiers of the BEF proudly adopted the moniker *Old Contemptibles*.

officers to coordinate the operations of First and Second armies, so critical to the Moltke-Schlieffen design.[57] Kluck and Kuhl simply planned "to cut the English off" from establishing contact with Lanrezac's Fifth Army.

They did not have long to wait. Friedrich Sixt von Arnim's IV Corps, Ferdinand von Quast's IX Corps, and Ewald von Lochow's III Corps blindly advanced from north to south along the twenty-meter-wide Mons-Condé Canal against Sir Horace Smith-Dorrien's II Army Corps.[58] Had Kluck finally turned toward the south as requested by Bülow? Not a word of this reached Second Army. At the bend in the British line at Mons, where it turned southeast toward Peissant, Manfred von Richthofen's* I Cavalry Corps was approaching Sir Douglas Haig's I Army Corps. Field Marshal French's role was to protect Lanrezac's left flank; Kluck's was to roll up the British left flank between Saint-Aybert and Jemappes.

The two armies were advancing through some of the ugliest real estate in Europe. Once a medieval textile town, Mons in 1914 was in the heart of the Belgian coalfields. It had all the flavor of the Industrial Revolution—polluted ditches, swamps, watercourses, and canals. Railroads and cobbled roads further dissected the fields and farms and willow forests. Pitheads and smoking slag heaps, some as high as thirty meters, rounded off the landscape.

This phase of the Battle of the Frontiers began inauspiciously enough near Casteau. Field Marshal French, wisely having rejected a plea from Lanrezac to wheel east to strike Bülow's Second Army in the flank and thus expose the BEF to Kluck's First Army, was advancing in the direction of Soignies, as Joffre had requested in Special Order No. 15 of 21 August. Suddenly, 4th Dragoon Guards of 2d Cavalry Brigade came upon riders of Kluck's 9th Cavalry Division; a small skirmish ensued. Owing to inadequate reconnaissance, neither commander suspected the imminent clash of their entire forces. Both were thus surprised when, between 9 and 10 AM on the misty and rainy morning of Sunday, 23 August, Quast's IX Corps blundered into Smith-Dorrien's II Corps near Mons. A furious battle ensued all along

---

* Not to be confused with the future air ace ("Red Baron") of the same name, then serving with German cavalry in East Prussia.

the grimy Mons-Condé Canal: While Quast's artillery mercilessly battered the BEF's lines with shell and shrapnel, Smith-Dorrien's Fourth Middlesex and Second Royal Irish riflemen endlessly directed their accurate Lee-Enfield fire ("fifteen rounds a minute") into wave after wave of gray German infantry coming at them in close formation. Corporal John Lucy later recalled the carnage:

> A great roar of musketry rent the air. . . . For us the battle took the form of well ordered, rapid rifle-fire at close range as the field of grey human targets appeared, or were struck down, to be replaced by further waves of German infantry who shared the same fate. . . . Such tactics amazed us, and after the first shock of seeing men slowly and helplessly falling down as they were hit [it] gave us a great sense of power and pleasure.[59]

Captain Walter Bloem of 12th Brandenburg Grenadiers also attested to the lethality of the battlefield. The gently undulating hills and meadows around the canal were "dotted with little grey heaps," fallen German infantrymen. "Wherever I looked, right or left," he noted, "were dead and wounded, quivering in convulsions, groaning terribly, blood oozing from fresh wounds."[60]

It was much the same story farther west at Jemappes, where Lochow's III Corps similarly fed its infantry into deadly enemy rifle fire. By day's end, the BEF had suffered sixteen hundred casualties; Kluck and Kuhl chose not to reveal German losses, which have been estimated at about five thousand. Although the British abandoned both Mons and Jemappes by nightfall and began to fall back toward Le Cateau, the day's battle had ended inconclusively. Kluck and Kuhl, who had wanted to sweep around the British left flank while anchoring their own left flank on Mons, felt cheated of victory over the BEF by Bülow's constant demands that First Army at all times maintain close contact with Second Army. Moreover, they were annoyed that the enemy had once again eluded encirclement and that their own infantry had shown such profound contempt for the enemy's firepower. Mons was thus best forgotten.

For the British—both soldiers and the public at home, both then and now—Mons became one of the great legends of the war. There were many stories of what occurred that day, but they all had some elements in common: At one point in the battle, when the waves of gray German infantry seemed about to sweep across the canal and mop up the remnants of Smith-Dorrien's "Old Contemptibles," the skies parted brightly to reveal a knight in shining armor mounted on a white horse (Saint George?) while archers from above showered the German lines with arrows and white-robed angels shielded the BEF from hostile fire. The "Angel of Mons"[61] thus became for the British both a sign of divine intervention on their behalf and a symbol of hope for the duration of the war.

As Kluck resumed his attack the next day, 24 August, the entire Allied front suddenly seemed to collapse. Lanrezac, upon receiving news that Namur had capitulated and that Hausen's Third Army was crossing the Meuse south of Dinant, had decided by ten o'clock on the night of 23 August to fall back along the line Givet-Maubeuge. He reached his decision without consulting Joffre and without informing Sir John French, thus further eroding an already shaky relationship with the British commander. Fifth Army's precipitous retreat caused a twelve-kilometer-wide gap to develop between French Fifth Army's left and the BEF's right. "Johnnie" French felt "left alone" by Lanrezac and poured out his bitterness to Joffre at GQG. At 2 AM on 24 August, he ordered a general retreat from Mons southwest to Le Cateau. Despondency seemed to have overtaken him. He queried Lord Kitchener about the possibility of falling back on Le Havre—and Britain? He toyed with the idea of sheltering his forces in Maubeuge.[62] And he threatened to withdraw the entire BEF behind "the lower Seine"—that is, behind Fortress Paris. For the Allies, the Great Retreat had begun.

The agony of defeat was recorded by future historian Marc Bloch, a sergeant with French 272d IR. The retreat for him began in the "stifling heat" of the morning of 25 August. In village after village on the left bank of the Meuse, he encountered fleeing French peasants. "Wrenched from their homes, disoriented, dazed, and bullied by the gendarmes, they were troublesome but pathetic figures." Men, women, and children passed by in silent marches taking what little they could in small hand-pulled wagons. On 26 August, the burning sunshine cruelly turned to steaming rain. The retreat, "the monotony of each day," plodded onward toward the west, "continually retreating without fighting." Where and how would it end? "Oh, what bitter days of retreat, of weariness, boredom, and anxiety!"[63]

THE DECISION IN THE campaign in the west still lay ahead, but it would be fought by a much-reduced German field army. For Moltke and his deputy chief of staff, Hermann von Stein, panicked by the unexpectedly rapid Russian advance in the east, stripped Bülow's Second Army of Max von Gallwitz's Guard Reserve Corps and Hausen's Third Army of Plüskow's XI Corps to derail the Russian steamroller. As the two corps marched east from Namur, Moltke, in what he pathetically called a "counter-movement," ordered Max von Boehn's IX Reserve Corps to depart Schleswig-Holstein and join Kluck's First Army.[64] Stein had vetoed a suggestion by Wilhelm Groener, chief of the Field Railway Section of the General Staff, to send Bavarian I Corps and Prussian XXI Corps from Lorraine to East Prussia instead, with the revealing comment, "One cannot expect Bavarians to defend East Prussia."[65] As well, Moltke and Stein ordered Kluck to leave Hans von Beseler's III Corps to cover Fortress Antwerp and one brigade of Hans von Gronau's IV Reserve Corps to garrison Brussels. Finally, Bülow had detached Hans von Zwehl's VII Reserve Corps as well as one brigade of Einem's VII Corps to lay siege to the French garrison of fifty thousand men at Maubeuge.[66]

Heat and exhaustion as well as almost uninterrupted combat had further weakened the two "strike armies." During the entire month of August, Kluck's First Army of 217,384 soldiers had lost 7,869 men wounded as well as 2,863 killed or missing. Slightly less than eight thousand men had reported sick—mostly from heatstroke and dehydration, but also from foot sores due to the extended march of some four hundred kilometers in thirty days.[67] Bülow's Second Army of 199,486 soldiers listed 12,151 wounded and 5,061 killed or missing for August. Almost nine thousand soldiers had reported sick for much the same reasons as those in First Army. There had been three suicides in each army.[68] But if one takes into account the figures for just the last ten days of August—that is, the period of the heaviest fighting in the Battle of the Frontiers—the totals for First Army were 4,932 wounded, 2,145 killed or missing, and 2,567 reported sick; and for Second Army, 8,052 wounded, 3,516 killed or missing, and 4,125 reported sick.[69] Paris was still more than 130 kilometers away.

Joffre was by far the principal loser. On 23 August, he flippantly notified War Minister Messimy that he had "terminated" his strategic plan.[70] In fact, that plan lay in tatters—at the cost of 260,000 casualties (including 75,000 killed) and the loss of 83 percent of France's iron ore, 62 percent of its cast iron, and 60 percent of its steel production. French First and Second armies had attacked in Lorraine on 14 August; six days later, a German counterattack had driven them back. Third and Fourth armies had attacked in the Ardennes on 21 August; two days later, they had staggered back to their jump-off positions. Fifth Army had advanced to the Sambre on 20 August; three days later, it had begun its retreat to Givet. Joffre had been decisively beaten in the Battle of the Frontiers and had lost the initiative to the Germans.

He took no responsibility.[71] Both at the time and subsequently in his memoirs, Joffre insisted that he had placed "the main body of his army against the most sensitive point of the enemy," and that he had secured "numerical superiority at this point." But the troops, despite this "numerical superiority," had not displayed the "offensive qualities" he had expected of them. Worse, there had been "many individual failures" and "grave shortcomings" among his commanders. All too many had not "understood" his Field Regulation; all too many had failed to display the Napoleonic *feu sacré;* and all too many had shown themselves to be cautious instead of bold. Messimy for a second time in two weeks went so far as to demand that ineffectual commanders ("old fossils") be summarily executed.[72] A shocked President Poincaré recalled his liaison officer to GQG for a dose of reality. "Is it defeat?" he bluntly asked Colonel Marie-Jean Pénelon. The reply was surprisingly* straightforward, "Yes, Mister President."[73] That Sunday, 23 August 1914, childhood memories of 1870–71 could not have been far from the mind of the statesman born in Bar-le-Duc, Lorraine, in 1860.

The greatest losers by far, of course, were the people and the land of Belgium. The country lay in ruins. Villages had been reduced to rubble and ashes. Hundreds of civilians had been summarily executed for reportedly firing on German troops, and tens of thousands had been forcefully deported to Germany. An endless sea of refugees, pulling their few remaining possessions in ancient small carts, flowed aimlessly away from the fighting fronts. Giant shell craters pock-

---

* The colonel had earned the nickname *April Smiles* for his ability to put a positive spin on any news, no matter how bad.

marked the landscape. Bridges, canals, railroad tracks, and telegraph wires had been destroyed. Crops were rotting in the fields. The bloated or blasted corpses of horses and cows were left in the sun. Will Irwin, an American reporter for *Collier's Weekly*, was struck by the grayness of "earth and land and sky": "gray transport wagons," "gray motorcycles," "gray biplanes," and "gray machines of men." Ever onward the German "gray machine of death" rolled. Irwin's most lasting memory was a prosaic one: "And over it all lay a smell of which I have never heard mentioned in any book on war—the smell of a half-million unbathed men, the stench of a menagerie raised to the nth power. That smell lay for days over every town through which the Germans passed."[74]

CHAPTER SIX

SQUANDERED CLIMACTERICS

———

*One must never fail to recognize that it is difficult to free
oneself from a concept once it is conceived and to throw
over board an entire operations plan once it appears that
the presuppositions on which it is based are no longer valid.*

—GERMAN GENERAL STAFF RIDE 1905/06

T HE BATTLE OF THE FRONTIERS WAS OVER BY 24 AUGUST. FOR
nearly two weeks, two million-man armies had been locked in murderous combat along a front roughly three hundred kilometers wide.
There had been planned offensives that quickly degenerated into wild
melees in Alsace-Lorraine, Belgium, the Ardennes, and the triangle of
the Sambre-Meuse rivers. There had been unexpected skirmishes and
unwanted surprises as the opposing forces ran into one another headlong in rugged terrain. There had been severe "wastage" due to senseless massed infantry assaults. Artillery and machine guns had proved
utterly lethal. France and Germany had each suffered roughly 260,000
casualties.

In boxing terms, the two contenders had sparred for four rounds—
at Nancy, Liège, Namur-Charleroi, and Mons. They had landed, and
absorbed, jabs and light blows. They had inflicted black eyes, cut lips,
and swollen cheeks on each other. But there had been no massive combination punches to the body or the head, no knockout blow. The
Germans stuck to their game plan—to remain on the offensive everywhere and to knock out their opponent by either a left hook in Lorraine or a right hook at Paris, or both. They circled their prey waiting
for an opening. The French had come out looking to land a knockout

punch in the first two rounds—in Alsace-Lorraine and then in the Ardennes. When that approach failed, they adopted a "rope-a-dope"* strategy, constantly retreating, conserving energy, allowing the opponent to strike them repeatedly in hopes of tiring him out, and waiting for an opportunity to counterattack.

Round Five had the potential to be deadly—to the French. Alexander von Kluck's First Army was chasing the retreating British Expeditionary Force (BEF) on the right flank. Crown Prince Rupprecht's Sixth and Seventh armies were resting and recuperating from a week of constant combat on the left flank, and preparing to drive past Nancy and across the Meurthe River. Crown Prince Wilhelm of Prussia's Fifth Army and Duke Albrecht of Württemberg's Fourth Army had given the French center a terrible pounding in the Battle of the Ardennes. The war's center of gravity now shifted once more to Charles Lanrezac's French Fifth Army. Pointing northeast into the apex (Namur) of the right angle formed by the Sambre and Meuse rivers, Lanrezac was the anchor of the French position. If he failed to hold the line, it would spell doom not only for Sir John French and the BEF on his left, but especially for Pierre Ruffey's Third Army and Fernand de Langle de Cary's Fourth Army on his right, which had been bludgeoned and was now pinned down in the Ardennes by German Fifth and Fourth armies. And, of course, for Paris.

LANREZAC HAD ALREADY CROSSED swords with Karl von Bülow at Charleroi and had come out the loser. German Second Army had chased French Fifth Army south across the Sambre and by 25–26 August was making a major effort to encircle it from the northwest. But Lanrezac's problems did not end with Bülow. For on his right flank, another German army was driving west, and it posed the greatest potential threat: Max von Hausen's Third Army. It was a force to be reckoned with: Saxon XII and XIX corps as well as XII Reserve Corps and Prussian XI Corps, a total of 113,000 infantry, 71,000 cavalry, 602 guns, and 198 machine guns.[1] For much of August, Third Army had advanced through the Belgian province of Namur on the left flank of Bülow's Second Army—both forming the spokes that connected the hub of Fourth and

* A term famously coined by Muhammad Ali for the "Rumble in the Jungle" against George Foreman in October 1974 at Kinshasa, Zaire.

Fifth armies in the Ardennes to the outer rim of First Army in Flemish Brabant. After ordering Hausen to surrender Otto von Plüskow's XI Corps to Second Army to besiege Namur, Army Supreme Command (OHL) on 20 August ordered him to head for the line Namur-Givet with his three remaining corps. His instructions were to support Second Army's advance west of Namur and to coordinate his actions with Prussia's senior field commander. Ahead lay the right flank of French Fifth Army.

Hausen's advance was fraught with both promise and danger. If he and Bülow drove home their attacks on Fifth Army, the Prussian from the north and the Saxon from the east, Lanrezac's forces could be taken between two pincers and crushed.[2] But if either Bülow or Hausen failed to press the enemy hard at all times and allowed Lanrezac freedom of action, there was a danger that especially Hausen's Third Army could be driven by French Fifth Army against Langle de Cary's Fourth Army in the Ardennes. Expert coordination between Bülow and Hausen and their respective staffs was essential to success. The man whose job it was to provide this, Chief of the General Staff Helmuth von Moltke, was still at Koblenz, 280 kilometers from the front.

Hausen took his time. It was stiflingly hot. The roads were narrow and dusty. The local population was hostile. In town after town, from Somme-Leuze to Erezée, and from Champlon to Hargimont, his commanders reported finding vast caches of revolvers, ammunition, and dynamite, as well as destroyed railroad tracks, telegraph wires, and bridges. They notified Hausen of "cowardly attacks" on the men of Third Army by the local militia, the Garde civique. In response, Hausen took estate owners, priests, and mayors hostage, burned manor houses and urban dwellings, and summarily executed those caught obstructing his advance.[3]

Beginning on 17 August, Bülow almost daily badgered Hausen and his chief of staff, Ernst von Hoeppner, to drive their right wing across the Meuse River and thus secure Second Army's left flank. On 20 August, Bülow frantically cabled: "Where 3. Army today?" Coordinated action by Second and Third armies was "urgently desired." But the next day, he sent a mixed signal: "2. Army will not attack today."[4] What was it to be, Hausen must have wondered, a combined-armies attack or individual operations? And where was the controlling hand of Moltke?[5]

As Third Army approached Achêne on the road to Dinant on the afternoon of 21 August, Hausen and Hoeppner called a meeting of their corps and division commanders. All agreed that Dinant was a formidable obstacle. There, the Meuse flowed deep and broad and swift in a gorge that ran from south to north across their path of advance. Its eastern shore consisted of a ridge of high, heavily wooded hills; its western bank, of a precipitous hundred-meter-high rock cliff topped by a massive stone citadel.* The city of seven thousand inhabitants was strung out along the west bank of the river and dominated by the onion-domed Cathedral of Notre Dame. French forces—Hausen suspected two army corps—occupied both banks of the river. Three major roads fed into Dinant from the east. The French could be counted on to blow up the Meuse bridges as soon as Third Army hoved into view.

It was further agreed at the meeting that Dinant could be taken only by way of a frontal assault. Moltke, having received news that five French corps had begun a concentrated attack in the Ardennes, instructed Hausen to coordinate his assault with Bülow for 4 AM† on 23 August. Accordingly, Hausen moved his headquarters up to Castle Leignon, fifteen kilometers east of Dinant, and pushed Karl d'Elsa's XII Corps and Maximilian von Laffert's XIX Corps straight toward the city. Hans von Kirchbach's XII Reserve Corps was to continue its advance on Third Army's right flank in place of XI Corps, recently dispatched to Namur.[6] Saxon field artillery began to "soften" Dinant for the infantry assault. Engineers gathered barges and brought up pontoon bridges to span the Meuse when the French, as expected, blew up its bridges. The weather continued hot and dry.

At 10:30 AM on 22 August, Bülow was back with another request: "Rapid advance 3. Army with right wing against Mettet urgently desired."[7] In plain language, Bülow demanded that Hausen shift the direction of his attack to the north of Dinant against Louis Franchet d'Espèrey's I Corps at Mettet. Hausen and Hoeppner spent the rest of the day drafting new attack orders. Then, at 10 PM, they received startling news from Fourth Army. Erich Tülff von Tschepe und Weidenbach, commanding VIII Corps on Duke Albrecht's right flank, reported to his northern neighbor, Laffert of Hausen's XIX Corps,

* Interestingly, in 1934 King Albert of Belgium died near Dinant while rock climbing.
† French (GMT) time. German records are in German General Time (one hour later).

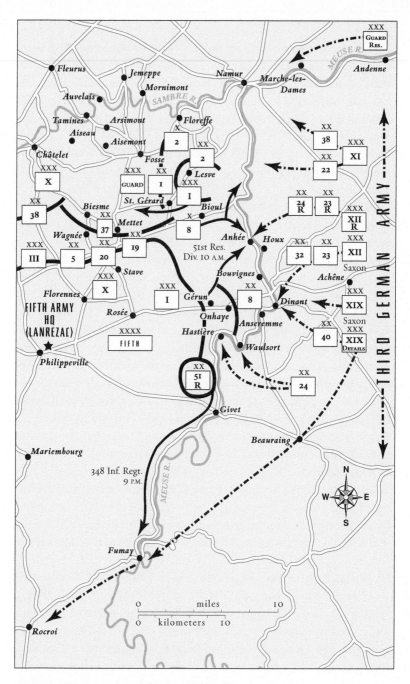

GERMAN THIRD ARMY'S ASSAULT ON DINANT

that the French seemed to have only three cavalry divisions in the area west of Dinant.[8] Albrecht's Fourth Army had turned southward to ward off the attack by Langle de Cary's Fourth Army and hence could not take advantage of the opening. Tülff strongly suggested that Hausen's Third Army bypass Dinant to the south, cross the Meuse, and drive a wedge between the joint of French Fifth and Fourth armies. Lanrezac's Fifth Army of 193 battalions and 692 guns might thus be crushed between the pincers of Bülow's Second Army and Hausen's Third Army.

What to do? Obey the wishes of Prussia's senior field commander? Heed the advice of a royal prince's corps commander? Seize the moment? Hausen prevaricated for much of the night. Then, at 4:50 AM on 23 August, fifty-seven Saxon artillery batteries opened fire on Dinant. It was a dreary, foggy morning. Hausen's spirits were raised immensely at 7:35 AM when he finally received instructions from Moltke: "Available units to be taken across Maas south of Givet." The news from Koblenz, Hausen recorded in the war diary, "produced great joy at Army Supreme Command 3."[9] It was one of those rare moments of opportunity that make history's great captains. At hand lay a golden opportunity to cut off Lanrezac's retreat from the Sambre and envelop French Fifth Army. Within the hour, Hausen ordered Laffert's XIX Corps to dispatch ten infantry battalions, nine artillery batteries, and three cavalry squadrons under Götz von Olenhusen south to Givet and on to Fumay, there to cross the Meuse and advance against Lanrezac's right flank.[10]

Hausen's bold action, of course, split his army into three groups. While Olenhusen's force—mainly 40th Infantry Division (ID)—marched off toward Givet, Kirchbach's XII Reserve Corps continued its advance north of Dinant toward Houx. That left a third group, d'Elsa's XII Corps, to storm the narrow medieval streets of Dinant and to seize the heights between Haut-le-Wastia, Sommière, and Onhaye.[11]

In daylong bitter fighting, Horst von der Planitz's 32d ID, followed by Alexander von Larisch's 23d Reserve Infantry Division (RID), crossed the Meuse on barges and pontoon bridges north of Dinant at Leffe. Karl von Lindemann's 23d ID advanced south of Dinant via Les Rivages. The French defense had been severely gutted as Lanrezac, hard-pressed by Bülow south of the Sambre, had ordered Franchet d'Espèrey's I Corps to turn northwest to come to the aid of Gilbert

Defforges's X Corps, heavily battered by the German Guard Corps at Arsimont. René Boutegourd's 51st RID and two brigades of Henri Deligny's 2d ID were all that stood between the Saxons and victory.

Fighting quickly degenerated into hand-to-hand combat. At Leffe, an industrial suburb north of Dinant, Planitz's 32d ID was met by a withering hail of bullets from Boutegourd's 51st RID and—according to both Hausen and the German official history—from the "fanatical" Belgian population, including women and children.[12] Lindemann's 46th Infantry Brigade (IB) managed to penetrate Dinant, where it, too, was greeted with heavy fire from French reserves and Belgian irregulars. When attempts to smoke out the francs-tireurs failed, Lindemann abandoned the city for an hour—and unleashed his artillery on the inhabitants.

Boutegourd frantically appealed to Franchet d'Espèrey for relief, informing I Corps' commander that one of his brigades had been "crushed by artillery fire, with heavy losses."[13] Franchet d'Espèrey at once realized the mortal danger to Fifth Army's right flank. Without consulting Lanrezac, he ordered I Corps to retrace its steps of the night before. Along the way, he ran across a colleague from the colonial wars, Charles Mangin, whose 8th Brigade stood in reserve. "General, the enemy has crossed the Meuse behind our right. The [51st] Reserve Division is giving ground. . . . Go immediately and take your two battalions." Franchet d'Espèrey promised to follow "as fast as I can with the main body of the corps."[14] It was Mangin's first appearance as a major actor on the Western Front.

In one of the few bright moments for the French in this early part of the campaign, Mangin picked up a cavalry regiment along the way and headed for Onhaye. En route, he encountered the shattered remains of French 33d Battalion stumbling back from Dinant. Trooper Christian Mallet, 22d Dragoons, was "stupefied" at seeing

terrifying beings, livid, stumbling along, with horrible wounds. One has his lips carried away, an officer has a crushed hand, another has his arm fractured by a shell splinter. Their uniforms are torn, white with dust, and drip with blood. Amongst the last comers the wounds are more villainous, in the wagons one sees bare legs that hang limp, bloodless faces.[15]

Mangin pushed on. Two kilometers west of Dinant, he reorganized Boutegourd's shattered reserve division and ordered a gallant bayonet charge that drove the enemy back from Dinant. The situation had been thus stabilized by the time Franchet d'Espèrey's I Corps arrived on the scene. Still, losses had been severe.

Among the thousand French casualties at Dinant was Lieutenant Charles de Gaulle, serving in Colonel Henri-Philippe Pétain's 4th IB. He later recalled the fierce fight around the city:

> Suddenly the enemy's fire was precise and concentrated. Second by second the hail of bullets and the thunder of the shells grew stronger. Those who survived lay flat on the ground, amid the screaming wounded and the humble corpses. With affected calm, the officers let themselves be killed standing upright, some obstinate platoons stuck their bayonets in their rifles, bugles sounded the charge, isolated heroes made fantastic leaps, but all to no purpose. In an instant it had become clear that not all the courage in the world could withstand this fire.[16]

To the south, Olenhusen's forces—in the strength of a brigade—had fallen prey to Carl von Clausewitz's "friction" of war and "fog of uncertainty." Advancing down the eastern shore of the Meuse, Olenhusen's troops planned to make Fumay by 23 August, and then to march southwest on Rocroi. But the troops never reached Fumay. The sun beat mercilessly on them. The roads were narrow and twisted, the woods dense, the slopes steep. Legs gave out. Horses collapsed. Units got lost. Orders were misread. West of Onhaye, it was this force that had the misfortune of running into Mangin's fierce bayonet charges. Their advance ground to a halt on the heights north of Bourseigne-Neuve.[17] And so, Hausen's opportunity to become a great captain was lost.

Late on 23 August, d'Elsa's XII Corps finally seized the smoking ruins of Dinant, lustily singing "Deutschland über alles." The Saxon 1st Jäger Regiment, bayonets fixed, stormed the citadel. Angered by having their anticipated easy march through neutral Belgium halted and having received reports of civilians firing on soldiers, d'Elsa's troops took their revenge.[18] For most, including Major Johannes Niemann of 9th Infantry Regiment (IR), this took the form of burning the homes of known resisters, executing suspected civilian shooters, and "requisitioning" stocks of "marmalade, pineapples, champagne, red wine, and other delicacies."[19] What then followed, in the words of historians John Horne and Alan Kramer, was "the systematic, premeditated elimination of presumed civilian resistance."[20] For those with historical interest, it was a repeat of 1466, when Charles the Bold had sacked the city and murdered its inhabitants.

Almost one resident in ten was killed. Corporal Franz Stiebing, 3d Company, 178th IR, noted the violence at Leffe: "We pushed on house by house, under fire from almost every building, and we arrested the male inhabitants, who almost all carried weapons. They were summarily executed in the street." Groups of suspected resisters were put up against city walls and shot; others were gunned down in the city's squares or in their places of work. An anonymous lieutenant in the same 178th IR wrote home on 21 August:

> The battle now becomes a wild melee, a street brawl. These mean-spirited brothers bring us assassin's losses from cellar windows, from apartments, from attics, from trees. The doors are broken down with rifle butts and hatchets, the houses searched with bayonets fixed, the guilty arrested. They are all taken down to the local prefecture. . . . The scoundrels are executed in groups in front of all witnesses. A terrible sight.[21]

Private Kurt Rasch informed his parents in Dresden that his battalion had been selected to storm Dinant with but one purpose: "to level everything in sight and to make one part [of the city] left of the Maas disappear from view." They did their jobs well. "Dinant has fallen, everything burned to the ground. . . . We shoot the men, plunder and burn down the houses."[22] A. Rückauer, a noncommissioned officer with 9th Foot Artillery Regiment, wrote home in a similar manner. Priests had led the civilian assaults on the Saxons. They were "rounded up and gunned down. [Dinant's] inhabitants lay about in heaps." Cattle and horses roamed the streets bellowing in terror. "By nightfall, Dinant resembled only a sea of fire and a heap of rubbish."[23] Eight villages on the ridge above the city likewise were ablaze.

On the Belgian side, Public Prosecutor Maurice Tschoffen recalled the manner of execution.[24] "The [Germans] marched in two columns down the deserted street, those on the right aiming their rifles at the

houses on the left, and inversely, all with their fingers on the trigger
and ready to fire. At each door a group stopped and riddled the houses,
especially the windows, with bullets." Almost as if to change the routine, other soldiers threw grenades and small bombs into the cellars of
homes.

The killings continued into 24 August. Some houses still burned;
others were already cold, smoking shells. Public and historic buildings
that had escaped the original orgy of destruction were systematically set
to the torch. The stench of bodies decomposing under the searing sun
became almost unbearable for inhabitants and occupiers alike. When it
was all over, somewhere between 640 and 674 civilians had been killed
and 400 deported to Germany. Two-thirds of the city's houses had been
torched; twelve hundred were but burned-out shells.[25]

At the height of the orgy of fire and death, around 5:30 PM, Bülow
rudely interrupted Hausen's operations: Another frontal assault by
Karl von Plettenberg's Guard Corps had been stopped cold at Saint-
Gérard. Relief by the right wing of Third Army was "urgently
wanted." The demand hit Hausen like a cold shower. Confusion and
uncertainty reigned at his headquarters. What to do? Follow Moltke's
orders to advance across the Meuse south of Dinant at Fumay? Recall
Olenhusen's units and rush them to Houx, north of Dinant, to come
to Plettenberg's aid? It was a cruel dilemma. Hausen resolved it as he
had done before: "giving ear to Second Army's distress," as Chief of
Staff von Hoeppner later put it,[26] Third Army grudgingly recalled
most of its units from the south. Chaos ensued as Olenhusen's weary
units dutifully about-faced to retrace their steps to Dinant.

Still, Hausen believed that all was not yet lost. Although having
sustained almost 1,275 dead and 3,000 wounded at Dinant, he planned
to drive his remaining forces southwest, belatedly to cross the Meuse
south of Givet and to strike French Fifth Army in the right flank.
Saxon XII Corps and XII Reserve Corps were to march on Rocroi,
XIX Corps on Fumay and Revin. But no sooner had Hausen issued his
orders than an emissary (Major von Fouqué) arrived from Bülow's
headquarters at 3 AM on 24 August and "urgently requested" that
Third Army wheel around on a westerly course toward Mettet to take
the pressure off Second Army's left wing. No fewer than five French
corps were assaulting Second Army.[27]

Sunrise was less than three hours away. A decision had to be made at once. For the second time in half a day, Bülow had directly interfered with Hausen's command. And for the second time in half a day, Hausen yielded. Within ninety minutes of Fouqué's arrival, he issued new orders for Third Army to fall into line with Bülow's demand. By then, the weakened vanguard of Third Army had failed in its attempt to cross the Meuse in force at Fumay, Revin, or Monthermé. French sappers had dynamited the bridges, and enemy infantry was entrenched on the river's west bank. In a bitter twist of fortune, six hours after Fouché's mission pleading "urgent" help from Third Army, Bülow cavalierly informed Hausen that Second Army was no longer in danger.[28]

Max von Hausen had failed to bring about the war's first "climacteric," to borrow a phrase from Winston S. Churchill. By his actions, as the German official history noted, Hausen "gave away the brilliant prospect of an operational pursuit" of Lanrezac's Fifth Army in order to "secure the tactical victory" scored at Dinant.[29] In truth, Third Army's commander had squandered a magnificent opportunity to help destroy an entire French army (or at least major parts thereof) because he could not bring himself to make an independent decision against the will of his Prussian superior.[30]

Artur Baumgarten-Crusius, the historian of Third Army, shifted the blame to Moltke. At no time had the chief of the General Staff offered Hausen the support he needed (and deserved). Prospects had been brilliant in the triangle of the Sambre and Meuse. While Max von Gallwitz's Guard Reserve Corps anchored the German front at Namur, Moltke should have ordered Hausen to deliver a "left hook" against Lanrezac by advancing from Givet to Rocroi; concurrently, he should have instructed First and Second armies to halt their advance southwest and instead to march from Mons to Maubeuge and deliver a "right hook" against Lanrezac. As well, he should have dispatched Manfred von Richthofen's I Cavalry Corps to Fumay, instead of wasting it on endless battles north of Binche as part of Bülow's Second Army.[31] French Fifth Army escaped the German "pincers" to fight another day. At Koblenz, Moltke incredibly informed the Saxon military plenipotentiary, Traugott Leuckart von Weißdort, "Operations are running . . . according to plan."[32]

Moltke's insouciance was no doubt occasioned by the flood of self-congratulatory reports that came in from the front.[33] On 23 August, Fifth Army's chief of staff, Konstantin Schmidt von Knobelsdorf, informed Moltke that the main French armies had been "reduced to rubble" (*zertrümmert*) and that the rest were in full flight.[34] Within hours, Duke Albrecht of Fourth Army was downright triumphalist in his report to Koblenz. "Total victory achieved; thousands of prisoners, including generals; and countless guns. Started pursuit of the beaten foe. . . . Troops fought valiantly; losses in many cases are great."[35] The next day, Bülow also signaled victory. "Enemy right wing decisively beaten by II Army"; and on 25 August, "II Army has decisively defeated the enemy." Hausen reported the French in "full retreat" and in danger of encirclement.[36] At the corps level, Max von Fabeck (XIII Corps) between 27 August and 2 September bombarded the OHL with a steady barrage of telegrams reporting French units "thrown back" from the front and "fleeing" the scene of battle; in short, a steady string of "unending victories against the Belgian-English army masses."[37]

The OHL readily accepted the rosy news from its field commanders. Colonel Wilhelm Groener, chief of the Field Railway Service, on 25 August crowed that the campaign in the west had been decided in Germany's favor. Lieutenant Colonel Gerhard Tappen, Moltke's chief of operations, cheerily announced: "The whole thing will be done in six weeks."[38] It seemed to be 1870–71 all over again. The French simply were no match for the Prussian-German war machine. They were soft and effeminate, too much devoted to food and wine. They bolted at the first serious "storm of steel" from the Krupp guns. They blanched and ran at the first sign of massed waves of field-gray warriors coming at them with bayonets fixed.

The euphoria was contagious. Karl von Wenninger, the Bavarian military plenipotentiary, reported to Munich that the French armies had been reduced to "riff-raff" already on the first morning of the Battle of the Saar.[39] Fritz Nieser, his counterpart from the Grand Duchy of Baden, informed Karlsruhe that "military circles" considered the campaign against France already won. "What is still to follow comes under [the heading] occupation measures."[40]

Moltke at last agreed with critics in the General Staff who stressed that the OHL needed to be closer to the front—but not too close! He remained concerned that the closer Wilhelm II was to the fighting, the more active the role he might take in command decision making. He felt personal responsibility for the kaiser's safety. And he was aware that General Moriz von Lyncker, chief of the Military Cabinet, since

9 August (!) had been interviewing candidates to succeed him in case of a major setback. Rather than Namur or Charleroi, Moltke settled on Luxembourg.[41]

It was a poor choice. Whereas Alfred von Schlieffen in 1908 had envisioned a distant, highly centralized command-and-control system, one in which the "modern Napoleon" would conduct operations from a "comfortable chair at a broad table" in a "house with roomy bureaus" by way of "wire and wireless telegraphy, telephone and signal apparatus, as well as hordes of trucks and motorcycles,"[42] Moltke on 30 August had to settle for a small, dingy girls' schoolhouse. "We have neither gas nor electric lights, only dim petroleum lamps," he wrote his wife that day.[43] An officer on Moltke's operations staff was brutal in his assessment of the new headquarters. "Work conditions were simply scandalous. Desks consisted of several rough boards and trestles. There was no light at all." Moltke worked out of a small schoolroom and Tappen out of an adjacent closet, "where operational discussions took place."[44] The "modern Napoleon's" communications system consisted of a single radio transmitter.

IN TRUTH, COMMUNICATIONS REMAINED the Achilles' heel of the German armies in the west. One scholar has acidly noted, "The war began with an end to communications."[45] The OHL's single Morse-type telegraph transmitter had a reach of just three hundred kilometers, which meant that by the time of the Battle of the Marne, Moltke could reach First Army only by way of relay stations at Péronne, Noyon, Compiègne, and Villers-Cotterêts; Second Army, only via Marle, Laon, and Soissons.[46] Unsurprisingly, transmission delays of up to twenty hours were not uncommon. As late as 3 September, German wire connections had been established only as far as Esch-sur-Alzette on the Luxembourg-Lorraine border. The Field Telegraph Corps was headed by a "total novice," General William Balcke, who had been promoted to the post from command of 82d IB and who neither understood nor cared about modern electronic communications.[47] Moreover, his corps of eight hundred officers and twenty-five thousand men was too small to handle the daily traffic emanating from seven armies and nearly two million soldiers. "Troops, individual units and private parties" all vied with headquarters for time on the radio-telegraph. The two critical "strike" armies on the German right wing were without radio connection to each other, much less to their individual corps. First Army established electronic connections to its corps headquarters only after the Battle of Mons. Second Army likewise failed to connect to its corps headquarters before the Battle of Saint-Quentin. Neither the four higher cavalry commanders nor any of the army's ninety-two infantry divisions possessed a telegraph section. To compound this neglect, what little existed in the way of communications was designed to function "from the bottom to the top, rather than the other way around," for the simple reason that army commanders wanted to be free of direct "interference" from General Staff headquarters. Finally, the Germans in the west, like the Russians in the east, sent most of their messages in clear because ciphers were cumbersome to use and speedy transmission was required.[48]

IN TERMS OF FUTURE operations, Moltke and Tappen on 27 August issued a new General Directive to their field commanders.[49] They assumed that the Belgian army was in a "complete state of disintegration," that the British would not be able to raise new armies "before from four to six months," and that the French center and northern armies were "in full retreat in a westerly or southwesterly direction, that is, on Paris." Thus, on the critical right wing, First Army was to advance to the lower Seine River, driving west of the Oise River; Second Army on Paris via La Fère and Laon; and Third Army on Château-Thierry by way of Neufchâtel-sur-Aisne. In the center, Fourth Army was to seize Reims on its way to Épernay, and Fifth Army to pass Châlons-sur-Marne and head for French army headquarters at Vitry-le-François. Sixth and Seventh armies were to secure the front in Lorraine—and, in case of a French withdrawal, to pursue the enemy across the Moselle River in the direction of Neufchâteau. Each army was to press the attack vigorously while simultaneously securing the flank of its neighbor(s). If the much anticipated French stand first along the Aisne and later along the Marne developed, *"a turn by the armies from a southwesterly to a southerly direction can be required."*[50]

Three conclusions are warranted. First, Moltke, Stein, and Tappen had basically abandoned Moltke's modified Schlieffen Plan. By 27 August, that concept had degenerated into individual operations by the various army commanders in the west, each designed to achieve local successes in a separate theater. Second, Moltke, Stein, and Tappen had also abandoned the concept of a vast envelopment of Paris from the north and the west. The right wing was now no longer pursuing an envelopment strategy, but simply one of flank protection. Third, the entire German advance had slid off in a general southeasterly direction, away from Paris. Moltke was "advancing on all points," but no longer southwest; rather, south and even southeast. This meant that if each army advanced as instructed by Moltke, securing the flank of its neighbor, "the overall alignment would be set by the left and by the centre, and not by the right."[51] The chief of the General Staff's instructions of 27 August—with their advance warning that the armies might be "required" to change course "from a southwesterly to a southerly direction"—were a vote of confidence for Bülow's concept of a purely tactical victory over Kluck's design of a strategic envelopment of the enemy. The nagging question at the OHL was whether the right wing—depleted by 265,000 casualties, by Hans von Beseler's III Corps detached to invest Antwerp, by Hans von Zwehl's VII Reserve Corps sent to seal off Maubeuge, and by XI Corps and Guard Reserve Corps dispatched to East Prussia—remained sufficiently strong to crush Allied forces still in the field.

JOSEPH JOFFRE HAD LOST the Battle of the Frontiers. At the Grand quartier général (GQG), his acolytes of the all-out offensive (*l'offensive à outrance*) were in a state of sudden and unexpected depression. Would the generalissimo be willing to recognize the full measure of the defeat? Would he be able to conjure up what Carl von Clausewitz called the "new and favorable factors" required of a great captain to avoid "outright defeat, perhaps even absolute destruction"?[52] Joffre's reputation, indeed his career, depended on his willingness and his ability to do so.

Reassessment began on the morning of 24 August. Joffre first laid out his future strategy in a candid letter to War Minister Adolphe Messimy.[53] "We are condemned to a defensive supported by fortified places and large-terrain obstacles." The immediate task was to surrender "the least possible" amount of terrain to the enemy; the longer-range aim was "to last as long as possible, while striving to attrit the enemy"; and the ultimate goal was "to resume the offensive when the [proper] moment arrives." Gone were the sweeping Napoleonic brushstrokes of vast offensives, and in their place came sensible and effective movements of men and machines as if on a vast chessboard. Messimy provided governmental support. "Take swift means, brutally, energetically, and decisively. . . . The sole law of France at this moment is: conquer or die."[54]

Joffre's first move was to pull forces on the French left wing back to the line Maubeuge-Mézières-Verdun.[55] This was followed by an accelerated shift of combat units from the right to the left—that is, from Alsace-Lorraine to the threatened region around Paris. Paul Pau's Army of Alsace was further cannibalized for troops. Railroads and bridges in Lorraine that could be of use to the Germans were destroyed. For much of the week after 24 August, Joffre took advantage of his interior lines and used his superb Directorate of Railways to move units north to face the menacing German right wing sweeping down on the capital. On 1 September, Victor Boëlle's IV Corps left Sainte-Menehould for Greater Paris in 109 trains; the next day, Pierre Dubois's IX Corps embarked at Nancy bound for Troyes in 52 trains; and Émile-Edmond Legrand-Girarde's XXI Corps departed Épinal for Gondrecourt in 74 trains.[56]

But what strategy to employ once the new formations were in place? Two alternatives dominated the discussions at GQG.[57] Deputy Chief of Staff Henri Berthelot suggested that any new army being organized behind the Allied left wing could best be used to attack German forces immediately threatening Paris—in particular, the inner, or eastern, wing of Bülow's Second Army. Joffre rejected Berthelot's scheme since it was based on the ability of Fifth Army and the BEF to keep the German right wing in check while a new army was being stood up. He had little faith left in either Charles Lanrezac or Sir John French. Thus, he opted for a much bolder design: to form a new army well to the west of German First Army and then to drive it eastward into Kluck's exposed outer right flank.

By 10 PM on 25 August, Joffre's staff had formalized his new plans in General Instruction No. 2.[58] After a cursory admission that it had been "unable" to carry out the "offensive maneuver originally planned," GQG defined the new strategy as being one

> to reconstruct on our left a force capable of resuming the offensive by a combination of the Fourth and Fifth Armies, the British Army and new forces drawn from the east, while the other armies hold the enemy in check for such time as may be necessary.

More sacred French soil—another hundred kilometers—would have to be abandoned as the planned withdrawal was extended farther into the interior to the line Amiens-Reims-Verdun. Rear guards of Third, Fourth, and Fifth armies were to cover the retreat by conducting "short and violent counterattacks" in which artillery was to be "the principal element employed." Belatedly, Joffre demanded a more "intimate combination of infantry and artillery." A new "group of forces," composed of at least one and perhaps even two army corps and four reserve divisions from Alsace-Lorraine and Paris, was to be assembled "before Amiens" or "behind the Somme." This was to be Joffre's "army of maneuver" (later designated Sixth Army), which was to envelop the German right wing. There, in a nutshell, was the genesis of the strategic plan for the Battle of the Marne.

But it would take time—perhaps too much time—and it was predicated on the entire Allied line holding fast. Joffre had two great fears. First, a gap had developed between Fourth and Fifth armies stumbling out of the Ardennes and back from the Sambre, respectively. The Germans, moving south on Hirson, on the Oise River, might discover this and attempt to break through. Thus, Joffre formed a Special Army Detachment under Ferdinand Foch—the future Ninth Army—out of two corps from Langle de Cary's Fourth Army and two divisions from Lanrezac's Fifth Army. Foch, recalled from the Grand Couronné de Nancy on 27 August, immediately moved to close the gap in the line. He would soon learn that both his only son, Cadet Germain, and his son-in-law, Captain Charles Bécourt, had been killed on 22 August as the Germans swept into Belgium.

Joffre's greatest fear, as always, was the British. Sir John French seemed bent on retreating from the Germans faster than they could pursue. Somehow, Joffre had to sell the field marshal on his General Instruction No. 2. In typical fashion, and in sharp contrast with the sedentary Moltke, on 26 August, Joffre raced off to British General Headquarters (GHQ) at Saint-Quentin. Lanrezac of Fifth Army, on the British right, and Albert d'Amade, commanding a group of territorial divisions on the British left, were also summoned. The meeting took place in a neo-Pompeian house with closed shutters and dimly lit rooms. Sir John French and Henry Wilson, representing Chief of Staff Archibald Murray, who was away at Le Cateau and ill, arrived late. Lanrezac, his pince-nez hanging over his ears "like a pair of cherries," was less than enthused about having to deal with the British at all. He found Joffre silent and dull, seemingly "wrapped in a cloak of enveloping dumbness."[59]

Predictably, the meeting became another disaster.[60] Sir John rattled off a long list of French failures, beginning with Joffre's refusal to accept the fact that the Germans had crossed the Meuse in force and ending with Lanrezac's failure to inform him of Fifth Army's sudden retreat from the Sambre. These French "blunders" had increased the burden on the BEF and decreased the field marshal's confidence in French decision making. Moreover, his army was exhausted and desperately needed a day of rest. He proposed falling back to Compiègne. A painful silence ensued. Lanrezac, bored by the British diatribe, merely shrugged. He cagily declined to inform the group that he had already ordered Fifth Army to "break contact with the enemy" and to continue its retreat twenty kilometers toward Laon prior to any counterattack he might mount.[61]

It was up to Joffre to save the day. He was in an unenviable position. His concentration plan, XVII, had been shattered by the Germans at great loss. Bülow's Second Army had advanced south from the Sambre and was about to cross the Oise. If it did so, and in the process routed French Fifth Army, the campaign in the west would be lost. He desperately needed to hold the line of the Oise River, and for that he desperately needed the BEF. Joffre pulled himself together. He patiently explained the gist of his Instruction général No. 2: After the planned withdrawal to the line Amiens-Reims-Verdun, he would form French Fourth and Fifth armies as well as the BEF as a "mass of manoeuvre" on the French left "capable of resuming the offensive"; all he asked of Sir John was that the BEF keep its place in the line and "conform" to the movements of French Fifth Army and d'Amade's Territorials. But he could not simply issue the field marshal a direct order: Sir John outranked him, and there existed no machinery to coordinate the actions of the British and French armies. As General Wilson translated Joffre's presentation, Lanrezac, shoulders stooped slightly, gave the impression that he was bored. The atmosphere was funereal.

Sir John French sprang into action. He was flummoxed. "I know nothing of this Order," he petulantly barked out. He turned to Henry Wilson. The latter allowed that he had received Joffre's instruction during the night, but had not studied it, much less translated it for Sir John. Joffre was livid, but he maintained his customary calm. The atmosphere had turned from ice cold to hostile. Another pained silence followed. Junior officers dared not speak. French and Lanrezac refused to speak to each other directly. When Sir John invited the group to lunch, Lanrezac declined.[62]

Charles Huguet, chief of the French Military Mission at GHQ, summarized the conference as having been conducted with "extreme coolness" and "lack of cordiality." It had "achieved no military result."[63] Later that night, Huguet informed Joffre, back at Vitry-le-François, that the BEF had not only lost a battle, but "all cohesion." It would require "serious protection" from the French army before it could reorganize.[64] Joffre moved with alacrity.[65] He enacted General Instruction No. 2, standing up French Sixth Army under Michel-Joseph Maunoury out of VII Corps and four reserve divisions around Amiens. He formally abolished Pau's Army of Alsace since most of its units had already been sent to Sixth Army. And with another stroke of the pen, he crossed off the hapless Army of Lorraine, sending its infantry divisions to Third Army and its staff to Sixth Army. It was Joffre at his best: decisive, resolute, unflappable.

Colonel Huguet's reference to a "battle lost" concerned Le Cateau. While the French and British held their desultory discussions at Saint-Quentin, advance guards of Kluck's First Army had, at dusk on 25 August, attacked the Coldstream Guards of Sir Douglas Haig's I Corps, withdrawing on the east side of the Forest of Mormal. In fact, Haig had callously disobeyed Field Marshal French's order to assist British II Corps. He instead prepared to shelter for a few hours in deserted army barracks at Landecries. There occurred several street fights with Kluck's advance guard that night. This minor, accidental encounter set off near panic at corps headquarters—where Haig's staff prepared to destroy the unit's records—and at Saint-Quentin—where French's chief of staff, Sir Archibald Murray, "completely broken down," could scarcely be sustained by "morphia or some drug" before "promptly" slipping into a "fainting fit."[66] Landecries was not Haig's finest hour. It was one of the rare occasions on which the normally steady Haig became "rattled," possibly the aftereffects of a severe bout of diarrhea from the night before. Standing on a doorstep, revolver in hand, he cried out to John Charteris, his chief of intelligence, "If we are caught, by God, we'll sell our lives dearly."[67] He was spared the sale. The I Corps continued its retreat toward the Aisne River the next morning.

Yet again, the greater danger faced Sir Horace Smith-Dorrien's II Corps, falling back on the west side of the Forest of Mormal. Delayed

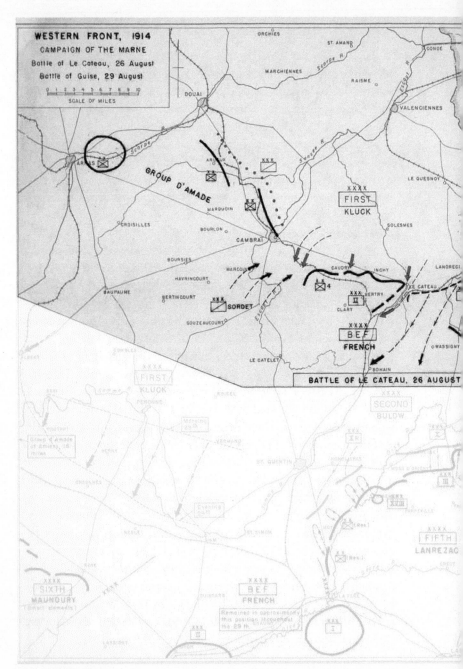

WESTERN FRONT, 1914
CAMPAIGN OF THE MARNE
Battle of Le Cateau, 26 August
Battle of Guise, 29 August

SCALE OF MILES

BATTLE OF LE CATEAU, 26 AUGUST

BATTLE OF LE CATEAU

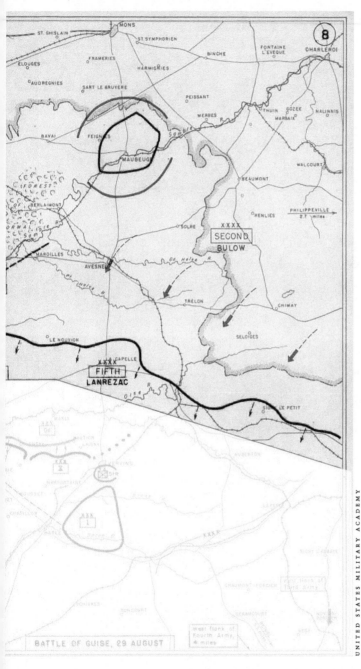

ST. GHISLAIN
MONS
ST SYMPHORIEN
FONTAINE
L'EVEQUE
CHARLEROI
8
BINCHE
ELOUGES
FRAMERIES
HARMIGNIES
AUDREGNIES
SART LE BRUYERE
PEISSANT
THUIN
GOZEE
NALINNIS
MERBES
MARBAIX
BAVAI
FEIGNIES
WALCOURT
MAUBEUGE
FOREST
BERLAIMONT
BEAUMONT
PHILIPPEVILLE
2.7 miles
ORMAL
SOLRE
RENLIES
XXXX
SECOND
BULOW
MAROILLES
AVESNES
TRELON
CHIMAY
LE NOUVION
SELOIGES
CAPELLE
XXXX
FIFTH
LANREZAC
OISE
SIGNE LE PETIT

BATTLE OF GUISE, 29 AUGUST

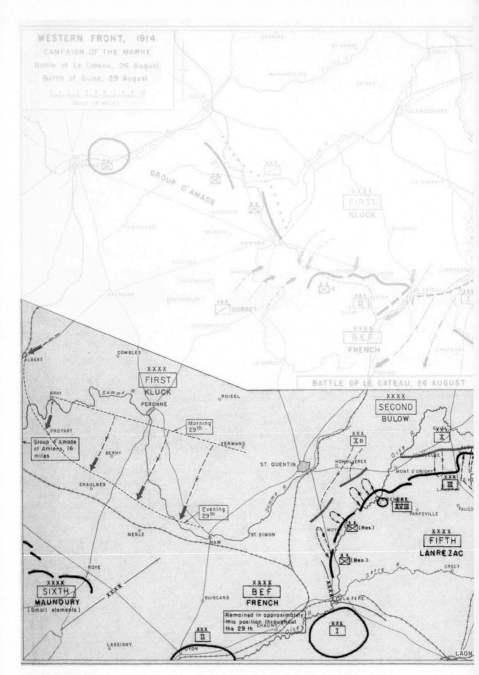

BATTLE OF GUISE

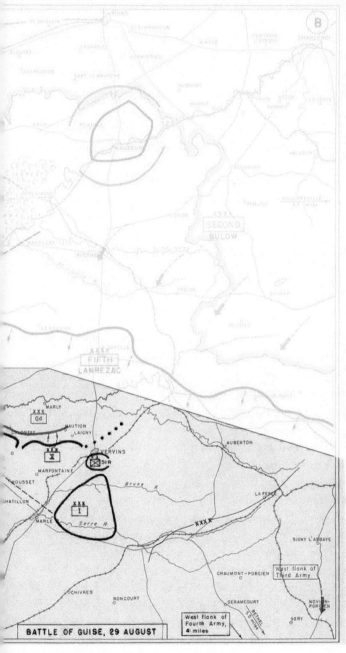

BATTLE OF GUISE, 29 AUGUST

by the passage of Jean-François Sordet's cavalry corps across its line of retreat, II Corps was itself harassed by more of Kluck's advance guards. It just managed to reach Solesmes, where it found cover under the guns of Sir Thomas Snow's newly arrived 4th ID. But late that night, Sir Edmund Allenby's cavalry division (CD) reported that Kluck was closing in on the BEF. Smith-Dorrien decided that his best chance lay in preparing his defenses and then "giving the enemy a smashing blow."[68] Twice he communicated his decision to GHQ. At 3:30 AM, he ordered his units to stand their ground on a low ridge running west of Le Cateau.

The Battle of Le Cateau coincidentally fell on the 568th anniversary of the Battle of Crécy, where Edward III of England had defeated the far superior army of Philip VI of France. But in 1914, fate favored the stronger battalions. At 6 AM, the guns of Kluck's First Army, sited on the heights above the town, unleashed a deadly barrage. At first, Smith-Dorrien's center managed to hold its own against the infantry assaults of Friedrich Sixt von Arnim's IV Corps. But on the right flank, left unprotected by Haig's retreat from Landecries, Ewald von Lo-chow's III Corps drove forward to envelop British II Corps. Furious counterattacks failed to repel the Germans, and 19th IB as well as 5th ID seemed threatened with destruction. On the left flank, too, the situation grew precarious as Georg von der Marwitz's II Cavalry Corps and two infantry divisions of Hans von Gronau's IV Reserve Corps attacked "Snowball" Snow's 4th ID. British II Corps was saved from possible annihilation by a timely sortie by Sordet's cavalry corps against Gronau's IV Reserve Corps and by an almost suicidal attack by Henri de Ferron's 84th Territorial Division against Alexander von Linsingen's II Corps moving up to join Gronau's units.

In contrast with the brutal offensive infantry assaults supported by massive artillery barrages at Charleroi, in the Ardennes, and in Lorraine, Le Cateau was a battle waged on open and largely treeless fields, in which British riflemen fought from prone positions and rarely had the luxury of digging rifle pits. It in many ways was more like a battle out of the U.S. Civil War or the Franco-Prussian War than the fighting one normally associates with World War I. Still, the British suffered 7,812 casualties at Le Cateau, their greatest battle (and losses) since Waterloo. The next day, gray and gloomy with heavy downpours, the commanders of two exhausted battalions surrendered rather than offering battle near Saint-Quentin.[69]

By 28 August, intensely hot again, the BEF had put the Oise River between itself and the pursuing Germans. Even the ever-optimistic Henry Wilson was seen at the new headquarters in Noyon mumbling, "To the sea, to the sea, to the sea."[70] French communications at Belfort intercepted Wilhelm II's ebullient radio message to the troops: "In its triumphant march, First Army today approaches the heart of France."[71] Still, Le Cateau was a bitter pill for Kluck to swallow. For a second time (after Mons), he had inflicted a tactical defeat on the British, but at great (unspecified) cost to his own forces and delay in the great sweep through northeastern France. And for a second time, due to poor intelligence and reconnaissance, he had failed to "achieve the desired annihilation."[72]

LE CATEAU STIRRED JOFFRE to still more feverish activity. Around 6 AM on 27 August, he dispatched an urgent appeal to Lanrezac, reminding the commander of Fifth Army to launch the counterattack against the Germans that Joffre seemingly had promised French at the conference in Saint-Quentin the day before.[73] The situation had grown more critical since then, given that Hausen's Third Army had crossed the Meuse at Dinant. Joffre called for an immediate strike northwest from the region of the Oise River between Hirson and Guise. Yet again, Lanrezac prevaricated. He preferred to withdraw another twenty kilometers south, there to regroup, and then to attack from around Laon. All the while, Huguet bombarded Vitry-le-François with ever more dire reports concerning the British army.[74] By early afternoon on the twenty-seventh, it had evacuated Saint-Quentin, exposing Lanrezac's left flank. At 5:45 PM, Huguet reported that the BEF's situation was "extremely grave" and that its retreat threatened to turn into a "rout." In a final communiqué later that evening, he informed Joffre that after Le Cateau, two British infantry divisions were "nothing more than disorganized bands incapable of offering the least resistance," and that the entire BEF was "beaten, incapable of a serious effort." At 8:10 PM, Joffre gave Lanrezac a direct order to attack toward Saint-Quentin.

It was a bold plan. Bülow's Second Army was moving in a southwesterly direction—Karl von Einem's VII Corps and Guenther von

Kirchbach's X Reserve Corps were approaching the British near Saint-Quentin—and thus offered an inviting flank for a counterattack. Of course, Joffre also knew that the plan was risky because he was asking much of a battered and exhausted army that had just marched almost three hundred kilometers first up to and then back from the Sambre. Fifth Army would have to execute a ninety-degree turn from northwest to west—while facing major enemy forces. Hence, Joffre dispatched one of his staff officers, Lieutenant Colonel Alexandre, to Lanrezac's headquarters at Marle to monitor the attack. Unsurprisingly, neither the professor from Saint-Cyr nor his chief of staff, Alexis Hély d'Oissel, was amused by being lectured by a junior officer. Lanrezac sent Alexandre back to Vitry-le-François with a brutal peroration: "Before trying to teach me my business, sir, go back and tell your little strategists to learn their own."[75]

Joffre's new deployment plan must have reminded Lanrezac of his recent trials and tribulations in the Battle of Charleroi. There, Fifth Army had been boxed into the triangle formed by the Sambre and Meuse. Now he was being asked to fight in a similar triangle around Guise, where the Oise River, after flowing east to west, turns sharply southwest. More, he would have to divide his forces: While Émile Hache's III Corps and Jacques de Mas-Latrie's XVIII Corps would drive west against Bülow's formations harassing the British around Saint-Quentin, a single corps, Gilbert Defforges's X, would have to secure the northern front toward Guise as well as to cover Fifth Army's right flank and rear. That would leave only Franchet d'Espèrey's I Corps in reserve.[76]

At 9 AM on 28 August, Lanrezac had a not-unexpected visitor: Joseph Joffre. The chief of staff was "shocked" by his commander's physical appearance: "marked by fatigue, yellow complexion, bloodshot eyes."[77] In what both officers later admitted was a "tense and heated" meeting, they exchanged views. Lanrezac, without informing Joffre of the dispositions he had made during the night to realign his corps according to GQG's new design, launched a biting attack on Joffre's overall strategic plan and reminded him of the great fatigue of Fifth Army and the overwrought "nerves" of some of its commanders. Joffre, fully aware that he could not afford either militarily or politically to have the BEF crushed on French soil, lost his customary calm. He exploded. "His rage was terrific," Lieutenant Edward Spears, British liaison officer with French Fifth Army, recorded. "He threatened to deprive Lanrezac of his command and told him that he must obey without discussion, that he must attack without his eternal procrastination and apprehensiveness."[78] When Lanrezac coldly countered that he possessed no written orders, Joffre sat down, seized paper and pen, and provided same. "As soon as possible, the Fifth Army will attack the German forces that were engaged yesterday against the British Army."[79]

By the time the story of the stormy meeting made the rounds in the seething political cauldron of Paris, President Raymond Poincaré noted in his diary that Joffre had threatened to have Lanrezac "shot" if he "disobeyed" this direct order.[80] A request that the BEF join Fifth Army's attack was readily accepted by Haig—but immediately rejected by Sir John French, who "regretfully" informed Huguet that his "excessively fatigued" troops needed 29 August to rest.[81] Huguet was shocked to learn that the field marshal was planning a "definite and prolonged retreat" south of Paris.[82] Lanrezac was incensed. *"C'est une félonie!"* reportedly was his kindest comment on Sir John and the British.[83]

Lanrezac counterattacked out of the triangle of the Oise around Guise in a thick mist at 6 AM on 29 August.[84] Yet again, he squared off against Bülow. Yet again, the weary soldiers of French Fifth Army and German Second Army were asked for another Herculean effort. Yet again, the terrain was miserable: woods and brush, ravines and streams. Yet again, Paris was the prize. And yet again, both sides had a different name for the battle: Guise to the French and Saint-Quentin to the Germans.

Lanrezac caught Bülow's Second Army off guard. As the sun slowly began to burn through the morning mist, it became readily evident that once more, what was intended to be a single, bold, decisive French counterattack had degenerated into a series of distinct localized battles. Hache's III Corps and de Mas-Latrie's XVIII Corps advanced about four kilometers west and northwest, respectively, before each was met by a withering storm of artillery, followed by massed infantry charges. By noon, their drive had stalled. French X Corps in the center of the line attacking north fared even worse. By 11 AM, General Defforges was pleading with Lanrezac to send him reinforcements. "I am very violently attacked on my whole front. They are getting around my right flank. I will hold at all costs. Get me support as soon as possible on my right and on my left."[85] Lanrezac countered that it was too early in the day to commit Franchet d'Espèrey's precious I Corps.

North of the Oise, Bülow was about to enter Saint-Quentin with his staff when the thunder of heavy guns erupted to the southeast. He drove toward the sound of the guns. Not only had Kirchbach's X Reserve Corps been heavily attacked east of Guise, but Emmich's X Corps and Plettenberg's Guard Corps were in a serious firefight around Audigny, south of Guise. Bülow and his chief of staff, Otto von Lauenstein, quickly appreciated that Second Army was conducting two major but separate battles: one at Guise in a southeasterly direction against the line of the Oise between Bernot and La Fère, and the other across the Oise from Guise to Vervins. By noon, a fifteen-kilometer-wide gap had formed between the two groups.[86]

A lieutenant (Dr. Trierenberg) with 2d Guard Regiment wrote home about the horror of battle around Le Sourd. Approaching the village through ripe orchards, the Guard was met by a withering hail of fire from houses and hedges and pinned down for two hours. When it finally resumed the advance, "the streets of Le Sourd offered a horrible picture. The dead and the wounded lay about in heaps. Pleading cries for help were directed toward us." Beyond Le Sourd, the fields had been set on fire by the artillery and were littered with abandoned machine guns and their dead crews. Not even a small wood offered protection, as it was repeatedly raked by French 75mm fire. "Bloody corpses rolled around on the ground." The heat was unbearable. Whenever the men spied even a dirty puddle of water in the clay soil, "they fell over it like a pack of wild animals." The wounded ran about in delirium, "wild eyed and foaming at the mouth." At the end of the day, 2d Guard Regiment was down to eight hundred men.[87]

The situation was critical. The French were tenaciously attacking Bülow's entire front. On the left flank, the Guard Corps was battling Defforges's X Corps east of Audigny. Unsurprisingly, Bülow hurriedly contacted Hausen's Third Army and requested that it attack the French "in the direction of Vervins" to relieve the pressure on Plettenberg's Guard Corps. Uncharacteristically, there was no ready reply from Hausen. In fact, Third Army was being hard-pressed by Dubois's IX Corps near Rethel. Moreover, the distance to Vervins was too great for Third Army to cover in a day. As well, Hausen allowed, his men were "extraordinarily impaired by the great heat on the waterless plateau of Château-Porcien."[88] There was nothing for Bülow and

Lauenstein to do but call in the last reserves: Kurt von dem Borne's 13th ID and Paul Fleck's 14th ID. Piecemeal, they fed their reserves into wherever the French threatened to break Second Army's front—at Audigny, at Le Mesnil, at Mont-d'Origny, at Sains-Richaumont.

By midafternoon, the crisis on Second Army's left flank had further intensified. Just after 1 PM Joffre, who had spent the morning with Lanrezac at Marle, released Fifth Army's iron reserve to be "engaged as circumstances best require in liaison with the 3rd and 10th Army Corps."[89] Finally unleashed, Franchet d'Espèrey did not disappoint. Believing both Hache and Defforges to have been beaten morally rather than physically, he pushed his forces in between III and X corps. What followed was grand theater. Mounted on a chestnut charger in the light of the setting sun, Franchet d'Espèrey ordered Alexandre Gallet's 1st ID, its bayonets fixed, colors unfurled, and bands playing "La Marseillaise," to sweep down the slope from Le Hérie against the German line. Obviously stirred by the sight, the men of III and X corps joined the attack. Only the onset of darkness prevented a systematic attempt to exploit the charge. Joffre had found a potential new army commander: "a man of energy and willpower."[90]

The western French front facing Saint-Quentin was dramatically less successful. Neither Hache nor de Mas-Latrie was cut from the same cloth as Franchet d'Espèrey. The more Hache clamored for reinforcements, the less inclined de Mas-Latrie was to press the attack against Saint-Quentin on the left flank of III Corps. And when German X Reserve Corps, commanded by Richard von Süsskind after Kirchbach had been wounded in a firefight, drove down the Oise against Justinien Lefèvre's 18th ID, de Mas-Latrie ordered a retreat. On his left flank, Einem's VII Corps at the same time crossed the Oise and chased Pierre Abonneau's 4th Reserve Division Group out of its positions between Choigny and Moy. Jules Champin, a soldier with French 36th IR, recalled the horror of the attack:

> German bullets whiz around my ears without stopping and shells fall on all sides, a bullet hits the ground just in front of me but doesn't touch me. . . . I noticed that I didn't have any more cartridges. When I asked my comrades who were 4–5 meters away, they didn't answer my calls. They were all dead.[91]

The assault on Saint-Quentin, the cornerstone of Joffre's grand design, had ended in failure.

As bloody 29 August came to a close, a depressed Bülow took stock of the situation. His center had held—but just barely. His right flank had chased Lanrezac's XVIII Corps and 4th Reserve Division Group from the field. But his left flank southeast of Guise gave cause for concern. A liaison officer from General von Plettenberg's headquarters reported around 8 PM that the Guard Corps had been stopped dead in its tracks by Defforges's X Corps and Franchet d'Espèrey's dramatic sunset charge; that its front was overextended to a width of eighteen kilometers; that it most likely would not be able to resume the attack the next day; and that in case of another French attack, it would have to fall back behind the river. Not prepared to have the kaiser's Guard Corps "totally bled to death" on the banks of the Oise, Bülow gave Plettenberg freedom of action, including the option of a full withdrawal.[92]

Bülow then turned his attention to a gift from the gods: That night at Mont-d'Origny, several precious documents had been taken from Colonel Gédéon Geismar, the captured chief of staff of III Corps— among them, Lanrezac's attack orders to his corps commanders. Bülow and Lauenstein were now fully informed. Whereas they had suspected that "at most 5 corps" had attacked Second Army that day, in truth the French had thrown thirteen divisions into the battle—against just six and one-half German divisions. More, the captured papers showed that Saint-Quentin was the main object of the French drive, and thus Plettenberg and the Guard Corps were not in danger of a renewed attack the next morning.[93]

In fact, the next day, 30 August, was anticlimactic. Bülow renewed the offensive into the triangle of the Oise. From Second Army headquarters at Homblières, he drove X Corps, Guard Corps, and X Reserve Corps forward with exhortations to "advance soon and energetically." By noon, Chief of Staff von Lauenstein was sure of victory. The Battle of Saint-Quentin, he wrote his wife, had taken a sudden and surprising turn in the last twelve hours. "I was certain of the issue around 12 o'clock noon." Bülow concurred. "Now the matter has been decided." He hailed his advancing troops, "Great victory! French totally defeated!" The "moral capacity to resist" of the French army, Lauenstein crowed, "apparently" had been "broken." German fliers reported large columns of French soldiers falling back on Crécy-sur-Serre and Laon. Lauenstein rose to giddy heights. "Our offensive surpasses even Napoleonic dimensions. If only Schlieffen could have witnessed this."[94] At 3:45 PM, Bülow issued his Order of the Day: "The enemy has been defeated along the entire front in the three-day [*sic*] Battle of Saint-Quentin."[95]

Lanrezac, fearing that German Third and First armies might join the battle in a pincer move against Fifth Army's flanks, at 5 PM on 31 August ordered his "fatigued" corps commanders to retreat south behind the Aisne River.[96] Three hours later, Joffre approved Lanrezac's request to break contact (lest his army be "captured," as Lanrezac put it to GQG) and to withdraw forty kilometers to a new line running from Compiègne to Soissons to Reims.[97]

Guise/Saint-Quentin had turned into another German tactical victory, albeit another bloody one. Lanrezac had failed to take advantage of Fifth Army's numerical superiority over German Second Army. He had held back Franchet d'Espèrey's I Corps for much of the day and had engaged it only after Hache's III and Defforges's X corps had been driven to the point of defeat. He had left Abonneau's cavalry and Boutegourd's 51st RID (up from Dinant) virtually idle on his right wing. Above all, he had failed to detect and then to exploit the fifty-kilometer gap that had developed between Bülow's left and Hausen's right—that is, to press home a devastating attack on the left wing of Plettenberg's battered Guard Corps on the morning of 30 August.[98] Historians who speak of Lanrezac's "unwilling victory" are off the mark.[99]

As great as Lanrezac's failings were, they paled compared with those of Bülow. For a second time (since Charleroi), he had blunted an attack by French Fifth Army. For a second time, he had driven that force back with heavy losses. And for a second time, he had an opportunity to pursue and perhaps finish off Fifth Army. As commander of both First and Second armies and with Third Army at his beck and call, he was well positioned to close the vise on Lanrezac: Kluck to drive against Fifth Army's left flank from the west, Hausen against its right flank from the east, and his Second Army against its rear from the north.

Bülow did nothing of the kind. Instead, he spent the afternoon of 30 August spreading the news of his victory. Kluck was first on the list. "Today 2 Army has decisively defeated the enemy. Large formations fell back on La Fère." Moltke was next: "Today, the second day of the Battle of St. Quentin, complete victory. French [forces] comprising four army corps and three divisions in full retreat." Hausen was last: "Major French forces decisively defeated in two-day Battle of St. Quentin and hurled back on La Fère and east [of there]."[100] More, instead of immediately ordering a potentially fatal pursuit of the "decisively defeated" French Fifth Army, Bülow let his troops rest the next day, 31 August, as well. Field kitchens arrived to serve the half-starved troops from steaming vats of soup with meat, potatoes, cabbage or beans, and roots or rice. Nearly six thousand soldiers needed medical attention or burial. Almost as an afterthought, Bülow nonchalantly suggested that First Army change direction and advance along the line La Fère–Laon and "fully exploit" Second Army's tactical victory. The Germans' second potential "climacteric" of the war had been squandered.

CHAPTER SEVEN

TO THE MARNE

It is essential for a general to be tranquil and obscure,
upright and self-disciplined. . . . He alters his management
of affairs and changes his strategies. . . . He shifts his
position and traverses indirect routes to keep other people
from being able to anticipate him.

—SUN-TZU

D ESPITE KARL VON BÜLOW'S FAILURE TO EXPLOIT HIS "TOTAL victory" at Saint-Quentin, Army Supreme Command (OHL) had every reason to believe that the campaign in the west had been won by late August. For nearly three weeks, its armies had steadily advanced, had blunted every enemy offensive, and had driven Joseph Joffre's armies ever deeper into France. From Nancy to Verdun, Namur to Charleroi, Guise to Saint-Quentin, and Mons to Le Cateau, the enemy seemed on the verge of collapse. Only "occupation measures," the OHL informed Fritz Nieser, Baden's military plenipotentiary to Imperial Headquarters, remained. On the morning of 4 September, advance guards of Second Army happily passed a road sign, PARIS 121 KM; by afternoon, another sign read, PARIS 95 KM.[1]

The opposing headquarters took time to reassess the flow of the campaign after Guise/Saint-Quentin. For Helmuth von Moltke, this meant setting in place a series of orders instructing his armies how to pursue the enemy and how to bring about the final, decisive victory. For Joseph Joffre, this meant a further falling-back toward Paris and frantic efforts to form up Michel-Joseph Maunoury's Sixth Army. And, of course, more dealings with the always difficult British.

—

SHORTLY AFTER NOON ON 28 August, having satisfied himself that Charles Lanrezac had the attack at Guise well under way, Joffre left Fifth Army headquarters at Marle. His driver, Georges Bouillot, sped him to Compiègne to confer with Field Marshal Sir John French.[2] As always, Joffre was concerned about his "fragile" left wing. If, Godspeed, Lanrezac advanced across the Oise against German Second Army, or if, God forbid, Bülow's infantry drove Fifth Army back on Laon, a serious gap would be created between Fifth Army and the British Expeditionary Force (BEF). More, if the latter continued to retreat, a second gap—between Fifth Army and Maunoury's nascent Sixth Army—would also open up. In short, it was imperative that Sir John halt his precipitous retreat and return to the line.

French had no desire to do either. Despite Joffre's most flowery pleading and cajoling—something totally out of character for the usually phlegmatic generalissimo—the field marshal would buy into neither General Instruction No. 2 nor the new plan to stand along the line Compiègne-Soissons-Reims. "No, no, my troops need forty-eight hours of absolute rest," French insisted.[3] All the while, Chief of Staff Archibald Murray, having recovered from his "dead faint" at Le Cateau, urged his chief to remain firm about withdrawing and not to endorse Joffre's design.

Joffre left Compiègne disappointed and bitter, but not defeated. He decided to appeal to President Raymond Poincaré to exert political pressure on John French. The latter made his feelings clear in a letter to Secretary of State for War Horatio Herbert Lord Kitchener on 30 August. "My confidence in the ability of the leaders of the French Army to carry this campaign to a successful conclusion is fast waning, and this is my real reason for the decision I have taken to move the British forces so far back." His three "shattered" corps required time to rest and refit.[4] Privately, he allowed that they needed "ten days of quiet."[5] For the next two days, the BEF made it its business to be always one day's retreat farther back than French Fifth Army on its right and Sixth Army slowly being assembled near Paris on its left.

In fact, "Johnnie" French was fast retreating into the eye of a political storm. Joffre's appeal to Poincaré resulted in the president contacting Sir Francis Bertie, and asking St. James's envoy at Paris to forward

Poincaré's "imperative" plea for action by the BEF to the field marshal. "I refused," was French's lapidary comment.[6] Poincaré was livid. "Eight days, eight days! Before eight days [are up] will the Germans not be in Paris?"[7] At the War Office in London, Kitchener became alarmed that Sir John's refusal to fall into line with Joffre's new strategy and the continuing rapid retreat of the BEF could lead to defeat of the French left flank and therewith collapse of the entire front, if not also of the Entente. Before daybreak on 1 September, Kitchener, with the approval of the cabinet, was aboard a Royal Navy destroyer bound for France; he summoned French to meet him and Bertie at the British embassy in Paris. The field marshal took along "old Archie" Murray and Charles Huguet, the French representative at British headquarters (GHQ). Poincaré sent Premier René Viviani and the new minister of war, Alexandre Millerand, to what was fast shaping up as the first Anglo-French "summit."

Secretary Kitchener's arrival at the British embassy in his blue field marshal's uniform was as dramatic as it was unfortunate. The "super-sensitive" Sir John French "immediately took it as an insult. Was Kitchener, who did not outrank him, trying to pull rank?"[8] Not unexpectedly, the meeting quickly became "heated." Kitchener, according to Huguet, remained "calm, balanced, reflective, master of himself"; French, on the other hand, was "sour, impetuous, with congested face, sullen and ill-tempered in expression."[9] As the exchange between the two British field marshals grew in volume and intensity, Kitchener asked Sir John to join him in an adjoining room. There is no record of the conversation. None is needed. Kitchener later that night recapitulated their discussion in a letter to Field Marshal French, of which he sent Prime Minister Herbert Henry Asquith a copy for good measure. It was blunt.

> French's troops are now engaged in the fighting line, where he will remain conforming to the movements of the French Army. . . . By being in the fighting line you of course understand I mean dispositions of your troops in contact with, though possibly behind, the French as they were to-day. . . . [10]

There was no more talk by Sir John of a withdrawal south of Paris. He resumed his place in the Allied line. Kitchener returned to London.

At Vitry-le-François, Joffre, resplendent as ever in baggy red breeches and crumpled black tunic, put the finishing touches on General Instruction No. 4 that same day.[11] Lanrezac's Fifth Army and Fernand de Langle de Cary's Fourth Army were to withdraw another hundred kilometers to the Seine and Aube rivers, and Maunoury's Sixth Army was to be stood up northeast of Paris. Joffre politely rejected Sir John French's suggestion that the Allies hold along the Marne River, fearing that this would inhibit his freedom of maneuver. He furiously drove his Directorate of Railways to rush four infantry divisions from Alsace-Lorraine to face the German assault on Paris. For he well knew the state of fatigue of his soldiers along the Marne. During a tour of the front of Third and Fourth armies on 30 August, he had noted red trousers faded to the color of "pale brick," coats "ragged and torn," shoes "caked with mud," the soldiers' eyes "cavernous in faces dulled by exhaustion," and their faces dark with "many days' growth of beard." Twenty days of campaigning had aged them "as many years."[12]

As well, Joffre instructed the War Ministry to comb the depots and barracks of France for replacements for the 260,000 men killed, wounded, or ill at the front. It estimated the numbers to be large—a "minimum" of 300,000 infantry, 30,000 artillery, and 20,000 cavalry recruits—but it would be weeks before they could be sufficiently formed into units, equipped, trained, and deployed. The same was true for the draftees of the Class of 1914, which by the end of August amounted to 180,000 deemed fit for combat training. Already in late August, War Minister Adolphe Messimy had concluded that while "human resources" were "considerable," the difficulties in clothing and equipping new recruits were "considerable, but not insurmountable." However, the acute shortage of officers, especially for the infantry, remained *"le point délicat."*[13]

The frantic pace of Joffre's activities after the Battle of the Frontiers has been well documented.[14] Ably chauffeured by Bouillot, Joffre crisscrossed the French countryside. On 26 August, he met with French, Lanrezac, and Albert d'Amade at Saint-Quentin; on the twenty-eighth, he saw Lanrezac at Marle; on the twenty-ninth, he met with French at Compiègne and Henry Wilson at Reims; on the thirtieth, he was at Pierre Ruffey's Third Army headquarters at Varennes; on 3 September, he visited Lanrezac again, this time at Sézanne; and on the fifth he met yet again with Sir John French, at Melun, on the Seine River. Everywhere Joffre went, he inspected, he ordered, and he disposed, much like an eighteenth-century enlightened despot. And he fired—among the infantry, the commanders of two armies, nine corps, and thirty-three divisions; among the cavalry, one corps and five divisional commanders.[15] On 30 August, he fired Ruffey of Third Army and replaced him with Maurice Sarrail, until then VI Corps commander. Four days later, he parted company with Lanrezac, dismissing the "lion of the French army" with two curt sentences and placing him under the military governor of Paris. Not surprisingly, Louis Franchet d'Espèrey, the tough-minded commander of I Corps, took over Fifth Army. For the upcoming counterpunch against the three German armies approaching Paris, Joffre needed leaders "who have faith in their success" and who thereby knew "how to impose their will on their subordinates and dominate events."[16] The "short and square" Franchet d'Espèrey, with a head like a "howitzer," straight jaw, high cheekbones, and "dark piercing eyes,"[17] fit the bill.

THERE WERE NO SIGNS of such frenetic activity at German headquarters in Luxembourg. Once in possession of Bülow's pronouncement of "total victory" over Lanrezac's Fifth Army, Moltke and his staff by the evening of 30 August believed that they had a clear picture of the situation. Despite small gaps among First, Second, and Third armies, the entire right pivot wing, or *Schwenkungsflügel,* was on the march again. Everywhere, Moltke assured nervous leaders in the German state capitals, the enemy was "in full flight."[18] And when First Army the following day reported that it had swept all opposing forces from the field, Moltke's concerns about a flanking movement out of Fortress Paris vanished. As did a sudden panic attack when the British landed four battalions (three thousand men) of marine light infantry and artillery under Sir George Aston at Ostend on 27–28 August to secure the BEF's supply base there and possibly to harass Kluck's lines of communication. For they were reembarked within seventy-two hours when Sir John French moved his main supply base to Saint-Nazaire in the Bay of Biscay.[19] All the Germans found at Ostend was a trainload of dead horses, shot because there had been no ships on which to evacuate them.[20] Most critically, during the night of 30–31 August, Moltke received the welcome news that Eighth Army had shattered General A. V. Samsonov's Russian

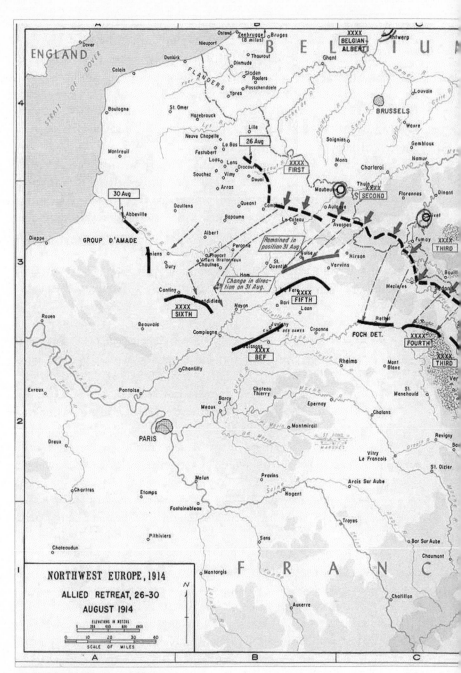

THE ALLIED RETREAT, 26–30 AUGUST 1914

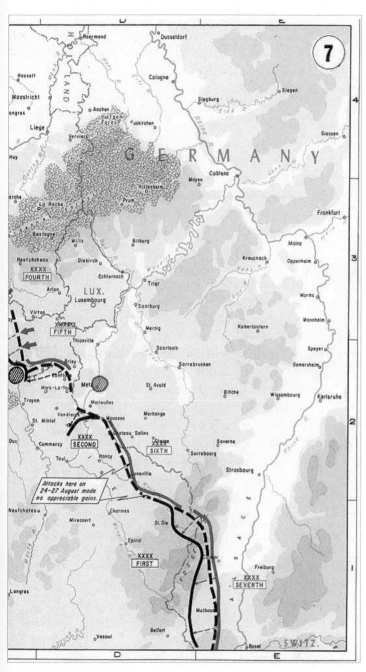

Attacks here on
24-27 August made
no appreciable gains.

Second Army at Tannenberg. Tales of Russian terror accompanied the news.* It was time to set all the major pieces in play for the final act in the great drama in the west.

Already by 30 August, Moltke and his chief of operations, Lieutenant Colonel Gerhard Tappen, were aware that the armies on the right wing were no longer advancing on a southwesterly course as originally prescribed, but rather more southerly. All thoughts of descending into the Lower Seine basin vanished. The immediate need now was to bring the movements of First and Second armies into concert with Third Army's slow advance along the line of the Aisne between Rethel and Semuy. Accordingly, the OHL directed Bülow to march on Reims and there to link up with Hausen's right flank. Bülow leisurely took La Fère, but halted his right wing at Marle.[21] Yet again, Moltke declined to give a direct order to his senior commander in the field to speed up the advance—all the while mumbling *"ordre—contre-ordre—désordre"*[†] before Tappen and his puzzled staff.[22]

The shift toward the south was reinforced on 1 September when Crown Prince Wilhelm's Fifth Army, straddling the Meuse River around Stenay, unexpectedly ran into a buzz saw. Was it a local attack? Or had Joffre mounted a major offensive out of the fortified region of Clermont-Dombasle-Verdun? German Fourth Army quickly provided the answer when it captured Langle de Cary's attack order: French Third and Fourth armies, in unison with Ferdinand Foch's special army detachment, had indeed launched a concerted counterattack against the center of the German line. Wilhelm's Fifth Army was in danger of being crushed on the Meuse—near the very place, Sedan, where forty-four years earlier Moltke's uncle had routed the Imperial Army of Napoleon III.

Moltke saw opportunity arising from the crown prince's predicament. He spied another chance at a Cannae and immediately ordered the right wing of Max von Hausen's Third Army to drive southeast from Château-Porcien across the Aisne, with Bülow's left wing to follow. All cavalry units within riding distance were "urgently urged" to attack the enemy "today, if possible."[23] If all went according to plan, Third, Fourth, and Fifth armies could crush Joffre's forces between

---

* The Reichsarchiv later set the total at 1,620 civilians killed or deported; 17,000 buildings torched; 135,000 horses, 200,000 pigs, and 250,000 cows slaughtered.
† "Order—counter-order—disorder."

Verdun and Reims. "There, in Moltke's estimation," Chief of the Military Cabinet Moriz von Lyncker noted in his diary, lies "the decision" in the war.[24] In a letter to his wife, Moltke noted the immediacy of the moment and the excitement of the possibility. "The center armies will engage today and tomorrow; it will be the decisive battle [of the campaign], on whose outcome incredibly much depends."[25] Throughout the morning of 1 September, he demanded "immediate, ruthless prosecution of the attack" southeast by Third and Fourth armies, for "today's success depends on this."

But Moltke was to be denied his Cannae as the French retreated more rapidly than his forces could advance. Shortly after 1:30 PM, Hausen reported that the enemy was rapidly withdrawing in great disorder to the Vesle River and that Third Army was "energetically" renewing its advance, "direction south." The small fortress of Givet had finally fallen to the Saxons. Duke Albrecht of Württemberg soon followed with similar news from Fourth Army headquarters, noting that "according to prisoner interrogations, dissolution is setting in among French troops." By 4 PM, even the erstwhile threatened Fifth Army informed the OHL that it had been victorious all along the line and that the adversary was "fleeing" the battlefield.[26]

Moltke was ecstatic. He had once more defeated the French. And on such a special day! That night, he wrote his wife: "Today, on the day of the Battle of Sedan [1870], we have once again achieved a great success against the French." The German official history of the war tartly noted: "And yet, basically nothing more had been achieved than that the enemy had once again escaped the hoped-for decisive blow by timely withdrawal."[27]

The fighting in the Ardennes remained vicious. The terrain was rocky and wooded. Artillery pounded poorly dug trenches. Bayonet attacks by both sides, accompanied by bloodcurdling yells, punctuated attack after attack. Eugen Röcker, a company commander fighting with Fourth Army "between Verdun and Reims," remembers the "hellish roar" of the French 75s as their shells whistled by and threw massive clumps of dirt through the air. A theology student at Tübingen University, Röcker screamed the words of Psalm 91★ above the din.[28]

★ "He will cover you with His wings; you will be safe in His care. . . . A thousand may fall dead beside you, ten thousand all around you, but you will not be harmed."

Despite the repeated proclamations of "decisive victories," the never-ending reports of "fleeing" French armies, and the hosannas that accompanied them at the OHL, there were doubters. One of these was Prussian war minister Erich von Falkenhayn. As early as 30 August, while visiting Sixth Army in Lorraine, he had expressed "doubts about the magnitude of successes to date." He then toured the fronts of the German center armies to gain firsthand knowledge of the course of the war. The "real war" stood in stark contrast with the news bulletins from the front. Early in September, after having inspected the right-wing armies, Falkenhayn grew even more apprehensive. What was being reported "is not a battle won; that is [a] planned withdrawal." There was no physical evidence of victory. "Show me the trophies or the prisoners of war," he viciously demanded of Moltke.[29]

While the chief of the General Staff rebuked the war minister for meddling in operational matters, privately he shared Falkenhayn's concerns. Although his armies had advanced to within ninety kilometers of Paris, Moltke confided his innermost fears to the banker Karl Helfferich. Somehow, the victories did not ring true. "We have had successes, but we have not yet won."[30] Victory, as Carl von Clausewitz had taught, "means the destruction of the opponent's strength to resist." And the French continued to "resist." As a young officer with 7th Grenadier Regiment, Moltke had experienced "decisive victory" and had seen "shattered armies" during the Franco-Prussian War of 1870–71 at Weißenburg, Wörth, and Sedan. In August 1914, there were too few captured guns, too few prisoners of war, he sadly noted. All signs seemed to indicate that the French were conducting an orderly retreat. "The hardest task is still ahead of us!" he warned Helfferich. But when Lieutenant Colonel Wilhelm von Dommes, chief of the General Staff's Political Section, suggested that "senior" members of the staff be dispatched to the fronts to gain personal insight into the overall situation, Moltke rejected this sensible idea. Neither his Supreme War Lord, Wilhelm II, nor his army commanders, he pathetically replied, "deserve such [a sign of] mistrust."[31]

NOT FORGOTTEN IN THE hectic drive "to the Marne" was the fact that the cherished Cannae might yet be achieved: on the German south wing, or *Südflügel*, in Lorraine. As early as 21 August, Moltke had sent Crown Prince Rupprecht and his chief of staff, Konrad Krafft von Dellmensingen, a General Directive for the further campaigns of Sixth and Seventh armies: "Pursue in the direction of Épinal." Krafft, who was doing his best to mount a full pursuit of the retreating French armies after the Battle of the Saar westward, was "thunderstruck" by this new order.[32] It made no sense to abandon that pursuit toward Nancy, to halt and reorganize the troops, and then to march them off in an almost straight southerly direction across the face of the French strongholds at Nancy and Lunéville. But Moltke was not impressed by this line of reasoning. Two days later, he informed Rupprecht and Krafft that if the French "continued to fall back," they were to charge after them "to the last breath of man a[nd] horse," to cross the Moselle between Toul and Épinal, and then to head for Neufchâteau, on the Meuse. He left the final mop-up of French forces to the discretion of the Bavarians: They could either break the right wing of Joffre's armies against the Swiss border or drive them into the waiting arms of German Fifth and Fourth armies in the Ardennes and the Argonne.[33] Chief of Operations Tappen was truly expansive. Such an offensive "in grand style" against the 100,000 to 120,000 French troops he believed still to be in the Vosges might even "end the war."[34] Indeed, visions of a gigantic Cannae—a double envelopment of the entire French army—now seduced the OHL. Might Joffre's forces not be crushed between German First and Second armies driving down from the north and Sixth and Seventh armies charging up from the south, while Third, Fourth, and Fifth armies "fixed" the rest of the French forces in the Ardennes and Argonne?

Such grand musings were rudely shattered just twenty-four hours after Rupprecht ordered Sixth Army to advance toward Charmes while Josias von Heeringen's Seventh Army encircled French forces from the north. For at 5 AM* on 25 August, Joffre's two armies in Lorraine mounted a counterattack toward the northeast from their positions south of the Meurthe River.[35] The initiative, won by Rupprecht in the Battle of the Saar, now returned to Joffre.

The Battle of the Trouée de Charmes (also known as the Battle of the Mortagne) was fought in rugged, hilly, wooded country crisscrossed by three major rivers—the Meurthe, the Mortagne, and the Moselle. The natural advantages all lay with the defenders, who, moreover, were familiar with the terrain from years of peacetime ma-

---

* French (GMT) time.

neuvers. Heavy fighting ensued for two days. The brunt of the attack by Édouard de Castelnau's XVI, XV, and XX corps of French Second Army fell on the Bavarian right wing (especially Oskar von Xylander's I Corps and Karl von Fasbender's I Reserve Corps). "Forward everywhere . . . *to the limit!*"[36] Castelnau admonished his corps commanders. Farther south, Yvon Dubail drove the two left corps of French First Army against Karl von Martini's Bavarian II Corps and Fritz von Below's Prussian XXI Corps around Serres, north of the Marne-Rhine Canal.

For a brief moment, Rupprecht's army was threatened with envelopment. A relief attempt by Ludwig von Gebsattel's Bavarian III Army Corps with 5th Infantry Division (ID) as well as 4th and 8th Ersatz divisions was rebuffed with heavy losses. Martini reported that many of his companies (normally 250) were down to thirty men, and that some infantry units of II Corps had sustained losses of up to 75 percent. Maximilian von Montgelas's 4th Bavarian ID was reduced to three thousand men, having lost almost nine thousand in the fighting in Lorraine. Bavarian 1st Infantry Regiment (IR) took a thousand casualties in two days. Only a heavy downpour on 26 August and the fact that French gunners routinely broke for lunch from 1 to 3 PM brought relief. At the height of the battle, Rupprecht learned that his eldest son, Luitpold, had died of infantile paralysis. That evening the OHL took away 8th Cavalry Division (CD) to beef up the front in East Prussia.

Fritz Burger, a deputy officer with Bavarian 1st Foot Artillery Regiment, noted the devastation around Blâmont on 27 August. "The broad, rolling countryside was a single sea of flames." Domèvre-sur-Vezouze, a small town of fifteen hundred inhabitants, was "completely reduced to ashes. . . . Left and right nothing but smoking ruins." The professor of art from Munich University mused: "Pompeii must have looked like this after the violent upheaval." War was truly hell. "The blood of those [francs-tireurs] shot after courts-martial still stuck to a wall on my right." Behind another smoldering ruin, he found the "bloody shirts and pants, knapsacks and rifles" of 190 French soldiers buried the day before. Once out of Domèvre, he came across "endless columns of wounded; wan, tired, sluggishly they moved along."[37] Major Rudolf von Xylander on Krafft's staff similarly was shocked by the devastation at Maixe. "It looked extremely horrific everywhere; the farmsteads burned down; in many fields the French [soldiers with their red pants] lay as if in a field of poppies; many just lay in the road; a great number of horses and a great deal of material laid about. It smells terrible."[38]

The Battle of the Trouée de Charmes ended in a bloody draw on 28 August.[39] Thereafter, the front in Lorraine stabilized for almost a week. While Joffre used the relative calm to transfer more units— Georges Levillain's 6th CD and Louis Comby's 37th ID—to buttress his left wing around Paris, Moltke and Tappen devised a new plan for the Bavarian army. It was now to abandon the breakthrough in the direction of Neufchâteau and instead to reduce *la position de Nancy,* a heavily fortified belt of fortresses, woods, and heights that surrounded the capital of 120,000 inhabitants of the Meurthe-et-Moselle.

The change in plans had been occasioned in part by Tappen's "displeasure" that Sixth Army had not already driven through the Charmes Gap.[40] Moltke also poured out his venom over the putative "inactivity" of the Bavarians. "You visited Sixth Army," he shot at General Karl von Wenninger on 30 August. "When will it finally attack?" Bavaria's military plenipotentiary had indeed just returned from a tour of the front and had been deeply shaken by what he had seen: "burned-down villages, overturned wagons, dead horses, fresh graves." The countryside was a wasteland of "still smoking, at times still burning ruins where there once were villages, animal corpses, wounded horses with deadly-sad eyes aimlessly wandering, the air filled with burning sweet smells" of the flesh of men and horses. Wenninger reminded Moltke that Rupprecht's soldiers had suffered greatly during nineteen days of consecutive combat against an enemy "double our strength." It elicited no sympathy. "That is also the case with other armies a[nd] still they attack!" Moltke snapped back. Growing more agitated by the minute, he accused the Bavarians of having used improper tactics. "Sixth Army's losses all too often were unnecessary; the corps simply ran into art[illery] fire—that must come to an end!"[41]

Moltke chose not to inform Wenninger that he had dispatched yet another emissary, Major Max Bauer, to Bavarian headquarters that very day. Bauer, strongly hinting that he was acting on Moltke's behalf, came up with another grand scheme. After storming *la position de Nancy,* Sixth and Seventh armies were "'simply' to pass through Charmes Gap" between Toul and Épinal, strike the French flank, and "drive the remainder of the Army of the Vosges into the arms of the

German Fifth Army" around Verdun. In this way, Bauer assured the Bavarians, they would "bring about the decision" in the war.[42] Flabbergasted by yet a further radical change in plans by the OHL, Krafft queried Bauer, Moltke's expert on artillery, as to how long it might take to reduce the fortifications at Nancy. "Oh well, after our experiences at Liège and Namur you should be able to reduce them within 3 days."[43] Bauer promised Rupprecht the remaining 150mm field artillery from the fortresses of Metz, Strasbourg, Germersheim, and Mainz. But since there were no draft horses available for transport, General Otto Kreppel, commander, Bavarian Field Artillery, had to secure railways to move the heavy batteries and twenty-six trains of shells to Nancy. Rupprecht sadly recorded that the Bavarian army had lost three hundred officers and ten thousand men by the end of August 1914.[44]

While Rupprecht and Krafft drafted plans for Bauer's small Cannae in the south, Major von Xylander just happened to be in Luxembourg. There, he learned "purely by accident" that the OHL no longer had "any desire" to take *la position de Nancy*. Lieutenant Colonel Tappen confirmed the rumor and added that Sixth and Seventh armies were just to "fix" French forces in equal numbers in Lorraine. Hardly had Xylander caught his breath than Deputy Chief of the General Staff Hermann von Stein let it be known that he expected the Bavarians "merely" to attack the "Bayon bridgehead" on the Moselle River, halfway between Nancy and Épinal to the south. Perhaps as early as "tomorrow."[45]

It was pure Alice in Wonderland. What was it to be? Reduction of the Nancy salient? The drive through the Charmes Gap? The attack on the Bayon bridgehead? Or all of the above? Rupprecht took matters into his own hands: On 31 August, he decided as theater commander and as scion of a royal house that he had no choice but to follow Wilhelm II's order to storm the Grand Couronné de Nancy, the natural three-hundred-meter-high protective ridge that extended from the German border to northeast of Nancy.

Krafft von Dellmensingen immediately did what any other good chief of staff would have done: He drove to Luxembourg to run Rupprecht's decision by the OHL. He found the mood there downright ebullient. Tappen led off. "Everywhere the enemy is retreating. . . . The entire western wing is advancing with greatest marching effort."

Kaiser Wilhelm II

THE GERMANS

Helmuth von Moltke, German chief of the general staff

General Alexander von Kluck, chief of staff, German 1st Army (center) with staff. General von Kuhl is on his right.

Erich Ludendorff,
deputy chief of staff,
German 2nd Army

General Karl von Bülow,
German 2nd Army

THE FRENCH

Raymond Poincaré,
president of France

General Ferdinand Foch,
French 9th Army

General Édouard de Castelnau,
French 2nd Army

THE FRENCH

General Joseph Joffre, French chief of general staff

General Fernand de Langle de Cary, French 4th Army (center). Joffre is at left.

General Charles Lanrezac, commander French 5th Army

THE FRENCH

General Auguste Yvon Edmond Dubail, French 1st Army

Joseph Galliéni, governor
of Fortress Paris

General
Michel-Joseph Maunoury

General Maurice Sarrail,
French 3rd Army

H. H. Asquith, prime minister of the United Kingdom

Horatio Herbert
Lord Kitchener,
secretary of state
for war, Great Britain
(center)

A recruiting
poster featuring
Lord Kitchener's
image

THE BRITISH

Field Marshal John French,
commander-in-chief,
British Expeditionary Force

Field Marshal Douglas Haig

Field Marshal Sir Henry Wilson, British deputy chief of staff

General Sir Horace Smith-Dorrien, British II Corps

Fort Loncin, Liège, Belgium, November 1918

The library at Louvain

He envied the men of First and Second armies. "Those people are conducting a promenade around France!" There would be "no holding along the Marne," he assured Krafft. The French would be herded off in a southeasterly direction and "driven against the Swiss border."[46] There was no need even to contemplate shuttling forces to northern France, Tappen concluded, as the right wing sweeping toward Paris would bring its crushing might to bear in a few days, perhaps even the very next day![47]

At noon on 1 September, Crown Prince Rupprecht called a meeting of his chief of staff and corps commanders. Krafft von Dellmensingen, as usual, favored offensive operations. La position de Nancy needed to be taken immediately so that Sixth Army could then break through the Charmes Gap and roll up the flank of the French forces facing Fifth and Fourth armies. To recall the heavy artillery being hauled up to the front would constitute "a definitive admission of defeat."[48] Oskar von Xylander spoke against Krafft. His I Corps had been badly battered in the advance on Nancy, and he feared that a "drawn-out, costly" siege could lead to the "disintegration" of his corps. The "only viable course was to withdraw."[49] Karl von Martini of II Corps was at the front and sent his chief of staff, Lieutenant Colonel Franz Stängl, in his stead. Stängl led off with a litany of problems: The corps had sustained heavy losses, especially among the infantry; it lacked heavy artillery; its front was spread too thin and in danger of cracking under a sustained counterattack. Krafft craftily agreed. But the attack had been ordered by the OHL, he noted, and there was nothing he could do about that.[50] The II Corps would just have to mount one final Herculean effort. Ludwig von Gebsattel of III Corps had "vainly" spoken the past week of "making Nancy a present" for King Ludwig III, but he now favored delaying the assault until his corps could be properly concentrated and the heavy artillery promised by Major Bauer was in place.[51] Rupprecht, who considered the assault—especially on the Grand Couronné guarding Nancy—to constitute "an irresponsible, difficult undertaking," readily took up Gebsattel's notion of a delay. The crown prince confided to his war diary that he and Krafft had undergone a "test of nerves" and had both "lost their patience" at the meeting.[52]

The attacks on Bayon and the charge through the Trouée de Charmes were canceled. The great host of 272 guns was to be assembled before the Grand Couronné. The attack was set for the night of 4–5 September. Gebsattel's Bavarian III Corps, which had largely been spared the fighting around Nancy and thus denied battle honors,[53] would spearhead the assault.

"NEVER DO WHAT THE enemy wants for the very reason that he wants it," the great Napoleon had counseled a century before. "Avoid a battle-ground that he has reconnoitered and studied, and with even more reason ground that he has fortified and where he is entrenched."[54] As is often the case, sound advice grounded in solid history was ignored. The Grand Couronné northeast of Nancy constitutes a plateau scarp that in the north is a mere ridge broken by buttes and mesas, but that near Nancy becomes wider and forms "an eastward projecting bastion measuring half a dozen miles from the [Moselle] to its apex." The entire plateau of the Grand Couronné is "breached by transverse stream valleys"[55] and erosion gaps. Attacking infantry from the north and northeast would have to batter their way across the plateau to assault Nancy. Key to the French defenders was the so-called Pont-à-Mousson Gateway, a broad opening in the Grand Couronné that cut the plateau east to the Moselle. It was protected by two pillars: the Mousson butte, to the north, and the Sainte-Geneviève Plateau, to the south.

As well, the French had carefully prepared the defenses around Nancy—and especially on the ridges of the Grand Couronné. It was one of the many ironies of the war that this work had been ordered by Foch, the apostle of the all-out offensive, after he assumed command of XX Corps at Nancy in August 1913. The French had left Nancy unfortified because it projected dangerously in front of the line of forts they had constructed in the 1880s through Toul, Épinal, and Belfort. Foch obviously thought Nancy worth saving from attack.

Specifically, Foch's engineers had extended the defensive works three kilometers out to the heights of Malzéville. They had studded every approach to the escarpment with forts, artillery, machine guns, and barbed wire. They had dug deep trenches across roads and rail beds to slow the enemy advance. They had calibrated every piece of ground for the heavy Rimailho artillery as well as the *soixante-quinzes*. They had concealed much of this firepower in the ravines that dissected the Grand Couronné. Even geography had played into their hands. To the north of Nancy, 150- to 200-meter-high ridges shot straight up from the western banks of both the Meurthe and Moselle rivers, offering defenders a natural bulwark. The fallback position west of Nancy across the Moselle trench was even more formidable: The high plateau of the Forest of Haye in the angle formed by the Meurthe and the Moselle bristled with artillery emplacements and concrete forts. In between lay three water obstacles: the Mortagne River, 8 to 15 meters wide and 1.2 meters deep; the Moselle, 70 to 100 meters wide and between 0.60 and 1.50 meters deep; and the Canal de l'Est, 18 to 22 meters wide and 2.2 meters deep. All three would have to be crossed by the Bavarians after they had seized Nancy.[56]

French units, refreshed after the Battle of the Trouée de Charmes, were assigned positions around Nancy for the expected German assault.[57] Castelnau deployed four corps of Second Army on the heights north and northeast of the city, with Jean Kopp's 59th Reserve Infantry Division (RID) at Sainte-Geneviève and Émile Fayolle's 70th RID at Amance. He then sited half of Pierre Dubois's IX Corps southeast of Nancy behind the Meurthe: Émile Brun d'Aubignosc's 68th RID at Saffais, Louis Espinasse's XV Corps at Haussonville behind the Mortagne, and Louis Taverna's XVI Corps as well as Louis Bigot's 74th RID near Belchamp. Dubail placed Joseph de Castelli's VIII Corps east of the Forest of Charmes and César Alix's XIII Corps around Rambervillers. Léon Durand's Second Reserves Group (three divisions) was divided among the active units. Émile-Edmond Legrand-Girarde's XXI Corps was the last to arrive.[58]

But this formidable concentration was short-lived. Joffre was so confident of Nancy's defenses that between 31 August and 2 September, he continued to strip his forces there to bolster the front around Paris. Unit by unit, Second Army had to surrender Espinasse's XV Corps, three brigades of Dubois's IX Corps, Justinien Lefèvre's 18th ID, Camille Grellet de la Deyte's 10th CD, and a chasseur brigade. First Army entrained Legrand-Girarde's XXI Corps, bound for Paris.[59] It now consisted mainly of Castelli's VIII Corps and Pierre Roques's XII Corps, 167,300 effectives and 5,400 sabers in all.[60] Joffre was no longer interested in tying down (*fixer*) German forces in Lorraine, but merely in making a stand (*durer*) east of Nancy.[61] By 4 August, Castelnau's Second Army consisted of Taverna's XVI Corps and Maurice Balfourier's XX Corps (nine infantry divisions), Foch's former unit, as well as the reserves (ten infantry divisions), roughly 120,500 soldiers as

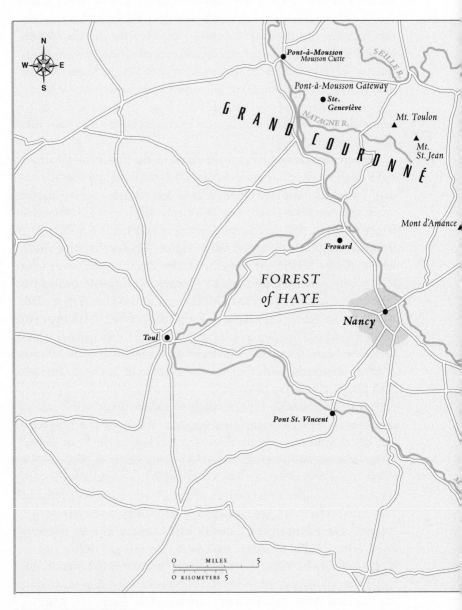

NANCY AND THE GRAND COURONNÉ

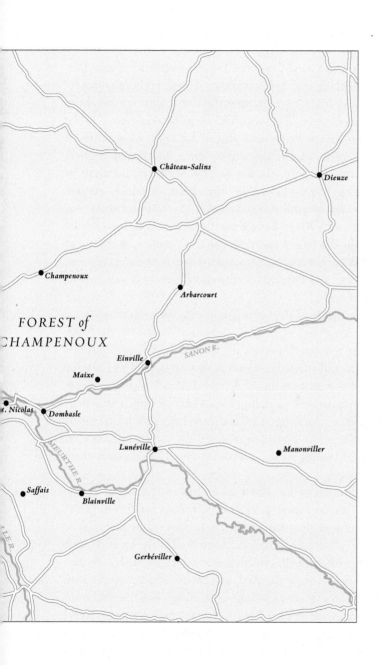

Château-Salins

Dieuze

Champenoux

Arbarcourt

FOREST of
CHAMPENOUX

Einville

SANON R.

Maixe

t. Nicolas

Dombasle

MEURTHE R.

Lunéville

Manonviller

Saffais

Blainville

ER.

Gerbéviller

well as 3,800 cavalrymen and 536 pieces of artillery.[62] Still, Second Army alone was superior to the attacking Bavarian Sixth Army.

THE ASSAULT ON THE Grand Couronné began a day ahead of schedule, in the heavy, humid night of 3–4 September. The air pressure caused by the massive artillery barrage was so powerful that it blew out the doors at Bavarian I, II, I Reserve, XIV, and XXI corps headquarters.[63] In the morning, Crown Prince Rupprecht pushed his right wing north of Nancy along the Saffais Plateau and sent his left against Épinal. As well, he ordered Seventh Army to advance on Rambervillers, northeast of Épinal. Comprising mostly Landwehr formations, it quickly became bogged down in vicious hand-to-hand combat. Heavy fighting also ensued along the Meurthe River. But the main assault consisted of a frontal infantry attack on the Grand and Petit Mont d'Amance, northeast of Nancy, as well as Forts Saint-Nicolas-de-Port and Pont-Saint-Vincent, southeast of Nancy, and Frouard, northwest of Nancy. It was now or never on the *Südflügel*.

The desperate nature of the fighting immediately became apparent. At Mandray, a village ten kilometers southeast of Saint-Dié, the battle raged from house to house.[64] French artillery on the Grand Couronné poured fire on the tight German waves as they attempted to cross the plains below. Chasseurs ferociously defended Mandray at every corner, finally retiring on the church. The soldiers of Eugen von Benzino's Ersatz division blew open its barricaded door. With trumpets sounding the charge, the Bavarians stormed the sanctuary. They set the wooden stairs leading to the steeple on fire. The chasseurs there never had a chance.

At Maixe, a hamlet of five hundred people on the Marne-Rhine Canal, German reserves took a terrible pounding for fifteen hours from well-hidden French artillery, accurately directed by fliers.[65] The Bavarian history of the war recorded, "Soon Hell broke loose. French heavy and light artillery shells whistled over our heads with their ear-shattering screams and their shrapnel, and the entire region was soon enveloped in a thick haze of smoke and dust." Even well-dug-in infantry companies were hit hard. "Human torsos and individual [body] parts flew through the air" from wagons that had been abandoned in the village square. "Everywhere there was horror and despair, death and perdition; everywhere, there were wild screams of pain and fear."

Horses, as if whipped, ran about in panic, taking with them wagons and artillery caissons. The wounded screamed horribly—and had to be abandoned.

On 4 September, Sixth Army concentrated its artillery fire on the front along the Meurthe between the Forest of Vitrimont and Courbesseaux, but could not drive the French out. The next day, Rupprecht's gunners shifted their fire to the area northeast of Nancy; roughly three thousand shells rained down on the Amance heights. Xylander's I Corps fired off a thousand howitzer rounds on 5 September. Day and night the deafening artillery duel continued. Wave after wave of gray-clad Bavarian infantry debouched from the Champenoux Forest under cover of darkness to storm the front of the Grand Couronné—only to be cut down by murderous cross fire from the French 75s concealed on reverse slopes of the Mont d'Amance mesa and the Pain de Sucre butte guarding the eastern and southern approaches to the Grand Couronné. Still, the future of *la position de Nancy* hung by a thread on the second day of Rupprecht's offensive.

Castelnau's earlier optimism evaporated. He feared a repetition of the Battle of the Saar—decimation of Second Army if it stubbornly clung to defending the Grand Couronné. Reports from Durand's reserve divisions and Balfourier's XX Corps revealed that Second Army, recently depleted by Joffre, could not long withstand the Bavarian assault. At 2:30 PM on 5 September, Castelnau telegraphed the Grand quartier général (GQG): "I cannot depend upon a prolonged resistance." He suggested a "timely withdrawal" behind the Meurthe and Moselle rivers, to the Forest of Haye or to the heights of Saffais and Belchamp—and perhaps even beyond.[66]

Joffre was not amused. Unlike his German counterpart, he never lost sight of the overall campaign and never gave in to momentary situations, no matter how dire they appeared. Thus, he began his *"très urgent"* epistle to Castelnau at 1:10 PM on 6 September with a lecture on strategy. "The principal mass of our forces is engaged in a general battle [along the Marne] in which the Second Army, too remote from the scene of operations, cannot take part." If Second Army suddenly retreated to the line Belfort-Épinal, the two French armies in Lorraine would be separated from each other and defeated piecemeal. If First Army joined Castelnau's retreat, all of Franche Comté, along with its capital, Besançon, and the major fortress Belfort, would be lost and the right wing threatened with envelopment and annihilation. Joffre deemed it "preferable" that Castelnau maintained his "present position" at Nancy "pending the outcome of this battle."[67] The "little monk in boots" well understood the understated meaning of the term *préférable*. Incredibly, after the war he would claim that he had heroically resisted Joffre's "order" to abandon Nancy. It became another legend of the Battle of the Marne.

Castelnau dug in. The French right in the area of Rehainviller-Gerbéviller held firm, staunchly defended by Taverna's XVI Corps and Espinasse's XV Corps, shattered earlier at Sarrebourg, as well as by Bigot's 74th RID and Charles Holender's 64th RID. The center and the left of the line from the Sânon River to the Forest of Champenoux saw the fiercest fighting, with outposts and villages frequently passing from one hand into the other.

The battle for Nancy reached its climax on 7 September. The Bavarians advanced out of the north from the Pont-à-Mousson Gateway and three times furiously stormed the north front of the Grand Couronné with flags unfurled and bands playing. The village of Sainte-Geneviève and the Mont Toulon ridge commanding the southern side of the gateway witnessed brutal bayonet charges throughout the night. If they could be taken, the way would be opened for the Bavarians to march up the Moselle to Nancy, storm the vital Mont d'Amance defensive works from the rear, and shatter the entire French defensive network on the Moselle Plateau.[68]

The German assault almost worked. Several units from 314th IR of General Kopp's French 59th RID accidentally abandoned Sainte-Geneviève, nicknamed the "Hole of Death" by its defenders.[69] But by 8 September, the French had retaken the village, thanks in large measure to the gallant counterattacks of Balfourier's XX Corps and the fact that the Bavarians had not detected the French withdrawal. More than eighty-two hundred German dead littered the battlefield; Baden XIV Corps suffered ten thousand casualties. The forests around Nancy had seen desperate bayonet charges. At one place, in the dark of night two Bavarian soldiers of Gebsattel's III Corps had bayoneted each other; next morning a patrol found their bodies thus "nailed" to two trees.[70]

General von Gebsattel had finally experienced the battle he'd yearned for so desperately. It was not at all the glorious venture that he had imagined. His corps had advanced into an "undoubtedly cleverly

prepared battlefield" studded with "far-ranging French guns." Bavarian artillery had been unable to gain any "significant advantage" because its spotters could not detect the sources of hostile fire. Each
night, the enemy had moved its units from one "well prepared position
into another." His own infantry had been unable to close with the
French. "Everywhere trenches and advance guards and rear-echelon
reinforcements."[71] It was siege-style warfare at its worst.

Violent fighting also occurred in the Forest of Champenoux.
Kopp's 59th RID and d'Aubignosc's 68th RID were hard-pressed between its ridges. Rupprecht drove his troops on to encircle them.
Castelnau wavered again—in part no doubt enervated by the news that
his son had died in battle several days earlier at Morhange. Joffre called
to rally Second Army. "I will try to hold out where I am," Castelnau
responded. But the prospect was not bright. "I feel that my army will
be lost." He again suggested "retreating immediately behind the
Moselle." And again, Joffre demurred. "Do nothing of the kind. Wait
twenty-four hours. You do not know how things are going with the
enemy. He is probably no better off than you are." Joffre's Order of
the Day was blunt: "You must not abandon the Grand Couronné, and
I formally order you to hold your present positions."[72]

Again, Castelnau dug in. More, on 10 September, amid thunder
and rain, he ordered an "energetic" attack by 59th RID and 68th RID
in the Forest of Champenoux and on La Bouzule, northeast of Nancy,
by Taverna's XVI Corps eastward out of Belchamp against Lunéville,
and by Balfourier's XX Corps against Réméréville.[73] Ever so slowly,
French pressure began to take its toll. German artillery, bound to rail
beds due to the lack of draft animals, was too inflexible to support infantry charges. The French 75s, on the other hand, were highly mobile and able to move up with the infantry. By the next day, French
fliers reported the Germans abandoning Lunéville, leaving behind
huge stores of arms and ammunition as well as countless wounded
in field hospitals. Second Army pushed forward—into Fraimbois,
Réméréville, Nomeny, and Pont-à-Mousson. French cavalry rode virtually uncontested into Einville-au-Jard, Serres, and Morville-sur-
Seille. Dubail's First Army advanced northward into abandoned
ground. The line of the Meurthe had been secured and Nancy spared
occupation.[74] Castelnau was promoted *grand-officier de la Légion d'honneur* on 18 September 1914.

The Battle of the Grand Couronné was as great a defeat for the Germans as Morhange had been for the French. There would be no triumphant entry into Nancy. There would be no breakthrough across the Moselle. There would be no small Cannae between Toul and Belfort. Instead, the Germans had suffered their first true setback in 1914. And the butcher's bill was savage. While neither side cared (or dared) to publish official figures, several unit diaries allow at least a glimpse into the frightful slaughter. On 11 September, Bavarian 14th IR lost a thousand men while retreating. Over the past week, 10th IR had suffered 70 percent casualties and 13th IR, around 50 percent. The Forest of Fraimbois was littered with the corpses of half-starved men and horses.

On the German southern left flank, Adolf Wild von Hohenborn, commanding 30th Division, XV Army Corps, wrote his wife that his troops were also withdrawing. He was delighted at finally being able to leave what he called "the pigsty Épinal." The battlefield was littered with the dead, stripped of valuables and some even of clothing. "The woods are full of corpses," he wrote. "The French dead lie in their trenches [packed] like sardines. The smell is so putrid that at [Saint-] Benoît the French built a bonfire to burn their dead."[75]

WHAT HAD HAPPENED TO the German assault? It had hardly been a "complete vindication of German tactical doctrine and training," as a recent book on the Battle of the Frontiers claims.[76] Apart from the fact that Rupprecht and Krafft von Dellmensingen had ordered a frontal infantry attack against a heavily fortified city without days of preliminary artillery bombardment, other areas of the front had demanded the OHL's immediate attention. Already by the second day of the offensive against the Grand Couronné, rumors of British landings on the Continent caused panic in Luxembourg. Moltke decided at once to create a new northern army, to remove General von Heeringen from the south to command it, and to assign one corps each from Sixth Army (Xylander's I Corps) and Seventh Army (Bertold von Deimling's XV Corps) to the new formation. He ordered Rupprecht to dispatch Ernst von Heydebreck's 7th CD as well. To the horror of his royal superior, Heeringen released XV Corps without asking or even informing Rupprecht.[77] And when Lieutenant Colonel Tappen demanded the immediate transfer of two corps from Lorraine to east of Paris on 5 September, Krafft von

Dellmensingen became despondent. "For us, the entire matter is most unfortunate. If that occurs [removal of the two corps], we will never overcome this passivity."[78] Crown Prince Rupprecht once more lectured the OHL that any withdrawal from Nancy now would be "highly detrimental to the morale of the troops."[79]

Wilhelm II arrived at Bavarian headquarters at this critical moment. He assured Rupprecht that he would personally "inhibit" any withdrawal of forces from Sixth Army. More, the pressure on the French from German Fourth and Fifth armies to the north would make itself felt within two to three days, with the result that "the enemy will be forced to give up [the battle] along the line of the Mosel."[80] But Rupprecht had lost all confidence in the kaiser's role as Supreme War Lord. He was shocked by what he termed Wilhelm II's "crass dilettantism" and "deficient knowledge" of the situation at the front.[81]

Rupprecht received more bad news from an irate General Ludwig von Sieger, chief of field munitions, who had arrived at Dieuze on 6 September to put an end to what he considered to be Sixth Army's "wasteful" expenditure of shells. Sieger now threatened to remove some of Rupprecht's heavy artillery if the attack on Nancy continued to stall. Before leaving Luxembourg, Sieger had mean-spiritedly barked at the Bavarian military plenipotentiary: "If they refuse to attack they hardly need that many artillery pieces."[82] And when Sieger on 8 September diverted six munitions trains bound for Sixth Army to Fifth Army—that is, from the Bavarian to the Prussian crown prince—royal relations reached their nadir. Rupprecht, "extremely angry," threatened to resign. Krafft agreed that this was yet another example of "haughty, brutal and encroaching Prussianism,"[83] but pleaded for his chief to remain at his post, citing the devastating impact that such a step would have both at home and abroad. Rupprecht agreed—on condition that he get an accounting from the OHL.

Krafft von Dellmensingen knew that the action against Nancy had unraveled and that the Bavarians would be blamed for the failure. He therefore penned a lengthy memorandum for posterity. Therein, he stressed the issue of troop morale. "Abandonment of the attack is a heavy moral blow for which *we* will *not* take responsibility." He crowed that he had not "fallen" into Sieger's "trap" by having the Bavarians concede failure. "The OHL *all by itself* must shoulder the responsibility for the entire idiocy of this on-again and off-again with regard to besieging Nancy."[84] He deplored how much modern warfare had degenerated in just one month. "This trench- and siege war is horrible!"[85] It reminded Rupprecht of another conflict—the Russo-Japanese War (1904–05).

There remained one final act to be played out in the tragicomic opera that was Lorraine. Crown Prince Rupprecht traveled to Luxembourg to appeal his case to Moltke and Tappen. Neither was willing to order the heir of the Reich's second largest kingdom to break off the assault on Nancy. Instead, they simply steered him toward that decision by restricting his supply of artillery shells. Moltke slyly informed Rupprecht to his "great surprise" that he could "proceed with the attack"—just as long as he suspended all other offensives, that he used his ammunition sparingly, and that he agreed to return all heavy artillery within six to nine days.[86]

That very moment, without informing Rupprecht, the last of the OHL's emissaries was on his way to Sixth Army headquarters. Major Erich von Redern, Tappen's chief of staff, painted a bleak picture of the war for Krafft. Russian units from Archangel had arrived in Britain and were on their way to northern France. "Hindus from India" had landed in southern France and likewise were headed for the front. To combat them, the OHL needed to draw down its forces in Lorraine. "It would be preferable," Redern stated, for Sixth Army "to break off contact with the enemy east of the Mosel" and to "recall" those units. Some could be redeployed to secure the line Metz-Strasbourg; the rest would be sent north. "The operations" at Nancy, Redern allowed, "had reached a dead point."[87] Upper Alsace was to be evacuated so that the Rhine Valley could be held. Krafft had no option but to call off the attack on the Grand Couronné. And to send Bavarian I Corps up north as requested.

One can only imagine Rupprecht's bitterness when, upon his return from Luxembourg, Krafft apprised him of the gist of Redern's instructions. In an angry telephone call from Dieuze to Luxembourg, Rupprecht demanded to know which advice to follow, Redern's or Tappen's? This brought a final piece of obfuscation: Redern's directives were valid, but Rupprecht could continue the assault on Nancy![88] A disillusioned Rupprecht formally suspended operations against Nancy. "They have totally lost control of their nerves at the OHL," he noted in his war diary.[89] He then ordered the bridges over the Meurthe River and all rail and communications centers destroyed.

THE BATTLE OF THE Frontiers in Lorraine ended in bitter recriminations (that were to last through the postwar period). Moltke's staff convinced themselves that Sixth Army had allowed Joffre to "dupe it" into believing that far greater numbers of French forces opposed them than in actuality; that Sixth Army simply had lacked the will to advance; and that by his "inaction" Rupprecht had brought great stress to the armies north of him. "As punishment for this incompetence," the OHL decreed, "Sixth Army needed to be disbanded."[90]

The Bavarians rose to the occasion in kind. Krafft von Dellmensingen decried the lack of clear direction from the OHL in general, and from Tappen in particular. He repeated his earlier accusation that Tappen had been nothing more than a "cipher" whom Erich Ludendorff had chosen as his successor "to keep the seat warm" at the Second Section for his return.[91] General von Wenninger stuck a dagger in the heart of the federal structure of the German army when he spoke of the unfortunate "anti-Bavarian" *Kollegium* that dictated operations: Tappen was a Prussian, Hentsch a Saxon, and Groener a Württemberger.[92]

The price for the command chaos in Lorraine was bloody stalemate. It was paid by the troops. While there never was a precise calculation of losses for the German armies in Alsace and Lorraine, Bavarian army historian Karl Deuringer "guesstimated" total casualties for the infantry at 60 percent and those killed at 15 percent. Since the Germans deployed fifty infantry brigades (three hundred thousand soldiers) in the area of the most violent battles between Pont-à-Mousson and Markirch, Deuringer calculated sixty-six thousand men killed or wounded, with seventeen thousand paying the ultimate price.[93] Given the savage nature of the fighting, one can hardly expect French losses to have been less.[94]

The German army's official ten-day medical reports (*Sanitätsberichte*) bear out Deuringer's findings. For Sixth Army, they set the casualty figure for August at 34,598—almost the size of a fully mobilized army corps—and the number of dead at 11,476. For September, half of which Sixth Army spent in transit from Lorraine to Belgium, the casualty total remains high at 28,957 (including 6,687 killed).[95] Most of this is due to the intense fighting around the Grand Couronné. Surprisingly, given that it was half the strength of Rupprecht's Sixth Army, Heeringen's Seventh Army suffered equally in terms of raw numbers: 32,054 casualties (10,328 killed) in August and 31,887 (10,384 killed) in September. On a percentage basis, Heeringen's unit of "weekend warriors" lost 70 percent of its original mobilized strength killed or missing in August, compared with 50 percent for Rupprecht's regulars.[96]

The Battle of the Frontiers in Lorraine had been central to neither the German nor the French deployment plan. It had simply gathered momentum and taken on a life of its own, at one time absorbing almost one-third of the forces on either side. Joffre had spied a chance for a frontal breakthrough of the *Moselstellung* between Metz and Thionville, with hopes of thereafter rolling up the German left wing and falling into the flank of Wilhelm's Fifth Army around Verdun. When that offensive failed, Moltke, for his part, had sought a German breakthrough of the Trouée de Charmes between Toul and Épinal, with hopes of a follow-up drive north against French Third and Fourth armies east of Vitry-le-François. Both designs failed to reach their objectives, and by early September the front in Lorraine had degenerated into trench warfare. Both Rupprecht and Heeringen had been reassigned to command newly constituted armies in northern France and Belgium. The southern flank was divided into a host of third-rate army detachment commands. The main decision would have to come elsewhere.

THE INABILITIES OF CROWN Prince Rupprecht, Crown Prince Wilhelm, and Max von Hausen to achieve their small Cannaes, combined with Bülow's inexplicable failure to pursue Lanrezac's badly knocked Fifth Army after Saint-Quentin, shifted the German center of gravity back to its original axis: First Army driving on Paris. Neither Alexander von Kluck nor his chief of staff, Hermann von Kuhl, was in high spirits at the end of August. Although as a reward for Le Cateau, Moltke on 27 August had restored First Army's independence, Kluck and Kuhl resented Bülow's constant demands for accountability, his ceaseless cries for assistance, and his petty reminders to maintain contact on the flanks. Twice—at Mons and at Le Cateau—they had allowed the British to elude them. In disgust, Kuhl, fearing that First Army might be pulled apart in an endless pursuit, decided to let the BEF go wherever it wanted on its southwesterly trajectory.

But could the German right wing in general and First Army in particular still achieve the primary mission? Alfred von Schlieffen had demanded a ratio of 7:1 between the German right and left wings, and Moltke still one of 3:1. The reality at the end of August 1914 was that while the left flank in Alsace-Lorraine (Sixth and Seventh armies) had a strength of 331,597 men, the right flank in northern France (First and Second armies) had just 372,240, or about one corps more. What was now the German center in the Ardennes and the Argonne (Third, Fourth, and Fifth armies) was greatest at 474,050 soldiers.[97] With specific reference to the critical pivot wing, during the initial battles of the war the *Schwenkungsflügel* (First, Second, and Third armies) had enjoyed an advantage of 100 infantry battalions and 175 artillery batteries over French Fifth Army and the BEF; by the time it reached the Marne, that ratio had been reversed, with the French left wing (Ninth, Fifth, and Sixth armies) superior to the German right wing (First and Second armies, and half of Third Army) by 200 battalions of infantry and 190 batteries of artillery.[98]

More, First Army was no longer the "strike" force that it had been at the start of the campaign, when it had put 217,384 men and 748 guns in the field. By the end of the month, it had lost 2,863 killed or missing, 7,869 wounded, and 9,248 ill.[99] The large number in the latter category was due to heat exhaustion, sunstroke, foot sores, and hunger. Most corps were down to half of their full strength by early September. And the farther First Army advanced, the more its supplies lagged behind. By 4 September, its railhead at Chauny was 140 kilometers behind the fighting front. Its motor transport companies had been driven so hard that 60 percent of their wood-rimmed trucks had broken down by the time First Army reached the Marne. There were on hand far fewer than the 924 fodder wagons required to haul two million pounds of hay and oats daily to its eighty-four thousand horses.[100] And given that the German army had gone to war with its reserves (Landwehr and Ersatz) in the line, it would be weeks if not months before suitable replacements were ready to fill the manpower holes. Leaving II Corps to besiege Antwerp and VII Reserve Corps to invest Maubeuge had further reduced First Army's combat strength to just 174,000 "rifles."

The soldiers of First Army were spent: tired, hungry, thirsty, and wounded. They had marched five hundred kilometers, often as much as thirty or forty per day, in searing heat. They had fought major battles with the British as well as with French rear guards. "Our men are done up," one of Kluck's infantry commanders noted. "They stagger forward, their faces coated with dust, their uniforms in rags. They look like living scarecrows." They sang as they marched, mainly to keep from falling asleep. "They drink to excess but this drunkenness keeps them going."[101] Walter Bloem, a company commander with 12th Brandenburg Grenadiers, wrote likewise of his men.

> Unshaved, and scarcely washed at all for days . . . faces covered with a scrubbly beard, they look like prehistoric savages. Their coats were covered with dust and spattered with blood from bandaging the wounded, blackened with powder-smoke, and torn threadbare by thorns and barbed wire.[102]

All Kluck could offer them were more forced marches. Paris was but sixty kilometers away.

The closer the German "strike" armies approached Fortress Paris, the more critical it became to coordinate their advance. Nothing of the sort happened. In fact, silence descended over the German front. The OHL at Luxembourg did not receive a single communication from either First or Second army on 1 September. Nor did it receive any news from either unit on 2 September. All it knew was that the two armies had generally changed from a southwesterly to a southerly direction of pursuit.

Around suppertime on 1 September, Moltke had dashed off a terse note to Kluck: "What is your situation? Request immediate reply."[103] No reply. During the afternoon of 2 September, the OHL intercepted a message from Second Army to First Army, informing the latter that the enemy was "in full retreat behind the Marne and to the south," and that Bülow intended to push his advance guards to the Marne the next day. Planning at Luxembourg thus remained based on "suspicions" rather than facts. On the basis of these "suspicions," Moltke and Tappen on the evening of 2 September reached a basic decision: The war would have to be decided by concentrating the German armies for an envelopment of the "main French forces"[104] somewhere in the area between Paris and Verdun—the region of the Marne. At 8:30 PM on 2 September, Moltke sent out his General Directive: "Intention Army

Supreme Command to drive the French away from the capital in southeasterly direction. 1 Army is to follow 2 Army in echelon and to continue to protect the army's flank."[105] Paris was to be bypassed to the east.

Specifically, Sixth and Seventh armies would continue to tie down French First and Second armies in Alsace-Lorraine; Fifth and Fourth armies were to keep the pressure up on French Third and Fourth armies in the middle of Joffre's line; and Third Army was to advance in concert with Second Army's left wing against Foch's Special Army Detachment. The knockout blow now was to be delivered by Bülow's Second Army, which would race south of Paris, cut off French Fifth Army's line of retreat, and roll up the enemy armies west of the Argonne. First Army's new role was to follow Second Army in echelon and guard its right flank against a possible attack out of the west. Satisfied with his labors, Moltke assured members of the kaiser's entourage that "the steamroller in France is moving ahead unstoppable."[106]

Unsurprisingly, Kluck and Kuhl, headquartered at Louis XV's château at Compiègne, were not thrilled with this turn of events. Quite on their own, the two had crafted a new role for First Army. Fully appreciating that it was no longer sufficiently powerful to attempt the march around Paris, and seeing in Lanrezac's retreat from Guise/Saint-Quentin a splendid chance at last to strike an enemy army in the flank, they turned First Army toward the Oise River along the line Compiègne-Noyon. Once more, their corps commanders were well ahead of Kuhl's staff work. By the morning of 3 September, both Ewald von Lochow's III Corps and Ferdinand von Quast's IX Corps had reached the Marne; advance guards crossed the river at Nanteuil-le-Haudouin, Charly, and Château-Thierry. Friedrich Sixt von Arnim's IV Corps stood on the Aisne at Crouy. Alexander von Linsingen's II Corps and Hans von Gronau's IV Reserve Corps had advanced across the Oise between Chantilly and Compiègne.[107] Later that afternoon Kuhl, perhaps anticipating Moltke's directive for First Army to follow Bülow's Second Army "in echelon," issued orders formalizing the new advance due southeast. In fact, Bülow after his victory at Saint-Quentin on 30 August had suggested that very move.

While this "deviation" is generally depicted as a spur-of-the-moment "bolt out of the blue," new documents discovered after the fall of the German Democratic Republic in 1990 prove this not to have been the case. For Kuhl, then in the grade of major, had gamed just such a scenario in Case "Freytag II" as part of Schlieffen's "General Staff Ride West 1905."[108] In short, the march-by east of Paris had been a major component in the master's great design.

Kuhl was not worried about a possible French sortie out of the capital as long as the "phantom Paris" did not become "flesh and blood."[109] But just to be on the safe side, he dispatched Gronau's IV Reserve Corps to Nanteuil-le-Haudouin to guard First Army's right flank— where, according to the latest intelligence, the only enemy formation was the BEF beating a hasty retreat. Indeed, he was sufficiently unconcerned about the area north and northeast of Paris not to send aerial reconnaissance there.

At this critical point of the campaign, with million-man armies either in panicked retreat or in hot pursuit, intelligence was at a premium. Where was the enemy? In what strength? And, especially, on what route of march? The French, like Bülow during the night of the first day of the Battle of Guise/Saint-Quentin, now received a "dramatic windfall." An officer with German Guard Cavalry Division, apparently fresh from Kluck's headquarters, had been ambushed and killed in his car by soldiers of French 310th Infantry Regiment. His haversack contained a blood-smeared map bearing numbers and pencil lines. Commandant Girard, head of the Deuxième Bureau, was ecstatic. He at once deduced that the numbers referred to German First Army's corps and the pencil lines, their lines of advance. It was the intelligence breakthrough that Joffre needed. For it was now clear to him that Kluck had changed his course toward the southeast.[110]

Kluck and Kuhl, having made their momentous decision to turn southeast without any input from the OHL, Bülow, or Hausen, in the morning of 4 September finally conveyed their new course of action to Moltke. The rambling message was a strange mix of information, accusation, and self-justification. It began, "First Army requests information about the situation at other armies." The duumvirate then testily reminded Moltke that they had heard only "news of decisive victories followed on many occasions with pleas for assistance." That was aimed directly at Bülow. First Army had at all times provided the requested assistance, which had entailed "sustained heavy fighting and [long] marches," and in the process had "reached the limits of its capabilities." Quast's IX Corps alone had allowed Bülow to cross the Marne and to force the enemy to retreat. "Hope now to exploit that success." Kluck and Kuhl bluntly informed Moltke that they could not heed his General Directive of 2 September to follow Second Army "in echelon" if they were to stove in the left flank of French Fifth Army. They requested immediate reinforcement in the form of Hans von Beseler's III Reserve Corps (guarding Antwerp) and Hans von Zwehl's VII Reserve Corps (besieging Maubeuge). And they demanded at all times to be kept abreast of the action of the other German armies. It took an incredible sixteen hours for the six-part message to be drafted, typed in clear text, enciphered, and transmitted.[111] Was it purposeful obfuscation? Moltke chose not to reply to this stinging epistle.

Lost in all the excitement of the "march to the Marne" were several German reconnaissance reports of French troop movements. On 31 August, a flier from First Army reported "strong masses," which he estimated at one army corps, marching in a southerly direction toward Villers-Cotterêts; "various columns" heading south out of the Forest of Compiègne; and "about a division" leaving the Oise Valley for Senlis.[112] Three days later, just after Moltke and Tappen had sent out their General Directive for First Army to march by Paris on its eastern side, fliers from Maximilian von Laffert's XIX Corps of Saxon Third Army sent in detailed reports of French troop movements. One spied "marching columns of all weapons formations" heading south on the roads near Sainte-Menehould. "Suippes full of troops." French infantry was being entrained at railroad stations at Suippes, Somme-Suippe, Cuperly, and Saint-Hilaire-au-Temple. "One army corps" and eight troop trains ready to roll were spotted at Châlons-sur-Marne; another four troop trains at Mairy. A second flier reported seeing forty-two and a half kilometers of roads bursting with French troops en route to Châlons, Épernay, and Montmirail.[113] The next day, twenty-three kilometers of roads still bristled with *poilus* heading south toward Épernay. Obviously, these French movements would impact the coming battle in the Reims-Verdun sector of the front.

The reports by Saxon fliers were buttressed by other reports. At 11 AM and again at 8:45 PM on 3 September, Prussian fliers noted enemy movements at Dammartin-en-Goële and Villeron, northeast of Paris—heading in the general direction of Gronau's IV Reserve Corps of First Army. Kluck and Kuhl ignored them and ordered reconnaissance for 4 September only toward the south. One of the aircraft strayed offcourse, and at 5:30 PM on 4 September reported hostile formations marching northward from Épiais-lès-Louvres, just north of Paris. There was no way to warn Gronau as IV Reserve Corps was without radio communications.[114] At Luxembourg, the OHL dismissed these reports as merely pertaining to French rear guards (*Nachhut*).

During that same period, Linsingen's II Corps skirmished with troops of Frédéric Vautier's VII Corps—previously known to have been in Alsace—and Georg von der Marwitz's II Cavalry Corps with fresh forces from Céleste Déprez's 61st RID, François Ganeval's 62d RID, and d'Amade's Territorials. Kluck and Kuhl refused to acknowledge that the French were undertaking major troop transfers. Like Moltke, they argued that Linsingen and Marwitz had simply stumbled upon isolated French rear guards.

"The left wing of the main French forces"—read, Fifth Army— remained of "decisive importance" to Kluck and Kuhl. It was to be "pushed away from Paris" and "outflanked."[115] If all went according to plan, First Army would at the eleventh hour again become the hammer that would strike the left flank of the French armies as they were driven south by the other German armies. This grand vision of a right hook against French Third, Fourth, and Fifth armies blinded Kluck and Kuhl to the formation of Maunoury's Sixth Army on their right flank. Day after day, they drove II, IV, and III corps forward in frontal charges against Franchet d'Espèrey's Fifth Army, withdrawing behind the Marne, as well as against the three British army corps retreating from Creil and La Ferté-Milon. Day after day, the French and the British refused to accept a decisive battle. On 3 September, an advance guard of Pomeranian Grenadiers of Linsingen's II Corps had reported—rather optimistically—that they were just eighteen kilometers east of Paris. At dusk the next day, Kluck's flanking cover, IV Reserve Corps, made contact with French units at the Ourcq River.

CHAPTER EIGHT

CLIMAX: THE OURCQ

———

War is a series of catastrophes that results in a victory.

——GEORGES CLEMENCEAU

IN 1914, ROUGHLY ONE IN TEN FRENCHMEN LIVED IN PARIS. THE CITY proper covered 80 square kilometers; with the surrounding Department of the Seine, it extended to 480. Paris was one of the few major fortified capitals in Europe.[1] One ring of fourteen inner forts had withstood the German siege of 1870–71, and it had been augmented with an outer ring of twenty-five forts by 1890. Both were designed to protect Paris in case of an attack—or of a domestic uprising. As the distant roar of Alexander von Kluck's heavy artillery became ever more audible, the government of Premier René Viviani fell. President Raymond Poincaré was able to secure the newfound "sacred union" by way of a cabinet reshuffle that left Viviani as premier but brought Alexandre Millerand in as the new minister of war, replacing Adolphe Messimy. To Joffre's great delight, Millerand, the former moderate Socialist who had helped him pass the Three-Year Law in 1913, quickly rallied to defend the generalissimo's autocratic style of command in the face of the Chamber of Deputies' attempts to gain insight into military operations.

On 30 August, a German Taube aircraft dropped three bombs and some leaflets on the Quai de Valmy. By next day, a state of panic existed in the capital. The staff of the Ministry of War was instructed to send families to the countryside and then to depart for Tours.[2] The mail was already three days late, when it arrived at all. The Central Telegraph Office had been cut off from London. Most newspapers had stopped publishing. Grand hotels were being turned into hospitals. An exodus of perhaps a hundred thousand people was in full swing. Automobiles and cabs could be seen rushing people and their most precious belongings to the southern and western railway stations. There, they jostled for space with incoming French wounded and German prisoners of war. By noon, the Montparnasse Station was packed with ten thousand Parisians seeking to board trains for Rennes, Saint-Malo, and Brest. At the Invalides Station, usually reserved for the military, enough people had booked for Brittany to fill the trains for a week.

On 2 September, the forty-fourth anniversary of the Battle of Sedan (1870), the government left Paris for Bordeaux. In its absence, Parisians turned to a sixty-five-year-old former colonial soldier for succor. As the newly appointed military governor of Paris, General Joseph-Simon Galliéni commanded four territorial divisions and the 185th Territorial Brigade. Over the coming days, he received reinforcements in the form of a marine artillery brigade and 84th Territorial Division as well as 61st and 62d reserve infantry divisions (RID).[3] Chief of the General Staff Joseph Joffre, conceding the imminent danger to the capital, dispatched Michel-Joseph Maunoury's newly formed Sixth Army, soon to be augmented by IV Corps from Third Army, to Paris and placed it at the disposal of the military governor.[4]

Galliéni did not disappoint. In his first public proclamation, on 3 September, he promised to defend Paris "to the last extremity."[5] That morning, he called out military engineers and civilian laborers armed with axes and saws to cut down the undergrowth of brush and hedges that obscured the line of fire of the capital's 2,924 guns—ranging from massive 155mm siege guns to rapid-fire 75s.[6] They likewise demolished houses and sheds that Galliéni deemed to obstruct his artillery. Munitions depots were stocked with a thousand shells per heavy gun. Hospitals and penitentiaries were evacuated and readied for the anticipated flood of wounded men. Fire departments were put on alert. Grocery stores were filled for the expected siege with bread wheat for forty-three days, salt for twenty, and meat for twelve. Gas to produce electricity for three months was requisitioned from the countryside.[7] Pigeons were placed under state control in case telegraph and radio communications broke down. For three days, thousands of tons of concrete were poured and millions of meters of barbed wire strung for new defensive lines. Galliéni, who had fought at Sedan in 1870 and thereafter been interned in Germany, was determined that the enemy, should it take Paris, would find little of value: The bridges over the Seine River were to be blown up, and even the Eiffel Tower was to be reduced to scrap metal. Former Captain (now Lieutenant Colonel) Alfred Dreyfus joined the artillery.

All the while, cavalry scouts and pilots from both the French Armée de l'air and the British Royal Flying Corps kept Galliéni abreast of the German advance on Paris from Creil, Senlis, Clermont-sur-Oise, the Forest of Compiègne, and Soissons. Just after 8 AM on 3 September, British aviators spied "a great column" of German artillery and infantry advancing from Verberie to Senlis.[8] Later that afternoon, the news took a dramatic turn: Fliers reported massive columns of gray-clad enemy infantry—four corps in strength—that had suddenly shifted onto a southeasterly course toward Château-Thierry, Mareuil-sur-Ourcq, and Lizy-sur-Ourcq.[9] A single German corps stood between Kluck and Paris in echelon formation south of Chantilly. This could mean only one thing: Kluck was advancing into the gap between French Fifth Army and the British Expeditionary Force (BEF) around Montmirail, screened just by Louis Conneau's newly created cavalry corps. Joffre, apprised of this by Galliéni as he was moving his headquarters to Bar-sur-Aube, remained imperturbable: The French army would continue to follow his General Instruction No. 4 of 1 September, as amended the following day.[10]

Late in the night of 3 September, Galliéni, as *commandant des armées de Paris,* made a key decision: If Kluck continued on a southeasterly trajectory, he would rally all available troops in the Paris Entrenched Camp and strike First Army's exposed right flank.[11] The following morning, French aviators confirmed that Kluck continued to head southeast. Without awaiting formal orders from Joffre, Galliéni sent word to Maunoury's Sixth Army to be ready to march east by afternoon. He placed Antoine Drude's newly arrived Algerian 45th Infantry Division (ID) at Maunoury's disposal, raising Sixth Army (reinforced by 7 September with IV Army Corps from Maurice Sarrail's Third Army) to about 150,000 soldiers. Galliéni planned to assault the western flank of the German army that "seemed to be gliding past Paris behind the front."[12]

At Bar-sur-Aube, Joffre had independently arrived at the same operational concept. The Germans, in the words of historian Robert

Doughty, occupied a "deep concave line between Paris, the Seine, the Aube, and Verdun." If Joffre could draw them farther into the salient between Paris and Verdun, perhaps he could cut them off with an attack on the "neck" of that salient in the direction of Meaux by Galliéni's garrison forces and Maunoury's Sixth Army.[13] Since Meaux lay thirty kilometers east of Paris on the Marne River, Joffre's concept closely paralleled Galliéni's. Rivers of ink would later be spilled as to which man first arrived at the operational concept that would unleash the Battle of the Marne. In the end, the decision was Joffre's to make.[14]

All that remained was for Sir John French to join the attack. The BEF, about to be augmented by 6th ID from Ireland and 4th ID from Britain, had crossed the Marne on 3 September and had finally stopped just east of Paris and south of Meaux. As ever, Joffre was concerned over what he politely termed the "fragility" of his left wing. Others were more direct in their dealings with the British. Galliéni, with Maunoury in tow, tried personal diplomacy. The field marshal was not at British headquarters at Melun, but off with his corps commanders at the Marne. Nor was General Henry Wilson at Melun. All Galliéni could get was what has been described as a "tedious" three hours of "talk and argument" with Archibald Murray.[15] Referred to even by his friends as "super-disciplined and super-obedient," the BEF's chief of staff refused to undertake anything until his boss was back. Galliéni returned to Paris dejected—and convinced that Murray was incapable of seeing the great strategic opportunity at hand. "Old Archie" Murray, revealing *"une grande répugnance"* toward Galliéni,[16] continued the British retreat southwest behind the Grand Morin River. The BEF constituted just 3 percent of Allied forces and had lost twenty thousand men along with half of its artillery.

That same day, Sir John French was supposed to discuss the situation with the new commander of Fifth Army, Louis Franchet d'Espèrey, at Bray-sur-Seine. But the field marshal was still with his corps commanders. In his stead, he sent Wilson, who was always willing to accommodate the French. Franchet d'Espèrey and Wilson quickly found common ground. There should be a joint attack in the direction of Montmirail: Below the Marne, French Fifth Army would approach Kluck's First Army from the south and the BEF from the west; north of the river, French Sixth Army would march eastward toward Château-Thierry.[17] Wilson set two conditions: that Sixth Army cover the BEF's flank and that it mount an "energetic attack" north of Meaux. Franchet d'Espèrey concurred—a bold act for a man in charge of Fifth Army for barely twenty-four hours.

In the meantime, Joffre, having spent hours in solitude under a tall weeping ash in the courtyard of the school that served as his headquarters, penned his Instruction général No. 5. He ordered Maurice Sarrail's Third Army, Fernand de Langle de Cary's Fourth Army, and Ferdinand Foch's Special Army Detachment (now formally designated Ninth Army) to halt their retreat, stand their ground, and, if possible, be ready to join in a full Allied counterattack on 6 September.[18] On 4 September, over his favorite dinner of Brittany leg of lamb at the Château Le Jard, Joffre received the news for which he had been desperately waiting: a note from Franchet d'Espèrey promising "close and absolute co-operation" between Fifth Army and the BEF, and assurance that Fifth Army, although "not in brilliant condition" after its recent encounters with German Second Army, would reach the Ourcq River the next day. "If not, the British will not march."[19] Joffre after the war gave full credit to Franchet d'Espèrey: "It is he who made the Battle of the Marne possible."[20]

With that welcome news in hand, Joffre delighted his staff: "Then we can march!"[21] At ten o'clock that night, he put the finishing touches to Instruction général No. 6. It set out the basic operations plan for the Battle of the Marne, to begin on the morning of 7 September. Maunoury's Sixth Army was to cross the Ourcq "in the general direction of Château-Thierry"; the BEF was to "attack in the general direction of Montmirail"; Franchet d'Espèrey's Fifth Army was to advance "along the line Courtacon-Esternay-Sézanne"; and Foch's Ninth Army was to cover Fifth Army's right flank around the Saint-Gond Marshes.[22] At Galliéni's urging, Joffre moved the date for the attack up to 6 September—something that he would later regret.[23] In London, the foreign ministers of Britain, France, and Russia signed a declaration that none of their governments would conclude a separate peace with either Germany or Austria-Hungary.

The next morning, 5 September, Joffre apprised War Minister Millerand of the seriousness of the hour. The "strategic situation," he began, was "excellent." He could not "hope for better conditions" for the offensive. He was determined "to engage all our forces without stint and without reservation to achieve victory." But he also reminded the newly appointed minister that nothing was ever certain in war. "The struggle in which we are about to engage may have decisive results, but it may also have very serious consequences for the country in case of a reverse."[24]

Joffre's final thoughts, as always, were with the British. Would they, as Franchet d'Espèrey had assured him, actually "march"? Or would French and Murray yet again find a reason to continue the BEF's retreat? Joffre moved on two fronts. First, he appealed to the government for a second time to use diplomatic channels to get London to stiffen Sir John's resolve. Next, he raced off to British headquarters at the Château Vaux-le-Pénil, nearly two hundred kilometers away at Melun, to meet with French. It was a dangerous journey through country infested with enemy cavalry patrols. Arriving at Melun around 2 PM, Joffre made one last appeal for cooperation. It was high drama. He informed Sir John that the French army, down to the "last company," stood ready to attack the invader to save France. "It is in her name that I come to you to ask for British aid, and I urge it with all the power that is in me." Growing more agitated with every sentence, Joffre reminded the field marshal that now was the time to move; that the next twenty-four hours would be decisive; that the time for retreating was over; that no man was to yield even a foot of French soil; and that those who could (or would) not advance "were to die where they stood." He then moved from appeal to taunt. "I cannot believe that the British Army, in this supreme crisis, will refuse to do its part—history would judge its absence severely." Finally, banging his fist on the table in the little Louis XV salon, Joffre moved from taunt to challenge: "Monsieur, le Maréchal, the honour of England is at stake!"[25] His face flushed with emotion and tears welling in his eyes, Sir John stumbled in vain over a few phrases in French. He then turned to one of his officers and inelegantly blurted out, "Damn it, I can't explain. Tell him that all that men can do our fellows will do."[26] History records that Joffre, upon reaching his new headquarters at Châtillon-sur-Seine, hailed his staff with the words "Gentlemen, we will fight on the Marne." That is pure legend.

THREE GERMAN ARMIES ADVANCED into the 250-kilometer salient between "the horns of Paris and Verdun." By 5 September, the critical sector bristled with seven opposing armies. From east to west, Foch's Ninth Army (IX and XI corps) at Mailly-Sézanne fronted Max von Hausen's Third Army (XII and XIX corps, XII Reserve Corps) and the left wing of German Second Army; Franchet d'Espèrey's Fifth Army (XVIII, III, I, X corps), north of Provins, was up against the bulk of Karl von Bülow's Second Army (VII and X corps, Guard Corps, X Reserve Corps, Guard Reserve Corps) and the left flank of German First Army; French's BEF (I, II, III corps), well behind Joffre's line south of Coulommiers, fronted the center of Kluck's First Army (II, III, IX, IX corps, IV Reserve Corps); and Maunoury's Sixth Army (VII Corps, Brigade Lamaze, Brigade Chasseurs, 45th Division) as well as units of Sarrail's IV Corps were poised to advance out of Paris toward Meaux against Kluck's right flank—specifically, Hans von Gronau's IV Reserve Corps at Saint-Soupplets–Monthyon–Penchard.

Numerically, the Germans were inferior to the Allies at the critical point, the right wing. Kluck's First Army of 128 battalions of infantry and 748 guns was ranged against 191 battalions and 942 guns of French Sixth Army and the BEF; Bülow's Second Army and half of Hausen's Third Army with 134 battalions and 844 guns faced 268 battalions and 1,084 guns of French Fifth and Ninth armies.[27] It was a stark reversal from August 1914.

While Kluck's First Army moved toward the Ourcq River northeast of Paris, German Second and Third armies advanced on the Aisne and Vesle rivers. As he approached Fismes on the Vesle, Bülow found the countryside littered with abandoned artillery caissons, rifles, ammunition, and uniforms. Hausen reported that he was heading toward Suippes "after fleeing enemy." Bülow ordered "ruthless pursuit" of the "shaken adversary" to the Marne. The French were to be "attacked without delay wherever [they] stood."[28] En route, Reims would be asked to surrender; if it refused, it was to be reduced "while sparing its cathedral."[29]

The German attack on Reims laid bare in microcosm Chief of the General Staff Helmuth von Moltke's failure to coordinate his armies. On the afternoon of 3 September, Hausen ordered Hans von Kirchbach's Saxon XII Reserve Corps to execute a bold strike (*Handstreich*) on Reims. Kirchbach decided on a nighttime attack by Alexander von Larisch's 23d RID. It totally surprised the city's garrison: 45th Reserve Brigade seized Fort Witry and 46th Brigade, Forts Nogent l'Abbesse

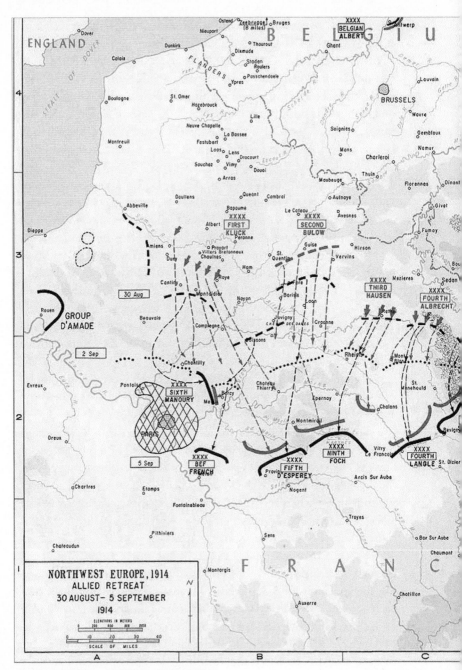

THE ALLIED RETREAT, 30 AUGUST–5 SEPTEMBER 1914

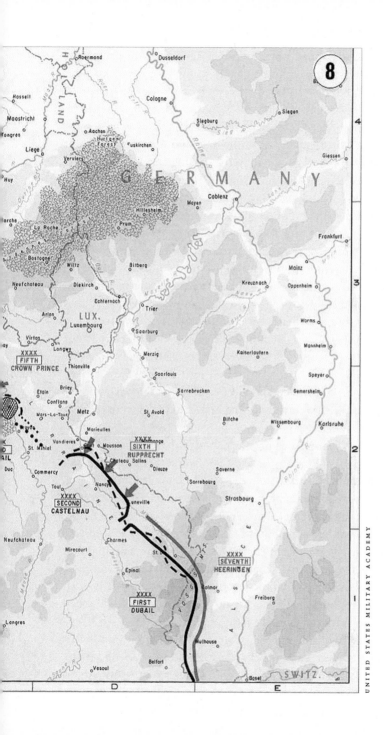

and La Pompelle, without firing a shot. A cavalry patrol penetrated into the heart of Reims. At midnight, Kirchbach informed Hausen, "Reims in the hands of XII Reserve Corps."[30]

Then, the totally unexpected: At 6:30 AM* the next day, Kirch- bach's units came under heavy artillery fire—from Karl von Pletten- berg's 2d Guard Division (GD) of Bülow's Second Army! Once again, communications had broken down. In the ensuing chaos, in which the Guard over forty-five minutes fired some 170 shells into the city, forty civilians were killed and the Notre-Dame de Reims Cathedral, in which French kings since Clovis had been crowned, was slightly dam- aged. Hausen at once informed Second Army: "Reims occupied by us. Cease fire."[31] Bülow stopped the shelling—and then imposed an "in- demnity" of fifty million francs on Reims, to be doubled if his terms were not accepted within forty-eight hours. Hausen was incensed. In his unpublished memoirs, he tried to imagine the "brouhaha" that would have resulted had their roles been reversed and Saxon artillery fired on the Prussian Guard. He found it "painful" that Bülow had not offered "a word of apology," not even an "explanation."[32] Interest- ingly, the minute German troops crossed into France, the reported incidents of francs-tireurs fire and German "reprisals"[33] abated. Still, Allied propaganda seized on the shelling of Reims to depict the enemy as "Huns" and "Vandals."

The debacle at Reims paled in comparison with Bülow's main con- cern: Kluck and First Army. For almost two weeks, Second Army had tenaciously hounded Charles Lanrezac's Fifth Army in brutal frontal attacks along the Sambre and Oise rivers. Moltke's General Directive of 2 September had left the final defeat of the French to Second Army. There would be no more bloody frontal assaults. Bülow looked for- ward to finally enveloping Fifth Army's left flank. He became angry on 3 September when he learned that Ferdinand von Quast's IX Corps of First Army had, in fact, crossed the Marne on his right wing directly in front of Karl von Einem's VII Corps. He grew downright livid when Kluck, pointedly "disobeying" Moltke's General Directive of 2 Sep- tember, late that night announced his intention to continue on a south- easterly course toward Montmirail.[34] This would force Second Army to halt its advance so as not to collide with Kluck's First Army. And it

---

* Greenwich Mean Time. German accounts give German General Time (one hour later).

would be at least 7 September before First Army's advance units could withdraw from the line Montmirail-Esternay. Kluck, Bülow moaned, had become "a thorn in his side."

The crisis on the Marne at last spurred Luxembourg into action. Late in the evening of 4 September, Moltke and his chief of staff, Lieutenant Colonel Gerhard Tappen, drafted a new General Directive for their field armies. To make certain that it reached the intended recipients, they had it delivered by automobile the next morning as well. The new orders began with a few general observations. The OHL conceded that Joffre had taken numerous formations out of his right wing at Toul-Belfort and shifted them to his left wing around Paris; that he had simultaneously removed units from in front of German Third, Fourth, and Fifth armies with similar intent; and that he most likely was standing up new formations on his left wing. The original design to "push the entire French army against the Swiss frontier," Moltke laconically wrote, "was no longer possible." The German right wing was now threatened as it hung in the air at Meaux. Worse still, there were agent reports of major French troop concentrations at Lille, of British landings at Ostend and Antwerp, and of eighty thousand Russians having been brought from Archangel to Britain for future deployment in France.

Of course, it was disinformation, all of it. But to Moltke, these "shadow" forces seemed all too real. He had committed all his active and reserve forces at the start of the war, and they now stood deep in France and East Prussia. The entire Kaiser Wilhelm Canal linking the North Sea to the Baltic Sea, the northwest German coast, and the border with Denmark were open to British invasion since he had moved IX Reserve Corps out of Schleswig-Holstein and attached it to Kluck's First Army. His prewar fears of a "three-front war" might yet be realized.

The new General Directive ordered Sixth and Seventh armies to tie down as many French forces as possible in Lorraine; Fourth and Fifth armies to continue to "drive" enemy forces facing them in the Argonne Forest "off in a southeasterly direction"; and First and Second armies to hold their positions east of Paris, to "parry offensively any enemy operations emanating from the region around Paris," and "to lend each other mutual support." Most opaquely, Third Army was to advance on Troyes–Vendeuvre-sur-Barse and, "as circumstances dictated," either support First and Second armies "across the Seine in a westerly direction," or turn south-southeast to buttress the German left wing in Lorraine.[35] There is no evidence to suggest that Moltke or Tappen seriously contemplated moving up to the front to direct the final phase of the campaign, or even to dispatch a senior officer from the General Staff for that purpose. One may remember that during the Battle of Guise/Saint-Quentin, Joffre had spent the entire morning at Fifth Army headquarters at Marle overseeing the main French attack.

In fact, Moltke's General Directive, when compared with Joffre's General Instruction No. 5 or No. 6, seems more like a theoretical staff exercise than a formal operations plan. It consisted of general observations on the campaign in the west and of vague suggestions for First and Second armies to hold their present positions and simply ward off enemy attacks; for Seventh and Sixth armies to "hold" on the left wing; and for Fifth, Fourth, and Third armies in the center of the line to operate in concentric sweeps south and southwest. It was an admission that the Schlieffen-Moltke operational concept of the *Schwenkungsflügel* (pivot wing) enveloping the entire left wing and center of the French army had been abandoned. There were no provisions for coordinating the actions of First and Second armies on the Marne, only obvious and nonspecific suggestions for Kluck and Bülow to "lend each other mutual support." Nor were there provisions to close the gap between Second and Third armies southeast of Reims. Hausen's instruction to deploy Third Army as he saw fit to support one of two German flanks some three hundred kilometers apart defied logic. Finally, the mere hint of rumors concerning British and Russian troop disembarkations in France stampeded Moltke into creating a new Seventh Army in Belgium under General Josias von Heeringen, hastily brought up from commanding the old Seventh Army in Lorraine. Once formed, it was to become the extreme right wing of the German line.

Within hours, the lack of command and control from Luxembourg became manifestly evident. At the very moment that Moltke and Tappen were drafting their General Directive calling on Third Army to drive on Troyes-Vendeuvre, Hausen at 5 PM on 4 September informed the OHL that he had ordered a day of rest for his forces. He repeated the message an hour later. "Troops desperately need a day of rest." He did not budge from his decision when the two flanking armies, Second and Fourth, informed him that they were resuming the offensive early the next morning. He stood firm even after he belatedly received Moltke's instruction to advance on Troyes-Vendeuvre at eight o'clock that night. Just before midnight, he informed the OHL for a third time in less than seven hours that Third Army would rest on 5 September.[36] Moltke raised no objections.

Hausen took pains, both at the time and in his memoirs, to justify his decision.[37] The men had reached the limits of their "psychological elasticity" as well as their "physical capability." Between 18 and 23 August, they had marched 190 kilometers to the Meuse, and thereafter 140 kilometers to the Aisne—much of it under a broiling sun and the last thirteen days during constant combat. Ammunition, food, and uniforms desperately needed to be hauled up to the front. The horses were short on oats and needed to be reshod. Hausen chose not to inform Moltke that there was also a personal reason: He had come down with what was diagnosed as a severe case of "bloody dysentery."

The German official history of the war later took Hausen to task.[38] By his action, he had exposed the flanks of his two neighboring armies—most precipitously, his halt had created a thirty-kilometer gap between his Third Army and Bülow's Second Army—and he had disrupted the planned seamless German advance on 5 September. But it failed to mention that with his action, Hausen had lost a splendid opportunity to exploit a twenty-five-kilometer gap that had developed between Foch's Ninth Army and Langle de Cary's Fourth Army. Especially Foch's Army Detachment had taken a terrible pounding from Hausen's two corps over the last two days: There had been heavy losses among infantry officers, the men were in a state of "serious fatigue" after "exhausting marches" and "the severity of the fighting," and many of the reserve formations were in what Foch termed "an extremely pitiable state." The entire region of Sommesous–Sompuis–Vitry-le-François was devoid of major French formations. From his headquarters at Sillery, Foch had informed Joffre that the Army Detachment, about to be reconstituted as Ninth Army, could at best survive two or three days of further attacks by German Third Army. It now gained twenty-four valuable hours in which to prepare its defensive line at the Saint-Gond Marshes and the heights south of Sézanne.[39]

It is difficult to disagree with the critique of Hausen. Every other German army had marched relentlessly under a searing sun during the last month. Every other army had suffered heavy casualties. Every other army needed rest and resupply. Some had in fact marched much greater distances than Third Army: First Army 500 kilometers and Second Army 440. Some, such as Second Army, had fought numerous more brutal engagements. It is hard to escape the verdict that Hausen simply was not made of the right stuff. For a second time since his failure to strike the flank of French Fifth Army south of Dinant, he failed to press a golden opportunity to break through the French line.

Above all, Moltke's General Directive was a rude shock for First Army, which received the relayed radiogram at 6 AM on 5 September. It entailed a painful retreat from advanced positions seized after long marches and heavy fighting between the Marne and Oise. Without direct radio communications either to the OHL or to Bülow's Second Army on his left flank, Kluck had advanced almost in a vacuum. He was thus without insight into the overall situation of the campaign in the west and about to collide with the left wing of Bülow's Second Army around Montmirail. He sent out no cavalry or aerial reconnaissance to the west, where French Sixth Army had been stood up, and was intent only on pursuing the British and French columns fleeing southward before him.

In the late afternoon, Kluck at Rebais had a visitor from Luxembourg: Lieutenant Colonel Richard Hentsch, chief of the OHL's Intelligence Section. It was Hentsch's first visit to the front, designed to establish better lines of communication among the field armies. Hentsch was not a bearer of good news. He informed Chief of Staff Hermann von Kuhl that Crown Prince Rupprecht's armies were tied down at Nancy and Épinal, unable to break through the Charmes Gap and drive north, and that Crown Prince Wilhelm's Fifth Army and Duke Albrecht's Fourth Army had made little progress around Verdun. Most likely, Joffre had used this stagnation of the fronts on the left and in the center of the German line to shuttle troops to the area around Paris, on Kluck's right.[40] First Army could expect an attack from the west any day.

Kuhl at once realized that he was "confronted with an entirely new situation." Without the "breakthrough on the upper Moselle," the giant Cannae being planned for the French army could not take place. The enemy "was by no means being held [down] everywhere" by Moltke's other armies; in fact, "large displacements of troops were in progress." The danger on First Army's right flank had come out of

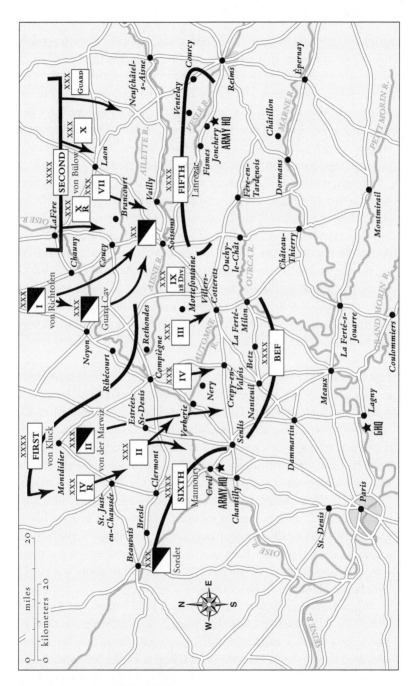

THE EVE OF THE BATTLE OF THE MARNE, 2 SEPTEMBER 1914

nowhere. It was real. It had to be addressed at once. "The suggestion, which we had made that morning, of first throwing the French back across the Seine, was finished."[41] Reluctantly, Kuhl agreed with Hentsch that First Army's four corps had to be withdrawn behind the Marne over the next two days "calmly and in orderly fashion" to a line Meaux–La Ferté-sous-Jouarre–La Ferté-Gaucher. This would then enable Second Army to swing around on its left and face Paris, its right wing on the Marne and its left wing on the Seine.

Having reached full agreement with First Army, Hentsch the next day traveled to Second Army headquarters at Champaubert. He repeated his (and Moltke's) bleak assessment of the German campaign in the west, and bemoaned the lack of four army corps "with which we could win the campaign."[42] One can only wonder whether he regretted the General Staff's earlier dispatch of Guard Reserve Corps and XI Army Corps to the Eastern Front, as well as of II Corps to besiege Antwerp, and of VII Reserve Corps to invest Maubeuge. It was now the thirty-fifth day of mobilization. Schlieffen had prescribed victory on the thirty-ninth or fortieth day.

THE BRUTAL HEAT FINALLY broke on 5 September. The first engagement in what came to be called the Battle of the Marne took place forty kilometers northeast of Paris. The future battlefield was bordered to the north by Villers-Cotterêts, the Bois du Roi, and Lévignen; to the east by the Ourcq River, which meandered on a southwesterly course from La Ferté-Milon to Lizy-sur-Ourcq before flowing into the Marne between Congis and Varreddes; and to the south by the Canal de l'Ourcq and the Marne. The land bordered by these three obstacles consisted of a hilly plateau studded with numerous villages, orchards, and grain fields. It was cut by three small streams: from north to south, the Grivelle, Gergogne, and Thérouanne. Each was embedded between gently rising wooded slopes of 80 to 120 meters; the chalky soil in places was dotted with bogs,[43] difficult terrain to do battle.

What Kuhl had called the "phantom Paris" became "flesh and blood" by 5 September. Early that warm and clear morning, General Maunoury, in accordance with Joffre's General Instruction No. 6, had advanced out of the Paris Entrenched Camp with Sixth Army. Once a ragtag collection of 80,000 reservists and second-line troops, Sixth Army now totaled 150,000 men: Victor Boëlle's IV Corps, Frédéric

Vautier's VII Corps, Henri de Lamaze's Fifth Group of 55th RID and 56th RID, Antoine Drude's 45th ID, Charles Ebener's Sixth Group of 61st RID and 62nd RID, and Jean-François Sordet's cavalry corps.[44] Maunoury placed 55th RID and 56th RID as well as a Moroccan brigade north of Dammartin-en-Goële; Étienne de Villaret's 14th ID of VII Corps and 63rd RID at Louvres; a brigade from the cavalry corps north of Claye-Souilly; and Raoul de Lartigue's 8th ID at the Marne on his right flank to maintain communications with Sir John French and the BEF. These were some of the units that German fliers had spotted on 3 and 4 September.

A slender, almost delicate soldier of sixty-seven, Maunoury had been wounded in the Franco-Prussian War (1870–71) and had served for a while as military governor of Paris. He was now all that stood between Kluck and the capital. He planned to march his ten infantry divisions to a position northeast of Meaux, and from there to strike Kluck's right flank the next day along the north bank of the Marne. Louis Gillet's reserve cavalry brigade had scouted Maunoury's route of advance toward Meaux and found no German forces.[45] It thus came as a total surprise when around noon a hail of 77mm artillery shells from the heights of Monthyon, northwest of Meaux, burst into the thick marching columns of 14th Infantry Division.

The unsuspected adversary was Hans von Gronau. Detached to guard First Army's right flank, IV Reserve Corps stood to the north of, and at right angles to, Kluck's main force around Barcy and Chambry. Gronau, at age sixty-four, was a Prussian artillery specialist. After several rotations through the General Staff in the 1880s and 1890s, he had commanded artillery regiments and brigades. Retired in 1911 and ennobled two years later, he was reactivated at the outbreak of the war.[46] At the Ourcq, Gronau commanded a much-depleted force: 43d Infantry Brigade (IB) had been taken from him to invest Brussels, with the result that IV Reserve Corps consisted of a mere fifteen (rather than the normal twenty-five) battalions of infantry and twelve batteries of light artillery.[47] It had neither aircraft nor electronic communications. With just 22,800 men, it was 12,000 under full strength. Moreover, Otto von Garnier's 4th Cavalry Division (CD) had but twelve hundred sabers, having been battered by British 1st Cavalry Brigade and Royal Horse Artillery around Néry on 1 September. Still, the vigilant Garnier kept up his patrols and detected French cavalry, some scouts, and a strong column of infantry marching toward Montgé-en-Goële, halfway between Paris and Meaux. Were these merely French advance guards? Or units of the Paris Garrison out on patrol? Or had Joffre somehow managed to cobble together a new army north of the capital?

Without aerial reconnaissance and with the western horizon blocked by a series of wooded hillocks between Saint-Soupplets and Penchard, the safe option was to stay put and await developments. But the wily Gronau threw out the textbook and made a quick decision that most likely would have resulted in failure at most staff colleges. "Lieutenant-Colonel, there is no other way out," he informed his chief of staff, Friedrich von der Heyde, "we must attack!"[48] Without delay, Gronau sent 7th RID and 22d RID to occupy the long, wooded ridge around Saint-Mard, Dammartin, and Monthyon. Their orders were simple: Attack any and all forces approaching out of the west. At 11:30 AM, Gronau's artillery spotted a mighty host of French infantry and artillery—de Lamaze's 55th RID and 56th RID as well as Ernest Blondlat's 1st Moroccan Brigade. They advanced northwest of Iverny along cobblestone roads lined with shimmering poplars, past gray stone farmhouses with gray slate roofs, and through fields of beets, mustard, wheat, and clover. As soon as they were within range, Gronau opened fire.

The battle raged fiercely throughout the day. A German artillerist (Hoyer) with 7th Reserve Field Artillery Regiment wrote home that the gun crews "were killed like flies." Some nearby batteries lost all their officers; his own unit, 70 percent. "And the horses!" In a nearby stable Hoyer found fifty dead in a single heap.[49] An anonymous noncommissioned officer with 26th Infantry Regiment (IR) remembered the horror of the battlefield. "The cadavers of animals of all kind lie everywhere and spread a horrible smell." After a brief rest and a two-hundred-liter barrel of red wine "liberated" at a "swampy farm," the men of the 26th moved on through "high grass, bushes and thickets." They found a small wood. "Sharp cracks beside us, ahead of us and above us. One shrapnel after another rains down on us. It covers the entire wood. We run from one large tree to another. . . . Countless wounded and dead lie all around us."[50] Darkness finally brought relief. German IV Reserve Corps held the ridge. Maunoury had not been able to cross the 120-meter-deep valley of the Ourcq River. Meaux remained well out of his reach.

CLIMAX: THE OURCQ · 243

Gronau's swift action proved critical to the course of the Battle of the Marne. It denied Joffre the all-important element of surprise.[51] Instead of Maunoury striking Kluck's right flank unawares, it was now French Sixth Army that had been taken by surprise. Moreover, the action had taken place a full eighteen hours *before* Joffre originally had planned to mount his great offensive between Verdun and Paris, thus throwing his overarching concept into question. Gronau and his band of valiant reservists, in the words of the German official history, had "with one bold stroke" finally brought clarity: "The German army's right flank was, in fact, seriously threatened."[52] And "with a rare appreciation of the strategic realities,"[53] Gronau understood that he was vastly outnumbered (about six to one) and withdrew IV Reserve Corps to relative safety ten kilometers behind the small Thérouanne stream. He would receive the coveted Pour le Mérite two years after he had first earned it at Monthyon.

Shortly before midnight on 5 September, the telephone rang at First Army headquarters at Rebais. It was Gronau with news of the encounter with Maunoury's Sixth Army. Chief of Staff von Kuhl, who at 7 PM had only received spotty news from Aircraft B65 that a minor engagement had occurred near Meaux,[54] at once grasped the gravity of the situation. There were but two choices—regroup and retreat to defensive positions to protect the German outer right flank, or blunt the French attack with a counteroffensive. Kuhl chose the latter. Kluck agreed: "Wheel 1. Army to the right at once, quickly form up on the right, attack across the Ourcq."[55] Just after midnight, Kluck and Kuhl ordered Alexander von Linsingen's II Corps to quick-march from south of the Marne to west of the Ourcq in the direction of Lizy-sur-Ourq and Germigny-l'Évêque, there to buttress Gronau's position behind the Thérouanne. Later on the afternoon of 6 September, they also dispatched Friedrich Sixt von Arnim's IV Corps to west of the Ourcq. It was a hard undertaking, as both corps had to cross two, and in some places three, river barriers. Yet the two corps incredibly managed two days of forced marches that stood out in the annals of the Prussian army: sixty kilometers on 7 September and seventy the following day, over bloated corpses of men and beasts alike, past columns of wounded and prisoners of war, through poplar woods and pear orchards.

It was a daring decision with potentially deadly ramifications. For, in the process, a fifty-kilometer-wide gap developed in First Army's line between Varreddes and Sancy-lès-Provins, at the southern limit of the German advance. Appreciating the danger, Kuhl rushed Manfred von Richthofen's I Cavalry Corps and Georg von der Marwitz's II Cavalry Corps into the breach. These rear guards were to defend first the trench of the Grand Morin River, then, if that fell, the trench of the Petit Morin, and finally the trench of the Marne. Gronau established a line of defense between Vincy-Manoeuvre and Varreddes. Knowing that major reinforcements were on the way, he sought out a comfortable ditch and took a nap.

AT DAWN ON 6 September, 980,000 French and 100,000 British soldiers with 3,000 guns assaulted the German line of 750,000 men and 3,300 guns between Verdun and Paris.[56] Joffre, who had been able to reinforce his armies with a hundred thousand reservists, issued the troops a stirring appeal. "The salvation of the country" was in their hands. There could be "no looking back." The sacred ground of France was to be held "at whatever cost"; "be killed on the spot rather than retreat." Anything even resembling weakness would not be "tolerated."[57] President Poincaré, at Bordeaux, had to get the text through unofficial channels. He understood the seriousness of the hour. "We are going to play our part for all we are worth in what will be the greatest battle humanity has ever known."[58] Charles Huguet, French military plenipotentiary to the BEF, for the first time in weeks detected cheer at GHQ now that the Great Retreat was finally over. "When day dawned on the ever-memorable morning of 6th September," Field Marshal Sir John French wrote, he had regained some of his earlier "great hopes" for victory. "The promise of an immediate advance against the enemy" sent "a thrill of exultation and enthusiasm throughout the whole force."[59] Deputy Chief of Staff Wilson giddily assured his French counterpart, Henri Berthelot, that the Allied armies would be in Germany "in 4 weeks."[60]

The most critical sector of the front was between Paris and the Marne. There, the battle would rage for four days. Much of it would be fought in a maze of waterways that served as tributaries to the Marne: the Ourcq, which flowed north and south on both sides of Maunoury's advance; the Petit Morin and the Grand Morin, which ran east and west across the line of advance of French Fifth Army and the

BEF; and finally the Saint-Gond Marshes, from which the Petit Morin arose and where Foch's Ninth Army stood.

At first, both Kluck and Bülow took the forces attacking Gronau's corps to be nothing more than French rear guards covering Joffre's withdrawal on Paris—at most a sortie designed to relieve pressure on the French armies south of the Seine. General von der Marwitz, in fact, asked the kaiser's court chaplain to prepare a suitable "entry text" for Paris, "but not too long!"[61] The Germans were disabused of the notion of encountering only French rear guards during the night of 6 September. Men from Duke Albrecht of Württemberg's 30th IB, Fourth Army, had found Joffre's stirring appeal to his troops near Frignicourt, south of Vitry-le-François.[62] Albrecht's headquarters, which had a telephone link to Luxembourg, immediately passed the document on to Moltke. Sometime around 8 PM, the chief of the General Staff sent it out to the other army commands. He did not counter it with a stirring appeal of his own. He was content simply to hand it over to the press with a quixotic message that the war needed to end with a peace that would "for all foreseeable future" see Germany "undisturbed by any foe."[63] There was now no doubt that the Allies' retreat had ended and that they had gone on the attack. Specifically, Gronau's battle with vastly superior French forces the day before pointed to an attempt to envelop the German right wing.

Chief of Operations Tappen, just promoted to the rank of colonel, was delighted. The "Day of Decision" was finally at hand. He burst into a meeting of his operations and intelligence officers: "Well, we finally get hold of them. Now it will be a fierce fight. Our brave troops will know how to do their job." No more retreats, no more avoiding battle by the enemy. It was now just a matter of applying "brute force."[64]

Kluck and Kuhl faced another major decision. Should they break off the battle and fall back from their advanced position in the acute angle of the Marne and the Ourcq? Should they, together with Bülow's Second Army, withdraw to defensive positions between the Marne and the Ourcq and there parry Joffre's flanking maneuver? Or should they continue the battle and seek a quick, decisive victory over Maunoury's Sixth Army? Yet again, both opted to blunt the French thrust with a counteroffensive. Realizing that First Army's three (understrength) corps on the Ourcq were too weak to mount a counterattack against 150,000 French soldiers, they turned to Bülow. Shortly after 8 AM on 7 September, they telegraphed Second Army headquarters at Champaubert: "II, IV and IV Reserve Corps heavily engaged west of the lower Ourcq. Where III and IX Army Corps? What is your situation?" No reply. They repeated the message, adding "Urgently request answer." It crossed paths with a radiogram from Second Army wishing to know, "What is your situation?" Finally, a third request from Kuhl, "Engagement III and IX Corps at the Ourcq urgently required."[65] No reply.

The German army's prewar neglect of communications and control was glaringly apparent.[66] During the Battle of the Marne, Luxembourg had direct telephone connections via Fourth Army with Fifth, Sixth, and Seventh armies on the relatively stagnant German left and center. But it could communicate with the fluid First and Second "strike" armies only by way of a single wireless set, which was prone to interruptions by weather and to jamming by French field stations and the Eiffel Tower. Messages often arrived so mutilated at Bülow's and Kluck's headquarters that they had to be re-sent three or four times. Field telegraph stations managed to get only twenty-nine of fifty-nine reports from First Army's fliers to Kluck and Kuhl between 1 and 5 September. There were no electronic ties between First and Second armies, or between them and their army corps and cavalry corps. A host of intelligence officers languished at the OHL and were not attached to the various corps commands where they might have done some good. No one thought of using airplanes to pass important orders along the line. The distance between Bülow's headquarters at Montmort and Kluck's at Vandrest (and later Mareuil), after all, was a mere fifty-five kilometers, or half an hour by air. The two commanders were thus effectively cut off from discussing the rapidly developing situation with each other—and with Moltke, who was 435 kilometers by automobile* away from Second Army headquarters and 445 from First Army headquarters.[67]

Interestingly, Tappen rejected all suggestions that the OHL, or at least a small operations staff, move up to the front behind the German right wing on the grounds of "technical difficulties as well as stodginess."[68] One can only speculate whether Moltke, for his part, remem-

---

* Or 230 kilometers by air.

bered that in 1866 his uncle had supervised the movements of his armies during the Battle of Königgrätz from the Roskosberg, above the Bistritz River, and that he had likewise led from the front in 1870 during the Battle of Sedan from a ridge high above the Meuse River near Frénois.

ALL THE WHILE, THE fighting west of the Ourcq raged on. Blondlat's Moroccan brigade and the right wing of Louis Leguay's 55th RID first went into action on the French right flank on 6 September. Linsingen's II Corps, just arrived, furiously counterattacked with heavy artillery. Soon the entire front from Barny to Trilport erupted with murderous artillery fire and spirited infantry charges. The French initially gained the upper hand, but by nightfall both sides fell exhausted into defensive positions. In the ensuing dark, the Germans could make out the glow of Paris's massive searchlights.

Linsingen urged greater speed on Sixt von Arnim's IV Corps; it arrived the next morning, 7 September. As senior corps commander, Linsingen took command and repositioned his forces: From right to left, Sixt von Arnim was to charge the front at Étavigny; Gronau was to hold the middle at Trocy-en-Multien; Kurt von Trossel with 3d ID and 22d RID was to cover Gronau's left near Germigny-l'Évêque; and Linsingen was to secure the left flank at Trilport. Maunoury in the meantime received reinforcements from Paris: Céleste Déprez's 61st RID, Drude's 45th ID, and the rest of Vautier's VII Corps, just up from Alsace. Unbeknown to the French commander, a German reserve infantry brigade under Rudolf von Lepel had been released by the surrender of Brussels and was marching south toward Nanteuil-le-Haudouin—against Sixth Army's left flank. Still, Maunoury enjoyed a numerical advantage of thirty-two infantry battalions and two cavalry divisions.

Maunoury vigorously resumed the offensive at 7 AM on 7 September.[69] In the middle of the front, Gronau's fatigued IV Reserve Corps, stiffened by the arrival of Sixt von Arnim's 15th Brigade, threw Léon Lombard's 63d RID into panic with a hurricane bombardment followed by massed infantry charges. Only a heroic counterattack by Colonel Robert Nivelle's 5th Artillery Regiment of 45th ID—firing shells from its 75s into the massed German infantry at the rate of twenty rounds per minute—prevented a complete collapse.* French Fifth Group of Reserve Divisions likewise was driven back, and its commander, de Lamaze, seriously considered falling back on Paris. On the southern flank, the men of 8th RID were "in a state of extreme fatigue," and Lartigue was forced to have the division stand down around noon. In the north, Sixt von Arnim's 16th Brigade shattered Déprez's 61st RID, but a combination of exhaustion after its nightlong forced march and a counterattack by Vautier's VII Corps prevented it from enveloping the French left flank. Still, 61st RID fell back as far as Nanteuil-le-Haudouin. Maunoury sent Louis de Trentinian's 7th ID from IV Corps to take its place in the left of his line. Galliéni rushed François Ganeval's 62d RID out to hold the line at the Ourcq.

At 10 AM on 7 September, First Army headquarters received word that an aviator had spotted two columns of British soldiers slowly moving north out of the Forest of Crécy toward the joint of German First and Second armies.[70] Kluck and Kuhl could wait no longer. Still without a reply from Bülow to their request for reinforcements, they seized the initiative and ordered Ewald von Lochow's III Corps and Quast's IX Corps, both temporarily assigned to Bülow, to leave Second Army's right wing in broad daylight and quick-march to the Ourcq.[71] For Kuhl had decided to master what now threatened to be assaults on both his wings by way of an all-out offensive on the right, designed to crush Maunoury's Sixth Army before the BEF could engage German First or Second army.

Incredibly, neither Kluck nor Kuhl was aware that General von Bülow shortly after midnight on 7 September had already pulled back his right wing, fearing that his soldiers were too exhausted to ward off another French frontal attack. Bülow withdrew III and IX corps of First Army as well as his own X Reserve Corps fifteen to twenty kilometers behind the shelter, such as it was, of the Petit Morin River— some eight hours *before* First Army's duumvirate ordered them to march to the Ourcq. Bülow radioed Moltke of his action at 2 AM. He declined to inform Kluck via dispatch rider. By his action, Bülow created a gap of some thirty kilometers between the right wing of Second Army and the left wing of First Army. Kluck and Kuhl, by recalling III

---

* In December 1916, Nivelle replaced Joffre as commander in chief of the French army.

and IX corps, widened that gap to about fifty kilometers. Failure to communicate once again bedeviled the German army commanders on the right pivot wing.

Having pulled back his right wing, Bülow next ordered an attack by his left wing. Realizing that Second Army was down to the strength of only three full corps, he once again enlisted the help of two Saxon infantry divisions from Hausen's Third Army.[72] General von Einem, commanding VII Corps on Second Army's right, thought the plan madness: At the very moment that the enemy might discover and then exploit the German gap astride the Petit Morin, "Bülow shifts the center of gravity to his left wing!" What use would victory there be, he mused, "if we are enveloped on the right and separated from First Army?"[73]

In fact, the German position on the Marne and the Ourcq defies rational analysis. Without firm direction from the OHL, both commanders had developed their own operational concepts. Bülow insisted that First Army's primary function, as laid down in Moltke's General Directive of 5 September, was to protect his right flank against a possible French sortie out of *le camp retranché de Paris*. Thus, it was paramount that Kluck break off the battle with Maunoury and shift his army left to join up with Second Army's right wing. As well, it was critical that Hausen's Third Army defeat Foch's Ninth Army on Bülow's left flank before Fanchet d'Espèrey's Fifth Army could exploit Second Army's exposed right flank. Kluck, on the other hand, insisted that the only way to break the French offensive was to destroy Maunoury's Sixth Army before the British, whose fighting capabilities he by and large denigrated, could take their place on the left flank of French Fifth Army south of the Grand Morin River. Bülow made no effort to coordinate the operations of the two "strike" armies or to bring Moltke fully into the calculus.[74] Just after 7 PM on 7 September, Richthofen's cavalry corps reported that British advance guards had crossed the Grand Morin at La Ferté-Gaucher. They were about to enter the gap in the German line.

For the Germans, 7 September was the critical day in the Battle of the Marne. Kluck and Kuhl, as noted previously, had hastily taken II and IV corps out of the line on the Marne and rushed them north to aid Gronau's corps on the Ourcq. Bülow had then withdrawn III and IX corps as well as X Reserve Corps behind the Petit Morin—only to have had Kluck and Kuhl eight hours later order III and IX corps to leave Bülow's right wing and to march north in order to help defeat Maunoury's French Sixth Army. None of these orders was shared, much less discussed beforehand. In the process, as is well known, Bülow, Kluck, and Kuhl had created a fifty-kilometer-wide gap between First and Second armies—one into which the BEF was slowly stumbling as it headed north between Changis, on the Marne, and Rebais, south of the Petit Morin. The eighth of September would thus see two distinct battles: Kluck versus Maunoury on the Ourcq, and Bülow versus Franchet d'Espèrey on the two Morins.

Kluck's bold, aggressive decision remains highly controversial. He had already "disobeyed" Moltke's General Directive to remain "echeloned" to the right and behind Second Army. Now he literally snatched two corps from Bülow's right wing and rushed them to the Ourcq. To Kluck, time was the critical factor. Could he defeat Maunoury before the BEF drove through the gap in the German line and into the back of either First Army or Second Army? How long could Richthofen's and Marwitz's cavalry corps hold the line of the Grand Morin against the three advancing British corps? When would Lepel's brigade finally arrive on the left flank of French Sixth Army? Kluck answered those rhetorical musings by ordering "every man and every horse" west of the Ourcq to deliver the final and fatal blow to Maunoury's Sixth Army. It was a last-minute, all-out gamble. The campaign in the west hung on it.

At Luxembourg, General von Moltke yet again was on the verge of panic. "Today a great decision will come about," he wrote his wife, Eliza, on 7 September, "since yesterday our entire army is fighting from Paris to Upper Alsace. Should I have to give my life today to bring about victory, I would do it gladly a thousand times." He lamented the "streams of blood" that had already been shed and the "countless" homes and lives that had been destroyed. "I often shudder when I think of this and I feel as though I need to accept responsibility for this dreadfulness. . . ."[75] These were not the words of a great captain.

GERMAN SECOND ARMY ON the Marne was a battered force. It had marched 440 kilometers under a broiling sun along dusty roads. Food and fodder had been irregular, and the half-ripe fruit and oats it found along the way only added to the misery of man and beast alike. It had fought most of the major engagements on the right wing—Liège, Namur, Charleroi, and Guise/Saint-Quentin. From around 260,000 soldiers at the start of August, it was down to 154,000 by the end of the month. About 9,000 men had succumbed to heat sores, exhaustion, and hunger; 12,151 were listed as wounded; and 5,061 had been killed.[76] After three days on the Petit Morin, Bülow informed the OHL, his army had shrunk from its initial seven to less than four corps, many at least 20 percent understrength.[77] In the only change in a major command undertaken by the German army during the "march to the Marne," Bülow replaced Guenther von Kirchbach with Johannes von Eben as commander of X Reserve Corps.

On 6 September, Eben's corps ran hard up against Gilbert Defforges's X Corps between Montmirail and Le Thoult as it came to the aid of Otto von Emmich's X Corps on his left. A violent battle ensued. Franchet d'Espèrey had admonished his troops not to surrender an inch of sacred soil. Fifth Army managed to advance five kilometers along its entire front, but at Le Thoult French X Corps was thrown five kilometers back across the Petit Morin. Both sides were at the limit of their physical capabilities. Richard von Süsskind, commanding 2d Reserve Guard Division with Eben's X Reserve Corps, reported, "The division is very exhausted. Though still able to attack, it is no longer in condition to continue the offense."[78] He spoke as well for many other division commanders.

When Bülow ordered First Army's III and IX corps as well as his own X Reserve Corps fifteen kilometers behind the Petit Morin early in the morning of 7 September, one of Eben's battalions of 74th Reserve Infantry Regiment (RIR) did not receive the order to withdraw. Quickly surrounded on all sides and with its back against the Petit Morin, it was mercilessly gunned down in what is called "the massacre of Guebarré Farm": 93 men surrendered and 450 lay dead. The French had ignored the white handkerchiefs that German soldiers had tied to their rifles and raised above the trenches as a sign of surrender.[79]

The situation on Bülow's left flank became critical. After an intensive night bombardment—unusual at this stage in the war—a brigade of Théophile Jouannic's 36th ID from Louis de Maud'huy's XVIII Corps around noon on 8 September surprised and threw terror into several companies of German VII Corps at Marchais-en-Brie, just northwest of Montmirail.[80] Although minor in itself, the brilliant

French tactical action at Marchais-en-Brie constituted what historian Sewell Tyng has labeled one of those "there the battle was won" defining moments of the large Battle of the Marne.[81] For the French assault had tremendous operational and even strategic ramifications. With German X Reserve Corps completely flanked from the west, Montmirail was indefensible. Moreover, Eben's IX Reserve Corps was outflanked on both sides. Of much greater concern to Bülow and his chief of staff, Otto von Lauenstein, was that Second Army's right wing, recently denuded of two corps bound for the Ourcq, was further jeopardized. They ordered VII Corps and X Reserve Corps to fall back ten kilometers east to the line Margny–Le Thoult. It was a major mistake. The two corps on Second Army's right flank now stood from north to south, facing west, and were thus utterly unable to shift right and close the gap with Kluck's First Army. In fact, that gap as a result had widened by fifteen kilometers.[82] Bülow's right wing "was no longer threatened, it was turned." The "path to the Marne" lay open for the left-wing corps of French Fifth Army—and the BEF.

Ever so slowly, Sir John French's forces, enhanced by William Pulteney's III Corps, on the morning of 6 September had begun its march to the front. It was headed for the open spaces of the Brie Plateau, a rich agricultural area best known for its cheeses. The plateau was cut east to west by the ravines of the Grand Morin, Petit Morin, Marne, Upper Ourcq, Vesle, Aisne, and Ailette rivers, passable only on bridges. To the north lay the three great forests of Crécy, d'Armainvilliers, and Malvoisine.[83] The BEF deployed in an easterly direction from Tournan-en-Brie, Fontenay-Trésigny, and Rozay-en-Brie (which the British called Rozoy), almost twenty kilometers behind the line where Joffre had wanted it to start. "Desperate Frankie," as the British jokingly called Franchet d'Espèrey, was furious and repeatedly demanded a more rapid advance. But at Rozoy, Sir Douglas Haig, feeling "uneasy about his left," where he suspected units of Marwitz's cavalry corps, halted the advance of I Corps, allowing Sixt von Arnim's IV Corps to make good its escape to the Ourcq.[84] Six pilots of the Royal Flying Corps found only open roads ahead of Haig. Thus, when Sir John French ordered Haig to resume his advance at 3:30 PM, I Corps unsurprisingly encountered only abandoned positions. This notwithstanding, by nightfall Haig was roughly twelve kilometers behind the day's objective. He had lost a mere seven men killed and forty-four wounded.

The next day, 7 September, aerial reconnaissance, in the stilted language of the British official history, again "confirmed the general impression that the enemy was withdrawing northward."[85] The day brought little action, just a continued hesitant advance by the BEF into the gap between German First and Second armies. Sir John had long ceased to be the dashing cavalry officer who had ridden to glory fourteen years earlier during the relief of Kimberley in the Boer War. "Old Archie" Murray, his chief of staff, continued to urge caution. The men tramped happily north singing "It's a Long Way to Tipperary" and certain of their guardian, the "Angel of Mons." Marwitz's thin cavalry screen could undertake only brief sorties to block the BEF crossing the Grand Morin.

Not only the French had become exasperated at the slow pace of the British advance. Lord Ernest Hamilton of Eleventh Hussars noted, "In the strict sense there was no battle during the British advance. The fighting . . . was desultory. . . . The advance at first was slow and cautious."[86] John Charteris, Haig's chief of intelligence, observed that although "keen," the men "moved absurdly slowly." The cavalry, Haig's true love, "were the worst of all, for they were right behind [!] the infantry."[87] Exasperated, Galliéni at Paris dispatched Lartigue's 8th ID south of Meaux to establish contact between the BEF and Franchet d'Espèrey's Fifth Army.[88] It was a murderous advance. The Germans held the seventy- to one-hundred-meter-high ridges above Meaux, their machine guns well concealed on the wooded crests of the Marne, and poured lethal fire into the French ranks crossing the valley floor below them.

On the diplomatic front, Joffre moved quickly to intervene when it seemed to him that Galliéni was driving the British too hard and thereby arousing "the touchiness of Field Marshal French." On 7 September, he cabled Horatio Herbert Lord Kitchener in London to extend his "warmest thanks" for Sir John's "constant," "precious," and "energetic" support of the Allied attack.[89] Alliance cohesion was secured.

At 10:10 AM on 8 September, German Aircraft B75 reported that the BEF was advancing "more rapidly" from La Ferté-Gaucher and

Rebais in the general direction of Saint-Cyr-sur-Morin. Horace Smith-Dorrien's II Corps was in the center of the line, flanked by Haig's I Corps on its right and "Putty" Pulteney's III Corps on its left.[90] It was another sunny day. By noon, the BEF had reached the Petit Morin, a shallow stream barely six meters wide. The Royal Flying Corps reported only small enemy columns ahead. Marwitz's cavalry corps fought a brief but gallant rear action—and headed north. Then a "violent thunderstorm" with "torrents of rain"[91] slowed the BEF's further advance. An impatient Joffre at 8 PM dashed off a communiqué to Sir John French confirming the gap between the two enemy armies and deeming it "essential" that the BEF exploit this by marching northeast before the Germans reinforced their cavalry with infantry and artillery. The BEF, in his opinion, should cross the Marne between Nogent-l'Artaud and La Ferté-sous-Jouarre, where the winding river was roughly sixty meters wide.[92] In three days and while outnumbering the enemy at least ten to one, "Johnnie" French's army had advanced just forty kilometers. The BEF's importance lay in its role as an "army in being," to borrow a naval term.

Joffre's problems were not, however, confined to the Germans. On 8 September, the generalissimo discovered to his chagrin that Galliéni, in his capacity as military governor of Paris, the previous day had cabled the government at Bordeaux for instructions on how to "evacuate the civilian population" of the capital's outlying suburbs and instructed prefects and the police to find "emergency locations" for the evacuees.[93] The usually aggressive governor, having pulled all units out of Paris to assist Maunoury on the Ourcq, for a brief moment was overcome by pessimism. If Maunoury were defeated, how could he hold the capital against Kluck's expected assault? Joffre, barely able to control his anger, cabled War Minister Millerand to "rescind" Galliéni's "dangerous" communication. "I remain the only judge of what is worth saying about the operations. . . . The Military Governor of Paris is under my orders, and therefore does not have the right to correspond directly with the Government."[94] It was vintage Joffre.

The Allied advance into the fifty-kilometer-wide space between First and Second armies drove Moltke ever deeper into despair. He issued no orders to either Bülow or Kluck on 6 or 7 September. Instead, he withdrew into a world of self-pity and grief. The "burden of responsibility of the last several days," he wrote his wife, was impossible even to name. "For the great battle of our army along its entire front has not yet been decided." The "horrible tension" of the last few days, the "absence of news from the far distant armies," and "knowing all that was at stake" was "almost beyond human power" to comprehend. "The terrible difficulty of our situation stands like an almost impenetrable black wall in front of me."[95] The only bright spot on the horizon was that on 6 September Hans von Zwehl had forced Fortress Maubeuge to surrender: 412 officers and 32,280 ranks were taken prisoner and 450 guns added to the German arsenal.[96] Zwehl's three brigades of VII Corps were now freed up, perhaps to plug the gap between the Marne and the Ourcq. Wilhelm II, returning from a tour of the front near Châlons-sur-Marne, was delighted by the news but alarmed by Moltke's pessimism. "Attack, as long as we can—not a single step backwards under any circumstances. . . . We will defend ourselves to the last breath of man and horse."[97]

THROUGHOUT HIS STAND AT the Petit Morin, Bülow had urged Hausen's Third Army to advance against Foch's Ninth Army around the Marais de Saint-Gond, the pivot of Joffre's line. Sixteen kilometers long and on average three kilometers wide, the marshes were an east-west barrier that was practically impassable. Only four narrow and low causeways running north to south traversed the marshes. Their broad expanse of reeds and grass was crisscrossed by drainage dikes cut into the clay basin. To the east was the dry, chalky plain of Champagne, broken only by scattered stands of pine.[98] Since the eighteenth century, it had been commonly called *la Champagne pouilleuse,* literally, the "louse-ridden and flea-bitten region of Champagne." Somewhere in the vicinity of the marshes, Salian Franks and Visigoths under the Roman general Flavius Aëtius and King Theodoric I had halted the advance of the Hunnic king Attila in AD 451.

Joffre ordered Foch to defend the Saint-Gond Marshes and thereby cover Fifth Army's right flank at all cost with Pierre Dubois's IX Corps (three divisions) and Joseph Eydoux's XI Corps (four divisions). Joffre's major concern was the gap between Foch's Ninth Army and Langle de Cary's Fourth Army. It was held only by Jean-François de L'Espée's 9th Cavalry Division, pending the arrival of Émile-Edmond Legrand-Girarde's XXI Corps, which on 2 September had embarked at Épinal in seventy-four trains.[99] Bülow's X Corps had pounded Dubois's IX

Corps at Saint-Prix and his Guard Corps had violently assaulted IX Corps at Bannes on 6 and 7 September; he now urged Third Army to exploit the gap. It would require a major effort by an army down to 2,105 officers and 81,199 ranks.[100]

Yet again, Hausen prevaricated. It was the dilemma of Dinant all over again. On his right, Plettenberg's 2d Guard Division had stalled at Normée. Bülow again called for relief. "Strongest possible support 3 Army urgently desired. The day's decision depends [on this]."[101] On Hausen's left, Heinrich von Schenck's XVIII Corps of Fourth Army likewise had been stopped in its tracks around Vitry-le-François, and Duke Albrecht called for assistance.[102] Whom to obey? A royal prince? Prussia's senior army commander? Or Moltke, who had ordered Third Army to march on Troyes-Vendeuvre? As at Dinant, Hausen decided to please all suitors: He divided his army. He ordered Maximilian von Laffert's XIX Corps to support Schenck's VIII Corps at Glannes; he approved Karl d'Elsa's prior decision to rush 32d ID as well as the artillery of 23d ID to aid the Guard Corps at Clamanges-Lenharré; and he instructed his remaining forces (mainly 23d ID and 24th RID released by the fall of Fortress Givet) to continue on to Troyes-Vendeuvre. He declined to use Fourth Army's direct telephone to Luxembourg to seek Moltke's input.

Hausen justified his actions in his unpublished memoirs. Orders were orders. He could not disobey a direct command from Bülow, or from Duke Albrecht, or from Moltke, even if it meant splitting his army into three separate entities.[103] For a third time since Fumay and Sommesous–Sompuis–Vitry-le-François, Hausen lost a splendid opportunity to drive an attack through the French line. The day of rest he had generously given his troops on 5 September now came home to roost: He was too far behind Second and Fourth armies on his flanks to rush to the immediate aid of either, and he was too far from the fighting front to penetrate Foch's weak spot. By dividing his forces, he forwent any attempt to envelop French Ninth Army. By having halted on 5 September, he had given away the chance to break through the fifteen-kilometer-wide gap between Foch's Ninth Army and Langle de Cary's Fourth Army.[104] One can only imagine what Hans von Gronau would have done under the circumstances.

None of Third Army's three groups made progress on 7 September, violently battered by Foch's 75s, the "black butchers" that often fired a thousand rounds each per day. In many places, officers had to rush to the front to get the men moving again.[105] Bülow announced that Second Army was pulling III and IX corps as well as X Reserve Corps behind the Petit Morin. At five o'clock that night Hausen, out of character and perhaps recognizing the lost opportunity of the previous day, reached a bold decision: He would assume the role of army-group commander. Until now, he confessed, Third Army had been little more than a "quarry of reserves" for Second and Fourth armies.[106] He determined to correct that situation.*

Knowing that the French had launched a major offensive between Verdun and Paris, Hausen reasoned that "the enemy cannot be strong and superior everywhere." Hence, the trick was to find the place where it was weakest. With Bülow being driven behind the Petit Morin by French Fifth Army and with Kluck fully engaged along the Ourcq by French Sixth Army, Hausen deduced that the weak spot had to be along the front of his army. And since his troops were being hammered by the French *les 75s*, he decided to "storm the enemy's artillery positions at dawn with the bayonet."[107] Such a ferocious charge would fortify the resolve of his Saxons for hand-to-hand combat. As well, he was concerned that inadvertent gunfire might alert the sleeping French soldiers. General d'Elsa was given overall command with his own XII Corps, Laffert's XIX Corps, and 23d ID. Kirchbach's XII Reserve Corps was to advance with 32d ID and 23d RID. Duke Albrecht agreed to attach Schenk's VIII Corps to d'Elsa's left wing; Bülow promised 2d GD (later also 1st GD) for Kirchbach's right wing. Hausen now commanded six and one-half army corps. He enjoyed a one-third numerical superiority over Langle de Cary's Fourth Army. At 9:15 PM, he informed the OHL of his plans; Moltke and Tappen radioed their approval shortly before midnight.[108]

At 2:45 AM on 8 September, Horst von der Planitz's 32d ID was ready. It was clear and dry. "*Seitengewehr aufgepflanzt! Sprung auf, marsch, marsch!*"† Orders had arrived at unit levels only thirty minutes before jump-off. The men advanced against Joseph Pambet's 22d ID and parts of Maurice Joppé's 60th RID between Sompuis and Vitry-

---

* Given the destruction by Allied air raids in 1945 of the records of Third Army's Strategic (Ia) and Tactical (Ib) sections, Hausen's unpublished memoirs are critical.
† "Fix bayonets! Advance by rushes!"

le-François with bayonets fixed, rifles unloaded, and breechblocks secured in their bread pouches. At 3 AM Arnold von Winckler's 2d GD
followed against René Radiguet's 21st ID, despite Winckler's initial
grave concern that Hausen's gamble could cost him his division. Larisch's 23d RID followed at 3:30 AM. A pale moon shone as the men
silently moved through "glorious vineyards" and marshes and over
chalky plains. As soon as they collided with the enemy, bugles and
drums called out the *attaque brutale*.

The 2d Guard waded across the Somme at Normée, and then
charged the French lines with "shouts of Hurrah, bugles blaring and
drums beating."[109] Concurrently, Planitz's Saxon 32d ID crossed the
Somme at Lenharrée. Despite the staggered starts, surprise was with
the Germans. Lenharrée fell by 4:45 AM, its defenders "exhausted,
wounded, taken prisoner, or fleeing."[110] The first light of dawn revealed the grisly sight of "green hillsides dotted as if with red and blue
flowers"—the tunics of dead French infantrymen.[111]

It was a "disastrous day" for Foch.[112] One French artillery battery
after another fled the German cold steel. Radiguet's 21st ID and Pambet's 22d ID were driven back by the furious assault, crashing into Justinien Lefèvre's recently arrived 18th ID. Next, Jules Battesti's 52d
RID had to fall back and d'Espée's 9th CD was forced to abandon
Sommesous. The marshes were effectively outflanked, their southern
exists uncovered. In short order, Mont Août, guarding the southern
Saint-Gond Marshes, fell. Foch rushed Paul Grossetti's 42d ID from
the left to the right flank to stanch the German advance. His entire
right wing seemed to have collapsed, Eydoux's XI Corps routed. Already at 6:15 AM, Eydoux ordered the four divisions of XI Corps to fall
back ten kilometers. Foch deemed its situation "critical." But, as historian Hew Strachan has put it, he "doggedly refused to admit it."[113] The
front held, battered but unbroken as it withdrew.

Around 9 PM, Foch and his chief of staff, Colonel Maxime Wey-
gand, appealed to Fifth Army to send a division to replace Grossetti's
shattered 42d ID on the right flank. Franchet d'Espèrey did better: He
sent Foch two infantry divisions and the artillery of Defforges's X
Corps.[114] As well, Joffre dispatched Antoine de Mitry's 6th CD to
Ninth Army; Legrand-Girarde's XXI Corps was expected any hour up
from Épinal. Therewith, Ninth Army's "broken" right wing could be
repaired and the gap between it and Fourth Army reduced to ten kilo-

meters.[115] Interestingly, Foch's putative comment, "Hard pressed on my right, my center is falling back, impossible to move, situation excellent. I attack," is yet another legend of the Battle of the Marne. But as President Poincaré noted in a reply to Foch's address to the French Academy in February 1920, while some authorities treated the text as "authentic, I have not the courage to disillusion them." After all, "if you never actually wrote this optimistic message it was anyhow in your thoughts."[116]

As dawn broke, Saxon 103d RIR entered Sommesous "at a magnificent run and with shouts of Hurrah."[117] Then reality hit. The men were hungry, as they had left their knapsacks behind to lighten the load. A hot sun began to beat down on them, and there was little water on the chalky Catalaunic plain to sustain an army. Foch ordered Dubois's IX Corps and Eydoux's XI Corps furiously to counterattack, even as they retreated.[118] The Germans had no artillery with which to subdue the flanking fire. During the nighttime crossing of the Somme, units had lost their way and tumbled chaotically together. The regiment lost 104 dead or missing and 224 wounded at Sommesous. By nightfall, it had not reached any of its goals for the day.

Hausen that night judged the attack to have gone "generally satisfactorily." Indeed, he had scored what seemed a stunning victory in one of the classic bayonet charges of the entire war.[119] Group Kirchbach's three divisions had pushed Foch's right wing back ten to thirteen kilometers along a twenty-kilometer front, and his center away from the southern exits of the Marais de Saint-Gond. Such a feat would not be repeated until the great German spring offensives of 1918. But privately, Hausen noted that the advance had been "a difficult and slow forward movement from one stand of woods to another, from farm to farm, from one hillock to another."[120] It was the sort of "siege-style" warfare that Deputy Chief of Staff Martin Köpke had warned Alfred von Schlieffen about in 1895.

Group d'Elsa's left wing also had made little progress. Winckler reported his 2d GD utterly "exhausted" after the "enormous tension" of the bayonet attack. "Officers and men fell asleep wherever they had stopped marching." The terrain had been too rugged for a coordinated assault; infantry units had lost their way in the dark and stumbled into other, unfamiliar units. The loss of officers had been "exceptionally high."[121] Hausen's spirited attack ground to a halt on the outskirts of

Montépreux. The men were physically drained. There were no reinforcements to exploit the initial advance. An evening rain turned the
fields into gray ooze and flooded the marshes. By next morning,
Hausen's forces had lost contact with the French.

Traugott Leuckart von Weißdort, the Saxon military plenipotentiary to the OHL, just happened to be with Third Army at Châlons-
sur-Marne during the bayonet attack. He reported to War Minister
Adolph von Carlowitz at Dresden that Hausen "considered his situation to be very serious, since [Third] Army had been pulled apart by
having to rush to the aid of both 2. and 4. Army." The danger of
French forces breaking through Third Army's thinly manned front was
"serious." Specifically, well-emplaced French artillery had mauled
Planitz's 32d ID. Shaken by what he had witnessed, Leuckart von
Weißdort conferred with Chief of Staff von Hoeppner and General
von Kirchbach, commanding XII Reserve Corps. Both agreed with
the Saxon military envoy. "[They] complain bitterly about heavy
losses, exhaustion of the troops due to daily battles and long marches,
and the fear that not enough artillery shells can be brought up to the
front."[122] It was a sobering document.

While Third Army released no casualty figures for that night's assault, overall losses were roughly 20 percent. The 2d GD recorded 179
officers and 5,748 men killed or wounded. Each regiment of 1st GD
lost about a thousand; many companies were down to just fifty
men.[123] For the period from 1 to 10 September, d'Elsa's XII Corps reported 3,621 killed and 3,950 wounded; Laffert's XIX Corps, 2,197
killed and 2,982 wounded; and Kirchbach's XII Reserve Corps, 766
killed and 1,502 wounded.[124] The most recent research gives only
broad figures: 4,500 casualties for Group Kirchbach and 6,500 for
Group d'Elsa.[125]

General von Hausen's supporters have depicted him as a "gifted
army commander" who sought to bring about a small Cannae at the
eleventh hour, and they have seen in his night attack an example of operational art to be emulated by the rest of the German army.[126] Yet
even at the tactical level, its wisdom remains questionable in light
of the fact that it was carried out across a river at night, without
reconnaissance of enemy positions, without prior shelling, without
artillery support during the advance, and with unloaded rifles. At the
operational level, it was even less spectacular. The staggered start

had resulted in an uneven advance. By 10 AM, Planitz's 32d ID lagged four kilometers behind Plettenberg's Guard Corps, marching on Connantray-Vaurefroy. Hour after hour, Plettenberg waited for Planitz to close ranks—in vain. When 2d GD took Fère-Champenoise at 4:30 PM, Saxon 32d ID was nowhere to be seen. Plettenberg was forced to halt his advance at Corroy for fear of exposing his left flank.[127] In fact, for reasons that neither Planitz, nor Kirchbach, nor Hausen explained after the war,★ for eight hours Planitz had "regrouped" 32d Division, echeloned in depth! It was the second major mistake in two days, following closely on the heels of Hausen's earlier splitting of his army. And like that earlier decision, it denied the Saxons the chance to exploit the gap between French Third and Fourth armies still guarded by only d'Espée's 9th Cavalry Division.[128]

Nor had the advance of Larisch's 23d ID been a model of operational effectiveness.[129] After jumping off late at 6 AM, it had advanced on Sommesous. At 1:30 PM, Kirchbach ordered it to point southeastward toward Montépreux. Larisch did not execute this order until 2:45 PM, and then marched through woods northeast of Montépreux. Kirchbach re-sent his order. Larisch advanced at 4:45 PM, but again toward the northeast. When he finally arrived at his designated rendezvous with Planitz, 32d ID was nowhere in sight. As a result, the Saxons missed an opportunity to break through the gap between Pambet's 22d ID and 23d RID and turn Foch's right flank. Hausen and Third Army, to stay with Winston Churchill's term, thus missed their third "climacteric."

ON THE OURCQ, TWO events straight from the pages of a Hollywood movie script took place during the night of 7–8 September. First, the French retreat to Nanteuil-le-Haudouin created a fascinating "what if?" scenario. Sordet's cavalry corps, battered and beaten, had joined Déprez's 61st RID in abandoning Sixth Army's left wing. Maunoury was furious. He ordered the cavalry corps back into line by way of a forced night march—and then relieved Sordet of command. The latter had failed to carry out Maunoury's explicit order to mount a raid into Kluck's rear around La Ferté-Milon. Gustave de Cornulier-Lucinière's 5th CD, with

---

★ Unfortunately, the loss of the war diary of 32d ID during the Allied bombing of Potsdam in 1945 denies clarity as to the motive for the halt.

sixteen hundred sabers, ten guns, and 357 troops riding bicycles, was then sent on that mission, the only one of its kind in the war. For two daring days, 5th Cavalry rode around the Forest of Viller-Cotterêts behind German lines. At 6 PM on 8 September, under "a dark red, cloudy sky," it attacked a German airfield near Troësnes. At that very moment, a cavalcade of cars arrived with First Army's staff. Kluck, Kuhl, and their aides "seized rifles, carbines and revolvers," flung themselves on the ground, and formed a broad firing line. The situation was cleared by the arrival of Arnold von Bauer's 17th ID, which "violently" dispatched the French riders, reducing 5th CD to half its original strength. General de Cornulier-Lucinière's "brave riders," in Kluck's words, had "missed a good prize!"[130]

Second, there took place that night what became the legend of the famous "taxis of the Marne," which "saved" Paris from the Germans. In truth, much of the artillery, the infantry, and the staff of Trentinian's 7th ID departed Paris for the Ourcq front by train and truck during the night of 7–8 September. But Governor Galliéni wanted to make sure that in case of a rail breakdown, not all reinforcements would be denied Maunoury; hence, he decided to dispatch 103d IR and 104th IR by automobile.[131] Police confiscated twelve hundred of the capital's black Renault taxicabs and eventually shuttled five hundred from the Invalides across Paris and west to Gagny. There, each picked up four or five *poilus* and made the fifty-kilometer trip to Nanteuil-lès-Meaux overnight. Galliéni's *"idée de civil"* was brilliant; its execution, dismal. Proceeding with dimmed lights and few maps, the taxis veered off the dark roads, ran into one another, missed road signs, and endured countless flat tires. After the lead cabs of the motorized exodus had unloaded their "passengers" at the front, they immediately turned back to Paris on the same roads to pick up more soldiers—only to run head-on into the slower taxi columns approaching Nanteuil. Roads became clogged, tempers flared, and many of the soldiers had to be discharged as far as two kilometers from their destination. It was great publicity for Galliéni; militarily it was insignificant. To this day, it remains a central part of the public's remembrance of the Great War.

For 8 September, Joffre ordered Sixth Army to "gain ground towards the north on the right bank of the Ourcq."[132] Instead, Maunoury decided to regain the terrain lost the previous night and to outflank German First Army from the north. It was a poor decision. After initially capturing some ground northeast of Nanteuil-le-Haudouin, the French advance was repulsed by Sixt von Arnim's IV Corps, reinforced by 6th ID from Lochow's III Corps. A second assault into the center of the enemy line at Trocy-en-Multien was shattered by German artillery. Gronau held the heights east of Étrépilly, but at great cost. "Nearly everything in the front lines became unraveled," he noted in the corps' war diary, "without Reserves [and] waiting in vain for relief and reinforcement in searing heat and without water or food."[133] And on the south of the line, Trossel's 3d ID, pressured both by Blondlat's Moroccan brigade and by other French forces moving up from the Marne, smartly withdrew to the heights of Congis above the Thérouanne, destroying the Marne bridges on its left. Another day ended in deadlock and extreme exhaustion for both sides.

Kluck remained downright dogged. His favorite maxim came from Julius Caesar: "In great and dangerous operations one must not think but rather act."[134] He decided that 9 September would be his supreme act. "The decision will be obtained tomorrow," he informed Moltke on the night of 8 September, "by an enveloping attack on the north under the command of General von Quast starting from the region of Cuvergnon." Lochow's III Corps and Quast's IX Corps had at last arrived on the Ourcq. To the north, Lepel's 43d Reserve Infantry Brigade had come down from Brussels.[135] At the eleventh hour, First Army would snatch victory from the jaws of stalemate.

Galliéni sensed as much. Perhaps still remembering the brief bout of pessimism that he had experienced the day before, Galliéni admonished Maunoury late on 8 September that it was "essential" to maintain his position and hold ground "with all your energy."[136] The commander of Sixth Army hardly needed the reminder. While conceding that his "decimated and exhausted" troops were no longer able to mount an offensive, he nevertheless assured Joffre, "I am resisting in all my positions." If the German pressure became too brutal, he would "refuse" his left flank "little by little," concentrate his force toward the north, and await "the offensive of the British and the Fifth Army" on Kluck's southern flank.[137] Joffre, fully appreciating Kluck's "very violent attacks," concurred. "Avoid any decisive action by withdrawing your left, if necessary, in the general direction of the Entrenched Camp of Paris."[138] More concretely, he dispatched Louis Comby's 37th ID from Fifth Army to buttress the Ourcq front, and he urged Albert d'Amade's group of territorial divisions standing east of Rouen to advance at great speed toward Beauvais and interdict Lepel's brigade.

Quast's IX Corps spent much of the morning of 9 September undertaking a leisurely attack on Clément Buisson's 1st CD and Aymard Dor de Lastours's 3d CD, then shifted to a bombardment of Boëlle's IV Corps while the infantry prepared for the decisive assault. Kluck grew impatient. Time was running out. Near daybreak, he had finally received word that Bülow had withdrawn his right wing north of the Petit Morin, from Montmirail to Margny to Le Thoult–Trosnay.[139] This further widened the gap between First and Second armies, guarded now as before only by 2d CD and 9th CD as well as by Richard von Kraewel's mixed brigade (units from Quast's IX Corps). Between 8:28 and 9:11 AM, Kluck and Kuhl had received several dire messages from Marwitz and Richthofen. "Strong infantry and artillery across the Marne bridge at Charly." The second was equally distressing, "Strong enemy infantry advancing via Charly and Nanteuil; 5th Cavalry Division and [2d Cavalry Division] have orders to attack." A third message, repeating the second, broke off with an ominous, "I must leave immediately."[140]

Kuhl called a staff meeting. It was agreed to press the attack on French Sixth Army. Kluck waited impatiently for Quast (and Sixt von Arnim) to mount the infantry assault that would decide the Battle of the Ourcq. To avoid immediate exploitation of his left flank by the BEF, the French cavalry corps, and de Maud'huy's XVIII Corps, now heading into the corridor between German First and Second armies, Kluck at 9:30 AM withdrew Linsingen's II Corps to the line May-en-Multien–Coulombs-en-Valois and ordered it to front the danger emanating from the Marne.[141] Just in time. Around noon, Bülow sent Kluck a dire message: "Airmen report advance of four long enemy columns toward the Marne. . . . Second Army initiates retreat, right flank on Damery [in fact, Dormans]."[142]

Still, Kluck, *furor Teutonicus* personified, pressed on with the attack. "Every man," he admonished one of Quast's staff officers, "must be convinced that the enveloping attack" on French Sixth Army "must bring the decision." He urged Quast to drive for the line Lévignen-Betz without delay. If the right wing reached Dammartin-sur-Tigeaux by nightfall, "all will have been won."[143] Once again, Quast ran up against Déprez's 61st RID, and once again he put it to flight. An aviator reported that Lepel's brigade had engaged Maunoury's left flank at Baron, northwest of Nanteuil-le-Haudouin. At that very moment, a visitor from the OHL arrived at First Army headquarters: Lieutenant Colonel Richard Hentsch, on what undoubtedly is the most famous staff tour in military history.

CHAPTER NINE

DECISION: THE MARNE

---

*I don't know who won the Battle of the Marne, but if it had
been lost, I know who would have lost it.*

—JOSEPH JOFFRE

"IF THE PESSIMISTIC OBERSTLEUTNANT HENTSCH HAD CRASHED INTO
a tree . . . somewhere on his journey of 8 September, or if he had
been shot by a French straggler, we would have had a ceasefire two
weeks later and thereafter would have received a peace in which we
could have asked for everything."[1] These pithy words, published in
1965 by Jenö von Egan-Krieger, who as Karl von Bülow's deputy adjutant had witnessed the Battle of the Marne at Second Army headquarters, in many ways encapsulate the most persistent myth of the
Marne. To wit, had Lieutenant Colonel Richard Hentsch of the General Staff not arrived at Bülow's headquarters at Montmort-Lucy late
that afternoon and by way of his pessimistic assessment of the situation
helped persuade Bülow to initiate Second Army's (and thereafter First
Army's) retreat behind the Marne River over the next two days, victory over France would have been secured. After all, lead elements of
Alexander von Kluck's First Army were just thirty kilometers from
Paris. Bülow's Second Army likewise seemed to be pressing on the capital. Max von Hausen's Third Army was poised to break through Ferdinand Foch's Ninth Army at the Saint-Gond Marshes. The French
government had fled to Bordeaux. Thus, for an entire school of German military officers and writers, the "miracle of the Marne" consisted
of Hentsch's fateful order to retreat.

This line of argumentation is to be found not only in the vast memoir literature, but also in the fourth volume of the German official history, *Der Weltkrieg 1914 bis 1918*. Usually factual and understated in its judgments, the official history loses its objectivity with Hentsch's mission—to which it dedicates about fifty pages.[2] Its depiction of the events of 8 and 9 September is one uninterrupted saga of victorious advances: in the Argonne and Ardennes forests, at the Marais de Saint-Gond, and along the Ourcq River. Every German unit is on the threshold of a breakthrough; every French on the point of defeat. Exit Hentsch from the story, and victory is assured. Beyond Germany, U.S. Army chief of staff Peyton C. March after the war expressed amazement that Germany's senior army commanders had readily obeyed orders from "a perfectly unknown lieutenant colonel . . . far exceeding his authority," and suggested that the Allies erect a monument in their "Hall of Fame" to honor Hentsch.[3]

BEFORE ANALYZING THE FINAL, dramatic turn of events of the Marne, I owe the reader three brief discourses: Who was Richard Hentsch; on what documentary evidence can we evaluate his mission; and how did it fit into the German staff system of 1914?[4] Born 18 December 1869, the son of an army sergeant in the Inspectorate of Barracks at Cologne in the Prussian Rhineland, Hentsch because of "difficult family relations" decided in 1888 to enter the Saxon rather than the Prussian army. After a brilliant performance at the War Academy in Berlin, he alternated assignments to both the Prussian and Saxon General Staffs with infantry commands. In 1912, he served with Saxon XII Army Corps and the following year, in the rank of major as operations officer, with Saxon XIX Corps at Leipzig. In April 1914, Hentsch was promoted to lieutenant colonel and returned to the Prussian General Staff in Berlin as chief of the Third Section (Intelligence). He was a heavy smoker and had developed gallbladder problems that made him irritable and almost unapproachable.

Supporters and detractors alike agree that Hentsch was a superb, if somewhat pessimistic, military analyst. Colonel Max von Mutius, aide-de-camp to Kaiser Wilhelm II in 1914, recalled Hentsch as "an exceptional, talented officer endowed with clear and sober judgment."[5] General Hermann von Kuhl, who as chief of staff of First Army in

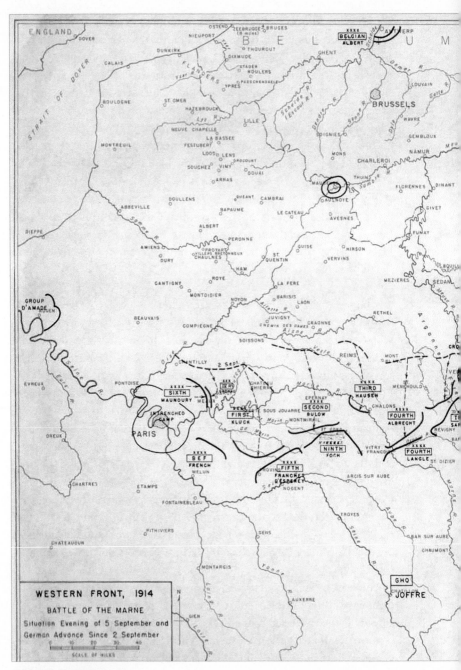

BATTLE OF THE MARNE, 1914

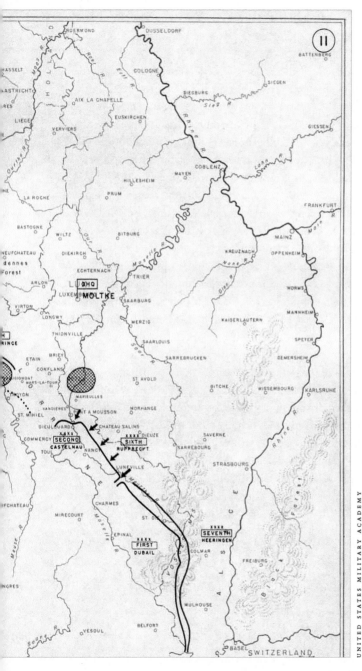

September "vigorously" argued with Hentsch about the order to retreat from the Ourcq, was fair in his postwar assessment. Hentsch on numerous occasions had worked under Kuhl at the General Staff—most recently in the Third Section, which Hentsch inherited from Kuhl. "I knew him as a very intelligent, prudent and reserved staff officer," Kuhl wrote, "in whom one could have absolute confidence."[6] Similarly, Gerhard Tappen, chief of operations in 1914, was not spare with praise after the war. He called Hentsch "an unusually gifted General Staff officer" who impressed on the basis of his "firm and precise nature" as well as his "calm, clear and convincing reasoning."[7] After the Marne, Hentsch served in the campaigns against Serbia and Romania (1915–17) and received the order Pour le Mérite while with Army Group Mackensen in September 1917. He died at Bucharest in February 1918 after a gallbladder operation.

For all the rivers of ink spilled about the so-called Hentsch mission,[8] there exists a single contemporary document: his report to the General Staff on 15 September 1914.★ This is extremely important in light of the fact that Chief of the General Staff Helmuth von Moltke never put his instructions to Hentsch on paper; that neither Moltke nor Hentsch made notes of their final discussion "under four eyes" before the lieutenant colonel left Luxembourg; that the only two officers who accompanied Hentsch in his staff car (Captains Georg König and Hans Koeppen) participated in just some of Hentsch's discussions with the various army commanders and their staffs; and that the other eyewitness accounts by General Staff officers Wilhelm von Dommes and Gerhard Tappen[9] were submitted to the Reichsarchiv a decade after the Marne as it produced the critical fourth volume, *The Marne Campaign—The Battle,* of its official history.† Indeed, the Hentsch mission remained shrouded in the "fog of uncertainty" even for the Reichsarchiv historians in the 1920s, when they discovered that the General

---

★ Moltke had been forced out of office the day before, and the rest of the senior staff was occupied with the withdrawal to the Aisne; none initialed Hentsch's report.

† Interestingly, Dommes was the "patriotic censor" who in May 1919 on behalf of the army and the Foreign Office convinced Moltke's widow, Eliza, not to publish the general's memoirs, titled *Responsibility for the War,* as their contents could bring about a "national catastrophe" at a time when the Allies were hammering out peace terms in Paris. Dommes (and Tappen) denied that Hentsch in September had been given "full power of authority" by Moltke. Both Dommes and Tappen after the war denied that Hentsch and Moltke had met privately shortly before Hentsch departed on his tour of the front. And both Dommes and Tappen were highly active in selecting materials for the Reichsarchiv to use in writing the volume dealing with the Battle of the Marne.

Staff's files on it "contained as good as nothing."[10] I have reconstructed Hentsch's staff tour on the basis of 1914 diary excerpts that were submitted to the Reichsarchiv by leading staff officers and front commanders in the early 1920s, and which became available only after the collapse of the German Democratic Republic in 1990.

Third, Hentsch's mission was not a "one-off," an isolated shot in the dark, but rather consistent with what one scholar has called the "Tappen method."[11] As noted in chapters 3 and 7, Moltke and Tappen had used "special emissaries" to communicate with Crown Prince Rupprecht of Bavaria's Sixth Army in Lorraine. Lieutenant Colonel Wilhelm von Dommes, Major Max Bauer, General Ludwig von Sieger, and Major Erich von Redern had all been sent to Rupprecht's headquarters not with specific written orders but simply with general talking points. All four had no authority to direct Sixth Army's operations. One, Dommes, had even been warned by Kaiser Wilhelm II "to avoid anything embarrassing that might give his planned 'suggestions' the impression of an 'order.' "[12] Yet in each case, Rupprecht and his chief of staff, Konrad Krafft von Dellmensingen, had understood the nature of those missions as representing the "thoughts" of the Army Supreme Command (OHL). Hentsch's mission was thus consistent with established General Staff practices.

THE MOOD AT THE OHL on the morning of 8 September can only be described as bordering on panic.[13] Moltke had received no word from First or Second armies the past two days. Both were reported to be within striking distance of Paris, yet one (First) had cut sharply across the front of the other (Second) at the Marne. French chief of the General Staff Joseph Joffre had launched a massive counterattack along the entire front from Paris to Verdun. A new French Sixth Army seemed to be trying to envelop First Army's right flank on the Ourcq. The British Expeditionary Force (BEF) ever so slowly was marching into the fifty-kilometer-wide gap between First and Second armies. Moltke, fearing that First Army had already been attacked in the rear and was in danger of being ground up between French Sixth Army and the BEF, desperately needed clarity. He believed that neither he nor Tappen could be spared at Luxembourg and hence decided to dispatch another emissary. Dommes, chief of the Political Section and just promoted to colonel, volunteered. Moltke instead chose Hentsch because he had visited both

Bülow's and Kluck's headquarters three days earlier and thus was better informed on the military situation at the Marne and the Ourcq.

During the intense discussions among the four officers—Moltke, Tappen, Hentsch, and Dommes—in Tappen's office, Moltke most likely gave Hentsch powers to initiate a general withdrawal of the right wing to the line Sainte-Menehould–Reims–Fismes–Soissons *if* First Army's predicament made such a move "necessary." Hentsch took this to constitute "full power of authority" (*Vollmacht*) to act in Moltke's name.[14] This certainly is what he shared with Captain König during their drive to the front. At a final meeting alone with Moltke sometime around 9 AM* on 8 September, Hentsch—according to Wilhelm II and half a dozen General Staff officers at the OHL—received no word to dissuade him of this interpretation.[15] At 10 AM Hentsch, along with Captains König and Koeppen, left Luxembourg to visit Fifth, Fourth, Third, Second, and First armies.[16] He decided on his own to undertake a grand tour of the entire front from the Argonne Forest to the Ourcq River rather than to proceed directly to Second and First armies. He was mentally "confident" and physically "fresh," and showed no signs of the gallbladder ailment. But, as he confided to Captain König, he regretted that Moltke had declined to issue him orders in writing and that the chief of the General Staff had not gone to the front in person, or at least sent a more senior officer, such as Deputy Chief of Staff Hermann von Stein or Colonel Tappen. He feared that he would be made the "scapegoat" for whatever action he took.[17]

The small motorcade arrived at Fifth Army headquarters in Varennes-en-Argonne at 1 PM on 8 September. Hentsch was pleased to learn that Crown Prince Wilhelm planned to storm Forts Troyon and Les Paroches the next day.[18] He then continued to Fourth Army headquarters, arriving at Courtisols, on the Vesle River, at 3:15 PM. He received the welcome news that Duke Albrecht would advance along the Marne-Rhine Canal the next day. In short, both armies were engaged in heavy fighting in the rugged Argonne terrain. Each hoped to mount flanking offensives by their respective right wings: Wilhelm to envelop French Third Army east of Revigny and Albrecht to surround French Fourth Army east of Vitry-le-François. Hentsch used Fourth Army's telephone link to inform Luxembourg that there was no urgency.[19]

* Greenwich Mean Time. German accounts give German General Time (one hour later).

Hentsch left Courtisols at 4:30 PM for Châlons-sur-Marne. Hausen was at the front, but Chief of Staff Ernst von Hoeppner optimistically reported that Third Army, despite the precarious position of its right wing due to having received its eighth and ninth SOS calls in two days from Second Army, was making "victorious but slow progress."[20] In fact, the audacious bayonet attack of Hausen's Third Army had been stopped by French Ninth Army. Still, for Hentsch, no urgency. Shortly before leaving Châlons at 5:45 PM, Hentsch radioed Moltke: "3. Army's situation and conception [of operations] entirely favorable."[21] Next, he was off to Second Army headquarters at Montmort-Lucy, where he arrived at 6:45 PM. Bülow returned from his command post at Fromentières half an hour later. The ensuing meeting was greatly to shape the Battle of the Marne.

On arriving at the Château de Montmort, Hentsch's cautious optimism waned. The shafts of the wagons of Second Army's headquarters staff all pointed north, an indication of a planned withdrawal.* He held a brief, first meeting with Chief of Staff Otto von Lauenstein. At first, Lauenstein tried to reassure Hentsch that all was well. That very afternoon Bülow had rushed to the front at Champaubert upon receiving word that Louis Franchet d'Espèrey's Fifth Army had broken through the seam between Otto von Emmich's X Army Corps and Guenther von Kirchbach's X Reserve Corps—only to return "laughing and in high spirits" because the report had proved to be false.[22] But then Lauenstein became more serious. The day's offensive by the left wing of Second Army had met with some success, but the right wing between Montmirail and Chézy had barely been able to maintain its positions and was in danger of being enveloped by French Fifth Army. Hentsch in the name of the OHL expressed the view that First Army would not be able to ward off French Sixth Army's offensive emanating from Paris, and that "enemy formations" were exploiting the fifty-kilometer-wide corridor between First and Second armies.[23]

Bülow then invited Hentsch, Lauenstein, and First General Staff Officer Arthur Matthes, as well as Captains König and Koeppen, into his study in the Renaissance castle. No protocol was kept. According to Hentsch's report of 15 September and Lieutenant Colonel Matthes's postmeeting notes, Bülow began with a description of Second Army's

---

* A junior staff officer had accidentally ordered this configuration of the baggage wagons.

situation.[24] It was "extremely serious and even dangerous." After a month of unceasing campaigning, Second Army's combat effectiveness had been reduced to the point where it was "in no condition" to deliver the "final and decisive blow" that was now being asked of it. Bülow, still without any reports from First Army headquarters at Mareuil, then turned his anger on Kluck. In nonobservance of Moltke's General Instruction of 5 September, First Army had turned southeast and crossed the Marne ahead of Second Army. Kluck now threatened to withdraw III and IX corps from Second Army's right flank, thereby widening the distance between the two armies by fifteen kilometers. The two cavalry corps and Jäger units that had been thrown into the breach would soon be overrun. Unless Kluck at once broke off the battle with Michel-Joseph Maunoury's Sixth Army at the Ourcq and closed up with Second Army, "hostile columns, brigades or divisions" could break through the gap. There were no reserves to fall back on. "First Army simply and solely is responsible for the current crisis."

At this point in the discussion, either Bülow or Matthes uttered what soon became a fateful word, *"Schlacke."*[25] Captain König reiterated this fact in formal replies to the historians of the Reichsarchiv in March 1925 and January 1926, and on both occasions testified that the word *cinders* had been applied to Second Army. The term would be central to all subsequent discussions, both at Montmort and Mareuil-sur-Ourcq. It undoubtedly stemmed from the fact that Second Army had been constantly on the march for a month, that it had fought at least three major engagements with French Fifth Army, that its right wing was being exploited by the enemy, that it already had to pull three corps behind the Petit Morin, that the men were at the end of their physical capabilities, and that Second Army's overall strength was little more than three corps.

Hentsch spoke next. In what Captains König and Koeppen described as "calm, measured terms," Hentsch described the state of Kluck's First Army east of Paris as "serious" and in danger of envelopment. It could not be counted on to prevent the enemy from crossing the Marne. It simply had to pull back from the Ourcq and he, Hentsch, "had the full power of authority to order this if necessary in the name of the Oberste-Heeresleitung." The boldness of the statement took Bülow by surprise. While conceding the potential "danger" east of

Paris, he remonstrated that a breakthrough "had not yet become reality." Again, he argued that the best solution was to order Kluck to close and protect Second Army's right wing. Hentsch demurred. First Army was no longer able to perform such a complicated maneuver in the midst of battle. Bülow countered that it was not yet too late. But time was fast running out for Kluck. If the Allies broke through at the Marne, Bülow lectured Hentsch, they would have two enticing options: "either to turn against the left flank and rear of First Army or against the right flank of Second Army; both could lead to a catastrophe." Hentsch agreed. He again reminded Bülow that he had "full power of authority" to order Kluck to withdraw from the Ourcq.

An orderly called Lauenstein to the telephone. Louis de Maud'huy's XVIII Corps had broken through Karl von Einem's VII Corps at Marchais-en-Brie and was threatening Montmirail. Bülow now became alarmed. Second Army's front was in danger of being breached. He immediately ordered his right wing (Kluck's III and IX corps as well as his own X Reserve Corps) to fall back fifteen to twenty kilometers behind Margny and Le Thoult-Trosnay to escape envelopment, at least for the moment. It should be noted that he did this *before* Kluck actually took back his III and IX corps and quick-marched them to the Ourcq. The plight of the German position was becoming ever more apparent. Bülow mused aloud that should the French "compel a retreat by force of arms" through a "hostile country in which practically every inhabitant might be armed," this could easily have "incalculable consequences."[26] Therewith, as Captain König clearly remembered, the word *retreat* had been uttered for the first time.[27]

All present at the meeting agreed that First Army's situation was "desperate"; none had faith that Kluck's right wing could envelop Maunoury's left. Furthermore, all agreed that the last possible moment to order a general retreat would come as soon as major Allied forces crossed the Marne. For reasons that he never explained, Hentsch decided to spend the night at Montmort rather than to push on to First Army headquarters. Unsurprisingly, the mood at dinner that night was "depressing." At 9:30 PM, just before going to bed, Hentsch sent off a cryptic note to Luxembourg: "Situation at 2. Army serious, but not desperate."[28] What was Moltke to make of that?

From 5 to 6 AM on 9 September, Hentsch, Lauenstein, and Matthes held a final meeting in the château's gardens. Bülow, undoubtedly exhausted from the previous night's momentous discussions, preferred sleep to another meeting with Hentsch, whom he described as the "horrible pessimist" from the OHL.²⁹ The talks merely fleshed out what had already been agreed upon: Second Army could hold its present position only if First Army disengaged at the Ourcq and withdrew eastward along the north bank of the Marne to link up with Bülow's right wing; if Kluck refused, Lauenstein was prepared to issue orders for Second Army to fall back behind the Marne. Hentsch concurred. At 6 AM, he departed Montmort for the eighty-kilometer drive to First Army headquarters at Mareuil. Moltke that day gave vent to his growing pessimism in a letter to his wife. "It goes badly. The battles east of Paris will not end in our favor. . . . And we certainly will be made to pay for all that has been destroyed."³⁰

Bülow, having risen and been briefed by Lauenstein and Matthes on their talks with Hentsch, reviewed the morning's reconnaissance report from Lieutenant Berthold of Flying Squadron 23. It confirmed his worst fears: "Advance by 5 hostile columns in a northerly direction in the region of Montmirail—La Ferté."³¹ They were obviously advancing from the Petit Morin toward the Marne into the gap between First and Second armies. For Bülow, the last moment to order a general retreat had arrived. "Second Army initiates retreat," he tersely informed Hausen and Kluck on his left and right, respectively, at 9:02 AM, "right flank on Damery [sic]."³² When shortly thereafter a message arrived from Mareuil stating that First Army was withdrawing its left flank (Alexander von Linsingen's II Corps) toward Coulombs, Bülow (incorrectly) assumed that this was because Hentsch had ordered Kluck also to begin the withdrawal.³³ Bad communications yet again bedeviled the Germans.

How does one account for the bizarre meeting at Montmort? On the surface, it seems ludicrous that a mere lieutenant colonel was able to move Prussia's most senior field commander into ordering his army to retreat without having suffered a major defeat. Even more ludicrous is that Bülow made absolutely no effort to contact either Moltke at Luxembourg or Kluck at Mareuil—by telegraph, rider, automobile, or airplane. Incredibly, four trains of Bülow's Telephone Section 2 sat idle at Dormans studying handbooks on how to install and repair lines and equipment; they took no steps whatsoever to establish telephone communications with Kluck, less than sixty kilometers away as the crow flies.[34] Surely, Bülow and Lauenstein could, and should, have overruled a lieutenant colonel and taken responsibility for coordinating their intended action with the OHL and First Army.

The truth of the matter is that the order to retreat was issued *not* by Hentsch or by Moltke, but by Bülow, with whom responsibility for setting in motion the German retreat from the Marne must rest. To be sure, Bülow was between a rock and a hard place by the evening of 8 September. Franchet d'Espèrey's Fifth Army was hammering Second Army's exposed right wing, over which it enjoyed a four-to-one numerical superiority. The BEF at last was advancing into the gap between the two German pivot armies and harassing Kluck's lines of communication. Could Bülow simply stand on the Marne for another day or two and hope and pray that Hausen's Third Army would yet defeat Ferdinand Foch's Ninth Army in the Saint-Gond Marshes; or that Kluck's right wing would sweep around the left flank of Maunoury's Sixth Army northeast of Paris? If either or both Hausen and Kluck were victorious, the campaign could be salvaged at the eleventh hour. If not, the sheer weight of numbers that favored Franchet d'Espèrey would crush Second Army's right wing—while the three corps of the BEF and the French cavalry corps would assault Kluck's rear on the Ourcq.

Some scholars have viewed Bülow's decision on the fourth day of the battle to avert a pending "catastrophe" by way of a timely retreat as "a sound one."[35] At the time, Lauenstein crowed to Deputy Chief of Staff von Stein that "Germany will one day thank General von Bülow that he issued the order to retreat."[36] Few German military writers, either at the time or subsequently, have agreed with either view. They are right. Quite apart from the sudden and impulsive nature of the decision and Bülow's refusal to seek input from Moltke or Kluck, it did not correspond to the situation on the ground. There had been no major breakthrough. Kluck was rallying his army corps to crush French Sixth Army on the Ourcq. Rudolf von Lepel's infantry brigade, marching southwest from Brussels, was about to strike Maunoury's left flank. Second Army had merely to close up its front and stand firm at the Marne. Time was not yet of the essence. Bülow, who had viewed Kluck and First Army as a "thorn in his side" ever since their turn toward the south after the Battle of Guise/Saint-Quentin, allowed emotions to dictate operations.

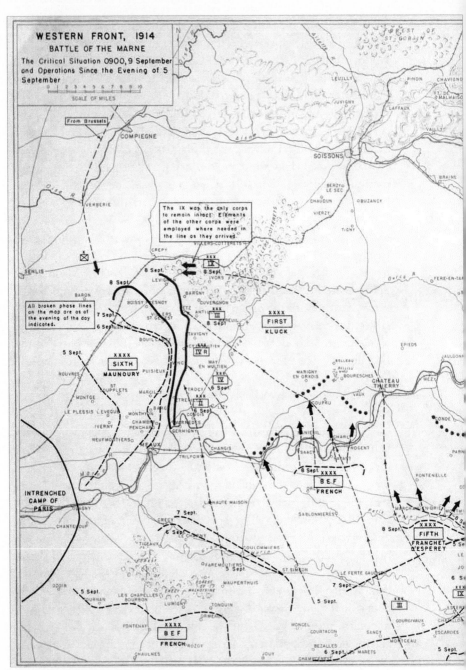

BATTLE OF THE MARNE, 9 SEPTEMBER 1914

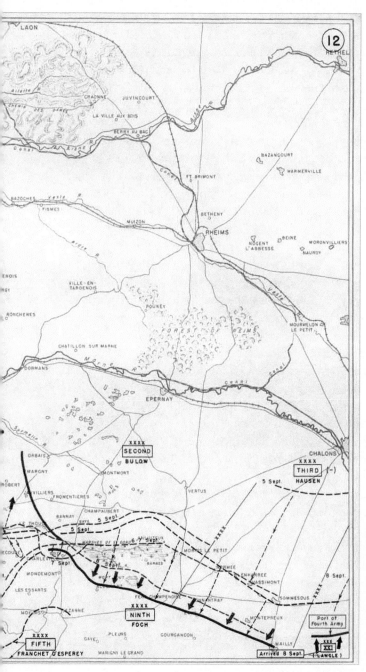

There remains the larger question concerning the fitness to command of Bülow and Lauenstein. The German official history and most eyewitnesses declined after the war to address the question, content merely to regurgitate "recollections" of what was said that 8 September. General Karl von Einem of VII Corps was an exception. After the war, he ruefully informed the historians of the Reichsarchiv, "General Lauenstein gave the impression of a sick man, Bülow was old and deaf."[37] The only military scholar to undertake "an attempt to elucidate psychological conditions" was Swiss lieutenant Colonel Eugen Bircher. After spending a decade sifting through every available scrap of French and German published sources, Bircher concluded that neither Bülow nor Lauenstein was in top form, physically or mentally, at the Marne.[38] Bülow, a first-rate organizer and reformer of Prussian army doctrine before the war, had long suffered from thyroid gland illness, which had left him with severe arteriosclerosis. Under extended combat and fatigue, this condition flared up anew and made him edgy, agitated, and hard of hearing. At age sixty-eight, he was four years beyond what constituted mandatory retirement in the French army. During the night after he made his momentous decision to retreat, Bülow suffered three "crying fits" at Saint-Quentin, his new headquarters. The next day, he extended a dour greeting to Pastor Paul Le Seur: "If you think that you are seeing the commander of Second Army, then you are mistaken! That, I once was."[39] Wilhelm II promoted Bülow to the rank of field marshal in January 1915 and three months later bestowed on him the order Pour le Mérite. That same year, Bülow suffered a stroke that paralyzed his left side; he died at Berlin on 31 August 1921.

Lauenstein, while in the rank of captain, had developed chronic thyroid eye disease,* which attacked his heart as well as nervous system; its symptoms included extreme nervousness, muscular tremors, palpitation of the heart, and protrusion of the eyeballs. Although only fifty-seven years old in 1914, the stress and strain of four weeks of constant combat had severely tested his nerves. Captain Koeppen, who was at the critical meeting in Montmort, later informed the Reichsarchiv that on 8 September, Lauenstein had made a "sick, almost apathetic impression" on him.[40] Bülow's chief of staff seemed to suffer

---

* Exophthalmic goiter, also known as Graves', Parry's, or Basedow's disease.

from heart palpitations during the meeting and managed to get through it only "with strong means, especially alcohol." Lieutenant Colonel Matthes, in fact, had taken Lauenstein's place in decision making. Incredibly, Wilhelm II awarded Lauenstein the Iron Cross, First Class, for his role in the Battle of the Marne. Lauenstein died of heart disease in 1916. The degree to which these physical ailments affected their decision making that 8 September remains an interesting, but open, question.

HENTSCH ARRIVED AT MAREUIL-SUR-OURCQ at 11:30 AM on 9 September after a five-hour detour via Reims, Fismes, and Fère-en-Tardenois. If the sight of wagon shafts turned away from the front had already alarmed him at Montmort, what he witnessed en route to Mareuil unnerved the staff officer.[41] At Fère-en-Tardenois, he encountered ammunition and supply trains, horse-drawn artillery, weary infantrymen, and columns of wounded cavalrymen fleeing from the front helter-skelter for fear of being cut off by advancing French forces. At Neuilly–Saint-Front, he could not get through, as the town was "plugged up" by countless people running in terror of what they thought to be bombs falling. Finally making his way through Neuilly "by the repeated use of force," Hentsch headed south. At Brumetz, he had to turn around when informed (incorrectly) that British cavalry was already in the area. Then panicked Landwehr soldiers fired at his car, taking it to be part of a French advance guard. At every stop, he was told that the enemy had driven German cavalry from the Marne and had crossed the river in pursuit.

General von Kuhl, First Army's chief of staff, met Hentsch on a dusty road at Mareuil. He quickly brought his former assistant up to speed: First Army that morning had been seriously threatened by Maunoury's attacks on the Ourcq; aviators had reported the British advance into the gap between the two German armies in the area north of the Petit Morin River stretching from Montmirail west to La Ferté-sous-Jouarre; and Hans von Gronau's IV Reserve Corps had been ground down in the fighting. But the arrival of Ferdinand von Quast's IX Corps and Friedrich Sixt von Arnim's IV Corps had stabilized the situation.[42] The two officers then entered Kuhl's operations room. No protocol was kept. Neither cared to send for General von Kluck, who was a mere two to three hundred meters away at his command post. Obviously, two General Staff officers could decide First Army's operations without its commander. Kuhl announced that First Army's right wing was about to turn Maunoury's left flank, and that he viewed the BEF's advance into the gap "not at all tragically" since the British had reeled back in confusion ever since Mons and Le Cateau. "We knew from previous experience," one of Kuhl's staff officers later stated, "how slowly the British operated." In any case, the two German cavalry corps would be able to "deal" with the BEF. A second staff officer recalled that Hentsch was "dumbfounded" by this optimistic evaluation of the situation.

Hentsch then made his formal presentation. Fifth Army was tied down at Verdun; Sixth and Seventh armies likewise were pinned at Nancy-Épinal; and Bülow's VII Corps had not "withdrawn" behind the Marne but had been "hurled" back across the river. To wit, the time for a general retreat had come. Third Army was to withdraw northeastward of Châlons, Fourth and Fifth armies via Clermont-en-Argonne to Verdun, Second Army behind the Marne, and First Army in the direction of Soissons and Fismes to close up with Second Army. A new German army was being formed at Saint-Quentin, whereupon the offensive could be renewed. Knowing that Bülow had ordered Second Army to fall back on Dormans, Hentsch took a charcoal pen and drew the lines of retreat for First Army on Kuhl's staff map.

Kuhl "vigorously" objected.[43] First Army's right wing was about to break Maunoury's left; the attack had to be given a chance to succeed; a retreat by his exhausted and disorganized forces was out of the question. And how, he demanded to know, had Bülow come to retreat behind the Marne? Hentsch obfuscated. "The decision to retreat," he coldly replied, "had been a bitter pill for Old Bülow to swallow." He then repeated the unsubstantiated but critical comment made by either Bülow or Matthes at Montmort that Second Army had been reduced to "cinders" by Franchet d'Espèrey's vicious attacks. Finally, Hentsch pulled his ace out of his sleeve: He had come with "full power of authority" and "in the name of the Oberste-Heeresleitung" ordered First Army to retreat. It was less than a clinical staff performance.

Kuhl was thunderstruck. If Second Army had indeed been reduced to "cinders" and was being forced to withdraw from the Marne, then "not even a victory over Maunoury" could spare First Army's left flank from certain destruction. In the terse verdict of the German official history, "The dice were cast." Kuhl had no direct telephone line to

Luxembourg, and he chose not to use one of his aircraft to send a staff officer to Montmort to confer with Bülow or Lauenstein. Later on, he simply informed Kluck of his discussion with Hentsch. "With a heavy heart, General von Kluck was obliged to accept the order."[44] Kuhl, who understood the inner workings of the General Staff system better than anyone, conceded at Hentsch's requested Court of Inquiry in April 1917 that the lieutenant colonel had "not exceeded his authority." Erich Ludendorff, then deputy chief of staff of the German army, concurred. "He [Hentsch] merely acted according to the instructions he received from the then Chief of the General Staff [Moltke]."[45]

Hentsch, "psychologically deeply shaken" by the gravity of his action and fearful that he would be "blamed for the unfortunate termination of the [Schlieffen-Moltke] operation,"[46] departed Mareuil at 1 PM—not to brief Second Army on his discussions with Kuhl but to inform Third, Fourth, and Fifth armies of the decision to retreat. Fifteen minutes later, Kluck issued formal orders "at the behest of the OHL" for First Army to break off the battle with French Sixth Army and to withdraw "in the general direction of Soissons."[47] Thus ended First Army's bloody thirty-day, six-hundred-kilometer advance on Paris.

There are times when senior military leaders have the right and the duty not to obey orders that make no sense, but to act in the best interests of their army and country. General Ludwig Yorck von Wartenburg was one such commander, who in December 1812 had signed a neutrality pact with Russia at Tauroggen rather than to continue to have the Prussian army serve as a hoplite force for Napoleon I. On 9 September 1914, Kluck and Kuhl owed it to their soldiers and their country to see the battle with French Sixth Army through to conclusion. For the last chance to win the campaign in the west rested with their decision. A simple demand for formal written orders from the kaiser or the chief of the General Staff would have done the trick since, given the deplorable state of German communications, it would have taken two days to send the message and to receive a reply from Moltke. Instead, we are left with the great "what if?" on the Ourcq.

LIEUTENANT COLONEL HENTSCH RETURNED to Luxembourg at 12:40 PM on 10 September. The atmosphere at the OHL was highly charged. The day before, while Hentsch was making his rounds, Moltke, hearing of the BEF's advance into the infamous gap by way of an intercepted wireless, had lost his nerve and recommended a withdrawal all along the line. The senior generals in the kaiser's entourage counseled continuation of the offensive. Wilhelm II agreed. He adamantly rejected Moltke's advice and demanded precise information on the status of the German right wing. But the discussions were "all superfluous," Chief of the Military Cabinet Moriz von Lyncker noted, since there existed no means of communication with Kluck.[48] Moltke, according to Deputy Chief of Staff von Stein, thereupon cracked. It was 1 August all over again, when the kaiser, upon receiving the (false) news that London would hold Paris out of the war if Germany did not attack France, had brusquely demanded that Moltke alter his entire operations plan and deploy against Russia alone. And as on that day, Moltke on 9 September became "extremely agitated." He reminded Wilhelm II that Bülow had already come out in favor of a withdrawal, and that Bülow "is one of the most experienced generals in the army."[49] The discussion raged furiously. The kaiser refused to cave in. "Despite [what I have heard], I will lead the army into [sic] France."[50] Unsurprisingly, Colonel Tappen sided with his Supreme War Lord. "Whoever now perseveres," he concluded, "is the victor."[51]

Hentsch's report on 10 September decided the issue. First Army, he informed Moltke, "was responsible for the entire retreat" because by removing III and IX corps from Bülow's right wing, it had allowed the distance between the two armies to widen by fifteen kilometers, and the enemy was now exploiting it. Disingenuously, he reported that First Army had already "issued orders to withdraw," and that he, Hentsch, had merely tried to steer that withdrawal into the direction desired by the OHL! Specifically, First Army was falling back on Soissons-Fismes and Second Army behind the Marne. Third Army could regroup south of Châlons-sur-Marne, while Fourth and Fifth armies could remain in their present positions.[52] Although we have no documentary evidence concerning Hentsch's claim that Kuhl had already "issued orders to withdraw," it is clear that he was putting the best possible spin on a decision that he had forced on First Army's chief of staff. Hentsch had left Luxembourg on 8 September convinced of the need for a general retreat and realignment of the armies in the west. His talks with Bülow and Lauenstein at Montmort had only reinforced that conviction. At Mareuil, Hentsch—with his talk of Second Army being little more than "cinders," of its already ongoing withdrawal, and of his "full power of authority" to issue orders to retreat "in the name of the Oberste Heeres-Leitung"—had left Kuhl no choice but to withdraw from the Ourcq. For that action, Hentsch was fully responsible.

Moltke was "pleasantly surprised" by Hentsch's report. The danger of Kluck's left wing being crushed by the BEF and the French cavalry corps had been removed; First Army's withdrawal to Fismes would allow it to link up with Second Army again and thus eliminate the fifty-kilometer gap; and Fourth and Fifth armies could hold their lines. "Thank God," Moltke cried out, "then the situation seems much better than I thought."[53] The offensive could be resumed just as soon as the new Seventh Army had been formed at Saint-Quentin. And when news arrived around 9 PM on 10 September that Paul von Hindenburg's Eighth Army had defeated P. K. Rennenkampf's Russian First Army at the Masurian Lakes, the mood swing at the OHL was complete. Still, the savvy Hentsch asked Moltke to visit Third, Fourth, and Fifth armies "to make sure that I did the right thing."[54] The chief of the General Staff agreed to set off early next morning. Württemberg's war minister, Otto von Marchtaler, caustically noted, "He should have done that earlier; too late!" on his envoy's report of Moltke's decision.[55] Perhaps to "punish" Kluck for his bold initiative (against express orders) in crossing the Marne ahead of Second Army, Moltke once again placed First Army under Bülow's command. He simply refused to accept that his most senior commander in the field had set in motion the entire chain of action that would lead to a general retreat from the Marne.

Moltke's temporary recovery of spirits belied his true state of mind. For there is no question that by 8–10 September, Helmuth von Moltke was a broken man, mentally and physically. The heart problems for which he had been treated in 1911, 1912, and 1913 and that had led to arteriosclerosis had returned, aggravated by the onset of a gallbladder infection.[56] His closest associates at the OHL noted his loss of energy, declining willpower, and inability to make decisions. To them, he looked tired and lethargic. They were not alone. Crown Prince Rupprecht of Bavaria, concerned that "the OHL has lost its nerves," had traveled to German headquarters on 8 September to discuss the assault on Nancy. He was shocked. Moltke gave the impression of being "a sick, broken man. His tall frame was stooped and he looked incredibly debilitated." He ruminated about "many mistakes having been committed," from the foolish rush of Josias von Heeringen's XIV and XV corps into Mulhouse in Alsace early in August, to Rupprecht's "failure" to shift parts of his Seventh Army to the German pivot wing (*Schwenkungsflügel*) near Paris.[57] Rupprecht left Luxembourg convinced that the German operations plan had failed.

The next day, War Minister Erich von Falkenhayn again wielded his acid-dripping pen. "Our General Staff has totally lost their heads," he noted in his diary. "Schlieffen's notes have come to an end and therewith also Moltke's wit."[58] Karl von Wenninger, Bavaria's military plenipotentiary to the OHL, also took up the theme of a squandered "Schlieffen Plan." Twice he sarcastically noted in his diary that Moltke and his "minions" had merely known how "to roll the camera" and let "Schlieffen's film play through." The "beaming faces" that he had encountered at Berlin on 31 July had turned to "down-cast eyes" at Luxembourg. "It is as quiet as a mortuary," he recorded on 10 September. "One tip-toes around . . . best not to address [General Staff officers], not to ask."[59]

Hans von Plessen, the kaiser's adjutant general and commander of Imperial Headquarters, also noted the charged atmosphere at Luxembourg. Moltke (and his wife) seemed "agitated, nervous and very depressed." The lack of contact with First and Second armies was vexing. Above all, "No one understands how the French, who have been beaten so many times, seem to muster the strength to [mount] such [new] advances."[60] General von Lyncker, who as chief of the Military Cabinet was responsible for all military appointments, ruminated about the "extremely serious" situation in France. "The armies have been pulled apart in a thin line [forming] a great arc from the Vosges [Mountains] to Paris." On 10 September, he concluded that the Schlieffen-Moltke Plan had unraveled. "In sum, one must appreciate that the entire operation—that is, the encirclement [of French forces] from the north and northwest—has been utterly unsuccessful." The campaign had instead degenerated into what he termed simple "frontal engagements." Ominously, Lyncker laid the blame squarely on the chief of the General Staff. "Moltke is totally crushed by events; his nerves are not up to the situation."[61]

IN CONTRAST WITH MOLTKE, Papa Joffre was firmly in control of operations. After his stirring appeal to the troops from a converted monk's cell at his headquarters at Châtillon-sur-Seine on 6 September, Joffre with an iron hand directed the great assault that he had waited two weeks to launch. He had used his interior lines to great advantage to re-supply and to expand his armies, with the result that he enjoyed a supe-riority of forty-one to twenty-three infantry divisions over the three German armies of the pivot wing.[62] The French official history speaks of a neat division of *les armées françaises* during the Battle of the Marne into two distinct combat phases: the "offensive maneuver" of Fifth and Sixth armies and the BEF on the left wing; and the "stationary battle" of Third, Fourth, and Ninth armies in the center of the line.[63] The light, mobile forces that had proved to be inadequate for the brutal front as-saults of the past were ideal for the redeployment that Joffre now under-took.

Specifically, Joffre admonished Yvon Dubail's First Army and Édouard de Castelnau's Second Army to continue to "fix" Crown Prince Rupprecht's Sixth and Seventh armies along the Meurthe and Moselle rivers in Lorraine; Maurice Sarrail's Third Army to keep Crown Prince Wilhelm's Fifth Army pinned down around Verdun; and Fernand de Langle de Cary's Fourth Army likewise to occupy Duke Albrecht's Fourth Army between the Marne and Vesle rivers north of Vitry-le-François.[64] A major breakthrough by any of these enemy forces would have disastrous consequences. Joffre most feared a pincer move by German Fourth, Fifth, and Sixth armies that could trap his Third and Fourth armies along the western banks of the Upper Meuse. Finally, he remained anxious about Sir John French and the BEF joining in the attack north from Melun across the Grand and Petit Morin rivers between French Fifth and Sixth armies.

In the center of the French front, Joffre ordered Foch's Ninth Army to hold the Saint-Gond Marshes while Franchet d'Espèrey's vastly re-inforced Fifth Army mounted constant pressure on Bülow's exhausted Second Army across the two Morins. This would allow Maunoury's Sixth Army, the so-called army of maneuver, to sweep around the right flank of Kluck's First Army and crush it along the Marne near Château-Thierry. Gronau's sighting of, and brilliant decision to attack, French Sixth Army with IV Reserve Corps on 5 September, as previ-ously noted, had tipped Joffre's hand and deprived him of the element of surprise. But there could be no turning back; the advance of more than one million men and three thousand guns could not suddenly

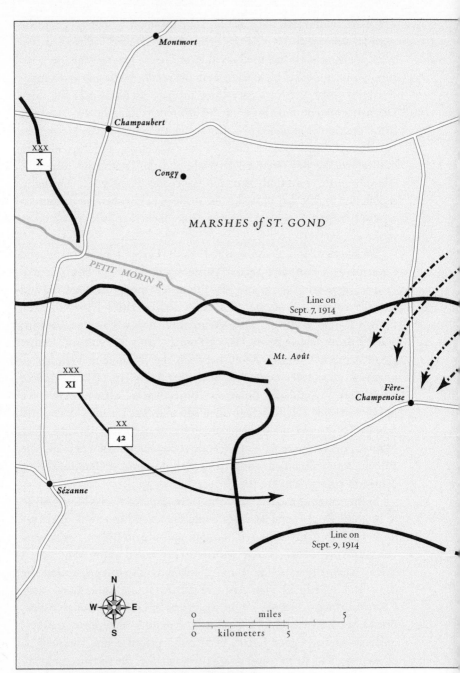

Montmort

Champaubert

Congy

MARSHES of ST. GOND

PETIT MORIN R.

Line on
Sept. 7, 1914

Mt. Août

Fère-
Champenoise

XXX
X

XXX
XI

XX
42

Sézanne

Line on
Sept. 9, 1914

N
W · E
S

| 0 | miles | 5 |
| 0 | kilometers | 5 |

FOCH AND FRENCH NINTH ARMY IN THE SAINT-GOND MARSHES

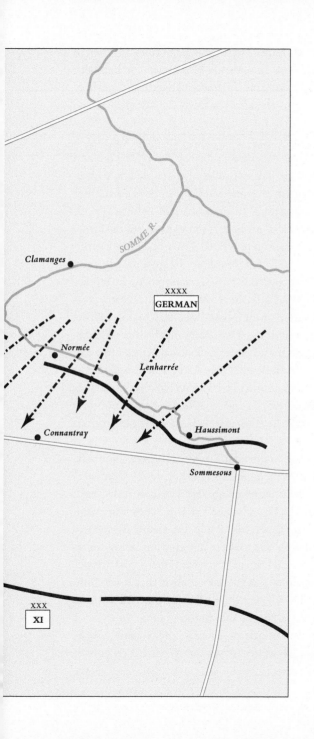

Clamanges

SOMME R.

XXXX
GERMAN

Normée

Lenharrée

Connantray

Haussimont

Sommesous

XXX
XI

be halted or even altered. Moreover, news was beginning to filter in of a great Russian victory over the Austro-Hungarians at Lemberg (Lwów).* This could only cause the Germans concern and perhaps force them to transfer some of their forces from the Western to the Eastern Front.

Early on the morning of 6 September, the confident attitude at Ewald von Lochow's III Corps encampment at La Ferté-Gaucher and that of Quast's IX Corps at Esternay was rudely interrupted by violent artillery bombardments. At first, they believed this to be only another French rearguard action, but reports from aviators of columns of infantry in the strength of at least an army corps marching against Esternay quickly convinced them that French Fifth Army had gone over to the attack. From noon until nightfall, Franchet d'Espèrey's left wing (XVIII, III, and I corps) engaged the two German corps in bloody fighting between Sancy and Châtillon-sur-Marne. Completely surprised by the enemy, and vastly outnumbered due to Kluck's decision to transfer II and IV corps a hundred kilometers north to the Ourcq, Quast and Lochow in the best tradition of the Prussian army ordered a smart counterattack, thereby limiting Fifth Army's advance to five kilometers. In fact, the French commander had deemed it crucial that Fifth Army begin the offensive with a success. Hence, he had not set it unrealistic goals and had ordered it to entrench once visible progress had been made.

The next day, 7 September, Franchet d'Espèrey renewed the attack, this time in the direction of Montmirail. On his left, Louis Conneau's II Cavalry Corps and the BEF marched against German rear guards near Rozay-en-Brie (Rozoy). The advance for the Allies was suspiciously easy. Were the Germans laying a trap for them? Were they withdrawing forces in order to undertake a flanking movement elsewhere? The British, as always, advanced most cautiously. Joffre twice called Sir John French's headquarters to make it clear that it was "important," indeed "indispensable," that the BEF drive forward without delay and debouch north of the Marne that night.

Content to let his advance guards halt at the Grand Morin, Franchet d'Espèrey took stock of the situation. What his reconnais-

---

* Grand Duke Nikolai Ivanov's Russian army took 130,000 prisoners and inflicted 300,000 casualties on Franz Conrad von Hötzendorf's forces between 26 August and 11 September 1914.

sance brought back was simply astounding: Bülow had ordered his entire right wing—III and IX corps as well as X Reserve Corps—to withdraw as far as twenty kilometers behind the Petit Morin, thereby further widening the gap between his Second Army and Kluck's First Army. When Maud'huy's XVIII Corps later that afternoon seized Marchais-en-Brie, thereby threatening Montmirail and Johannes von Eben's X Reserve Corps with envelopment, Bülow undertook yet another fateful repositioning, moving VII Corps and X Reserve Corps to a north-south line between Margny and Le Thoult-Trosnay. The right wing of German Second Army had been turned.[65]

But Franchet d'Espèrey, who had distinguished himself as a corps commander at Guise/Saint-Quentin with his bold infantry charge, now seemed bedeviled by Carl von Clausewitz's "fog of uncertainty." Joffre's General Instruction No. 7 of 7 September had been clear: "The Fifth Army will accelerate the movement of its left wing and will employ its right wing to support the Ninth Army."[66] And Joffre's Special Order No. 19 the following day had again shown Franchet d'Espèrey the way: "The main body of the Fifth Army, marching due north, will drive the forces opposed to it beyond the Marne."[67] But instead of using his numerical superiority as a "breakthrough force" (*armée de rupture*) to destroy a retreating foe—either by envelopment or breakthrough—"Desperate Frankie" advanced only "methodically"[68] and with Fifth Army in echelon, its right (!) wing in advance. Fortunately for Franchet d'Espèrey, Bülow strangely chose not to destroy the Marne bridges after his units retreated over them.

During the early hours of 8 September, Kluck ordered III and IX corps (as II and IV corps before them) up to the Ourcq. The Allies had reached their first "climacteric" of the war: The BEF, Conneau's cavalry corps, and the left wing of French Fifth Army were poised to charge through the wide gap in the German line between Meaux and Château-Thierry. All that stood between them and annihilating either (or both) German First or Second army were four divisions of Georg von der Marwitz's and Manfred von Richthofen's thin and weary cavalry screen—augmented by Richard von Kraewel's mixed brigade (34th Infantry Brigade and two batteries of field artillery).[69]

The Allied breakthrough remained a mirage. Despite Joffre's constant exhortations, the BEF moved north at a snail's pace, still some thirty kilometers behind Joffre's desired jump-off line. Douglas Haig

(I Corps) and Horace Smith-Dorrien (II Corps) consistently spied phantom German formations in front of them. On 9 September, Haig halted I Corps until nightfall at the mere sighting of Karl von Ilsemann's 5th Cavalry Division (CD) and IX Corps' baggage train. Smith-Dorrien, not to be outdone, likewise stopped his advance after British 5th Infantry Division (ID) had encountered Kraewel's mixed brigade at Montreuil-aux-Lions. Smith-Dorrien engaged only two brigades of 5th ID and two companies of 3d ID against a vastly inferior force. Farther to the west, "Putty" Pulteney's III Corps failed to cross the Marne near La Ferté-sous-Jouarre. The German screen held the right bank of the Marne and destroyed most of the bridges in this sector. As at Meaux, the Germans expertly deployed their light guns on reverse slopes and their machine guns in the wooded ravines and trenches of the north bank of the Marne Valley. The four service pontoons with British III Corps were insufficiently equipped to span the seventy to ninety meters of the Marne. As darkness fell, only about half of 4th Division's battalions had crossed the river on a makeshift floating bridge made of trestles, pontoons, barrel piers, and boats.[70]

British cavalry, in the words of historian Hew Strachan, "was entirely out of the equation."[71] Edmund Allenby's 1st CD was content just to maintain contact with Franchet d'Espèrey's left flank, and Hubert Gough's 2d CD likewise with Maunoury's right wing. The dense woods, rivers, and ravines in the area seemed to dictate caution rather than bold pursuit. By nightfall, the BEF was still ten kilometers behind Joffre's *original* departure line. In historian Sewell Tyng's stinging words, Sir John French's army had "exercised no effective intervention" at the "point of greatest strategic significance and at the crucial moment of the battle." In strategic terms, its advance into the German gap "remained no more than a threat which was never translated into decisive action."[72] Except, of course, by Hentsch, Bülow, and Kuhl.

Nor did the French cavalry corps distinguish itself in the effort to break through the German corridor. Following on the heels of British cavalry, Conneau's riders crossed the Marne at Château-Thierry in the afternoon of 9 September. They encountered no opposition. But when he received the news that only a single German cavalry division (the 5th) was to the north, Conneau halted his advance. General de Maud'huy, coming across Camille Grellet de la Deyte's 10th CD resting by the roadside south of the Marne, asked for the latest reconnaissance reports. Upon being told that there were none, he exploded. "It's a disgrace to the French cavalry. My divisional cavalry has already told me there is no one at Château-Thierry and you tell me you know nothing! You're good for nothing!" He informed Grellet that he was going to storm Château-Thierry with a regiment of African Zouaves. "You can follow behind if you like, but at least don't get in my way!"[73]

In all fairness to the soldiers and cavalrymen of the BEF, French Fifth Army, and the French cavalry corps, much had already been asked, and was still being asked, of them. After days of marching to the front in mid-August, they had charged the enemy—only to have had to endure weeks of miserable retreat under a broiling sun and along dusty roads. Then they had about-faced and held off an enemy victorious and confident. Since 6 September, they had attacked yet again. They had suffered horrendous casualties. Tens of thousands were dead or wounded as well as ill from foot sores, heat exhaustion, sunstroke, thirst, and dysentery. Especially Jean-François Sordet's cavalry corps; having covered a thousand kilometers since the war began, it simply was too exhausted to push on ahead. Christian Mallet, a trooper with Colonel Félix Robillot's 22d Dragoons, later recalled the suffocating heat, gnawing hunger, intolerable thirst, and utter fatigue of those days. "The exhausted men, covered with a layer of black dust adherent to their sweat, looked like devils. The tired horses, no longer off-saddled, had large open sores on their back."[74] In fact, French riders, unlike their British counterparts, stayed in the saddle rather than save their horses by occasionally dismounting. In Foch's caustic words, they seemed to have "their brains in their legs."[75] Finally, German rear guards and cavalry fought a tenacious retreat throughout 7–8 September, further hampering the Allied advance.

The tide had turned. The German day of decision in the west, 6 September, was gone. With the German retreat from the Marne and the Ourcq in full swing, the initiative was now completely with the British and the French. The ninth of September would turn out to be the decisive day of the Battle of the Marne for the Allies. Franchet d'Espèrey was aware of the importance of the moment. Once more, he drove Fifth Army forward. Once more, he urged his soldiers on with a clarion call. In a forced appeal to history, he called on them to rid "the

Motherland" of the "barbarians," just as they had done a century before with "the Prussians of Blücher."* Still, he warned against overconfidence. "The enemy is shaken but not completely beaten. Great tests of your endurance lie ahead of you, you will have to carry out many long marches, to take part in many bitter fights."[76] In fact, with four German army corps having first moved north to the Ourcq, and now retreating northeast in the direction of the Valley of the Aisne, the going was unsurprisingly easy. French Fifth Army, having waded across the narrow Petit Morin the day before, at 2:30 PM on 9 September crossed the Marne southwest of Château-Thierry. Concurrently, British cavalry seized several Marne bridges between La Ferté-sous-Jouarre and Château-Thierry.

Joffre immediately spied the opportunity awaiting the Allies. The magnitude of his new design became apparent late in the night of 9 September. Until then he had concentrated his efforts on trying to push the BEF and the left wing of Fifth Army to exploit the gap between German First and Second armies, but the slow pace of their advance and the enemy's withdrawal had cost him that opportunity. Joffre returned to his former offensive optimism. He shifted focus from breakthrough to envelopment. His Instruction particulière No. 20 "suggested" that Sir John and the BEF, with their flanks covered by Raoul de Lartigue's 8th ID and Maud'huy's XVIII Corps, seize the heights of the south bank of the Clignon River between Bouresches and Hervilliers and attack Bülow's Second Army with all due energy and speed.[77] The Particular Instruction ordered Fifth Army to drive the enemy "back toward the north"; all the while, Gilbert Defforges's X Corps was to maintain contact with Foch's Ninth Army. This would free Maunoury's Sixth Army, "resting its right on the Ourcq," to attack northward "to seek to envelop the enemy." Eugène Bridoux's V Cavalry Corps was to harass "the flank and the rear" of Kluck's "fleeing" First Army. Remembering the nervous state of the government at Bordeaux, Joffre dashed off a reassuring cable: "General situation is satisfactory. . . . Battle is engaged in good condition and should lead to a decisive result."[78] By the night of 9 September, the Allies were on the offensive along a broad front stretching from Meaux to Châlons-sur-Marne.

---

* In 1813–15, Field Marshal Gebhard von Blücher had fought with the Duke of Wellington against Napoleon I.

THE FRENCH CENTER ALONE caused Joffre concern. Langle de Cary's Fourth Army, fronting Duke Albrecht's Fourth Army, was stretched out in a wide arc between Humbauville, southwest of Vitry-le-François, and Revigny-sur-Ornain. On its left wing, the Mailly Gap, some twenty kilometers wide, separated it from the right flank of Foch's Ninth Army southeast of the Saint-Gond Marshes; on its right, the smaller Revigny Gap had opened between Fourth Army and Sarrail's Third Army. Joffre rushed reinforcements up from Lorraine—Louis Espinasse's XV Corps and Émile-Edmond Legrand-Girarde's XXI Corps—to plug the gaps. His one worry was that an enemy breakthrough there could jeopardize his left wing behind the Seine River.

Indeed, on 6 September, Duke Albrecht planned to attack southeast from Vitry-le-François along the Marne-Rhine Canal with VI, VIII, and XVIII corps as well as VIII and XVIII reserve corps to relieve the pressure on German Sixth Army before Nancy. At dawn, a violent French artillery attack preempted his plan. Although Albrecht at first believed that this was simply one last, desperate French attempt to secure their line by way of a brazen offensive, aviators' reports of the arrival of fresh formations (Joseph Masnou's 23d ID from XII Corps in the south) quickly brought the realization that the French had gone to the attack in the east as well. Erich Tülff von Tschepe und Weidenbach's exposed VIII Corps stood in danger of being enveloped; hence, as mentioned earlier, Duke Albrecht appealed to Third Army for aid. Hausen, as ever, responded positively. He divided his army, sending Maximilian von Laffert's XIX Corps and 23d ID from Karl d'Elsa's XII Corps to buttress Fourth Army's right wing. For three days, Langle de Cary's soldiers fought a vicious battle in the land between the Ornain and Marne rivers. Neither side gained an advantage.

On 8 September, Duke Albrecht had declined to take part in Hausen's nighttime bayonet attack on French artillery positions; by the time he attempted it the next morning after a lengthy artillery barrage, he had lost the critical element of surprise. At ten-thirty that night, Langle de Cary confidently informed Joffre that "all together, the general situation at the close of day is good." The enemy had thrown everything it had at Fourth Army, Langle de Cary reported, and French fliers reported no German reserves moving up to the front.

"Physical state of troops: good. Moral state: much improved, is now actually excellent." The arrival of Legrand-Girarde's XXI Corps from Épinal augured well for the next day, when Langle de Cary planned to attack Albrecht's right flank, with "a good chance of bringing about a decision."[79] The German retreat in the afternoon of 9 September made that "chance" more than reasonable.

In fact, a sharp dispute had broken out between the German center armies. While Duke Albrecht called on Fifth Army to support his left wing in an attempt to envelop the left flank of Langle de Cary's Fourth Army, Crown Prince Wilhelm instead wanted Fourth Army to tie down Langle de Cary's right wing while he forced his way through the Revigny Gap. Appeals for resolution to Luxembourg brought no relief. Studiously careful not to get ground up in a spat between two royals, Moltke managed a Solomon-like decision: "Mutual support between 4. and 5. Armies desirable."[80] Albrecht eventually yielded, after Wilhelm appealed the matter directly to his father, the kaiser.

While the German royals squabbled, Joffre struck. On the morning of 6 September, Sarrail's Third Army, with its pivot on Verdun and its main body about twenty kilometers southwest of the fortress, had advanced against German Fifth Army as part of the great Allied offensive.[81] Expecting the enemy to continue its advance southward from Clermont-en-Argonne and Sainte-Menehould, Joffre had ordered Sarrail to "attack the flank of the enemy forces . . . west of the Argonne Forest."[82] But the German crown prince had shifted his advance onto a southeasterly course toward Bar-le-Duc, with the result that the two armies clashed head-on. Frédéric Micheler's V Corps, entrusted with guarding the Revigny Gap, took the brunt of the German attack by Kurt von Pritzelwitz's VI Corps—the same unit that had so badly mauled the French colonials at Rossigny. And just as at Rossigny, Pritzelwitz's corps again stove in a French division—this time the 10th of Micheler's V Corps—shot its commander, General Charles Roques, and captured most of its staff.[83] Espinasse's XV Corps had arrived just in time to take part in Third Army's debacle.

Joffre, true to fashion, blamed the setback on Third Army's commander. He struck out furiously. He railed against "the mediocre military value" of some of Sarrail's units. He accused them of having committed "grave errors such as abandoning rifles, ammunition and rucksacks along the roads or in bivouacs." He charged that especially

173d Infantry Regiment (IR) had purposefully "broken war material." All too many infantry officers "have no authority over their men"; staff officers failed to show "sufficient activity." Joffre closed his blistering epistle with the dire admonition that "General Command of Third Army reestablish order, taking whatever measures necessary."[84]

By 8 September, the Germans had stormed the Meuse heights and thrown the French line back from Revigny, Laheycourt, and Laimont. Joffre, concerned that the enemy would now break through the Revigny Gap, late on the night of 8 September ordered a chastened Sarrail to withdraw his right wing and break off contact with *la région fortifée de Verdun*.[85] Sarrail churlishly refused. He would later claim that he had heroically refused the "order to abandon Verdun" and assume the title of "Savior of Verdun." In fact, Verdun with its mighty ring of forts, 350 heavy and 442 light guns, and 65,774 soldiers had little to fear from the German crown prince.[86] With his stubborn refusal to obey Joffre's order, Sarrail had momentarily imperiled the entire French attack by failing to maintain contact with the right wing of Langle de Cary's Fourth Army.[87]

Crown Prince Wilhelm on 10 September made a final bid for breakthrough. His Fifth Army had taken a frightful battering from the *soixante-quinzes*—5,263 dead and missing and 9,556 wounded in the last ten days.[88] General Frédéric-Georges Herr, in charge of VI Corps' artillery brigade, expertly directed French fire from aircraft and balloons.[89] In a single day, the 75s of Martial Verraux's VI Corps destroyed eleven batteries (sixty-six guns) of Bruno von Mudra's XVI Corps. To silence the "black butchers," Wilhelm, like Hausen two days before, decided on a nighttime bayonet attack by VI, XIII, and XVI army corps. Using his telephone line from Varennes to Luxembourg, he obtained Moltke's sanction.[90] But as Bavarian casualties before Nancy mounted dramatically, the chief of the General Staff rescinded his approval. Wilhelm and his chief of staff, Konstantin Schmidt von Knobelsdorf, took the matter to Chief of Operations Tappen and again threatened to seek an imperial ruling.

Moltke relented. At 2 AM on a cold and rainy 10 September, almost one hundred thousand *Landser,* with rifles unloaded and bayonets fixed, stormed French positions around Vaux-Marie, north of Sainte-Menehould.[91] The charge, like that of George Pickett at Gettysburg in July 1863, was shattered by enemy artillery. Well into daybreak, the

75s of Micheler's V Corps and Verraux's VI Corps poured their deadly fire into the packed gray ranks of German infantry. At 7:45 AM, the French counterattacked a demoralized and decimated enemy. Some German units panicked; others ran about in the darkness leaderless and in utter confusion; few dared return the enemy's fire for fear of shooting their own men.[92] A large proportion of Fifth Army's fifteen thousand casualties over the first ten days of September occurred that night. At the company and battalion levels, officer losses were as high as 40 percent.

The war diary of Max von Fabeck's Württemberg XIII Corps reveals the full terror of that dreadful night.[93] Hinko von Lüttwitz's 12th RID "failed completely to reach its assigned line," in the process blocking the advance of 38th Reserve Infantry Regiment (RIR). In the confusion, the two units fired on each other almost at point-blank range. The aforementioned French counterattack "totally demolished" 38th RIR. Elsewhere, Bernhard von Pfeil und Klein-Ellguth's 27th ID also failed to reach its assigned target line. Mudra's XVI Corps blindly shot at German units advancing on its flanks. By morning, Fabeck's units were in total disarray, hopelessly intertwined with those of XVI Corps and 52d Infantry Brigade. Most were down to one-third of full strength. "Nowhere," the war diary of XIII Corps concluded, had the original goal of silencing the French batteries "been achieved."

Near the end of that savage butchery, at around 9 AM, Lieutenant Colonel Hentsch arrived at Varennes on the return leg of his tour of the front. Arguing that Second Army had been reduced to "cinders," that the enemy had driven a wedge between German First and Second armies, and that a full withdrawal was under way, he ordered Fifth Army to fall back to the line Sainte-Menehould–Clermont. Crown Prince Wilhelm and Schmidt von Kobelsdorff vehemently refused to obey the order and demanded such written instruction from Wilhelm II or Moltke.[94] On the French side, Sarrail tersely assured Joffre at the end of the day, "Situation satisfactory."[95] At 2 PM on 11 September, Joffre was sufficiently confident of victory to inform War Minister Alexandre Millerand, *"La bataille de la Marne s'achève en victoire incontestable."*[96] The clarity of the statement requires no translation.

AT 4 AM (GMT) on a cold and damp 11 September, Moltke left Luxembourg with Colonels Tappen and von Dommes to visit his field armies.

Heavy northerly winds prohibited travel by air, and even the horses had trouble finding their footing in the "bottomless" mud. At Varennes, Moltke and Crown Prince Wilhelm conducted what eyewitnesses termed "an agitated and embarrassing" interview. The crown prince was in no mood for the chief of staff's pessimistic assessment of the situation. He cheerily informed the gloomy Moltke that the *attaque brutal* with the bayonet on the morning of 10 September had been a "great success" and that Fifth Army was ready to "exploit" this triumph.[97]

The trio motored on to Suippes and at 11 AM briefly conferred with Hausen. The mood at Suippes was "depressing." Hausen's 32d ID had recently been shattered by Foch's violent counterattacks, and his 24th RID had been battered by Ninth Army's advance guards the night before near Connantray-Vaurefroy. If the word *cinders* (*Schlacke*) applied to anyone, it was to Third Army, which had lost 14,987 men in the first ten days of September.[98] There was nothing to fall back on, as Dresden had already sent out all available reserves—111 officers, 351 noncommissioned officers, 4,050 ranks, and 330 horses.[99] Incredibly, Hausen stated that Third Army, stretched across a forty-kilometer front, could hold its position until the new offensive with Seventh Army commenced. Moltke, although convinced that the French were about to mount a major assault to "pierce the right and center of Third Army" and afraid that Hausen's forces "were no longer combat effective," concurred.[100]

Sometime before 1 PM, Moltke arrived at Fourth Army headquarters at Courtisols. The mood there was "confident." Duke Albrecht assured Moltke that although he had lost 9,433 men in the last ten days, he could spare forces to shore up Hausen's battered Third Army. His chief of staff, General Walther von Lüwitz, lectured Moltke that a major withdrawal would have a decimating "moral effect" on the troops.[101] Then the proverbial bolt from the blue: Just as Tappen was drafting orders for Fifth, Fourth, and Third armies to maintain their positions, his staff overheard a relayed radio message from Bülow at Second Army headquarters to the OHL. "Enemy appears to want to direct his main offensive against the right flank and center of Third Army" in an obvious attempt to break through at Vitry-le-François.[102] A "deeply shaken" Moltke saw no reason to doubt Bülow. The only countermeasure was to withdraw the entire German center to the line Suippes–Sainte-Menehould until the new offensive (with Seventh

Army) could be launched on the right wing. Moltke and Tappen, appreciating that Second Army had sustained 10,607 casualties between 1 and 10 September, agreed. It was only fitting that Bülow, who had set the retreat in motion on 8 September, likewise initiated the final decision to undertake a general retreat all along the front.

Moltke was fearful that not only his right wing but now also his center stood on the point of collapse. He rushed back to Suippes. Hausen was incapacitated due to illness, now correctly diagnosed as typhus. Hoeppner, his chief of staff, was at the front. Thus, a Major Hasse on Third Army's staff confirmed Bülow's dire prognosis: Foch's Ninth Army was threatening the entire front of Third Army. No sooner had Hasse completed his briefing than Third Army's radio operators intercepted a call from Duke Albrecht's Fourth Army to the OHL: "Strong enemy forces marching against Vitry-le-François and Maisons-en-Champagne."[103] There was not a moment to lose. At 1:30 PM, Moltke made what he later called "the hardest decision of my life, [one] which made my heart bleed,"[104] the general order to retreat in echelon. He instructed Second Army to fall back to Thuizy (southeast of Reims), Third Army to the line Thuizy-Suippes, Fourth Army to Suippes–Sainte-Menehould, and Fifth Army to east of Sainte-Menehould. This would essentially become the stationary trench line of the Western Front.

Moltke dispatched Dommes to bring the unwelcome news to Fourth and Fifth armies, where Dommes in horror discovered that their army corps were down to but ten thousand infantrymen each. Moltke, for his part, motored on to Bülow's headquarters. Lieutenant Colonel Matthes, who basically had taken over operational decisions from the "sick, almost pathetic" Lauenstein, never forgot the chief of staff's shaken state. "Constant nervous facial twitching betrayed his extremely strained condition to all those present."[105] Moltke declined to motor on to First Army. Perhaps finally acknowledging the lack of leadership on the German right wing, he placed Heeringen's new Seventh Army at Saint-Quentin under his most senior army commander—Karl von Bülow.[106]

Moltke returned to his headquarters in the Hôtel de Cologne at Luxembourg in a driving downpour around 2 AM on 12 September. His first order was to relieve the severely ill Max von Hausen of command of Third Army. He next briefed Wilhelm II on his tour of the front. According to Hans von Plessen, chief of Imperial Headquarters, the kaiser became enraged, "slammed his fist on the table and forbade any further retreat."[107] Moltke then went to bed, where he was comforted by several of his staff officers—and by his wife, Eliza.

In a belated bid to reverse what they considered to be the rapidly escalating disaster occasioned by Moltke's order to retreat, Deputy Chief of Staff von Stein and Chief of Operations Tappen set off early in the morning of 13 September on a tour of army headquarters. At Montmédy, they came across Dommes, returning from Fourth and Fifth armies. The trio quickly agreed on a last-ditch effort to save the German campaign in the west: They would plug the still-twenty-kilometer-wide gap between First and Second armies by withdrawing one army corps each from Third, Fourth, and Fifth armies. They informed Wilhelm II of their plans by telegraph at 8 PM. There is no record of the kaiser's response.

General von Einem, until then commander of VII Corps and now head of Saxon Third Army, offered up XII Corps and Duke Albrecht's XVIII Corps from Fourth Army. Chief of Staff Schmidt von Knobelsdorf of Fifth Army grudgingly agreed to release VI Corps—which was, in fact, fighting with Albrecht's Fourth Army. Even then, he did so only on condition that it first be given a day of rest and not be subjected to "long marches." Bülow, when informed of the plan, believed it might effect at least a "much desired moral success."[108] Whether the three corps' exhausted men and horses could even have made the 100-to-150-kilometer march must remain an open question, as must their possible deployment once there, for the fronts were rapidly moving during the German retreat from the Marne. Whatever the case, by the time Stein, Tappen, and Dommes returned to Luxembourg "frozen through and through" at 5:15 AM on 15 September, events there had overtaken their plan.

For on 14 September, Chief of the Military Cabinet von Lyncker had informed Wilhelm II that "Moltke's nerves are at an end and [he] is no longer able to conduct operations."[109] The kaiser had agreed and in what has been depicted as "a terrible scene" had ordered Moltke to step down on grounds of "ill health."[110] Deputy Chief of Staff von Stein, in Moltke's words, was also "sacrificed."[111] The decision took Moltke completely by surprise. "I refuse to do this! I am not sick. If H[is] M[ajesty] is unhappy with the conduct of operations, then I will go!"[112] But in the end he accepted what he twice called his "martyr-dom" to spare both his Supreme War Lord and the nation embarrass-ment.[113] Prussian war minister von Falkenhayn was to succeed Moltke, but the change in command would not be made public until 20 January 1915 to conceal the defeat at the Marne. Indeed, when Falkenhayn on 28 September requested that the Foreign Office publish a General Staff report on the debacle at the Marne, Chancellor Theobald von Bethmann Hollweg forbade such disclosure.[114]

On 11 September, Einem, en route to taking over Third Army, by chance had come across Moltke at Reims. "I met a totally broken and disconcerted man." Incredibly, Moltke began the conversation by ask-ing Einem, "My God, how could this possibly have happened?" Einem lost his composure. "You yourself ought to know the answer to that best of all! How could you ever have remained at Luxembourg and al-lowed the reins of leadership totally to slip from your hands?" Moltke was taken aback. "But, dear Einem, I could not possibly have dragged the Kaiser through half of France during our advance!" Einem's "harsh" reply was meant to cut to the quick. "Why not? The Kaiser most likely would not have had anything against it. And if your Great Uncle could square it with his sense of responsibility to take his King right onto the battlefields of Königgrätz [1866] and Sedan [1870], you and the Kaiser could at least have come sufficiently close to the front to keep the reins in your hands."[115] For Moltke, the war thus ended as it had begun—with a brutal, negative comparison to his uncle, the Elder Moltke.

To the German soldiers at the sharp end of the stick, the order to re-treat seemed grotesque. They did not feel like a beaten army. Georg Wichura, whose 5th ID for days had valiantly held up the advance of the BEF and the French cavalry corps between Monbertoin and Montreuil-aux-Lions, was "decimated" by the order. The "mood swing" among his men was "terrible, everywhere confused looks." "A thousand serious thoughts went through their heads," the division's diary noted. "Legs like lead. Silent and exhausted, as if in a trance, the column plods on ahead."[116] Similar reactions were noted at Third Army. The order to retreat arrived like a "bolt of thunder" at 133d RIR. Its commander, Lieutenant Colonel Schmidt, recalled, "I saw many men cry, the tears rolled down their cheeks; others simply expressed amaze-ment." Lieutenant Colonel Wilke of 178th IR noted "understandable shrugging of shoulders, sad shaking of heads. . . . Finally, it all turned into a dumbfounded silence filled with ominous anticipation."[117] The general feeling among the Saxon troops was that "it was not our fault, we stood our ground."[118]

At Second Army, Oskar von Hutier, commanding 1st Guard Division, refused to obey the order to retreat.

I ordered my mount in order to rush up to the front. I already had my left foot in the stirrup when the Division's Deputy Adjutant . . . leaped from his horse and came over to me with a deadly pale look. When I asked him what was wrong, he whispered in my ear: "We must all retreat immediately."

Hutier's reply: "Have they all gone crazy?"[119] Paul Fleck, commanding 14th ID, VII Corps, likewise was dumbfounded. "This could not be. . . . Victory was ours." He obeyed the order only after having it confirmed by Second Army's chief of staff, von Lauenstein.[120] Colonel Bernhard Finck von Finckenstein, commanding the prestigious 1st Kaiser Alexander Guard-Grenadier-Regiment, remonstrated that the enemy was "in wild flight" from the front. The order to retreat "hit us like the blow of a club. Our brave troops had to give up the bloody victory only so recently achieved and to surrender the battlefield to the enemy. That aroused bitter feelings."[121] Major von Rantzau of 2d Grenadier Regiment even toyed with insubordination: "Colonel, I respectfully report that we have lost confidence in our leadership [OHL]."[122] Captain Walter Bloem of 12th Brandenburg Grenadiers with Kluck's First Army dismissed the French "Victory of the Marne" as an "utter fraud." He and the men of B Company took solace in draining ninety bottles of claret in four hours.[123] Only the hope in a new offensive brought some relief.

The first order of business for the German armies after their retreat from the Marne was to resupply the troops and salvage whatever war materials had been damaged or abandoned. By 10 September, the Prussian War Ministry issued formal orders for full-scale scavenging to begin.[124] Cavalrymen were to be buried only in their "underwear and pants," with boots, tunics, and equipment gathered for reuse. Dead and wounded infantrymen were to be stripped of all ammunition and weapons "already in the front lines." Casings from artillery shells, broken machine guns, shattered artillery pieces, caissons, and harnesses were to be gathered up. All parts from downed aircraft and Zeppelins likewise were to be retrieved. "War Socialism" was in full flower at the front.

FOR JOFFRE, THE ORDER of the Day was straightforward and urgent— "to pursue energetically and leave the enemy no respite: victory depends on the legs of our infantry."[125] Abandoning his plan to envelop the German right wing, Joffre now ordered French Third to Sixth and Ninth armies and the BEF to pursue the retreating Germans in echelon on a northeasterly course.[126] Specifically, Sixth Army was to advance on Soissons, the BEF on Fismes, Fifth Army on Reims, and Ninth Army on Sommesous and Châlons. As well, he called Joseph de Castelli's VIII Corps up from Charmes and Bayon in Lorraine to press the attack. For four days, Joffre's armies fought a bloody battle of pursuit against dogged German rear guards over fields littered with the stinking remains of men and beasts, broken war equipment, burning villages, and streams of refugees. But the legs of the French infantry were as tired as those of the German, and slowly the enemy slipped out of Joffre's grasp.

The Battle of the Marne ended in anticlimax. On 11 September, torrents of rain and a sudden cold snap further dogged the already exhausted troops. Heavy clouds and dense mist grounded Joffre's aircraft. Deep mud slowed the horse-drawn artillery. In the confusion, Douglas Haig's gunners mistakenly shelled their own infantry. All along the line, the Allied armies advanced barely fifteen kilometers a day against a retreating enemy. By 13–14 September, the erstwhile German pivot wing, reinforced by the new Seventh Army from Saint-Quentin, had dug in on the commanding heights along the northern bank of the Aisne River. On 13 September, Maunoury informed Joffre that Sixth Army, "which has not had a day of rest in about fifteen days, very much needs 24 hours rest."[127] Franchet d'Espèrey the next day refused to obey Joffre's order to mount a major offensive northward toward Berry-au-Bac, Gernicourt, and Neufchâtel. "It is not rear guards that are in front of us," he testily lectured the generalissimo, "but an organized [defensive] position."[128] Even the feisty Foch informed GQG the next day that Ninth Army was meeting "great resistance" along its "entire front."[129] And at the lowest stratum of command, Sub-Lieutenant J. Caillou of 147th IR matter-of-factly noted that while his unit had received 2,300 reinforcements since August, by the time it reached the Aisne it had suffered 2,800 casualties "out of a complement of 3,000."[130]

The Valley of the Aisne constitutes a deep depression with the river running east to west and in many places too deep to ford. Its slopes consist of rough woods and thickets. A ridge, 150 meters above the river and traversed by a forty-kilometer road, the Chemin des Dames, built by Louis XV for his daughters, provided German artillery with superb observation posts. For four soggy and bloody days, Franchet d'Espèrey's Fifth Army, Maunoury's Sixth Army, and Sir John French's BEF assaulted the German defensive line, moving over battle-scarred terrain littered with abandoned wounded, munitions, supplies, stragglers, and thousands of drained wine bottles—to no avail. By 18 September, a "surprised" Joffre scaled back the Battle of the Aisne as it became clear that frontal assaults on well-dug-in German artillery, machine-gun, and infantry positions ("very serious fortifications") had dashed all "hope for a decision in open terrain."[131]

In the center of the French line, neither Third Army nor Fourth Army made any appreciable progress. Once more, Joffre took out his frustration on Sarrail. "I do not understand how the enemy was able to get away 48 hours ago without your being informed of it," he acidly lectured the general by telephone. "Kindly institute an inquiry immediately on this matter and let me know the results at once."[132] Sarrail evaded a formal inquiry by having his staff telephone GQG with a routine progress report.[133] Foch, freshly invigorated, drove Ninth Army in pursuit north-northeast with the aim of "destroying" the German army.[134] Pounding rain rendered the chalky roads of the Champagne virtually impassable. At Fère-Champenoise, Foch's soldiers found ransacked wine cellars and the streets strewn with empty wine bottles. At 8 PM on 11 September, Justinien Lefèvre's 18th ID entered Châlons-sur-Marne; at 7:45 AM the next day it began to cross the Marne.[135] The Germans' retreat had been so hasty that they had not had time to activate the demolition charges attached to the bridges. That night Foch dined at the Hôtel Haute-Mère-Dieu, where the night before the chefs had prepared a "sumptuous meal" for Saxon crown prince Friedrich August Georg and his staff.[136]

In truth, men, horses, and supplies had been exhausted. On 20 September, Franchet d'Espèrey dejectedly instructed his corps commanders simply to "stand and hold."[137] The next day Joffre in a "lapidary manner" instructed Foch by telephone, "Postpone the attack. Inform [commanders] to economize ammunition."[138] What the French official history of the war calls a "threatening ammunition crisis" had developed for the artillery. *Les 75s* had started the war with 1,244 shells per gun, but those stocks had been fired off and the daily production of at best 20,000 shells did not begin to meet the requirements for the three thousand *soixante-quinzes* in service.[139] An obvious "shell crisis" was at hand well before the end of September 1914. To the great relief of British and French commanders, the Germans were equally fatigued. The III Corps of Kluck's First Army, to give but one example, between 17 August and 12 September had marched 653 kilometers with full combat packs, had fought the enemy for nine full days, and had had zero days of rest.[140]

In a final bid for victory, Joffre used his superb railroad system to shift forces (IV, VIII, XIV, and XX corps) from his right to his left. In a feat of logistical brilliance, the Directorate of Railways moved the corps in about four to six days on roughly 105 to 118 trains each.[141] Yet again, the sought-after final victory eluded Joffre. He blamed it on "the slowness and the lack of skilled maneuvering displayed by the two flank armies and Fifth Army."[142] His staff calculated that the French army in September had suffered 18,073 men killed, 111,963 wounded, and 83,409 missing.[143] Several belated attempts by each side between 17 September and 17 October to turn the flank of the other—the so-called race to the sea—ended in deadly deadlock.* The great war of maneuver turned into siege-style warfare in the blood-soaked fields and trenches of Artois, Picardy, and Flanders.

---

* The French official history gives the dates 20 September–15 October for *la course à la mer*. AFGG, 4:127.

EPILOGUE

———

Everything in war is very simple, but the simplest thing is difficult.

—CARL VON CLAUSEWITZ

THE BATTLE OF THE MARNE WAS A CLOSE-RUN THING. IT CONFIRMED yet again the Elder Helmuth von Moltke's famous counsel that no plan of operations "survives with certainty beyond the first encounter with the enemy's major forces."[1] And it reified yet again Carl von Clausewitz's dictum that "war is the realm of uncertainty; three quarters of the factors on which action in war is based are wrapped in a fog of greater or lesser uncertainty."[2] Nothing about the Marne was preordained. Choice, chance, and contingency lurked at every corner.

Senior commanders on both sides did not at first understand the magnitude of the decision at the Marne. It seemed simply a temporary blip on the way to victory. The armies would be rested, reinforced, resupplied, and soon again be on their way either to Berlin or to Paris. Below headquarters and army as well as corps commands, a million men on either side likewise had no inkling of what "the Marne" meant—except more endless marches, more baffling confusion, and more bloody slaughter. Future historian Marc Bloch, a sergeant with French 272d Infantry Regiment, on 9 September recalled marching down a "tortuously winding road" near Larzicourt on the Marne at night, oblivious to the fact that the great German assault had been blunted. "With anger in my heart, feeling the weight of the rifle I had never fired, and hearing the faltering footsteps of our half-sleeping men echo on the ground," he drearily noted, "I could only consider

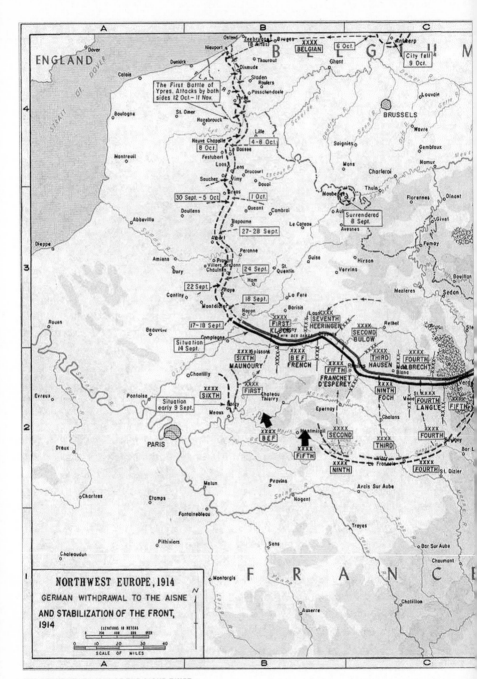

NORTHWEST EUROPE, 1914
GERMAN WITHDRAWAL TO THE AISNE
AND STABILIZATION OF THE FRONT,
1914

ELEVATIONS IN METERS
0   200   400   600   METER

0   10   20   30   40
SCALE OF MILES

THE FRONT STABILIZES AT THE AISNE RIVER

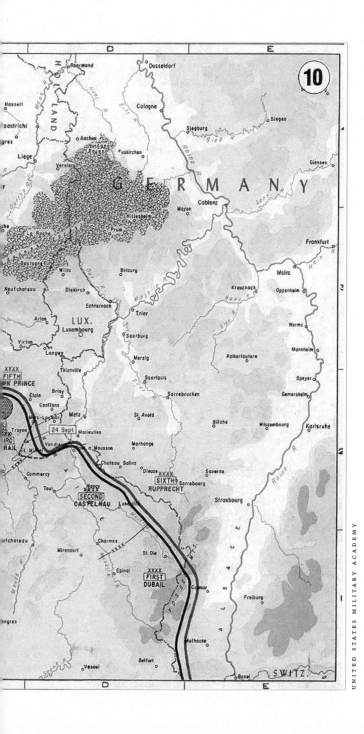

myself one more among the inglorious vanquished who had never shed their blood in combat."[3]

The Battle of the Marne did not end the war. But if it was "tactically indecisive," in the words of historian Hew Strachan, "strategically and operationally" it was a "truly decisive battle in the Napoleonic sense."[4] Germany had failed to achieve the victory promised in the Schlieffen-Moltke deployment plan; it now faced a two-front war of incalculable duration against overwhelming odds. A new school of German military historians[5] goes so far as to suggest that Germany had lost the Great War by September 1914.

Still, "what if?" scenarios abound. What if Germany had not violated Belgium's neutrality; would Britain still have entered the war? What if Helmuth von Moltke had not sought a double envelopment of the enemy in Alsace-Lorraine *and* in northern France; could at least half of the 331,000 soldiers on the left wing have helped the right wing to victory? What if he had not sent III and IX army corps to the east; could one of those have filled the famous gap between Second and First armies on the Marne, and the other helped Third Army break French Ninth Army's fragile front at the Saint-Gond Marshes? What if the commanders of German First and Second armies had simply refused to follow Lieutenant Colonel Richard Hentsch's "recommendation" to retreat from the Marne; could German First and Second armies have held on the Ourcq and Marne rivers, with possibly war-ending results?

What if Joseph Joffre had not been the French commander in chief? What if he had been cashiered in late August after he had been soundly defeated in the Battle of the Frontiers and after his deployment Plan XVII had totally collapsed? What historian Sewell Tyng called Joffre's "inscrutable, inarticulate calm," his "placid, unsophisticated character," and his "far-sighted, unsentimental, determined" leadership were among the major reasons why the French did not repeat their collapse of 1870–71.[6] After the war, Marshal Ferdinand Foch paid due tribute. Immediately after the loss of the Battle of the Frontiers, Joffre had recognized that "the game had been poorly played." He had broken off the campaign with every intention of resuming it as soon as he had "repaired the weaknesses discovered." Once clear on "the enemy's ultimate intentions" by marching across Belgium, Joffre had shifted forces from his right wing to his left, had cashiered general officers whom he found to be "not up to standard," had orchestrated an orderly withdrawal behind the Marne and Seine rivers, had created Michel-Joseph Maunoury's new "army of maneuver" in the west, and had launched his great attack between "the horns of Paris and Verdun" when he deemed the moment favorable. "When this moment arrived, he judiciously combined the offensive with the defensive after ordering an energetic about-face," Foch opined. "By a magnificently planned stroke he dealt the invasion a mortal blow."[7] The contrast with the lethargic, doubting, distant, "physically and mentally broken" Younger Moltke need not be belabored.

What if French morale had cracked after the Battle of the Frontiers? Campaigns are not fought against lifeless bodies. The enemy reacts, innovates, surprises, and strikes back. Were it not for the "emotions" and the "passions" of the troops, Carl von Clausewitz reminds us, wars would not escalate and might not even have to be fought. "Comparative figures" of opposing strengths would suffice to decide the issue without having to resort to "the physical impact of the fighting forces." Put differently, "a kind of war by algebra."[8] But in 1914, the French *poilu* surprised the Germans with what Moltke called his *élan*. "Just when it is on the point of being extinguished," he wrote his wife at the height of the Battle of the Marne, it "flames up mightily."[9] Karl von Wenninger, the Bavarian military plenipotentiary at Imperial Headquarters, likewise expressed his surprise at the enemy's tenacity. "Who would have expected of the French," he wrote his father on 9 September, "that after 10 days of luckless battles a[nd] bolting in open flight they would attack for 3 days so desperately."[10] General Alexander von Kluck gave the adversary his full respect in 1918. "The reason that transcends all others" in explaining the German failure at the Marne, he informed a journalist, was "the extraordinary and peculiar aptitude of the French soldier to recover quickly." Most soldiers "will let themselves be killed where they stand"; that, after all, was a "given" in all battle plans.

> But that men who have retreated for ten days . . . that men who slept on the ground half dead with fatigue, should have the strength to take up their rifles and attack when the bugle sounds, that is a thing upon which we never counted; that is a possibility that we never spoke about in our war academies.[11]

Perhaps the greatest "what if?" scenario: What if Kluck's First Army had indeed turned the left flank of Maunoury's Sixth Army northeast of Paris? For most German military writers and the German official history of the war, *Der Weltkrieg 1914 bis 1918,* this was a "certainty." Victory assured. End game. War over. But Moltke's chief of operations, Gerhard Tappen, stated after the war that he was not so sure. He, the Gabriel ever trumpeting victory throughout August and early September 1914, conceded that even Kluck's triumph at the Ourcq River would not have been "decisive" to the overall war effort. Given the dogged "tenacity" of the British and their "well known war aims," the war would have dragged on.[12] Even if thereafter First Army had pivoted on its left and squared off with the three army corps of the BEF and Louis Conneau's cavalry corps, the end result likely would have been utter exhaustion for the armies on both sides. Stalemate. An honest appraisal from one not known for candor. And yet, did Kluck not owe it to both his troops and the nation to have fought the battle through to conclusion?

The campaign in the west in 1914 revealed two distinct command styles. Moltke was content to remain at Army Supreme Command headquarters far removed from the front—first in Koblenz and then in Luxembourg—and to give his field commanders great latitude in interpreting his General Directives. He chose not to exercise close control over them by way of telephones, automobiles, aircraft, or General Staff officers. After all, they had conducted the great annual prewar maneuvers and war games and as such could be counted on to execute his "thoughts." Already, in peacetime, Moltke had let it be known that it sufficed for "Commanding Generals" simply to be "informed about the intentions of the High Command," and that this could easily be accomplished "orally through the sending of an officer from the Headquarters."[13] The reality of war proved otherwise. Some commanders failed the ultimate test, war, mainly because of a lack of competence (Max von Hausen); some partly because of advanced age (Karl von Bülow); and others partly because of ill health (Helmuth von Moltke, Otto von Lauenstein).

General Moriz von Lyncker, chief of the Military Cabinet, struck at the heart of the matter on 13 September. "It is clear that during the advance into France the necessary tight leadership on the part of the Chief of the General Staff had been totally lacking."[14] The next day he convinced Wilhelm II to place Moltke on "sick leave." But while more than thirty German generals were relieved of command of troops in 1914, there was no general "housecleaning" at the very top. Three army commanders were beyond reach, of course, because they were in line for future crowns: Wilhelm of Prussia led Fifth Army until August 1916, when he took command of Army Group Deutscher Kronprinz for the rest of the war; Rupprecht of Bavaria headed Sixth Army until August 1916, when he was given charge of Army Group Kronprinz Rupprecht until November 1918; and Albrecht of Württemberg stayed with Fourth Army until February 1917, when he assumed command of Army Group Herzog Albrecht for the duration.

Not even the two most controversial army commanders were sacked after the Battle of the Marne. Karl von Bülow, who had shown less than boldness first at the Sambre and then at the Marne, not only was promoted to the rank of field marshal in January 1915 and awarded the order Pour le Mérite, but was rewarded for his mediocre performance by (again) being given command of First Army and then of Seventh Army as well. He led Second Army until April 1915, when he was temporarily relieved of command due to a stroke. He was forced to retire two months later; his pleas to be reinstated fell on deaf ears. Alexander von Kluck, who had disobeyed Moltke's orders and turned in southeast of Paris, commanded First Army until March 1915, when near Vailly-sur-Aisne he was severely injured in the leg by shrapnel. He turned seventy while recuperating and in October 1916 was retired. Max von Hausen was the only army commander relieved of duty, and that came about mainly due to a severe case of typhus. His desperate appeals to be reinstated also went unanswered.

After the Battle of the Marne, the German army of 1914 was gone forever. Its tidy division into federalist Baden, Bavarian, Prussian, Saxon, and Württemberg contingents ended, never to be revived. In the words of former Prussian war minister Karl von Einem, the new commander of Third Army, "The army totally loses its wartime separateness. Everything is moved about, divisions and brigades are thrown together. It is living from hand to mouth."[15] In short, a true "German" army fought the Great War for the next four years.

Joseph Joffre, on the other hand, played a highly active, indeed intense, role in French decision making. Apart from issuing a host of General Instructions, Special Instructions, and Special Orders, he showered his army commanders with hundreds of "personal and secret" memoranda, telephone calls, and individual orders. He used his driver and automobile to great advantage, constantly on the road to inspect, to order, to encourage, and, where necessary, to relieve. In fact, Joffre filled a park with so-called *limogés*. * These included, by his reckoning, two army, ten corps, and thirty-eight division commanders.[16] Some (Charles Lanrezac) he fired because he considered them to be overly pessimistic or willing to challenge his orders; others (Pierre Ruffey) because he found them to be unnecessarily "nervous" and "imprudent" in their dealings with subordinates. He maintained in command a core of loyal and aggressive army commanders (Fernand de Langle de Cary, Yvon Dubail, Édouard de Castelnau), and he promoted several corps commanders (Louis Franchet d'Espèrey, Ferdinand Foch, Maurice Sarrail) who had "faith in their success" and who by "mastery of themselves" knew how to "impose their will on their subordinates and dominate events."[17] He never regretted his sometimes unjustified firings. He declined after the war to engage the "victims" in a war of memoirs.

Ironically, given the Elder Moltke's strategic use of railways in 1866 and again in 1870–71, it was Joffre who in 1914 brilliantly used his Directorate of Railways and interior lines to great advantage. When by 24 August, he realized that he had lost the Battle of the Frontiers, that his concentration plan, XVII, lay in tatters, and that the Germans were indeed sweeping through Belgium, Joffre altered "the centre of gravity of his dispositions so as to achieve at last a substantial numerical superiority at the western extremity of the front which he had come to recognize as the decisive point."[18] As early as 26 August, he dissolved the ineffective Army of Alsace, reconstituted much of it as Frédéric Vautier's VII Corps, and then sent it to reinforce the Entrenched Camp of Paris. Two days later, as the Battle of the Trouée de Charmes wound down, he dispatched Georges Levillain's 6th Cavalry Division and Louis Comby's 37th Infantry Division to the capital. And then he orchestrated a staggering transfer of forces from Lorraine to Greater Paris between 31 August and 2 September: from First Army, Edmond Legrand-Girarde's XXI Corps; from Second Army, Louis Espinasse's

---

* Ineffective commanders were "retired" to Limoges, four hundred kilometers southwest of the nerve center of Paris.

XV Corps, Pierre Dubois's IX Corps, Justinien Lefèvre's 18th ID, and Camille Grellet de la Deyte's 10th Cavalry Division; and finally, from Third Army, Victor Boëlle's IV Corps.[19] The Younger Moltke, by contrast, eschewed major transfers of forces from his left to his right wing due to "technical" difficulties and downright "stodginess."

The carnage was frightful. Although the French army published no formal casualty lists, its official history, *Les armées françaises dans la grande guerre*, set losses for August at 206,515 men and for September at 213,445; those for the ten days at the Marne surely must have approached 40 percent of the latter figure.[20] The chapel of the École spéciale militaire de Saint-Cyr, before its destruction in World War II, had only a single entry for its dead of the first year of the war: "The Class of 1914." In terms of natural resources and industrial production, France had lost 64 percent of its iron, 62 percent of its steel, and 50 percent of its coal.[21]

The German army likewise published no official figures for the Marne. But according to its ten-day casualty reports,[22] the armies in the west sustained 99,079 casualties between 1 and 10 September:

ARMIES	ACTUAL STRENGTH	SICK	WOUNDED	DEAD AND MISSING	TOTAL
First	162,100	1,904	5,817	5,533	13,254
Second	134,264	2,205	5,015	3,387	10,607
Third	117,700	2,156	8,170	4,661	14,987
Fourth	77,961	938	5,168	3,326	9,433
Fifth	225,859	4,615	9,556	5,263	19,434
Sixth	240,187	8,865	9,054	3,281	21,200
Seventh	128,527	3,547	4,651	1,966	10,164

Unsurprisingly, the army corps that took the brunt of the fighting during that ten-day period suffered most heavily: Hans von Gronau's IV Reserve Corps with First Army (2,676 killed or missing and 1,534 wounded); Otto von Emmich's X Corps with Second Army (1,553 killed or missing and 2,688 wounded); and Maximilian von Laffert's XIX Corps with Saxon Third Army (2,197 killed or missing and 2,982 wounded).[23] Taking together all five German armies between Verdun and Paris, roughly 67,700 *Landser* were rendered hors de combat in the Battle of the Marne.[24] Total British casualties at the Marne were 1,701.

Horses died in equally horrid numbers. For the first year of the war, no one bothered to keep records: The historians of the Reichsarchiv at Potsdam in the 1920s could not find the files of a single cavalry division with regard to "sickness or loss of horses."[25] Only 22d Infantry Division kept tabs from the start of the war in Belgium, and it reported a loss rate of roughly 30 percent. Most were the result not of combat but rather of exhaustion, colic, saddle sores, lung disease, withers' fistulas, and improper shoeing. And since there yet existed no veterinary clinics, sick or wounded animals were simply shot in the field—and thus escaped official records. During the course of the Great War, Germany lost an estimated one million horses dead and seven million wounded.

Artillery ruled the battlefield. The German 105mm and 150mm howitzers, called "cooking pots" (*marmites*) by the French and "Jack Johnsons" by the British, and the lighter 77mm guns ripped men and horses alike into shreds of flesh and deposited their remains as mounds of pulp. The French 75s, dubbed "black butchers" by the Germans, filled the air with shrieking shrapnel shells (*rafales*) that exploded above the enemy and drenched those below with thousands of iron balls. For four weeks, "crude, stinking, crowded ambulance wagons" jostled the wounded back to barns and churches hastily converted into field hospitals, where the unfortunates lay for hours "in a cloud of flies drinking [their] blood." For days, in words historian Robert Asprey addressed to the "common soldier" of 1914, "you ate nothing, drank nothing, no one washed you, your bandages went unchanged, many of you died." The living moved on, a mass of stinking humanity advancing through "a reeking foul air of dead and dying cattle and mutilated horses" to fight another battle, another day.[26]

The murderous nature of industrialized warfare changed the common soldiers who conducted it. Regardless of social, regional, or religious origin, they wrote home of the filth and dirt, horror and fear, of their frontline experiences. Some remembered the initial euphoria of marching through fall-clad orchards, the camaraderie among soldiers, the welcome mail calls, the "playing at cowboys and Indians" while advancing through woods, and the "liberating" of wonderful wine cellars. Most remembered the constant nagging hunger and thirst, the endless marches by day and night, the choking dust, the searing heat, then the cold rain and oozing mud, the burning villages, the groaning of the wounded, and the deathly rattle of the dying.

An anonymous German soldier, presumably a former miner, wrote to the *Bergarbeiter-Zeitung* in Bochum just after the Marne, "My opinion about the war itself has remained the same: it is murder and slaughter, and it is still incomprehensible to me today that humankind in the twentieth century could commit such slaughter."[27] A university professor, "von Drygalski," at about the same time expressed his feelings of the war experience in similar but more prosaic terms. "I have seen so much that is grand, beautiful, monstrous, base, brutal, heinous, and gruesome, that like all the others I am totally stupefied. To see people die hardly interrupts the enjoyment of the coffee that one has triumphantly brewed in stark filth while under artillery fire."[28]

A French *poilu,* the future renowned violoncellist Maurice Maréchal, expressed much the same disillusion with the war in early September. His initial "beautiful, innocent joy" at news of "Victory! Victory!" at the Marne quickly "took flight" as he surveyed the battlefield:

> There, a lieutenant of the 74th [Infantry Regiment], there, a captain of the 129th, all in groups of three or four, sometime singly and still in the position of firing prone, red pants. These are ours, these are our brothers, this is our blood. . . . Oh! Horrible people who wanted this war, there is no torment enough for you![29]

Three weeks later, Maréchal reflected again on the war. "Oh, this is long and monotonous and depressing." The "energy" and the "heroism" of 1870–71 were absent on the Western Front in 1914. "The heroism of today: hide as best as possible." Only the carnage was the same. "We feel small, so small, in the face of this frightening thing, some with bloody arms, others with boots ripped to shreds by red holes." The meaning of it all escaped him. "We do not know, not really, if we have done anything of use for the country."[30]

The newly promoted Adjutant Bloch of French 272d Infantry Regiment by year's end had overcome his "war euphoria" of August. "I led a life as different as possible from my ordinary existence: a life at once barbarous, violent, often colorful, also often a dreary monotony combined with bits of comedy and moments of grim tragedy."[31] Thereafter, he experienced primarily the "dreary monotony" of what he called the "age of mud": constant downpours, caved-in trenches, and unrelieved dampness. "Our clothing was completely soaked for days on end. Our feet were chilled. The sticky clay clung to our shoes, our clothing, our underwear, our skin; it spoiled our food, threatened to plug the barrels of our rifles and to jam their breeches."[32] Typhoid fever, contracted in the damp netherworld of the trenches, came almost as a relief to him in January 1915.

Above all, the Battle of the Marne destroyed once and for all romantic notions of war. "Wish it were a fresh and jolly [*frisch und fröhlich*] tussle," Robert Marcus, a German student, wrote his parents from the Argonne Forest, "rather than this malicious, gruesome mass assassination." Mines, hand grenades, and flamethrowers had reduced warfare to a new form of barbarism. "Is such a manner of warfare still compatible with human dignity?" he rhetorically asked his parents.[33]

Yet, despite the savage nature of warfare in the west, morale held. There were no widespread refusals to obey the call-ups in August 1914; large numbers of volunteers (even if grossly exaggerated for public consumption) rushed to the recruiting depots; and no major "rebellions" or "strikes" took place either at home or at the front. None of the armies kept statistics on "fragging" (shooting of officers) or on desertions. Wherever casualties were broken down under the headings of "cause," possible deserters were lumped into the generic category of "missing," which likely referred primarily to prisoners of war. Statistics for the seven German armies in the west show 21 suicides for August and a mere 6 for September 1914. The highest incidence was in Bavarian Sixth Army, with 8 suicides (among 228,680 soldiers); of these, 6 occurred before the army had even marched off to the front. Alcohol and fear of not being up to the task that lay ahead figured in most cases; almost all involved gunfire.[34] And if one considers that Germany in 1914 suffered 800,000 casualties (including 18,000 officers), then the 251 suicides (including 19 officers) for that period[35] are statistically insignificant and further proof of the inner steadfastness of those forces.

The Battle of the Marne did not, of course, dictate another four years of murderous warfare. If anything, it prefigured the resilience of

European militaries and societies to endure horrendous sacrifices. To be sure, some historians have suggested that Chancellor Theobald von Bethmann Hollweg's infamous "war-aims program"* of 9 September, at the very height of the struggle at the Marne, committed Germany to push on to victory regardless of the cost.[36] But there were those at Imperial Headquarters who fully understood that the time had come in the fall of 1914 to end the Great Folly. Field Marshal Gottlieb von Haeseler, activated for field duty at the tender age of seventy-eight, advised Wilhelm II to sheath the sword. "It seems to me that the moment has come which we must try to end the war."[37] The kaiser refused the advice. Moltke's successor, Erich von Falkenhayn, by 19 November had reached the same conclusion as Haeseler before him. Victory lay beyond reach. It would be "impossible," he lectured Bethmann Hollweg, to "beat" the Allied armies "to such a point where we can come to a decent peace." By continuing the war, Germany "would run the danger of slowly exhausting ourselves."[38] The chancellor rejected the counsel.

It began at the Marne in 1914. It ended at Versailles in 1919. In between, about sixty million young men had been mobilized, ten million killed, and twenty million wounded. With the 20/20 vision of hindsight, the great tragedy of the Marne is that it was strategically indecisive. Had German First Army destroyed French Sixth Army east of Paris; had French Fifth Army and the BEF driven through the gap between German First and Second armies expeditiously; had French Fifth Army pursued German Second Army more energetically beyond the Marne; then perhaps the world would have been spared the greater catastrophe that was to follow in 1939–45.

---

* The chancellor demanded German domination of Central Europe "for all imaginable time," annexation of Luxembourg, reduction of France and Russia to second-rate powers, "vassal" status for Belgium and the Netherlands, and a German colonial empire in Central Africa.

ACKNOWLEDGMENTS

T
HE FEDERAL STRUCTURE OF THE GERMAN LAND FORCES IN 1914
forced me to trace down all the various army, corps, brigade, division, and regiment primary materials for this book. The task was made much easier by the cheerful and professional assistance that I received from a host of archivists in all parts of Germany: the Bayerisches Hauptstaats-archiv, III Geheimes Hausarchiv, and IV Kriegsarchiv, at Munich; the Generallandesarchiv at Karlsruhe; the Hauptstaatsarchiv at Stuttgart; and the Sächsisches Hauptstaatsarchiv at Dresden. The Bundesarchiv-Militärarchiv at Freiburg proved a veritable treasure trove with the new record Group RH 61: Kriegsgeschichtliche Forschungsanstalt des Heeres, consisting of some three thousand Prussian and German army files previously thought destroyed by Allied bombing raids on Potsdam in 1945.

For French archival records, I am grateful to my research assistant, Dr. Stephanie Cousineau of the University of Northern British Columbia, who gave up what little free time she had from teaching to research the files of the Service Historique de la Défense at the Château de Vincennes; the Historial de la Grande Guerre at the Château de Péronne; and the Document Service of Le Mémorial de Verdun. As well, she checked countless of my inelegant French translations and cheerfully collected French books and pamphlets either out of print or recently reprinted (and generally unavailable outside France).

Truly yeoman service above and beyond the call of duty was carried out by the staff of the Document Delivery/Interlibrary Loan Services of the University of Calgary. For two years, they chased down 153 of even the most obscure requests that I made of them—and never complained (much less faltered) even once. Conversely, I wish to thank their (to me anonymous) colleagues at the University of Alberta at Edmonton, who sent to Calgary virtually all the memoir literature for both French and German military and political leaders as well as the weighty tomes of the German official history, *Der Weltkrieg 1914 bis 1918. Die militärischen Operationen zu Lande,* and its French counterpart, *Les armées françaises dans la grande guerre,* all in record time.

Special thanks are due three people who made this book happen: Rob Cowley, founding editor of *MHQ: The Quarterly Journal of Military History,* who first proposed the topic to me; Jonathan Jao, editor at Random House, who expeditiously approved and encouraged the project; and Linda McKnight, my literary agent at Westwood Creative Artists in Toronto, who as always crossed all the *t*'s and dotted all the *i*'s of the contract. They were a pleasure to work with.

The Social Sciences and Humanities Research Council (SSHRC) of Canada has funded my research since 1990. Without this steadfast support, research at the numerous German archives would not have been possible. And finally, I once again owe more than I can express to my severest critic and dearest wife, Lorraine Parrish Herwig, who read far too many drafts of this work. As always, what errors remain are all of my own making.

ABBREVIATIONS

AFGG	*Les armées françaises dans la grande guerre,* 11 *tomes,* 111 annexes (Paris: Imprimerie nationale, 1922–37)
AOK	Armeeoberkommando (German army command)
BA-MA	Bundesarchiv-Militärarchiv, Freiburg
BEF	British Expeditionary Force
BHStA-GH	Bayerisches Hauptstaatsarchiv, Geheimes Hausarchiv, Munich
BHStA-KA	Bayerisches Hauptstaatsarchiv-Kriegsarchiv, Munich
CD	Cavalry division
GD	Guard division
GHQ	General Headquarters (British)
GLA	Generallandesarchiv, Karlsruhe
GQG	Grand quartier général (French military headquarters)
HGW-MO	*History of the Great War: Military Operations,* 23 vols. (London: Macmillan, 1922–48)
HHStA	Haus-, Hof- und Staatsarchiv, Vienna
HstA	Hauptstaatsarchiv, Stuttgart
IB	Infantry brigade
ID	Infantry division
IR	Infantry regiment
Joffre	Joseph Joffre, *Mémoires du maréchal Joffre (1910–1917)* (Paris: Plon, 1932), 2 vols.
KTB	*Kriegstagebuch* (war diary)
Moltke	Helmuth von Moltke, *Erinnerungen Briefe Dokumente 1877–1916. Ein Bild vom Kriegsausbruch, erster Kriegsführung und Persönlichkeit des ersten militärischen Führers des Krieges,* ed. Eliza von Moltke (Stuttgart: Der Kommende Tag, 1922)
OHL	Oberste Heeresleitung (German Army Supreme Command)
RID	Reserve infantry division
RIR	Reserve infantry regiment
SHD	Service Historique de la Défense (formerly Service historique de l'armée de terre), Château de Vincennes
SHStA	Sächsisches Hauptstaatsarchiv, Dresden
WK	Reichsarchiv, *Der Weltkrieg 1914 bis 1918. Die militärischen Operationen zu Lande* (Berlin: E. S. Mittler, 1925–56), 14 vols.

A NOTE ON SOURCES

Historians of the German armies in World War I for decades were restricted to archives accessible in the Federal Republic of Germany. These mainly centered on documentary records for the federal armies of Baden, Bavaria, and Württemberg, housed at Karlsruhe, Munich, and Stuttgart, respectively. Unlike those of the Prussian army at Potsdam, they were not destroyed by the Allied bombing offensives of World War II and hence witnessed a great deal of first-class research. I began by working through these materials.

For XIV Army Corps of the Grand Duchy of Baden, which provided most of the units fighting in Alsace, I consulted its war diary (*Kriegstagebuch,* or KTB) at the Generallandesarchiv at Karlsruhe (GLA). Deputy Commander Hans Gaede's XIV Corps reports to Grand Duke Friedrich II are in 59 Weltkrieg 1914—Schriftwechsel Gaede 316. A summary of fortress shelling is in 59 Denkschrift der Beschiessungen der Forts 1914, General v. Bailer 365. Brigade commands are in 456 F58 Brigadebefehle 27. A special collection of war letters and diaries was most useful: S Kriegsbriefe und Kriegstagebücher 52, 53. Of greatest value were the war diaries of the various regiments and their battalions in Alsace, under the general file 456: F37 Inf. Regt. 111; F38 Inf. Regt. 112; F39 Inf. Regt. 113; F42 Inf. Regt. 169; F43 Inf. Regt. 170; and F58 Inf. Regt. 40. All service records were cross-checked in the regimental muster rolls: 456 D Kriegsrangliste. At the military-political level, the reports by Baden's acting military plenipotentiary to the Army Supreme Command (OHL) were most useful: 222 Politische Berichte des Großherzogl. Gesandten in Berlin und München über den Kriegsausbruch 34816.

Research into Duke Albrecht of Württemberg's Fourth Army, which was closely linked in all but name with the Prussian army and in 1914 was composed largely of Prussian formations, and into Württemberg XIII Army Corps, which fought under Crown Prince Rupprecht of Bavaria in Lorraine, was conducted at the Hauptstaatsarchiv Stuttgart (HStA), Landesarchiv Baden-Württemberg. The reports of its military plenipotentiary to General Headquarters are in M 1/2 Berichte des Militärbevollmächtigten beim Grossen Hauptquartier und des stellv. Militärbevollmächtigten in Berlin August–September 1914, vols. 54–58. The war diary of XIII Army Corps is in M 33/2 Gen. Kdo. XIII A.K. 1914–1918, Kriegstagebuch 28.7.14–21.1.15, vol. 884; and its operational orders in ibid., vol. 9. Württemberg war losses were tabulated by the War Ministry in M 1/11 Kriegsarchiv, Kriegsverluste, vol. 1048; the War Ministry also recorded all matters pertaining to war equipment in M 1/4 Kriegsminsterium, Allg. Armee-Angelegenheiten 1524. A special postwar collection of studies, M 738 Sammlung zur Militärgeschichte, dealt with issues such as communications during the war (36) and battalion histories (23). Given the near-total destruction of the records of the Prussian General Staff in 1945, of special value was a compendium of fifty situation reports by the chief of the General Staff to the Württemberg

War Ministry: M 1/2 Kriegsministerium 109, Mitteilungen des Chefs des Feldheeres Nr. 1–50, 27.7.1914–3.1.1915.

One of the richest veins for historians is the military records of Crown Prince Rupprecht's Sixth Army at the Bayerisches Hauptstaatsarchiv, IV, Kriegsarchiv (BHStA-KA), Munich. Bavarian forces were initially deployed in Lorraine and then shunted to the right flank of the German armies in Picardy, Artois, and Flanders. Critical files consulted included its war diary: Armeeoberkommando 6, Kriegstagebuch der 6. Armee 2.8.14–14.3.1915; as well as its prewar mobilization orders in Folder 369, Gedanken über die ersten Operationen der 6. und 7. Armee and Aufmarsch-Anweisungen. The Sixth Army KTB was then checked against the war diaries of the General Commands of the various Bavarian Army Corps: Generalkommando I AK, KTB 31.7.14–28.2.15; Ge. Kdo. II. bayer. AK, KTB 1.8.1914–31.12.1914; Generalkommando III AK, Kriegstagebuch 29.7.14–31.12.1914; and the war diary for Bavarian I Reserve Army Corps, Auszug aus dem Kriegstagebuch des Generals d. Inftr. Ritter von Fasbender, komd. General I.b.R.K. Extremely valuable was the rich war diary of Sixth Army's chief of staff, Konrad Krafft von Dellmensingen: KTB 1914, Nachlaß Krafft von Dellmensingen 145; and the (albeit fragmentary) diary of one of his brightest staff officers in Nachlaß Rudolf von Xylander 12, Kriegstagebuch 1914/18. An incomplete list of Bavarian war dead for 1914 is in AOK 6, Feldzug 1914, Verlustliste. The reports of the Bavarian military plenipotentiary to the OHL are at the Bayerisches Hauptstaatsarchiv-Ministerium des Äußeren: MA 3076–3085 Militärbevollmächtigter Berlin, Tagebuch Karl von Wenninger. Most critically, I am indebted to Dr. Gerhard Immler for garnering permission from HRH Prince Luitpold, head of the House of Wittelsbach, for me to research Crown Prince Rupprecht's war diary: Tagebuch Rupprecht, Nachlaß Kronprinz Rupprecht 699, at the Bayerisches Hauptstaatsarchiv, III, Geheimes Hausarchiv (BHStA-GH).

Over the past three decades, I researched fragments of personal files pertaining to leading figures of the General Staff and senior military commanders at the Bundesarchiv-Militärarchiv (BA-MA) in Freiburg: Beseler (N 30); Boetticher (N 323); Dommes (N 512); Einem (N 324); Groener (N 46); Haeften (N 35); Kluck (N 550); Moltke (N 78); Schlieffen (N 43); Tappen (N 56); and Wild v. Hohenborn (N 44). A very few prewar records from the Prussian army also exist in PH 3, Großer Generalstab: 256 Aufmarsch und operative Absichten der Franzosen in einem zukünftigen deutsch-französischen Kriege; 443 Mobilmachungsplan für das deutsche Heer zum 1. April 1914; 663 Große Generalstabsreise 1905/06; and 6546 Berichte über fremde Armeen, 1907–1911. Data on general officers were gleaned from the roughly twenty-volume collection MSg 109. Soldiers' letters came from several files, including MSg 2/3112 and 2/4537.

The collapse of the German Democratic Republic in 1989–90 proved to be a boon to scholars of World War I. First and foremost, its demise allowed research in the records of the Saxon Third Army at the Sächsisches Hauptstaatsarchiv (SHStA) at Dresden. The reports of the Saxon military plenipotentiary at General Headquarters are in 11250 Sächsischer Militärbevollmächtigter in Berlin Nr. 71. Geheimakten A: Verschiedenes. Third Army Commander Max von Hausen left two sets of personal recollections: 12693 Personalnachlaß Max Klemens Lothar Freiherr von Hausen (1846–1922) Nr. 38 and Nr. 43b; and 12693 "Meine Erlebnisse u. Erfahrungen als Oberbefehlshaber der 3. Armee im Bewegungskrieg 1914" Nr. 43a. The latter was most valuable as it contains the general's handwritten memoirs, penned in July 1918; much of this material (and especially the critical sections) was exorcised from his published memoir, *Erinnerungen an den Marnefeldzug 1914* (Leipzig: K. F. Koehler, 1920). I also worked through the war diary of Third Army Supreme Command, 11353 Armee-Oberkommando 3. Unfortunately, the files for its Strategic (Ia) and Tactical (Ib) Sections were lost, most likely during Allied bombing raids on Potsdam in 1945 (see below). Fortunately, I was able to compensate for this by researching the records of the

General Commands of Third Army, 11355 Generalkommando des XII Armee-Korps, as well as those of XII Reserve Corps, 11356 Generalkommando des XII Reservekorps Nrs. 139 and 273, which contain copies of Hausen's most important orders. The SHStA also has several superb collections of war diaries and letters: 11372 Militärgeschichtliche Sammlung, Nrs. 103, 105, and 371. All service records were cross-checked in the *Ehrenrangliste des ehemaligen Deutschen Heeres auf Grund der Ranglisten von 1914* (Berlin: E. S. Mittler, 1926), 2 vols. Saxon regimental histories were published as *Erinnerungsblätter deutscher Regimenter Sächsischer Armee* (Dresden: v. Baensch, 1921–39), 88 vols.

While it was widely assumed by Western historians that the Royal Air Force's bombings of the Kriegsgeschichtliche Forschungsanstalt on 14 February 1945 and of the Reichsarchiv on 14 April 1945 (both at Potsdam) had totally destroyed the archives of the Prussian army, that in fact was not the case. Although East German officials steadfastly maintained for half a century that as a "peaceful socialist country" they maintained no "military archives," a great number of files from the former Kriegsgeschichtliche Forschungsanstalt had escaped the bombing and been taken to Moscow by the Red Army. In 1988 the Soviet Union returned forty tons of documents—including some three thousand Prussian and German army files—to the Militärarchiv der Deutschen Demokratischen Republik, also at Potsdam.

To both the surprise and the delight of scholars, in 1994 these documents were removed to the BA-MA in Freiburg, where they were initially deposited as Special Collection W-10 and where they are now being recataloged as RH 61: Kriegsgeschichtliche Forschungsanstalt des Heeres, Teil 1, Teil 2. The unfortunate outcome is a confusing crescendo of old "W-10" and new "RH 61" file numbers. For prewar planning by the Prussian General Staff, the most important collections include: 96 Aufmarschanweisungen für die Jahre 1893/94 bis 1914/15; 406 Die militärpolitische Lage Deutschlands in den letzten 5 Jahren vor dem Kriege; and 50315 Gemeinsame Kriegsvorbereitungen Deutschland-Österreich-Ungarn. Frage eines gemeinsamen Oberbefehls im Kriege. As well, much of Alfred von Schlieffen's war planning survived in N 323/9, Nachlaß Boetticher, Gr. Generlstabsreise 1905.

Fragmentary documentary records for the first year of the war in general and for the Battle of the Marne in particular are in a series of compilations in RH 61: 83 Vorgänge im Großen Hauptquartier des Generalstabes 1914–1915; 84 Beurteilung der Lage zwischen den Flügeln der 1. und 2. Armee am 9.9.1914; 161 Die Fahrten Moltkes, Dommes, Steins und Tappens zur Front am 11., 12., 13. und 14.9.1914; 948 Der Krieg im Westen 1914–1916; 50443 Die Finanzierung des ersten Kriegsjahres 1914/15; 50603 Kriegsverluste, Verstärkungen, Munitionsverbrauch und Kriegsgefangene im Ersten Weltkrieg; 50631 Tagebücher Beseler; 50634 Generaloberst v. Einem; 50635 Falkenhayn-Tagebuch; 50652 Kriegserinnerungen von General v. Kuhl; 50656 Tagebuch v. Plessen; 50661 Kriegserinnerungen und Kriegstagebuch des Generalleutnants v. [sic] Tappen; 50676 Der Krieg im Westen 1914–1916; 50677 Auszüge aus Feldbriefen von Januar 1914—November 1918; 50730 Der Chef des Generalstabes von Moltke; 50739 Generalleutnant von Stein, der Generalquartiermeister der sechs ersten Kriegswochen; 50775 Die Verluste an Pferden 1914–1918; 50850 Die Tätigkeit der Feldfliegerverbände der 1. und 2. Armee 2.–9. September 1914; and 51060–064 Die OHL und die Marne-Schlacht vom 4.–9.9.1914. Countless others are to be found in the chapter notes.

During the 1920s, the senior commanders of especially the Bavarian and Prussian armies conducted a vitriolic paper war concerning both roles and responsibilities for the campaign in the west in 1914. A great many of their personal papers were circulated to fellow officers and to the Reichsarchiv at Potsdam. The result was a plethora of war diaries copied and annotated by postwar investigators. Wherever possible, I used only the original war diaries.

Given that neutral Belgium was truly a victim rather than an instigator of the July Crisis, I eschewed research in the General State Archives at Brussels and instead relied on several solid histories based on that country's documentary record for 1914: Émile Joseph Galet, *S. M. le Roi Albert, commandant en chef devant l'invasion allemande* (Paris: Plon, 1931); Marie-Rose Thielemans and Emile Vandewoulde, *Le Roi Albert au travers de ses lettres inédites, 1882–1916* (Brussels: Office international de librairie, 1982); Luc de Vos, *Het effectief van de Belgische krijgsmacht en de militiewetgeving, 1830–1914* (Brussels: Koninklijk Legermuseum, 1985); and *Histoire de l'armée belge* (Brussels: Editions Centre de Documentation historique des forces armées, 1982–88), 2 vols. The German invasion and occupation of 1914 are detailed at length by Jeff Lipkes, *Rehearsals: The German Army in Belgium, August 1914* (Leuven: Leuven University Press, 2007).

The major documentary collections that I have worked through over the past three decades in Great Britain are mostly at the National Archives (formerly the Public Record Office), Kew. They include the files of the Foreign Office: 800/49 Various Ministers' and Officials' Papers Grey, France 1905–1906; 800/87 Admiralty 1905–1913; 800/94 Foreign Office, memoranda 1912–1914; 800/100 Prime Minister 1909–1916. Also, those of the Cabinet: CAB 2 Committee of Imperial Defence and Standing Defence Subcommittee, Minutes 1902–1936; CAB 4 Committee of Imperial Defence, Miscellaneous Memoranda 1903–1938; and CAB 42 War Council and Successors 1914–1916. Of special interest in the latter group were the files pertaining to Despatch of the British Expeditionary Force (CAB 42/1/3) and to Home Defence (CAB 42/1/4). CAB 2/2 includes the minutes of the critical meeting on strategy of the CID on 23 August 1911. Of value at the Bodleian Library, Oxford University, are the Papers of Herbert Henry Asquith 1892–1928, especially A.2 Cabinet letters: Copies of Asquith's cabinet letters to the King, 1908–16.

For France, Dr. Stephanie Cousineau of the University of Northern British Columbia conducted research at the Service Historique de la Défense (SHD), formerly the Service historique de l'armée de terre, at the Château de Vincennes. Its vast holdings include the formal correspondence between the War Ministry (Messimy, Millerand) and the Grand quartier général (Joffre), as well as that for the military governor of Paris (Galliéni) for August and September 1914. Specifically, the personal collections researched were K 79 boxes 1 and 2, K 88 box 1, K 93 box 1, K 97 boxes 1, 2, 4, and 5, K 268 box 1, and K 802 box 1; the general collections included 5 N 66, 6 N 9, 7 N 4, 16 N 1551 as well as 1552 and 1674, 19 N 1142 and 1539, 21 N 15, 22 N 99 and 420, and 24 N 385 and 468. A good deal of the this material was published between 1922 and 1937 in the French official history, *Les armées françaises dans la grande guerre* (see below). Most important for this book were the narrative volumes (1, 2, and 3) of *tome* 1, the single annex of documents for volume 1, the two annexes for volume 2, and the four annexes for volume 3. SHD at Vincennes also houses a vast treasure trove of private *papiers* of many of the commanding generals of 1914. The most important are those for Fabry, Ferry, Foch, Grasset, Joffre, Journée, Regnault, Pétain, Pierrefeu, Pugens, and Ruffey; as well, there is the George Collection dealing with the Battle of Mulhouse; the Papiers Sauve (170th Infantry Regiment) in the Archives de Castelnau; and the Papiers Ferry (Grand Couronné). It is a mixed bag at best: some are repetitious, others mere summaries of battle orders, and many are postwar self-justifications and scurrilous attacks on Joffre.

Dr. Cousineau also researched war letters of common soldiers at the Historial de la Grande Guerre at the Château de Péronne and at the Document Service of Le Mémorial de Verdun. The massive, annotated collection of war letters by Jean Norton Cru was recently reprinted: *Témoins: Essai d'analyse et de critique des souvenirs de combatants édités en français de 1915 à 1928* (Nancy: Presses Universitaires de Nancy, 2006). Other published collections of war letters include *La dernière lettre écrite par des soldats français tombés au champ d'honneur, 1914–1918* (Paris: Flammarion, 1921); *Paroles de poilus: lettres et carnets du front 1914–1918*, eds. Jean-Pierre Guéno and Yves Laplume (Paris: Librio, 1998); *Les violettes des tranchées: lettres d'un poilu qui n'aimait pas la guerre,* ed. Étienne Tanty (Paris: Éditions-Italiques, 2002); "*Si je reviens comme je l'espère*": *lettres du front et de l'arrière,* eds. Madeleine and Antoine Bosshard (Paris: B. Grasset, 2003); and *Mon papa en guerre: lettres de poilus, mots d'enfants 1914–1918,* ed. Jean-Pierre Guéno (Paris: Librio, 2004).

Of course, military historians for a long time have had access to official as well as semi-official histories of the Great War undertaken by the warring nations after 1918. These include:

Baden. *Die Badener im Weltkrieg 1914/1918,* ed. Wilhelm Müller-Loebnitz (Karlsruhe: G. Braun, 1935).

Bavaria. *Die Bayern im Großen Krieg 1914–1918. Auf Grund der amtlichen Kriegsakten dargestellt* (Munich: Verlag des Bayerischen Kriegsarchivs, 1923), 3 vols.

————. *Das Bayernbuch vom Weltkriege 1914–1918. Ein Volksbuch,* ed. Konrad Krafft von Dellmensingen (Stuttgart: Chr. Belser, 1930), 2 vols.

————. *Die Schlacht in Lothringen und in den Vogesen. Die Feuertaufe der Bayerischen Armee,* ed. Karl Deuringer (Munich: Max Schick, 1929), 2 vols.

Belgium. *La campagne de l'armée belge (31 juillet 1914–1er janvier 1915) d'après les documents officials* (Paris: Bloud et Gay, 1915). In English: *The War of 1914: Military Operations of Belgium in Defence of the Country and to Uphold Her Neutrality: Report Compiled by the Commander-in-Chief of the Belgian Army, for the Period July 31st to December 31st, 1914* (London: W. H. & L. Collingridge, 1915).

France. Armée. Service historique. *Les armées françaises dans la grande guerre* (Paris: Imprimerie nationale 1922–37), 11 *tomes* and 111 annexes.

Germany. Marine-Archiv. *Der Krieg in der Nordsee* (Berlin: E. S. Mittler, 1921–37), 6 vols.

————. Reichsarchiv. *Der Weltkrieg 1914 bis 1918. Die militärischen Operationen zu Lande* (Berlin: E. S. Mittler, 1925–56), 14 vols.

————. *Der Weltkrieg 1914 bis 1918. Kriegsrüstung und Kriegswirtschaft* (Berlin: E. S. Mittler, 1930), 2 vols.

————. *Schlachten des Weltkrieges in Einzeldarstellungen* (Oldenburg and Berlin: Gerhard Stalling, 1921–33), 38 vols.

————. *Der Sanitätsdienst im Gefechts- und Schlachtenverlauf im Weltkriege 1914/1918* (Berlin: E. S. Mittler, 1934–38), vol. 2.

————. *Sanitätsbericht über das Deutsche Heer im Weltkriege 1914/1918* (Berlin: E. S. Mittler, 1934), vol. 3.

Great Britain. *History of the Great War: Military Operations,* ed. J. E. Edmonds (London: Macmillan, 1922–48), 23 vols.

————. *History of the Great War: Naval Operations,* eds. J. Corbett and H. Newbolt (London: Longmans, Green, 1920–31), 5 vols.

Saxony. *Sachsen in großer Zeit. Gemeinverständliche sächsische Kriegsgeschichte und vaterländisches Gedenkwerk des Weltkrieges,* ed. Johann Edmund Hottenroth (Leipzig: R. Max Lippold, 1923), 3 vols.

————. *Die Marneschlacht insbesondere auf der Front der deutschen dritten Armee,* ed. Artur Baumgarten-Crusius (Leipzig: Lippold, 1919).

Württemberg. *Württembergs Heer im Weltkrieg* (Stuttgart: Berger, 1939), 20 vols.

Additionally, some contemporary documents were published in the United States: *Source Records of the Great War,* ed. Charles F. Horne (USA: National Alumni, 1923), 7 vols. Two compilations stand out for France: *Histoire illustrée de la guerre de 1914,* ed. Gabriel Hanotaux (Paris: Gounouilhou, 1915–24), 17 vols.; and *La grande guerre sur le front occidental,* ed. Barthélemy Edmond Palat (Paris: Chapelot, 1917–29), 14 vols.

The principal leaders of the governments and armies of 1914 also left a flood of memoirs and personal papers. The most important Belgian works include those of King Albert I, *Les carnets de guerre d'Albert 1er, roi des Belges* (Brussels: C. Dessart, 1953); of his military advisers, Antonin Selliers de Moranville, *Du haut de la tour de Babel: Commentaire sur la preparation à la guerre et la situation stratégique de la Belgique en 1914* (Paris: Berger-Levrault, 1925); Louis de Ryckel, *Mémoires du lieutenant général Baron de Ryckel* (Paris: Chapelot, 1920); Émile J. Galet, *Albert, King of the Belgians, in the Great War* (New York: Houghton Mifflin, 1931); and of the commandant at Liège, Gérard Leman, *La rapport du général Leman sur la défense de Liège en août 1914* (Brussels: Palais des academies, 1960).

Britain's statesmen and soldiers likewise did not spare with their reminiscences. Important collections include John French, *1914* (London: Constable, 1919), 2 vols.; Douglas Haig, *War Diaries and Letters, 1914–1918*, eds. Gary Sheffield and John Bourne (London: Weidenfeld & Nicolson, 2005); David Lloyd George, *War Memoirs of David Lloyd George, 1914–1918* (London: Nicholson & Watson, 1933–36), 6 vols.; Archibald Murray, *Sir Archibald Murray's Despatches* (London and Toronto: J. M. Dent, 1920); Horace L. Smith-Dorrien, *Memories of Forty-Eight Years' Service* (London: J. Murray, 1925); *Field Marshal Sir Henry Wilson: His Life and Diaries*, ed. C. E. Callwell (London: Cassell, 1927), 2 vols.; Winston S. Churchill, *The World Crisis* (New York: Scribner, 1923–31), 6 vols.; and *H. H. Asquith: Letters to Venetia Stanley*, eds. Michael Brock and Eleanor Brock (Oxford and New York: Oxford University Press, 1982).

For France, the most important works on military matters include Yvon Dubail, *Quatre années de commandement, 1914–18: Journal de campagne* (Paris: Fournier, 1920); Louis Conneau, *Historique des corps de cavalerie commandés par le général Conneau du 13 août 1914 au 2 mars 1917* (Paris: Plon, 1924); Émile Fayolle, *Cahiers secrets de la grande guerre* (Paris: Plon, 1964); Ferdinand Foch, *Mémoires pour server à l'histoire de la guerre de 1914–1918* (Paris: Plon, 1931), 2 vols.; Joseph Galliéni, *Mémoires du maréchal Galliéni: défense du Paris (25 août–11 septembre 1914)* (Paris: Payot, 1920); Charles Julien Huguet, *Britain and the War: A French Indictment* (London: Cassell, 1928); Joseph Joffre, *Mémoires du maréchal Joffre (1910–1917)* (Paris: Plon, 1932), 2 vols.; Fernand de Langle de Cary, *Souvenirs de commandement, 1914–1916* (Paris, Payot, 1935); Charles Lanrezac, *Le plan de campagne français et le premier mois de la guerre (2 août–3 septembre 1914)* (Paris: Payot, 1921); Charles Mangin, *Lettres de guerre, 1914–1918* (Paris: Fayard, 1950); Adolphe Messimy, *Mes souvenirs* (Paris: Plon, 1937); Raymond Poincaré, *Au service de la France—neuf années de souvenirs* (Paris: Plon, 1926–33), 10 vols.; and Poincaré, *Comment fut déclarée la guerre de 1914* (Paris: Flammarion, 1939).

German commanders spent much of the decade of the 1920s writing memoirs to justify their actions during the war in general, and during the campaign of 1914 in particular. Those of the chiefs of the General Staff include the (posthumously published) recollections of Chief of the General Staff *Helmuth von Moltke. Erinnerungen, Briefe, Dokumente, 1877–1916. Ein Bild vom Kriegsausbruch, erster Kriegsführung und Persönlichkeit des ersten militärischen Führers des Krieges*, ed. Eliza von Moltke (Stuttgart: Der Kommende Tag, 1922); *Helmuth von Moltke, 1848–1916. Dokumente zu seinem Leben und Wirken*, ed. Thomas Meyer (Basel: Perseus Verlag, 1993), 2 vols.; and Erich von Falkenhayn, *Die Oberste Heeresleitung, 1914–1916, in ihren wichtigsten Entschliessungen* (Berlin: E. S. Mittler, 1920).

The collections by army commanders include Crown Prince Wilhelm, *Meine Erinnerungen aus Deutschlands Heldenkampf* (Berlin: E. S. Mittler, 1923); Crown Prince Rupprecht of Bavaria, *Mein Kriegstagebuch* (Munich: Deutscher National Verlag, 1929), 3 vols.; Karl von Bülow, *Mein Bericht zur Marneschlacht* (Berlin: A. Scherl, 1919); Karl von Einem, *Erlebnisse und Betrachtungen aus der Zeit des Weltkrieges* (Leipzig: K. F. Koehler, 1919), and *Ein Armeeführer erlebt den Weltkrieg. Persönliche Aufzeichnungen* (Leipzig: Hase & Koehler, 1938); Max von Gallwitz, *Meine Führertätigkeit im Weltkriege 1914/16* (Berlin: E. S. Mittler, 1929);

Max von Hausen, *Erinnerungen an den Marnefeldzug 1914* (Leipzig: K. F. Koehler, 1920), and *Generaloberst Max Freiherr von Hausen, ein deutscher Soldat. Nach seinen Tagebüchern, Aufzeichnungen und Briefen,* ed. Artur Brabant (Dresden: v. Baensch, 1926); and Alexander von Kluck, *Der Marsch auf Paris und die Marneschlacht 1914* (Berlin: E. S. Mittler, 1920). Some diaries and letters from the kaiser's military entourage have recently been sorted and edited by Holger Afflerbach, *Kaiser Wilhelm II. als Oberster Kriegsherr im Ersten Weltkrieg. Quellen aus der militärischen Umgebung des Kaisers 1914–1918* (Munich: R. Oldenbourg, 2005).

Important memoirs by General Staff officers involved in the decision-making process of 1914 include Max Bauer, *Der grosse Krieg in Feld und Heimat. Erinnerungen und Betrachtungen* (Tübingen: Osiander'sche Buchhandlung, 1921); Wilhelm Groener, *Lebenserinnerungen. Jugend, Generalstab, Weltkrieg,* ed. Friedrich Frhrr. Hiller von Gaertringen (Göttingen: Vandenhoeck & Ruprecht, 1967); Hermann von Kuhl, *Der Marnefeldzug, 1914* (Berlin: E. S. Mittler, 1921); Fritz von Loßberg, *Meine Tätigkeit im Weltkrieg, 1914–1918* (Berlin: E. S. Mittler, 1939); Erich Ludendorff, *Meine Kriegserinnerungen, 1914–1918* (Berlin: E. S. Mittler, 1919); Hermann von Stein, *Erlebnisse und Betrachtungen aus der Zeit des Weltkrieges* (Leipzig: K. F. Koehler, 1919); Gerhard Tappen, *Bis zur Marne 1914. Beiträge zur Beurteilung der Kriegführung bis zum Abschluss der Marne-Schlacht* (Oldenburg: Gerhard Stalling, 1920); and Rudolf von Xylander, *Deutsche Führung in Lothringen 1914. Wahrheit und Kriegsgeschichte* (Berlin: Junker und Dünnhaupt, 1935).

NOTES

PROLOGUE: *"A Drama Never Surpassed"*

1. *Die Badener im Weltkrieg 1914/1918,* ed. Wilhelm Müller-Loebnitz (Karlsruhe: G. Braun, 1935), 20–21. The Peugeot Memorial at Joncherey today memorializes the spot.

2. Holger H. Herwig, "The Marne," *MHQ: The Quarterly Journal of Military History* (Winter 2000): 10–11.

3. Ritter to Hermann Witte, 15 May 1917. *Gerhard Ritter. Ein politischer Historiker in seinen Briefen,* eds. Klaus Schwabe and Rolf Reichardt (Boppard: H. Boldt, 1984), 202–03.

4. Report for *Collier's Weekly;* cited in Mark Sullivan, *Our Times, 1900–1925* (New York and London: Charles Scribner's Sons, 1936), 5:26.

5. "Foreword" to Edmund Spears, *Liaison 1914: A Narrative of the Great Retreat* (London: Eyre & Spottiswoode, 1930), vii.

6. A first effort was undertaken by Basil Liddell Hart, *Reputations, Ten Years After* (Boston: Little, Brown, 1928).

7. Joffre, 1:420.

8. Sewell Tyng, *The Campaign of the Marne 1914* (New York and Toronto: Longmans, Green, 1935), 81.

9. *Die graue Exzellenz: Zwischen Staatsräson und Vasallentreue. Aus den Papieren des kaiserlichen Gesandten Karl Georg von Treutler,* ed. Karl-Heinz Janßen (Frankfurt, Berlin, Vienna: Ullstein, 1971), 167.

10. BA-MA, Nachlass Admiral Georg Alexander von Müller, N 159, 4:292. Diary entry for 4 September 1914.

11. Cited in Holger H. Herwig, *The First World War: Germany and Austria-Hungary, 1914–1918* (London: Arnold, 1997), 406.

12. This is the "minimalist" war-aims program that Chancellor Theobald von Bethmann Hollweg drafted on 9 September, the day of climax for the Battle of the Marne. See Fritz Fischer, *Griff nach der Weltmacht. Die Kriegszielpolitik des kaiserlichen Deutschland 1914/18* (Düsseldorf: Droste, 1961), 113ff.

13. *Les batailles de la Marne de l'Ourcq à Verdun (1914 et 1918)* (Soteca: Éditions, 2004), 11.

14. Tyng, *Campaign of the Marne,* 342ff.

15. To the best of my knowledge, the concept was first popularized by Gustave Babin in *L'Illustration* on 11 October 1915.

16. Louis E. Muller, *Joffre et la Marne* (Paris: G. Crès, 1931), 113ff.

17. WK, 4:541.

18. Erich Ludendorff, *Das Marne-Drama. Der Fall Moltke-Hentsch* (Munich: Ludendorffs Verlag, 1934).

19. Fritz Fischer's "Introduction" to Karl Lange, *Marneschlacht und deutsche Öffentlichkeit 1914–1939. Eine verdrängte Niederlage und ihre Folgen* (Düsseldorf: Bertelsmann Universitätsverlag, 1974), 7.

CHAPTER I. War: *"Now or Never"*

1. Cited in Zara Steiner, *Britain and the Origins of the First World War* (New York: St. Martin's Press, 1977), 215.

2. J. J. Ruedorffer [Kurt Riezler], *Grundzüge der Weltpolitik der Gegenwart* (Stuttgart and Berlin: Deutsche Verlagsanstalt, 1914), 219.

3. Christopher Andrew, "France and the German Menace," in Ernest R. May, ed., *Knowing One's Enemies: Intelligence Assessment Before the Two World Wars* (Princeton, NJ: Princeton University Press, 1984), 144.

4. Holger H. Herwig, *The First World War: Germany and Austria-Hungary, 1914–1918* (London: Arnold, 1997), 6–7.

5. Werner Maser, *Adolf Hitler. Legende, Mythos, Wirklichkeit* (Munich: Bechtle, 1974), 12.

6. Graydon A. Tunstall Jr., "Austria-Hungary," in Richard F. Hamilton and Holger H. Herwig, eds., *The Origins of World War I* (Cambridge: Cambridge University Press, 2003), 112–49.

7. Letter dated 28 June 1914. Gina von Hötzendorf, *Mein Leben mit Conrad von Hötzendorf. Sein geistiges Vermächtnis* (Leipzig: Grethlein, 1935), 114.

8. Hugo Hantsch, *Leopold Graf Berchtold. Grandseigneur und Staatsmann* (Graz: Styria Verlag , 1963), 2:558–59.

9. Dated 18 August 1914. Gina von Hötzendorf, *Mein Leben mit Conrad,* 118.

10. Dated 30 June 1914. *Juli 1914. Die europäische Krise und der Ausbruch des Ersten Weltkriegs,* ed. Imanuel Geiss (Munich: Deutscher Taschenbuch Verlag, 1965), 39–40. Italics in the original.

11. Franz Joseph's letter to Wilhelm II, 5 July 1914. HHStA, PA VII Gesandschaft Berlin 196.

12. *Österreich-Ungarns Letzter Krieg 1914–1918,* eds. Edmund Glaise von Horstenau and Rufolf Kiszling (Vienna: Verlag der Militärwissenschaftlichen Mitteilungen, 1931–38), 8:250–61, 306–07, 319ff., 381.

13. Ambassador Hans von Schoen to Minister-President Count Georg Hertling, 18 July 1914; Geiss, ed., *Juli 1914,* 110.

14. *Protokolle des Geheimen Ministerrates der Österreichisch-Ungarischen Monarchie (1914–1918),* ed. Miklós Komjáthy (Budapest: Akadémiai Kiadó, 1966), 141–50.

15. Cited in Geiss, ed., *Juli 1914,* 68. Berchtold had, in fact, developed this stratagem already on 8 July 1914.

16. Cited in Samuel R. Williamson Jr., *Austria-Hungary and the Origins of the First World War* (New York: St. Martin's Press, 1991), 204.

17. Bunsen to Grey, 8 August 1914. HHStA, PA VIII England, Berichte 1913, Weisungen Varia 1914.

18. Williamson, *Austria-Hungary,* 1, 6.

19. Fritz Fischer, *Griff nach der Weltmacht. Die Kriegszielpolitik des kaiserlichen Deutschland 1914/18* (Düsseldorf: Droste, 1961); expanded in Fischer, *Krieg der Illusionen. Die deutsche Politik von 1911 bis 1914* (Düsseldorf: Droste, 1969).

20. John C. G. Röhl, "Admiral von Müller and the Approach of War, 1911–1914," *Historical Journal* 12 (1969): 651–73.

21. For the "September program," see Fischer, *Griff nach der Weltmacht,* 113ff.

22. Fischer, *Krieg der Illusionen,* 684.

23. Bethmann Hollweg, 7 April 1913. *Verhandlungen des Reichstages. XII. Legislaturperiode, I. Session,* 189:4512–13; Wolfgang J. Mommsen, "The Topos of Inevitable War in Ger-

many in the Decade Before 1914," in Volker R. Berghahn and Martin Kitchen, eds., *Germany in the Age of Total War* (London: Croom Helm, 1981), 23–45.

24. Herwig, *First World War,* 22; and Herwig, "Germany," in Hamilton and Herwig, eds., *Origins of World War I,* 166ff.

25. Herwig, *First World War,* 21–22.

26. Theobald von Bethmann Hollweg, *Betrachtungen zum Weltkriege* (Berlin: Reimer Hobbing, 1919–21), 2:133.

27. Herwig, *First World War,* 20; and Herwig, "Germany," in Hamilton and Herwig, eds., *Origins of World War I,* 166.

28. Letter dated 14 March 1914. BA-MA, RH 61/406, "Die militärpolitische Lage Deutschlands in den letzten 5 Jahren vor dem Kriege," 46.

29. Memorandum dated 28 July 1914. Moltke, 3–7.

30. Diary entry dated 28 July 1914. BA-MA, RH 61/50635, Tagebuch v. Falkenhayn.

31. Stig Förster, "Der deutsche Generalstab und die Illusion des kurzen Krieges, 1871–1914: Metakritik eines Mythos," *Militärgeschichtliche Mitteilungen* 54 (1995): 92.

32. *Julikrise und Kriegsausbruch 1914. Eine Dokumentensammlung,* ed. Imanuel Geiss (Hanover: Verlag für Literatur und Zeitgeschehen, 1964), 2:299.

33. Ibid., 2:373.

34. Ibid.

35. Diary entry dated 1 August 1914. BA-MA, RH 61/50635, Tagebuch v. Falkenhayn.

36. Herwig, *First World War,* 28–29.

37. Diary entry dated 2 August 1914. Bernd F. Schulte, "Neue Dokumente zu Kriegsausbruch und Kriegsverlauf 1914," *Militärgeschichtliche Mitteilungen* 25 (1979): 142.

38. Evelyn Princess Blücher, *An English Wife in Berlin: A Private Memoir of Events, Politics, and Daily Life in Germany Throughout the War and the Social Revolution of 1918* (London: Constable, 1920), 14.

39. The following is from Moltke's notes of November 1914. Moltke, 19–23.

40. Diary entry dated 1 August 1914. BA-MA, RH 61/50635, Tagebuch v. Falkenhayn.

41. Notes by Moltke's adjutant, Hans von Haeften, dated November 1914. *Helmuth von Moltke 1818–1916. Dokumente zu seinem Leben und Wirken,* ed. Thomas Meyer (Basel: Perseus, 1993), 1:404.

42. Eugenia C. Kiesling, "France," in Hamilton and Herwig, eds., *Origins of World War I,* 227–65.

43. Robert Doughty, *Pyrrhic Victory: French Strategy and Operations in the Great War* (Cambridge, MA, and London: The Belknap Press of Harvard University Press, 2005), 53.

44. Joffre, 1:128.

45. John F. V. Keiger, *France and the Origins of the First World War* (New York: St. Martin's Press, 1983); and Keiger, "France," in Keith Wilson, ed., *Decisions for War 1914* (London: UCL Press, 1995), 121–49.

46. Luigi Albertini, *The Origins of the War of 1914* (London: Oxford University Press, 1952–57), 2:193.

47. Keiger, *France and the Origins of the First World War,* 153.

48. Albertini, *Origins of the War of 1914,* 2:536–39.

49. J. F. V. Keiger, *Raymond Poincaré* (Cambridge: Cambridge University Press, 1997), 175.

50. Keiger, "France," 145.

51. Ibid., 139–42.

52. Ibid., 132.

53. Paul M. Kennedy, *The Rise and Fall of the Great Powers: Economic Change and Military Conflict from 1500 to 2000* (New York: Random House, 1987).

54. Donald Kagan, *On the Origins of War and the Preservation of Peace* (New York: Doubleday, 1995), 199, 202–04, 206–14.

55. David Lloyd George, *War Memoirs of David Lloyd George, 1914–1918* (Boston: Little, Brown, 1933–37), 1:57–60.

56. Wilson, "Britain," in Wilson, ed., *Decisions for War,* 200.

57. Ibid., 188–89. Also J. Paul Harris, "Great Britain," in Hamilton and Herwig, eds., *Origins of World War I,* 266–99.

58. Wilson, "Britain," 191; Harris, "Great Britain," 282.

59. Elie Halévy, *A History of the English People in the Nineteenth Century* (New York: Barnes & Noble, 1961), 1:438.

60. Kagan, *Origins of War,* 202.

61. Asquith to Stanley, 2 August 1914. *H. H. Asquith: Letters to Venetia Stanley* (Oxford and New York: Oxford University Press, 1982), 146.

62. Kagan, *Origins of War,* 202–03.

63. Keiger, *France and the Origins of the First World War,* 162.

64. Barbara W. Tuchman, *The Guns of August* (New York: Ballantine Books, 1994), 133.

65. Wilson, "Britain," 201–02.

66. Ibid., 139.

67. George Allardice Baron Riddell, *Lord Riddell's War Diary, 1914–1918* (London: Nicholson & Watson, 1933), 6.

68. Wilson, "Britain," 199; Harris, "Great Britain," 286; Bernard Wasserstein, *Herbert Samuel: A Political Life* (Oxford: Clarendon Press, 1992), 163.

69. *Hansard's Parliamentary Debates,* 5th Series, 65 (1914): 1809–27; Sir Edward Grey, *Twenty-Five Years, 1892–1916* (London: Hodder & Stoughton, 1935), 2:16–17.

70. Steiner, *Britain and the Origins of the First World War,* 245.

71. Geiss, ed., *Juli 1914,* 347.

72. Bernhard von Bülow, *Denkwürdigkeiten* (Berlin: Ulstein, 1931), 4:556.

73. Wilson, "Britain," 199.

74. Lloyd George, *War Memoirs,* 1:32, 59, 52.

75. Gina von Hötzendorf, *Mein Leben mit Conrad,* 30–31.

76. Ivan S. Bloch's six-volume classic, *La guerre* (Paris: Guillaumin, 1898); Engels's comments from December 1887 in Karl Marx and Friedrich Engels, eds., *Werke* (Berlin: Dietz, 1962), 21:350–51.

77. BA-MA, RM 61/150, Denkschrift über die Ersatzgestellung für das Deutsche Heer von Mitte September bis Ende 1914.

78. Paul Plaut, "Psychographie des Krieges," *Beihefte zur Zeitschrift für angewandte Psychologie* 20 (Leipzig: Johann Ambrosius Barth, 1920): 10–14.

79. Herwig, *First World War,* 35, 80.

80. Adolf Hitler, *Mein Kampf* (Munich: F. Eher Nachf., 1939), 165.

81. Joachim Remak, *The Origins of World War I* (New York: Holt, Rinehart and Winston, 1967), 148.

82. Herwig, *First World War,* 80.

83. Asquith to Stanley, 4 August 1914. *Letters to Venetia Stanley,* 150.

84. John Gooch, *The Plans of War: The General Staff and British Military Strategy, c. 1900–1916* (New York: Wiley, 1974), 300.

85. Hew Strachan, *The First World War* (Oxford: Oxford University Press, 2001), 1:159–62.

86. A few among the many include Jean-Jacques Becker, *1914, comment les Françaises sont entrés dans la guerre: contribution à l'étude de l'opinion publique printemps-été 1914* (Paris: Presses de la Fondation nationale des sciences publiques, 1977); Wolfgang Kruse, *Krieg und nationale In-*

tegration. Eine Neuinterpretation des sozialdemokratischen Burgfriedensschlusses 1914/15 (Essen: Klartext, 1993); Thomas Raithel, *Das "Wunder" der inneren Einheit.* Studien zur deutschen und *französischen Öffentlichkeit bei Beginn des Ersten Weltkrieges* (Bonn: Bouvier, 1996); and Jeffrey Verhey, *The Spirit of 1914: Militarism, Myth and Mobilization in Germany* (Cambridge: Cambridge University Press, 2000).

87. Verhey, *Spirit of 1914,* 232.

88. Jon Lawrence, "The Transition to War in 1914," in *Capital Cities at War: Paris, London, and Berlin, 1914–1919,* eds. Jay Winter and Jean-Louis Robert (Cambridge: Cambridge University Press, 1997), 139ff.

89. Fritz Nieser report dated 3 August 1914. GLA, 233 Politische Berichte des Großherzogl. Gesandten in Berlin und München über den Kriegsausbruch 34816.

90. Axel Varnbüler to Karl von Weizsäcker, 3 August 1914. HStA, M 1/2 Berichte der sächsischen und württembergischen Gesandschaften in Berlin an ihre Regierungen zwischen dem 28. Juni und 5. August 1914, vol. 54.

91. Kruse, *Krieg und nationale Integration,* 30–41.

92. Becker, *1914,* 270–357.

93. *Deutsche Quellen zur Geschichte des Ersten Weltkrieges,* ed. Wolfdieter Bihl (Darmstadt: Wissenschaftliche Buchgesellschaft, 1991), 49.

94. Diary entries dated 1 and 2 August 1914. BA-MA, MSg 2/4537, Tagebuch Schulin.

95. SHStA, 11372 Militärgeschichtliche Sammlung Nr. 371, Nachlaß Martin Nestler.

96. Marc Bloch, *Memoirs of War, 1914–15* (Ithaca, NY, and London: Cornell University Press, 1980), 78–79.

97. Marc Ferro, *The Great War, 1914–1918* (London: Routledge & Kegan Paul, 1973), 147–49.

98. Letter to his wife, Helene, dated 23 August 1914. BA-MA, N 43, Nachlaß Groener, folder 31.

99. Diary entry dated 1 August 1914. BA-MA, RH 61/50635, Tagebuch v. Falkenhayn.

CHAPTER 2. *"Let Slip the Dogs of War"*

1. George F. Kennan, *The Decline of Bismarck's European Order: Franco-Russian Relations, 1875–1890* (Princeton, NJ: Princeton University Press, 1979), 3.

2. Henry Kissinger, *Diplomacy* (New York: Simon & Schuster, 1994), 201ff.

3. Arden Bucholz, *Moltke, Schlieffen and Prussian War Planning* (New York and Oxford: Berg, 1991), 109ff.

4. Gerhard Ritter, *Staatskunst und Kriegshandwerk. Das Problem des "Militarismus" in Deutschland* (Munich: R. Oldenbourg, 1965), 2:244.

5. Speech of 14 May 1890. *Stenographische Berichte über die Verhandlungen des Reichstages* (Berlin: J. Gittenfeld, 1890/91), 114:76–77.

6. Michael E. Nolan, *The Inverted Mirror: Mythologizing the Enemy in France and Germany, 1898–1914* (New York and Oxford: Berghahn Books, 2005), 41.

7. Jules Verne, *Les cinq cents millions de la Bégum,* vol. 18, *Les Œuvres de Jules Verne* (Geneva: Editions de l'Agora, 1981).

8. The standard for decades was Gerhard Ritter, *Der Schlieffenplan. Kritik eines Mythos* (Munich: R. Oldenbourg, 1956); in English, *The Schlieffen Plan: Critique of a Myth* (London: O. Wolff, 1958).

9. BA-MA, RH 61/663, Grosser Generalstab, Grosse Generalstabsreise 1905/06; Ritter, *Schlieffenplan,* 20–45, 145–95.

10. Oliver Stein, *Die deutsche Heeresrüstungspolitik 1890–1914. Das Militär und der Primat der Politik* (Paderborn: Ferdinand Schöningh, 2007), 106.

11. Hans Delbrück, *History of the Art of War* (Lincoln and London: University of Nebraska Press, 1975), 1:315ff.

12. Hans von Seeckt, *Gedanken eines Soldaten* (Berlin: Verlag für Kulturpolitik, 1927), 17.

13. BA-MA, RH 61/347, Wilhelm Dieckmann, "Der Schlieffenplan"; Robert T. Foley, ed., *Alfred von Schlieffen's Military Writings* (Portland, OR: Frank Cass, 2003); and especially Gerhard P. Groß, "There Was a Schlieffen Plan," in *Der Schlieffenplan. Analysen und Dokumente,* eds. Hans Ehlert, Michael Epkenhans, and Gerhard P. Groß (Paderborn: Ferdinand Schöningh, 2006), 117–60. The German deployment plans from 1893 to 1914 are reproduced in ibid., 345–484.

14. WK, 1:142–44.

15. Große Generalstabsreise 1905/06. BA-MA, PH 3/663, Großer Generalstab.

16. Aufmarsch 1905/06. Ehlert, Epkenhans and Groß, eds., *Schlieffenplan,* 394–99.

17. BA-MA, N 323/9, Nachlaß Boetticher, Gr. Generalstabsreise Mai 1905, 3–7; Groß, "There Was a Schlieffen Plan," 139–40.

18. Yehuda L. Wallach, *The Dogma of the Battle of Annihilation: The Theories of Clausewitz and Schlieffen and Their Impact on the German Conduct of Two World Wars* (Westport, CT, and London: Greenwood, 1986), 58.

19. Ritter, *Schlieffenplan,* 68; Stig Förster, "Der deutsche Generalstab und die Illusion des kurzen Krieges, 1871–1914. Metakritik eines Mythos," *Militärgeschichtliche Mitteilungen* 54 (1995): 78.

20. Holger H. Herwig, *The First World War: Germany and Austria-Hungary, 1914–1918* (London: Arnold, 1997), 48–50.

21. BA-MA, RH 61/346, Dieckmann, "Der Schlieffenplan," 53–57; BA-MA, N 43/101, Nachlaß Schlieffen, "Der Krieg in der Gegenwart."

22. Terence Zuber, "The Schlieffen Plan Reconsidered," *War in History* 6 (July 1999): 262–305. Zuber expanded on this in *Inventing the Schlieffen Plan: German War Planning, 1871–1914* (Oxford: Oxford University Press, 2003).

23. Diary and letters to Helene dated 22, 23, and 29 August, 13 and 15 September 1914. BA-MA, N 43, Nachlaß Groener, folders 22, 31.

24. Tagebuch Rupprecht dated 15 August and 9 September 1914. BHStA-GH, Nachlaß Kronprinz Rupprecht 699.

25. Hans von Zwehl, *Erich von Falkenhayn, General der Infanterie. Eine biographische Studie* (Berlin: E. S. Mittler, 1926), 66.

26. Müller-Loebnitz to Tappen, 29 December 1920. BA-MA, N 56/2, Nachlaß Tappen.

27. Ernst Rudolf Huber, *Deutsche Verfassungsgeschichte seit 1789* (Stuttgart: Kohlhammer, 1963), 3:882ff.

28. Müller-Loebnitz to Tappen, 29 December 1920. BA-MA, N 56/2, Nachlaß Tappen.

29. The most recent assessment is by Annika Mombauer, *Helmuth von Moltke and the Origins of the First World War* (Cambridge: Cambridge University Press, 2001), 46ff. The standard biography remains Eberhard Kessel, *Moltke* (Stuttgart: K. F. Koehler, 1957). Given the near-total postwar destruction of Moltke's papers by "patriotic self-censors," this work remains pivotal. The Moltke materials that escaped destruction have been published as *Helmuth von Moltke 1848–1916. Dokumente zu seinem Leben und Wirken,* ed. Thomas Meyer (Basel: Perseus, 1993), 2 vols. Some succor can be found in the discovery of eighteen of Schlieffen's and six of Moltke's "staff problems" (*Schlußaufgaben*) in the National Archives, College Park, MD, Records of the War Department General and Special Staffs, RG 165, Box 620. They had been collected and translated in 1928 by Colonel A. L. Conger, U.S. military attaché to Berlin.

30. For a critical analysis, see Helmut Zaner, "Der Generalstabschef Helmuth von

Moltke d.J. und das theosophische Milieu um Rudolf Steiner," *Militärgeschichtliche Zeitschrift* 62 (2003): 423–58.

31. Letter to his wife dated 23 July 1904. Moltke, 296.

32. Stein, *Deutsche Heeresrüstungspolitik,* 40, 255.

33. Annika Mombauer, "Der Moltkeplan: Modifikation des Schlieffenplans bei gleichen Zielen?" in Ehlert, Epkenhans, and Groß, eds., *Schlieffenplan,* 79–99.

34. See Robert T. Foley, "Preparing the German Army for the First World War: The Operational Ideas of Alfred von Schlieffen and Helmuth von Moltke the Younger," *War & Society* 22 (October 2004): 9ff.

35. *Die Große Politik der europäischen Kabinette 1871–1914. Sammlung der Diplomatischen Akten des Auswärtigen Amtes,* eds. Johannes Lepsius, et al. (Berlin: Deutsche Verlagsgesellschaft für Politik und Geschichte, 1922–27), 33:303.

36. Moltke to Conrad, 21 January 1909. BA-MA, RH 61/50315, Gemeinsame Kriegsvorbereitung Deutschland-Österreich-Ungarn. Frage eines gemeinsamen Oberbefehls im Kriege, 14–15.

37. Moltke to Bethmann Hollweg, 21 December 1912. BA-MA, RH 61/406, Die militärpolitische Lage Deutschlands in den letzten 5 Jahren vor dem Kriege, 63.

38. Ibid., 70.

39. Dated 5 August 1914. Mombauer, "Der Moltkeplan," 87.

40. See Foley, "Preparing the German Army," 20ff.

41. BA-MA, RH 61/406, Die militärpolitische Lage Deutschlands, 71–73.

42. BA-MA, RH 61/96, Aufmarschanweisungen für die Jahre 1893/94 bis 1914/15.

43. Aufmarsch 1913/14. Ibid.

44. Memorandum dated 28 December 1912. BA-MA, N 43/101, Nachlaß Schlieffen.

45. Ritter, *Schlieffenplan,* 185.

46. BA-MA, RH 61/50739, Generalleutnant von Stein, der Generalquartiermeister der sechs ersten Kriegswochen, 9.

47. Ritter, *Schlieffenplan,* 145ff.

48. BA-MA, RH 61/96, Aufmarschanweisungen für die Jahre 1893/94 bis 1914/15. In raw terms, the left wing was strengthened by eighty-five and the right wing weakened by ninety-six battalions.

49. David Kahn, *Hitler's Spies: German Military Intelligence in World War II* (London: Hodder and Stoughton, 1978), 32–34; Hilmar-Detlef Brückner, "Schulga von Rastenfeld," *Newsletter of the International Intelligence History Study Group* 6 (Winter 1998): 1–5.

50. BA-MA, RH 61/406, Die militärpolitische Lage Deutschlands in den letzten 5 Jahren vor dem Kriege, 33.

51. BA-MA, RH 61/96, Aufmarschanweisungen für die Jahre 1893/94 bis 1914/15.

52. See Jürgen Angelow, *Kalkül und Prestige. Der Zweibund am Vorabend des Ersten Weltkrieges* (Cologne: Böhlau, 2000), 382–84.

53. Report by the Saxon military plenipotentiary to Berlin, Hermann von Salza und Lichtenau, 6 September 1905. SHStA, Militärbevollmächtigter 1426, folder 45.

54. BA-MA RH 61/150, Denkschrift über die Ersatzstellung für das Deutsche Heer von Mitte September bis Ende 1914.

55. BA-MA, RH 61/50850, Die Tätigkeit der Fliegerverbände der 1. und 2. Armee 2.–9. September 1914, 6.

56. See Dennis E. Showalter, *Tannenberg: Clash of Empires* (Hamden, CT: Archon Books, 1992), 117–21.

57. Militärgeschichtliches Forschungsamt, *Handbuch zur deutschen Militärgeschichte 1648–1945* (Munich: Bernard & Graefe, 1979), 3:159.

58. Hew Strachan, *The First World War* (Oxford: Oxford University Press, 2001), 1:239.

59. Erich Günter Blau, *Die operative Verwendung der Deutschen Kavallerie im Weltkrieg 1914–18* (Munich: C. H. Beck, 1934), 4, 13, 23.

60. See, for example, the case of the 1st (Mecklenburg) Dragoon-Regiment Nr. 17 at Waremme on 6 August 1914. Gerhard Wagner, *Die deutsche Stahlrohrlanze* (Reutlingen: Steinach, 2005), 5.

61. Stefan Kaufmann, *Kommunikationstechnik und Kriegführung 1815–1945. Stufen telemedialer Rüstung* (Munich: Wilhelm Fink, 1996), 139.

62. On 25 July, War Minister von Falkenhayn opined: "Generally speaking, a state of war is declared already with the announcement of a threatening state of danger of war as well as with mobilization." HStA, M 1/4, Kriegsministerium, Allg. Armee-Angelegenheiten 1524.

63. Diary entry dated 1 August 1914. BA-MA, RH 61/50661, Kriegserinnerungen des Generalleutnants v. [*sic*] Tappen, 13.

64. WK, 1:145; Arden Bucholz, *Moltke, Schlieffen, and Prussian War Planning* (New York and Oxford: Berg, 1991), 278; Herwig, *First World War,* 58–59, 74.

65. Evelyn Princess Blücher, *An English Wife in Berlin: A Private Memoir of Events, Politics, and Daily Life in Germany Throughout the War and the Social Revolution of 1918* (London: Constable, 1920), 14.

66. BA-MA, RH 61/815, Finanzierung der Mobilmachung, 1–3.

67. Figures vary greatly. Those given are from the official Bavarian history, *Die Bayern im Großen Kriege 1914–1918* (Munich: Verlag des Bayerischen Kriegsarchivs, 1923), 1:5, 2 (appendix 1). See also *Das Bayernbuch vom Weltkriege 1914–1918. Ein Volksbuch,* ed. Konrad Krafft von Dellmensingen (Stuttgart: Chr. Belser, 1930), 1:9; and *Die Schlacht in Lothringen und in den Vogesen 1914. Die Feuertaufe der Bayerischen Armee,* ed. Karl Deuringer (Munich: Max Schick, 1929), 1:30–31.

68. From *Die Badener im Weltkrieg 1914/1918,* ed. Wilhelm Müller-Loebnitz (Karlsruhe: G. Braun, 1935), 13–14, 22, 24–25.

69. Ibid., 13–14.

70. GLA, S Kriegsbriefe und Kriegstagebücher 53.

71. GLA, 456 F41 Kriegstagebuch Inf. Regt. "Prinz Wilhelm" Nr. 112, 171.

72. Max von Hausen, *Erinnerungen an den Marnefeldzug 1914* (Leipzig: K. F. Koehler, 1920), 101–07, appendix 2; *Sachsen in großer Zeit: Gemeinverständliche sächsische Kriegsgeschichte und vaterländisches Gedenkwert des Weltkrieges in Wort und Bild,* ed. Johann Edmund Hottenroth (Leipzig: R. M. Lippold, 1920), 3 vols.

73. HStA, M 660/038, Nachlaß von Soden, Die Leistungen der Württemberger im Weltkrieg; also, *Württembergs Heer im Weltkrieg. Einzeldarstellungen der Geschichte der württembergischen Heeresverbände* (Stuttgart: Berger, 1939), 20 vols.

74. Sewell Tyng, *The Campaign of the Marne, 1914* (New York and Toronto: Longmans, Green, 1935), 80.

75. Mob.-Termin Kalender 1914/15. Ehlert, Epkenhans, and Groß, eds., *Schlieffenplan,* 478–84.

76. BHStA-KA, AOK 6/369, Aufmarsch-Anweisungen. Italics in the original.

77. Eugenia C. Kiesling, "France," in Richard F. Hamilton and Holger H. Herwig, eds., *The Origins of World War I* (Cambridge: Cambridge University Press, 2003), 229, 246. Comments by Gaston Doumerge (January 1914) and Maurice Paléologue (July 1914).

78. Ralph R. Menning, ed., *The Art of the Possible: Documents on Great Power Diplomacy, 1814–1914* (New York: McGraw-Hill, 1996), 247.

79. SHD, 7 N 1535, Renseignements données par le Général Gilinski au Général Joffre

dans la conference préliminaire du 30 juillet–12 août 1913. I have profited greatly from two recent publications by Robert A. Doughty: "French Strategy in 1914: Joffre's Own," *Journal of Military History* 67 (2003): 427–54; and *Pyrrhic Victory: French Strategy and Operations in the Great War* (Cambridge, MA, and London: The Belknap Press of Harvard University Press, 2005).

80. Jan Karl Tanenbaum, "French Estimates of Germany's Operational War Plans," Ernest R. May, ed., *Knowing One's Enemies: Intelligence Assessment Before the Two World Wars* (Princeton, NJ: Princeton University Press, 1984), 153, 158–59.

81. Dated 15 February 1908. AFGG, 1:33–38; and 1-1:4–7. Since all volumes from the French official history, *Les armées françaises dans le grande guerre,* used in this book are from the first of eleven multivolume *tomes,* the relevant *tome* number has simply been omitted. For the three narrative volumes of the series consulted, the single number 1, 2, or 3 designates the volume; a hyphenated number (1-1 or 2-1 or 3-1) designates the volume as well as its documentary annex; all numbers after the colon are for pages.

82. Ibid., 1-1, 7-11.

83. Ibid., 1:38; Doughty, *Pyrrhic Victory,* 14.

84. Joffre, 1:117.

85. Ibid., 1:190.

86. SHD, 7 N 1778; AFGG, 1:53ff., 77ff.; AFGG 1-1:21–35; Joffre, 1:169–80.

87. Cited in Doughty, *Pyrrhic Victory,* 19.

88. Tyng, *Campaign of the Marne,* 26–31.

89. Doughty, *Pyrrhic Victory,* 26.

90. Ibid., 22.

91. Ibid., 23.

92. Ibid., 27.

93. Anthony Clayton, *Paths of Glory: The French Army, 1914–18* (London: Cassell, 2003), 37.

94. Tanenbaum, "French Estimates," 166.

95. Ibid., 143.

96. Ibid., 95.

97. Cited in Doughty, *Pyrrhic Victory,* 34.

98. AFGG, 1:106, and 1-1:58; Joffre, 1:222; Raymond Poincaré, *Comment fut déclarée la guerre de 1914* (Paris: Flammarion, 1939), 119–20.

99. Jean-Baptiste Duroselle, *La France et les français 1900–1914* (Paris: Éditions Richelieu, 1972), 82–85; Strachan, *First World War,* 1:206.

100. Charles de Gaulle, *France and Her Army* (London: Hutchinson, n.d.), 90–91.

101. Jean-Jacques Becker, *Le carnet B; les pouvoirs publics et l'antimilitarisme avant la guerre de 1914* (Paris: Klincksieck, 1973).

102. Henri Desagneaux, *A French Soldier's War Diary, 1914–1918* (Morley, UK: Elmfield Press, 1975), 5.

103. Joffre, 1:236.

104. Instruction générale No. 1, 8 August 1914. AFGG, 1-1:124–26.

105. Joffre, 1:205.

106. *Field-Marshal Sir Henry Wilson: His Life and Diaries,* ed. C. E. Callwell (London: Cassell, 1927), 1:78–79.

107. Joffre, 1:122–24.

108. Michael Howard, *The Continental Commitment: The Dilemma of British Defence Policy in the Era of the Two World Wars* (London: Temple Smith, 1972), esp. 31–52.

109. Diary entry dated 18 November 1914. Douglas Haig, *War Diaries and Letters, 1914–1918,* eds. Gary Sheffield and John Bourne (London: Weidenfeld & Nicolson, 2005), 82.

110. Grey to Bertie, 15 January 1906. Grey Papers, FO 800/49, National Archives, Kew.

111. Keith Wilson, *The Policy of the Entente: Essays on the Determinants of British Foreign Policy, 1904–1914* (Cambridge: Cambridge University Press, 1985), 63.

112. Niall Ferguson, *The Pity of War* (London: Allen Lane, 1998), 65.

113. David Herrmann, *The Arming of Europe and the Making of the First World War* (Princeton, NJ: Princeton University Press, 1997), 156–57.

114. See Paul Hayes, "Britain, Germany, and the Admiralty's Plans for Attacking German Territory, 1906–1915," in *War, Strategy, and International Politics: Essays in Honour of Sir Michael Howard,* eds. Lawrence Freedman, Paul Hayes, and Robert O'Neill (Oxford: Oxford University Press, 1992), 95–116.

115. Samuel R. Williamson Jr., *The Politics of Grand Strategy: Britain and France Prepare for War, 1904–1914* (Cambridge, MA: Harvard University Press, 1969), 307.

116. Asquith to the king, 2 November 1911. Asquith Papers I/6, Bodleian Library, Oxford University. I am indebted to Professor Keith Neilson of the Royal Military College, Canada, for this reference.

117. Williamson, *Politics of Grand Strategy,* 364–67.

118. Strachan, *First World War,* 1:202.

119. Cited in *Sir Henry Wilson,* 1:158.

120. HGW-MO, 1:10.

121. Following from Ian V. Hogg, *British Artillery Weapons and Ammunition, 1914–1918* (London: Ian Allan, 1972), 80–81, 102–03, 116–17.

122. HGW-MO, 1:6–8.

123. Bruce Gudmundsson, *The British Expeditionary Force, 1914–1915* (Oxford, 2005), 72–73.

124. Nikolas Gardner, *Trial by Fire: Command and the British Expeditionary Force in 1914* (Westport, CT: Praeger, 2003), 20–27; also Andrew J. Risio, "Building the Old Contemptibles: British Military Transformation and Tactical Development from the Boer War to the Great War, 1899–1914," unpublished MA thesis, U.S. Army Command and General Staff College, Fort Leavenworth, KS, 2005, 31–82.

125. Timothy Travers, *The Killing Ground: The British Army, the Western Front, and the Emergence of Modern Warfare, 1900–1918* (London and New York: Routledge, 1993), 37–42.

126. *History of the Great War, Naval Operations,* ed. Sir Julian Corbett (London: Longmans, Green, 1920–31), 1:72–82.

127. HGW-MO, 1:31–50.

128. The following from Luc de Vos, "Belgien: Operationsplanungen und Taktik eines neutralen Landes," in Ehlert, Epkenhans, and Groß, eds., *Schlieffenplan,* 293–310. The run-up to 1914 is in Luc de Vos, *Het effectief van de Belgische krijgsmacht en de militiewetgeving, 1830–1914* (Brussels: Koninklijk Legermuseum, 1985); also, Centre de Documentation historique des forces armées, *Histoire de l'armée belge,* vol. 1, *de 1830 à 1919* (Brussels: Editions Centre de Documentation historique des forces armées, 1982).

129. Émile Galet, *Albert, King of the Belgians in the Great War: His Military Activities and Experiences Set Down with His Approval* (Boston and New York: Houghton Mifflin, 1931), 10ff.

130. Strachan, *First World War,* 1:208.

131. BA-MA, RH 61/96, Aufmarschanweisungen für die Jahre 1893/94 bis 1914/15.

132. Marie-Rose Thielemans and Emile Vandewoude, *Le Roi Albert au travers de ses lettres inédites, 1882–1916* (Brussels: Office International de librairie, 1982), 85.

133. Galet, *Albert, King of the Belgians,* 86.

134. Cited in ibid., 18–20.

135. Ibid., 32.

136. Luc de Vos, "Belgien," 303–04.

137. Galet, *Albert, King of the Belgians*, 73.

CHAPTER 3. *Death in the Vosges*

1. *The Commentaries of Caesar*, ed. William Duncan (London: J. Cuthell, 1819), 1:263–72. Hans Delbrück, *History of the Art of War* (Lincoln and London: University of Nebraska Press, 1990), 1:483–85, places the battle closer to Colmar and Schlettstadt (Sélestat).

2. Otto Pflanze, *Bismarck and the Development of Germany* (Princeton, NJ: Princeton University Press, 1990), 1:487.

3. AFGG, 1-1:21; Joffre, 1:252.

4. Sewell Tyng, *The Campaign of the Marne, 1914* (New York and Toronto: Longmans, Green, 1935), 61.

5. AFGG, 1:221.

6. Anthony Clayton, *Paths of Glory: The French Army, 1914–18* (London: Cassell, 2003), 20.

7. AFGG, 1:222–23.

8. Michael S. Neiberg, *Fighting the Great War: A Global History* (Cambridge, MA: Harvard University Press, 2005), 22; Joffre, 1:247–48.

9. *Die Badener im Weltkrieg 1914/1918*, ed. Wilhelm Müller-Loebnitz (Karlsruhe: G. Braun, 1935), 22–30.

10. WK, 1:159–68.

11. War diary dated 9 August 1914. GLA, 456 F38 KTB des Inf. Regt. 112, Nr. 146.

12. War diary dated 9 August 1914. Ibid., 456 F42 KTB des Inf. Regt. 169, Nr. 126.

13. Ibid., 456 F42 KTB des Inf. Regt. 169, Nr. 128.

14. Ibid., D Kriegsrangliste des Inf. Regt. 169, Nr. 180.

15. Messimy, 10 August 1914, SHD, 1 K 268; and Messimy, 15 August, AFGG, 2-2:68.

16. War diary dated 12 August 1914. GLA, 456 F43 KTB des Inf. Regt. 170, Nr. 345.

17. War diary dated 11 and 12 August 1914. Ibid., 456 F43 KTB des Inf. Regt. 170, Nr. 317.

18. Brigade Order dated 31 August 1914. Ibid., 456 F58 Brigadebefehle, Nr. 27.

19. Moltke's "Gedanken über die ersten Operationen der 6. und 7. Armee" of 6 August 1914, BA-MA, RH 61/96, Aufmarschanweisungen für die Jahre 1893/94 bis 1914/15; also Wenninger to War Ministry, 15 August 1914, BHStA-KA, Nachlaß Krafft von Dellmensingen 187.

20. See Dieter Storz, " 'Dieser Stellungs-und Festungskrieg ist scheußlich!' Zu den Kämpfen in Lothringen und in den Vogesen im Sommer 1914," in *Der Schlieffenplan. Analysen und Dokumente*, eds. Hans Ehlert, Michael Epkenhans, and Gerhard P. Groß (Paderborn: Ferdinand Schöningh, 2006), 161–204.

21. BHStA-KA, AOK 6, Gedanken über die ersten Operationen der 6. und 7. Armee 369; and ibid., Aufmarsch-Anweisungen 369.

22. *Keiner fühlt sich hier mehr als Mensch . . . Erlebnis und Wirkung des Ersten Weltkriegs*, eds. Gerhard Hirschfeld and Gerd Krumeich (Essen: Klartext, 1993), 94–95.

23. Ibid., 95, 107. Also WK, 1:169–70.

24. *Die Bayern im Großen Kriege 1914–1918*, ed. Bayerisches Kriegsarchiv (Munich: Verlag des Bayerischen Kriegsarchivs, 1923), 1:17.

25. Diary entry dated 9 August 1914. BHStA-KA, KTB 1914, Nachlaß Krafft von Dellmensingen 145.

26. *Die Bayern im Großen Kriege,* 1:20; WK, 1:192.

27. Diary dated 13 August 1914, BHStA-KA, KTB 1914, Nachlaß Krafft von Dellmensingen 145.

28. Joffre's instruction to First and Second armies dated 11 August 1914. AFGG, 1-1:188–89; Joffre, 1:253.

29. AFGG, 1:144–45, 229–30; and 1-1:171.

30. See the critique by Lieutenant Colonel Pont, head of the Third Bureau. AFGG, 1:147–48.

31. Castelnau to Joffre, 6 February 1914. AFGG, 1:295.

32. Yves Gras, *Castelnau ou l'art de commander 1851–1944* (Paris: Denoël, 1990), 149–74.

33. Instruction particulière No. 5, 13 August 1914, AFGG, 1-1:239–40; Tyng, *Campaign of the Marne,* 64.

34. Rudolf von Xylander, *Deutsche Führung in Lothringen 1914. Wahrheit und Kriegsgeschichte* (Berlin: Junker und Dünnhaupt, 1935), 34; Thomas Müller, *Konrad Krafft von Dellmensingen (1862–1953). Porträt eines bayerischen Offiziers* (Munich: Kommission für Bayerische Landesgeschichte, 2002), 318–19.

35. BHStA-KA, AOK 6, KTB 2.8.14—14.3.1915, folder 369, 48. Italics in the original.

36. BHStA-KA, KTB 1914, Nachlaß Krafft von Dellmensingen 145; Müller, *Krafft von Dellmensingen,* 328.

37. Diary entry dated 14 August 1914. Tagebuch Rupprecht, BHStA-GH, Nachlaß Kronprinz Rupprecht 699; Crown Prince Rupprecht, *Mein Kriegstagebuch* (Munich: Deutscher National Verlag, 1923), 1:9.

38. Diary entry dated 15 August 1914. Tagebuch Rupprecht, BHStA-GH, Nachlaß Kronprinz Rupprecht 699; BA-MA, RH 61/50739, Generalleutnant von Stein, der Generalquartiermeister der sechs ersten Kriegswochen, 11.

39. The German official history lists Sixth Army at 183 battalions of infantry and 1,068 guns; Seventh Army at 145 battalions and 698 guns. French forces ranged against them were set at 218 battalions of infantry and 864 guns for Second Army; 202 battalions and 734 guns for First Army. WK, 1:646.

40. AFGG, 1:271ff.

41. See 26th Division's report dated 14 August 1914. AFGG, 1-1:330–31.

42. Second Army reports dated 15 August 1914. AFGG, 1-1:316–17.

43. Charles de Gaulle, *France and Her Army* (London: Hutchinson, 1945), 91.

44. Robert Doughty, *Pyrrhic Victory: French Strategy and Operations in the Great War* (Cambridge, MA, and London: The Belknap Press of Harvard University Press, 2005), 62. "The fighting thus far has demonstrated the admiral offensive qualities of our infantry."

45. Joffre, 1:252, 273.

46. GLA, 456 F41 KTB des Inf. Regt. 112, Nr. 171. Goering served with 8th Company at Mulhouse, Sarrebourg-Morhange, and Nancy-Épinal.

47. GLA, 456 D Kriegsrangliste Bad. Inf. Regt. Prinz Wilhelm Nr. 112. Goering transferred to the air force for the rest of the Great War and ended forty-sixth on the list of "aces" with twenty-two "kills."

48. Formalized in Instruction générale No. 4, 19 August 1914. AFGG, 1-1:492.

49. Ibid., 528.

50. WK, 1:205; *Die Bayern im Großen Kriege,* 1:27.

51. Diary entry dated 15 August 1914. BHStA-GH, Tagebuch Rupprecht, Nachlaß Kronprinz Rupprecht 699; Rupprecht, *Mein Kriegstagebuch,* 1:11.

52. War diary dated 19 and 22 August 1914. GLA, 456 F58 KTB des Inf. Regt. 40 Stab, Nr. 27.

53. Ibid., Nr. 115.

54. GLA, S Kriegsbriefe und Kriegstagebücher 53.

55. Dominik Richert, *Beste Gelegenheit zum Sterben. Meine Erlebnisse im Kriege 1914–1918* (Munich: Knesebeck & Schuler, 1989), 28–29.

56. Letter dated 19 August 1914. GLA, 456 F58 KTB des Inf. Regt. 40 Stab, Nr. 52.

57. Gaede to Friedrich II of Baden dated 20 August 1914. GLA, 59 Weltkrieg 1914–Schriftwechsel Gaede, Nr. 316.

58. Diary entry dated 17 August 1914. BHStA-KA, KTB 1914, Nachlaß Krafft von Dellmensingen 145.

59. Diary entry dated 17 August 1914. Tagebuch Rupprecht, BHStA-GH, Nachlaß Kronprinz Rupprecht 699.

60. Diary entry dated 17 August 1914. BHStA-KA, KTB 1914, Nachlaß Krafft von Dellmensingen 145. Italics in the original.

61. Ibid.

62. BHStA-KA, AOK 6, KTB 2.8.14–14.3.1915, 7.

63. Diary entry dated 17 August 1914. Tagebuch Rupprecht, BHStA-GH, Nachlaß Kronprinz Rupprecht 699.

64. Diary entry dated 17 August 1914. BHStA-KA, KTB 1914, Nachlaß Krafft von Dellmensingen 145. Italics in the original.

65. Diary entry dated 17 August 1914. Tagebuch Rupprecht, BHStA-GH, Nachlaß Kronprinz Rupprecht 699.

66. Diary entry dated 18 August 1914. BHStA-KA, KTB 1914, Nachlaß Krafft von Dellmensingen 145; WK, 1:210–11.

67. Wenninger to Falkenhayn, 19 August 1914. BHStA-KA, Nachlaß Krafft von Dellmensingen 187.

68. AFGG, 1:275ff.; Joffre, 1:281–83.

69. See Maréchal Foch, *Mémoires pour server à l'histoire de la guerre de 1914–1918* (Paris: Plon, 1931), 1:61–62, 65.

70. Rupprecht, *Mein Kriegstagebuch,* 1:25.

71. Diary entry dated 19 August 1914. BHStA-KA, KTB 1914, Nachlaß Krafft von Dellmensingen 145.

72. B. H. Liddell Hart, *Foch: The Man of Orléans* (Westport, CT: Greenwood, 1931), 85.

73. Cited in Clayton, *Paths of Glory,* 24.

74. AFGG, 1:328–29; and 1-1:263; Joffre, 1:284–86.

75. Tyng, *Campaign of the Marne,* 70.

76. *Die Bayern im Großen Kriege,* 1:45–54.

77. Graevenitz to War Minister Otto von Marchtaler, 22 August 1914. HStA, M 1/2 Berichte des Militärbevollmächtigten beim Grossen Hauptquartier und des stellv. Militärbevollmächtigten in Berlin, vol. 54.

78. Diary entry dated 20 August 1914. Wenninger's reports are at the BHStA-Ministerium des Äußeren, Nachlaß Wenninger, MA 3076–3085. They were published in full by Bernd Schulte, "Neue Dokumente zu Kriegsausbruch und Kriegsverlauf 1914," *Militärgeschichtliche Mitteilungen* 25 (1979): 123–85, hence I cite this work.

79. Hew Strachan, *The First World War* (Oxford: Oxford University Press, 2001), 1:224.

80. Henri Desagneaux, *A French Soldier's War Diary, 1914–1918* (Morley, UK: Elmfield Press, 1975), 7.

81. Letters dated 27 August and 14 September 1914. Madeleine Bosshard and Antoine Bosshard, eds., *"Si je reviens comme je l'espère": lettres du front et de l'arrière, 1914–1918* (Paris: Grasset, 2003), 32, 36. Italics in the original.

82. Dated 22 August 1914. Joffre, 1:293.

83. Diary entries dated 21, 22, and 23 August 1914. Tagebuch Rupprecht, BHStA-GH, Nachlaß Kronprinz Rupprecht 699.

84. John Horne and Alan Kramer, *German Atrocities, 1914: A History of Denial* (New Haven, CT, and London: Yale University Press, 2001), 63–65. Karl Deuringer, *Die Schlacht in Lothringen und in den Vogesen. Die Feuertaufe der bayerischen Armee* (Munich: M. Schick, 1929), 1:185, gives a much different version in the Bavarian semiofficial history.

85. Horne and Kramer, *German Atrocities,* 65–66.

86. Ibid., 66–67.

87. BHStA-KA, AOK 6, Feldzug 1914, Verlustliste.

88. Deuringer, *Die Schlacht in Lothringen,* 2:459. The official history, *Die Bayern im Großen Kriege,* 1:69, states laconically: "The burning city of Lunéville lit up the night far and wide following this bloody day."

89. Diary entry dated 25 August 1914. BHStA-KA, Kriegstagebuch 1914/18, Nachlaß R. Xylander 12. Unfortunately, Xylander's diary exists only for 22–25 August 1914; the rest was burned by the family as the Russians entered Berlin in 1945.

90. Diary entry dated 28 August 1914. Tagebuch Rupprecht, BHStA-GH, Nachlaß Kronprinz Rupprecht 699.

91. Reports dated 22 and 26 August 1914. GLA, 233 Politische Berichte des Großherzogl. Gesandten in Berlin und München über den Kriegsausbruch 34816.

92. WK, 1:279.

93. Letter dated 20–21 August 1914. GLA, S Kriegsbriefe und Kriegstagebücher 53.

94. Aufzeichnungen von Karl Gruber über die ersten Kriegstage 1914, 23–24 August 1914. BA-MA, MSg 2/3112, 22.

95. Deuringer, *Die Schlacht in Lothringen,* 1:354–55.

96. Ibid., 531–32.

97. Ibid., 544.

98. WK, 1:301, 575, 582.

99. *Das Bayernbuch vom Weltkriege 1914–1918. Ein Volksbuch,* ed. Konrad Krafft von Dellmensingen (Stuttgart: Chr. Belser, 1930), 2:11–23.

100. Deuringer, *Die Schlacht in Lothringen,* 1:366–67.

101. Friedrich Stuhlmann, *Die deutsche Feldpost in Geschichte und Tätigkeit* (Berlin: R. Claassen, 1939), 14ff. There exist no figures for the Bavarian mail.

102. Bernd Ulrich, *Die Augenzeugen. Deutsche Feldpostbriefe in Kriegs- und Nachkriegszeit 1914–1933* (Essen: Klartext, 1997), 45–46.

103. *Das Elsass von 1870–1932,* ed. J. Rossé et. al (Colmar: Alsatia, 1936), 1:337.

104. Gaede to Friedrich II, 10 October 1914. GLA, 59 Weltkrieg 1914–Schriftwechsel Gaede 316.

105. Ordre particulière No. 18, 21 August 1914, AFGG, 1-1:693–94; Joffre, 1:286.

106. See AFGG, 2:426–32.

107. For a detailed eyewitness account, see General Otto Kreppel in *Das Bayernbuch,* 2:49–51; also Rupprecht, *Mein Kriegstagebuch,* 1:59, 63–65.

108. Letter dated 1 September 1914. GLA, S Kriegsbriefe und Kriegstagebücher 53.

109. War diary entry dated 27 August 1914. Tagebuch Rupprecht, BHStA-GH, Nachlaß Kronprinz Rupprecht 699.

110. Wenninger to War Ministry, 31 August 1914. Berichte Ml. Bev. Wenninger, BHStA-KA, Nachlaß Krafft von Dellmensingen 145.

111. WK, 1:569.

CHAPTER 4. *The Bloody Road West: Liège to Louvain*

1. D. J. Goodspeed, *Ludendorff: Soldier: Dictator: Revolutionary* (London: Hart-Davis, 1966), 1.

2. Cited in Sewell Tyng, *The Campaign of the Marne, 1914* (New York and Toronto: Longmans, Green, 1935), 53.

3. WK, 1:105–06.

4. Jeff Lipkes, *Rehearsals: The German Army in Belgium, August 1914* (Leuven: Leuven University Press, 2007), 42.

5. Ibid., 90–103; Maximilian v. Poseck, *Die Deutsche Kavallerie 1914 in Belgien und Frankreich* (Berlin: E. S. Mittler, 1921), 10–11.

6. WK, 1:109–10.

7. Ibid., 108.

8. Ibid., 111–13, 115.

9. Ibid., 111; Lipkes, *Rehearsals,* 61.

10. Joffre, 1:286–87.

11. Cited in *Source Records of the Great War,* ed. Charles F. Horne (USA: National Alumni, 1923), 2:49.

12. BA-MA, RH 61/50220, Wilhelm Dieckmann, "Der Schlieffenplan," 53–57.

13. WK, 1:112.

14. John Horne and Alan Kramer, *German Atrocities, 1914: A History of Denial* (New Haven, CT, and London: Yale University Press, 2001), 13; Lipkes, *Rehearsals,* 110ff.

15. Erich Ludendorff, *Meine Kriegserinnerungen 1914–1918* (Berlin: E. S. Mittler, 1919), 29.

16. Ibid., 29.

17. Moltke, 24.

18. Cited in Tyng, *Campaign of the Marne,* 56.

19. Research report dated 11 April 1938. BA-MA, RH 61/50739, Generalleutnant von Stein, der Generalquartiermeister der sechs ersten Kriegswochen, 7, 9.

20. *Ein Armeeführer erlebt den Weltkrieg. Persönliche Aufzeichnungen des Generalobersten v. Einem,* ed. Junius Alter (Leipzig: Hase u. Koehler, 1938), 35–37; *Keiner fühlt sich hier mehr als Mensch . . . Erlebnis und Wirkung des Weltkriegs,* ed. Gerhard Hirschfeld and Gerd Krumeich (Essen: Klartext, 1993), 88–89.

21. Diary entries dated 8 and 11 August 1914. *Ein Armeeführer erlebt den Weltkrieg,* 35–37.

22. Barbara Tuchman, *The Guns of August* (New York: Ballantine Books, 1994), 226.

23. WK, 1:120.

24. Ludendorff, *Kriegserinnerungen,* 31.

25. "German Letter from an Officer in the Assault," undated. Cited in *Source Records of the Great War,* 2:48.

26. Émile Galet, *Albert, King of the Belgians in the Great War: His Military Activities and Experiences Set Down with his Approval* (Boston and New York: Houghton Mifflin, 1931), 126.

27. WK, 1:120.

28. There is much debate on the matter. German commanders after the war argued that Liège caused them no delay. French and Belgian military histories insist on a delay of ten days. The British official history suggests a halt of "four or five days." HGW-MO, 1:35, n. 1.

29. AFGG, 1:158–59; Harald van Nes, "Die 'Kavalleriedebatte' vor dem Ersten Weltkrieg und das Gefecht von Halen am 12. August 1914," *Militärgeschichte* 3 (1993): 25–30.

30. The only biography remains Artur Brabant, *Generaloberst Max Freiherr von Hausen: Ein deutscher Soldat* (Dresden: v. Baensch, 1926).

31. Peter Graf Kielmansegg, *Deutschland und der Erste Weltkrieg* (Frankfurt: Athenaion, 1968), 34.

32. Diary entries dated 16 and 17 August 1914. Tagebücher General von Wenninger, BHStA-KA, HS 2543–46. Published in Bernd F. Schulte, "Neue Dokumente zu Kriegsausbruch und Kriegsverlauf 1914," *Militärgeschichtliche Mitteilungen* 25 (1979): 146–49.

33. *The Kaiser and His Court: The Diaries, Note Books and Letters of Admiral Georg Alexander von Müller, Chief of the Naval Cabinet, 1914–1918,* ed. Walter Görlitz (New York: Harcourt, Brace & World, 1959), 22–23.

34. WK, 1:258.

35. Ibid., 187, 259; Robert T. Foley, "Preparing the German Army for the First World War: The Operational Ideas of Alfred von Schlieffen and Helmuth von Moltke the Younger," *War & Society* 22 (October 2004): 19.

36. Detailed in Lipkes, *Rehearsals,* 125–70, 171–206.

37. Military Plenipotentiary Traugott Leuckart von Weißdort to War Minister Adolph von Carlowitz, 17 August 1914. SHStA, 11250 Sächsischer Militäbevollmächtigter in Berlin 71. Geheimakten A: Verschiedenes.

38. Diary entries dated 20 and 21 August 1914. BA-MA, N 324/11 and N 324/26, Nachlaß v. Einem.

39. Entry dated 19 August 1914. Joffre, 1:277–78.

40. WK, 1:186.

41. Tyng, *Campaign of the Marne,* 96.

42. See Antonin Selliers de Moranville, *Pourquoi l'armée belge s'est-elle retirée vers la position fortifiée d'Anvers le 18 août 1914* (Brussels: Dewit, 1921).

43. Brand Whitlock, *Belgium Under the German Occupation: A Personal Narrative* (London: W. Heinemann, 1919), 1:81.

44. Entry dated 21 August 1914. Evelyn Princess Blücher, *An English Wife in Berlin: A Private Memoir of Events, Politics, and Daily Life in Germany Throughout the War and the Social Revolution of 1918* (London: Constable, 1920), 21.

45. From Horne and Kramer, *German Atrocities,* 39–42; Lipkes, *Rehearsals,* 401ff.

46. Hugh Gibson, *A Journal from Our Legation in Belgium* (Toronto: William Briggs, 1917), 155–59.

47. Alexander von Kluck, *Der Marsch auf Paris und die Marneschlacht 1914* (Berlin: E. S. Mittler, 1920), 24.

48. BA-MA, RH 61/208, Franktireurkrieg in Belgien 1914; WK, 3:328–29.

49. Peter Paret et al., eds., *Persuasive Images: Posters of War and Revolution from the Hoover Institution Archives* (Princeton, NJ: Princeton University Press, 1992), 25.

50. Horne and Kramer, *German Atrocities,* 41.

51. Ibid., 74.

52. See *La guerre de 1914. L'action de l'armée belge pour la defense du pays et le respect de sa neutralité: rapport/du commandement de l'armée (periode du 21 juillet au 31 decembre)* (Paris: Chapelot, 1915).

53. WK, 1:408.

54. Ibid., 223; Max von Hausen, *Erinnerungen an den Marnefeldzug 1914* (Leipzig: K. F. Koehler, 1920), 112–13.

55. Cited in Tyng, *Campaign of the Marne,* 100.

56. WK, 1:401, 406, 416.

57. GLA, 59, Nr. 365, Denkschrift der Beschiessungen der Forts 1914, General v. Bailer, 12. Bailer was with the Engineer Corps.

58. Galet, *Albert, King of the Belgians in the Great War,* 146. The German official history gives slightly different totals: six thousand soldiers, forty heavy guns, and one hundred trucks captured. WK, 1:512.

59. Letter dated 20 August 1914. SHStA, 11356 Generalkommando des XII. Reservekorps 139.

60. *Keiner fühlt sich hier mehr als Mensch,* 101–02.

61. Letter dated 23 August 1914. SHStA, 11372 Militärgeschichtliche Sammlung Nr. 105.

62. The following from Horne and Kramer, *German Atrocities,* 35–36.

63. Report dated 24 August 1914. SHStA, 11356 Generaldommando des XII. Reservekorps 139.

CHAPTER 5. *Deadly Deadlock: The Ardennes*

1. WK, 1:354.
2. Ibid., 366–67.
3. Dated 13 August 1914. AFGG, 1:165–66; and 1-1:240–41; Joffre, 1:269.
4. Ibid., 1:266–68; Anthony Clayton, *Paths of Glory: The French Army, 1914–18* (London: Cassell, 2003), 46–47.
5. Sewell Tyng, *The Campaign of the Marne, 1914* (New York and Toronto: Longmans, Green, 1935), 191–92.
6. AFGG, 1:163.
7. Cited in Gabriel Rouquerol, *La bataille de Guise* (Paris: Berger-Levrault, 1921), 110.
8. Charles Lanrezac, *Le plan de campagne français et le premier mois de la guerre (2 août–3 septembre 1914)* (Paris: Payot, 1921), 77.
9. Instruction particulière No. 10, 15 August 1914. AFGG, 1-1:307–08.
10. Instruction particulière No. 13, 18 August 1914. AFGG, 1-1:424–25.
11. AFGG, 1-1:529; Joffre, 1:273–76; Robert A. Doughty, *Pyrrhic Victory: French Strategy and Operations in the Great War* (Cambridge, MA, and London: The Belknap Press of Harvard University Press, 2005), 65.
12. AFGG, 1-1:598; Joffre, 1:289.
13. Hew Strachan, *The First World War* (Oxford: Oxford University Press, 2001), 1:225.
14. Joffre to Messimy, 21 August 1914. AFGG, 1:205.
15. Barbara W. Tuchman, *The Guns of August* (New York: Ballantine Books, 1994), 258.
16. AFGG, 1:503–04. Joffre, 1:270–71, speaks bravely of "covering" the BEF's movements.
17. Charles J. Huguet, *Britain and the War: A French Indictment* (London: Cassell, 1927), 51; AFGG, 1:504–05.
18. *Field-Marshal Sir Henry Wilson: His Life and Diaries,* ed. C. E. Callwell (London: Cassell, 1927), 1:164. French chose to leave these discussions with Joffre and Lanrezac out of his memoirs: *1914* (Boston and New York: Houghton Mifflin, 1919), 34–36.
19. AFGG, 1:509.
20. HGW-MO, 1:10.
21. Tyng, *Campaign of the Marne,* 369.
22. *Field-Marshal Sir Henry Wilson,* 1:165.
23. AFGG, 1:474.
24. Ibid., 1:479.

25. Ibid., 1:484ff.

26. Lanrezac to Joffre, 22 August 1914. AFGG, 1-1:729. "L'armée W" refers to the BEF guarding Lanrezac's left flank.

27. AFGG, 1:498.

28. *The Commentaries of Caesar,* ed. William Duncan (London: J. Cuthell, 1819), 1:422–25.

29. Ordre particulière No. 17 to Third and Fourth armies, 21 August 1914. AFGG, 1-1:604.

30. Tyng, *Campaign of the Marne,* 82.

31. Cited in ibid., 79.

32. Official German figures as of 22 August 1914. Fourth Army was listed as 117 battalions and 640 guns; Fifth Army as 119 battalions and 680 guns. WK, 1:646.

33. Ibid., 1:306.

34. Crown Prince Wilhelm, *Meine Erinnerungen aus Deutschlands Heldenkampf* (Berlin: E. S. Mittler, 1923), 46. He would later blame the failure to achieve his "Cannae" on Bruno von Mudra's XVI Corps for interpreting the royal order to advance as one to withdraw, after having been attacked by superior French forces.

35. Tyng, *Campaign of the Marne,* 81.

36. Edmond Valarché, *La bataille des frontiers* (Paris: Berger-Levrault, 1932), 136.

37. For the attack, see Barthélemy Edmond Palat, *La grande guerre sur le front occidental* (Paris: Chapelot, 1917–29), 3:173ff. AFGG, 1:369ff.

38. WK, 1:472.

39. AFGG, 2:255.

40. Tuchman, *Guns of August,* 284–85; AFGG 1:376ff.

41. Jean Galtier-Boissière, *En rase campagne, 1914. Un hiver à Souchez 1915–1916* (Paris: Berger-Levrault, 1917), 48, 54.

42. AFGG, 1:387–88.

43. Ibid., 2:248ff.

44. Ibid., 1:401ff.

45. See Bruce I. Gudmundsson, "Unexpected Encounter at Bertrix," in Robert Cowley, ed., *The Great War: Perspectives on the First World War* (New York: Random House, 2003), 25–36.

46. Cited in Jean-Pierre Guéno and Yves Laplume, eds., *Paroles de poilus: lettres et carnets du front 1914–1918* (Paris: Librio, 1998), 27–28.

47. Report dated 23 August 1914. AFGG, 1-1:871.

48. Gudmundsson, "Unexpected Encounter," 26, 35.

49. Langle de Cary to Joffre, 1 September 1914. AFGG, 2-2:315.

50. *Sanitätsbericht über das deutsche Heer im Weltkriege 1914/1918* (Berlin: E. S. Mittler, 1934), 3:36, 37–38.

51. Letter to his wife dated 24 August 1914. BA-MA, RH 61/948 Der Krieg im Westen 1914–1916.

52. WK, 1:399.

53. Letter to his wife dated 24 August 1914. BA-MA, RH 61/948 Der Krieg im Westen 1914–1916.

54. WK, 1:394.

55. Ibid., 1:399.

56. Robin Neillands, *The Old Contemptibles: The British Expeditionary Force 1914* (London: John Murray, 2004), 2.

57. WK, 1:420.

58. The detailed British account is in HGW-MO, 1:7ff.; the German, in Raimund

von Gleichen-Rußwurm, *Die Schlacht bei Mons* (Oldenburg: Gerhard Stalling, 1919), 1–68.

59. John F. Lucy, *There's a Devil in the Drum* (London: Faber, 1938), 734.

60. Walter Bloem, *The Advance from Mons 1914* (London: Peter Davies, 1930), 60, 63.

61. David Clarke, *The Angel of Mons: Phantom Soldiers and Ghostly Guardians* (Chichester: John Wiley & Sons, 2004), 1–2.

62. Huguet, *Britain and the War,* 58–59.

63. Marc Bloch, *Memoirs of War, 1914–15* (Ithaca, NY, and London: Cornell University Press, 1980), 81–85.

64. Diary entry dated 25 August 1914. BA-MA, RH 61/50661 Kriegserinnerungen des Generalleunants v. [*sic*] Tappen, 29.

65. BA-MA, RH 61/50739 Generalleutnant von Stein, der Generalquartiermeister der sechs ersten Kriegswochen, 17.

66. Tyng, *Campaign of the Marne,* 136.

67. *Der Sanitätsdienst im Gefechts- und Schlachtenverlauf im Weltkriege 1914/1918* (Berlin: E. S. Mittler, 1938), 2:31. Some battalions reported as many as four hundred men down with foot sores.

68. Ibid., 2:93.

69. *Sanitätsbericht über das Deutsche Heer im Weltkriege 1914/1918,* 3:36.

70. Joffre to Messimy, 23 August 1914. AFGG, 1:213.

71. Joffre to Messimy, 24 August 1914. AFGG, 2:1, 124–25. Also Doughty, *Pyrrhic Victory,* 75.

72. Messimy to Joffre, 24 August 1914. SHD, 1 K 268.

73. Raymond Poincaré, *Au service de la France* (Paris: Plon, 1928), 5:155.

74. Cited in Mark Sullivan, *Our Times, 1900–1925* (New York and London: Charles Scribner's Sons, 1936), 5:26.

CHAPTER 6. *Squandered Climacterics*

1. Roland Kleinhenz, "La percée saxonne sur le front du centre," *Les batailles de la Marne de l'Ourc à Verdun (1914 et 1918)* (Soteca: Éditions, 2004), 147.

2. Undated letter from Hausen's chief of staff, Ernst von Hoeppner. SHStA, 12693 Personennachlaß Max Klemens Lothar Freiherr von Hausen 43b.

3. Max von Hausen, *Erinnerungen an den Marnefeldzug 1914* (Leipzig: K. F. Koehler, 1920), 108, 117.

4. "Meine Erlebnisse u. Erfahrungen als Oberbefehlshabers der 3. Armee im Bewegungskrieg 1914," SHStA, 12693 Personalnachlaß Max Klemens Lothar Freiherr von Hausen (1846–1922) 43a, 39, 41, 46. This is Hausen's unexpurgated handwritten memoir of July 1918, and will be used in place of the "cleansed" published version cited in note 3.

5. Ibid., 42.

6. WK, 1:371.

7. Hausen, "Meine Erlebnisse," SHStA 12693, 54.

8. WK, 1:372.

9. Hausen, "Meine Erlebnisse," SHStA 12693, 56.

10. Ibid. The best account of Hausen at Dinant is by Artur Baumgarten-Crusius, *Die Marneschlacht insbesondere auf der Front der deutschen dritten Armee* (Leipzig: R. M. Lippold, 1919), 28ff.

11. WK, 1:373–74.

12. Ibid., 1:379.

13. Sewell Tyng, *The Campaign of the Marne, 1914* (New York and Toronto: Longmans, Green, 1935), 115.

14. Ibid.

15. Christian Mallet, *Impressions and Experiences of a French Trooper, 1914–1915* (London: Constable, 1916), 33.

16. Cited in Paul-Marie de la Gorce, *The French Army: A Military-Political History* (London: Weidenfeld & Nicolson, 1963), 102.

17. WK, 1:381–82.

18. The terror of Dinant is detailed in Jeff Lipkes, *Rehearsals: The German Army in Belgium, August 1914* (Leuven: University of Leuven Press, 2007), 257–377.

19. Johannes Niemann, *Das 9. Königlich Sächsische Infanterie-Regiment Nr. 133 im Weltkrieg 1914–18* (Hamburg-Grossflottbek: Selbstverlag, 1969), 10.

20. John Horne and Alan Kramer, *German Atrocities, 1914: A History of Denial* (New Haven, CT, and London: Yale University Press, 2001), 43–53.

21. *Wir Kämpfer im Weltkrieg. Selbstzeugnisse deutscher Frontsoldaten,* ed. Wolfgang Foerster and Helmuth Greiner (Berlin: F. W. Peters, 1937), 39.

22. Letters dated 22 and 25 August 1914. SHStA, 11372 Militärgeschichtliche Sammlung Nr. 105.

23. Letter dated 6 September 1914. Ibid.

24. Cited in Horne and Kramer, *German Atrocities,* 48.

25. See the initial compilation by Édouard Gérard, *Tod Dinants. Geschichte eines Verbrechens* (Brussels: Brian Hill, 1919), 39–40. Lipkes, *Rehearsals,* gives figures of 685 civilians killed and eleven hundred homes and buildings burned.

26. Hoeppner to Hausen, undated (1918?). SHStA, 12693 Personennachlaß Hausen 43b.

27. Hausen, "Meine Erlebnisse," SHStA 12693, 67–68. Also, war diary dated 24 August 1914. SHStA, 11356 Generalkommando des XII. Reservekorps 139.

28. Hoeppner to Hausen, 30 March 1918. SHStA, 12693 Personennachlaß Hausen 43b.

29. WK, 1:384–85.

30. This was also the verdict of Hausen's successor as commander of Third Army: Karl v. Einem, *Ein Armeeführer erlebt den Weltkrieg. Persönliche Aufzeichnungen* (Leipzig: v. Hase & Koehler, 1938), 58.

31. Baumgarten-Crusius, *Die Marneschlacht,* 40–42.

32. Dated 24 August 1914. SHStA, 11250 Sächsischer Militärbevollmächtigter in Berlin 71. Geheimakten A: Verschiedenes.

33. WK, 1:402–03.

34. Ibid., 1:566.

35. Ibid., 1:337.

36. Ibid., 1:438–39.

37. Reports, 27 and 31 August, 2 September 1914. HStA, M 33/2 General Kommando XIII. Armee Korps 1914–1918, vol. 9, Operationsakten, Meldungen vom 26.8–7.9.1914.

38. Diary entry dated 24–25 August 1914. BA-MA, RH 61/83, Vorgänge im Großen Hauptquartier des Generalstabes 1914–1915.

39. Letter to his father dated 20 August 1914. Bernd Schulte, "Neue Dokumente zu Kriegsausbruch und Kriegsverlauf 1914," *Militärgeschichtliche Mitteilungen* 25 (1979): 153.

40. Dated 31 August 1914. GLA, 233 Politische Berichte des Großherzogl. Gesandten in Berlin und München über den Kriegsausbruch 34816.

41. War diary, General Hans von Plessen, 24 and 29 August 1914. Cited in Holger Afflerbach, ed., *Kaiser Wilhelm II. als Oberster Kriegsherr im Ersten Weltkrieg: Quellen aus*

der militärischen Umgebung des Kaisers 1914–1918 (Munich: R. Oldenbourg, 2005), 647, 651.

42. BA-MA, Nachlass Schlieffen, N 43/101, "Der Krieg in der Gegenwart." Later published in *Deutsche Revue* 34 (January 1909): 13–24.

43. Moltke, 382.

44. Tappen to General Staff, 13 July 1919. BA-MA, RH 61/51060 Die OHL und die Marneschlacht vom 4.–9.9.1919; WK, 3:190.

45. See Hans Georg Kampe, *Nachrichtentruppe des Heeres und Deutsche Reichspost. Militärisches und staatliches Nachrichtenwesen in Deutschland 1830 bis 1945* (Waldesruh: Dr. Erwin Meißler, 1999), 172.

46. From "Die Nachrichtenverbindungen zwischen den Kommandobehörden während des Bewegungskrieges 1914," General Schniewindt 1928. HStA, M 738 Sammlung zur Militärgeschichte 36.

47. Kampe, *Nachrichtentruppe,* 170, 172.

48. John Ferris, ed., *The British Army and Signals Intelligence During the First World War* (Phoenix Mill, UK: Alan Sutton, 1992), 4–5, suggests that British and French intelligence intercepted at least fifty radio messages in plain language from German armies, corps, and divisions between September and November 1914.

49. WK, 3:8–9.

50. Ibid. My italics.

51. Hew Strachan, *The First World War* (Oxford: Oxford University Press, 2001), 1:245.

52. Carl von Clausewitz, *On War,* eds. Michael Howard and Peter Paret (Princeton, NJ: Princeton University Press, 1976), 271.

53. Letter dated 24 August 1914. AFGG, 2-1:124–25. Joffre's reassessment has been laid out by Robert A. Doughty, *Pyrrhic Victory: French Strategy and Operations in the Great War* (Cambridge, MA, and London: The Belknap Press of Harvard University Press, 2005), 76–78.

54. Joffre, 1:303–04.

55. Ibid., 1:300.

56. See the compilation in AFGG, 3-4:846.

57. Joffre, 1:310.

58. Instruction général No. 2, 25 August 1914. AFGG, 2-1:278–80.

59. Robert B. Asprey, *The First Battle of the Marne* (Philadelphia: Lippincott, 1962), 72.

60. Joffre, 1:317–20.

61. AFGG, 2:121, 466; Doughty, *Pyrrhic Victory,* 78.

62. Edward Spears, *Liaison 1914: A Narrative of the Great Retreat* (London: Eyre & Spottiswoode, 1930), 228–31.

63. Charles J. Huguet, *Britain and the War: A French Indictment* (London: Cassell, 1928), 67.

64. Huguet to GQG, 16 August 1914. AFGG, 2-1:429.

65. Order dated the night of 25–26 August 1914. AFGG, 1-1:999; and 2:115–16.

66. Keith Jeffrey, *Field Marshal Sir Henry Wilson: A Political Soldier* (Oxford: Oxford University Press, 2006), 135.

67. John Charteris, *At G.H.Q.* (London: Cassell, 1931), 17.

68. Cited in *Field-Marshal Sir Henry Wilson: His Life and Diaries,* ed. C. E. Callwell (London: Cassell, 1927), 1:169.

69. Strachan, *First World War,* 1:223.

70. *Field-Marshal Sir Henry Wilson,* 1:170.

71. Sent "afternoon" of 28 August 1914. AFGG, 2-1:659.

72. Hermann von Kuhl, *Der Marnefeldzug 1914* (Berlin: E. S. Mittler, 1921), 82.

73. AFGG, 2:53–54; and 2-1:547. Also Joffre, 1:322–23.

74. Huguet to Joffre, 27 August 1914, SHD, 1 K 268; AFGG, 2-1:550–52; Joffre, 1:328–29; Doughty, *Pyrrhic Victory,* 78–79.

75. Cited in Tyng, *Campaign of the Marne,* 150.

76. Lanrezac's General Order of 27 August 1914. AFGG, 2-1:592–93.

77. Joffre, 1:332.

78. Spears, *Liaison 1914,* 252.

79. Joffre's order to Fifth Army, 9 AM, 28 August 1914. AFGG, 2-1:663; Joffre, 1:332.

80. Raymond Poincaré, *Au service de la France* (Paris: Plon, 1928), 5:206.

81. Huguet to GQG, 28 August 1914. AFGG, 2-1:671–72.

82. Huguet, *Britain and the War,* 72.

83. Barbara Tuchman, *The Guns of August* (New York: Ballantine Books, 1962), 448.

84. Lanrezac's orders of 28 August, AFGG, 2-1:706–07; attack in AFGG, 2:68ff.

85. Defforges to Lanrezac, 10 AM, 29 August 1914. AFGG, 2-1:866.

86. WK, 3:154–55.

87. Letter dated 29 August 1914. *Wir Kämpfer im Weltkrieg,* 57–61.

88. War diary dated 30 August 1914. SHStA, 11356 Generalkommando des XII. Reservekorps 139; Hausen, "Meine Erlebnisse," 108.

89. Particular Order to I, III, and X corps. AFGG, 2-1:827.

90. Joffre, 1:339.

91. Cited in Leonard V. Smith, *Between Mutiny and Obedience: The Case of the French Fifth Infantry Division During World War I* (Princeton, NJ: Princeton University Press, 1994), 55–56.

92. WK, 3:168.

93. Ibid., 3:168–69.

94. Lauenstein's letters dated 31 August and 3 September 1914. BA-MA, RH 61/948 Der Krieg im Westen 1914–1916.

95. WK, 3:175.

96. Lanrezac's General Order, 6 PM, 31 August 1914. AFGG 2-2:196–98.

97. Berthelot to Lanrezac, 31 August 1914. AFGG, 2-2:160.

98. Tyng, *Campaign of the Marne,* 160.

99. John Terraine, *The Western Front, 1914–1918* (London: Hutchinson, 1964), 131. A tactical victory belongs to the commander who gains and then holds the battlefield, not to the one who abandons it without plan or purpose. Moreover, Bülow's appeal for help was not the determining factor in Kluck's turn to the southeast.

100. WK, 3:177, 179, 186.

CHAPTER 7. *To the Marne*

1. BA-MA, RH 61/948, Der Krieg im Westen 1914–1916.

2. Joffre, 1:340–41.

3. Sewell Tyng, *The Campaign of the Marne, 1914* (New York and Toronto: Longmans, Green, 1935), 181.

4. Ibid.

5. *Field-Marshal Sir Henry Wilson: His Life and Diaries,* ed. C. E. Callwell (London: Cassell, 1927), 1:173.

6. Tyng, *Campaign of the Marne,* 182.

7. Raymond Poincaré, *Au service de la France* (Paris: Plon, 1928), 5:222.

8. Robert Cowley, ed., *What If? The World's Foremost Military Historians Imagine What Might Have Been* (New York: Berkley Books, 2000), 281.

9. Charles J. Huguet, *Britain and the War: A French Indictment* (London: Cassell, 1928), 84.

10. Ibid., 85.

11. Dated 1 September 1914. AFGG, 2-2:286–87; Joffre, 1:359–60.

12. Barbara Tuchman, *The Guns of August* (New York: Ballantine Books, 1962), 460.

13. Messimy's undated "note," probably around 25 August 1914. AFGG, 2-1:264–66.

14. Tyng, *Campaign of the Marne*, 187–88.

15. Joffre, 1:421.

16. Ibid., 1:370; Robert A. Doughty, *Pyrrhic Victory: French Strategy and Operations in the Great War* (Cambridge, MA, and London: The Belknap Press of Harvard University Press, 2005), 85.

17. Edward Spears, *Liaison 1914: A Narrative of the Great Retreat* (London: Eyre & Spottiswoode, 1930), 384.

18. Moltke's "top secret" report of 1 September 1914. HStA, M 1/2 Kriegsministerium 109, Mitteilungen des Chefs des Feldheeres Nr. 1–50, 27.7.1914–3.1.1915.

19. Julian A. Corbett, *Naval Operations: History of the Great War Based on Official Documents* (Uckfield: Naval & Military Press, n.d.), 1:95–97, 123–24; AFGG, 2:809.

20. BA-MA, RH 61/50661, Kriegserinnerungen des Generalleutnants v. [*sic*] Tappen, 32.

21. WK, 3:186, 220.

22. Ibid., 3:609.

23. Ibid., 3:225.

24. Diary entry for 31 August 1914. BA-MA, RH 61/948, Der Krieg im Westen 1914–1916.

25. Letter of 31 August 1914. Moltke, 383.

26. WK, 3:225–26.

27. Moltke, 383; WK, 3:227.

28. Dated 2 September 1914. Philipp Witkop, ed., *Kriegsbriefe gefallener Studenten* (Munich: Georg Müller, 1928), 309.

29. Holger Afflerbach, *Falkenhayn. Politisches Denken und Handeln im Kaiserreich* (Munich: R. Oldenbourg, 1994), 181–82.

30. Dated 4 September 1914. Karl Helfferich, *Der Weltkrieg* (Berlin: Allstein, 1919), 2:18.

31. WK, 1:605.

32. Diary entry for 21 August 1914. BHStA-KA, KTB 1914, Nachlaß Krafft von Dellmensingen 145.

33. Diary entry for 23 August 1914, ibid.; BHStA-KA, AOK 6, KTB 2.8.14–14.3.1915, 13. Also Crown Prince Rupprecht, *Mein Kriegstagebuch* (Munich: Deutscher National Verlag, 1923), 1:37–38, 41; Karl Deuringer, *Die Schlacht in Lothringen und in den Vogesen. Die Feuertaufe der bayerischen Armee* (Munich: M. Schick, 1929), 2:372–74, 583; WK, 1:575–76, 583.

34. Diary entry for 23 August 1914. Tagebuch Rupprecht, BHStA-GH, Nachlaß Kronprinz Rupprecht 699.

35. Joffre, 1:312–13.

36. Castelnau to XV and XVI Corps, 3 PM, 25 August 1914. AFGG, 2-1:291.

37. Dated 27 August 1914. GLA, S Kriegsbriefe und Kriegstagebücher 53.

38. Diary entry for 24 August 1914. BHStA-KA, Kriegstagebuch 1914/18, Nachlaß R. Xylander 12.

39. AFGG, 2:374.

40. Diary entry for 29 August 1914. BA-MA, RH 61/50661 Kriegserinnerungen des Generalleutnants v. [*sic*] Tappen.

41. Wenninger's letter to his father, 30 August 1914, BHStA-KA, HS 2662 Wenninger; and Wenninger's report to Munich, 31 August 1914, in Bernd Schulte, "Neue Dokumente zu Kriegsausbruch und Kriegsverlauf 1914," *Militärgeschichtliche Mitteilungen* 25 (1979): 160.

42. Diary entry dated 30 August 1914, BHStA-KA, KTB 1914, Nachlaß Krafft von Dellmensingen 145; Deuringer, *Die Schlacht in Lothringen,* 2:584–85; WK, 1:593, and 3:285; Thomas Müller, *Krafft von Dellmensingen (1862–1953). Porträt eines bayerischen Offiziers* (Munich: Kommission für Bayerische Landesgeschichte, 2002), 352–53.

43. Diary entry dated 30 August 1914. BHStA-KA, KTB 1914, Nachlaß Krafft von Dellmensingen 145.

44. Diary entries dated 30 and 31 August 1914. Tagebuch Rupprecht, BHStA-GH, Nachlaß Kronprinz Rupprecht 699.

45. Diary entry dated 31 August 1914, BHStA-KA, KTB 1914, Nachlaß Krafft von Dellmensingen 145; BHStA-KA, AOK 6, KTB 2.8.1914–14.3.1915, 15. Also Rudolf von Xylander, *Deutsche Führung in Lothringen 1914. Wahrheit und Kriegsgeschichte* (Berlin: Junker und Dünnhaupt, 1935), 153; WK, 3:286–87.

46. Diary entry dated 2 September 1914. BHStA-KA, KTB 1914, Nachlaß Krafft von Dellmensingen 145.

47. Diary entry dated 2 September 1914; ibid.

48. Diary entry dated 31 August 1914; ibid.

49. Diary entry dated 1 September 1914, ibid.; BHStA-KA, Generalkommando I AK, KTB 31.7.14–28.2.15; diary entry dated 1 September 1914, Tagebuch Rupprecht, BHStA-GH, Nachlaß Kronprinz Rupprecht 699.

50. Diary entry dated 1 September 1914. BHStA-KA, Generalkommando II AK, KTB 1.8.1914–31.12.1914.

51. Diary entry dated 1 September 1914. BHStA-KA, Generalkommando III AK, Kriegstagebuch 29.7.14–31.12.1914. The comment concerning the "present" of Nancy to Ludwig III is in diary entry dated 26 August 1914, Tagebuch Rupprecht, BHStA-GH, Nachlaß Kronprinz Rupprecht 699.

52. Diary entries dated 26 August and 1 September 1914; ibid.

53. "Gebsattel wants to have his battle." BHStA-KA, Kriegstagebuch 1914/18, Nachlaß R. Xylander 12.

54. Cited in Tyng, *Campaign of the Marne,* 68.

55. Douglas Wilson Johnson, *Battlefields of the World War: Western and Southern Fronts; A Study in Military Geography* (New York: Oxford University Press, 1921), 431, 437.

56. Reconnaissance report of 1 September 1914 by Colonel Karl von Nagel, chief of staff to I Corps. BHStA-KA, Generalkommando I AK, KTB 31.7.14–28.2.15.

57. *Die Bayern im Großen Kriege 1914–1918* ed. Bayerisches Kriegsarchiv (Munich: Verlag des Bayerischen Kriegsarchivs, 1923), 1:61.

58. See AFGG, 3:1159–61.

59. Details in ibid., 2:388, 390, 393.

60. Ibid., 3:1244.

61. Dated 28 August 1914. Ibid., 2:509; and 2-2:667; Joffre, 1:337.

62. AFGG, 3:1154–56.

63. Diary entry dated 4 September 1914. Tagebuch Rupprecht, BHStA-GH, Nachlaß Kronprinz Rupprecht 699.

64. Deuringer, *Die Schlacht in Lothringen,* 1:635; AFGG, 3-1:579.

65. AFGG, 2:434, 445; ibid., 3:1165.

66. Ibid., 3-1:97; Joffre, 1:398–99.

67. AFGG, 3-1:193.

68. Johnson, *Battlefields of the World War,* 485.

69. AFGG, 3:1186.

70. Diary entry dated 14 September 1914. Tagebuch Rupprecht, BHStA-GH, Nachlaß Kronprinz Rupprecht 699.

71. Diary entry dated 7 September 1914. BHStA-KA, Generalkommando III AK, Kriegstagebuch 29.7.14–31.12.1914.

72. 7 September 1914. Joffre, 1:407–08.

73. AFGG, 3:1210ff.

74. See WK, 4:492–93.

75. Dated 6–7 September 1914. *Adolf Wild von Hohenborn. Briefe und Tagebuchaufzeichnungen des preußischen Generals als Kriegsminister und Truppenführer im Ersten Weltkrieg,* ed. Helmut Reichold (Boppard: H. Boldt, 1986), 17.

76. Terence Zuber, *The Battle of the Frontiers: Ardennes 1914* (Stroud, UK: Tempus, 2007), 127.

77. WK, 4:148.

78. Diary entry dated 5 September 1914. BHStA-KA, KTB 1914, Nachlaß Krafft von Dellmensingen 145.

79. Diary entry dated 5 September 1914. Tagebuch Rupprecht, BHStA-GH, Nachlaß Kronprinz Rupprecht 699.

80. Ibid.; BHStA-KA, AOK 6, KTB 2.8.14–14.3.15.

81. Diary entry dated 5 September 1914. Tagebuch Rupprecht, BHStA-GH, Nachlaß Kronprinz Rupprecht 699.

82. Wenninger diary dated 6 September 1914. Schulte, "Neue Dokumente," 167.

83. Diary entry dated 8 September 1914. BHStA-KA, KTB 1914, Nachlaß Krafft von Dellmensingen 145.

84. Ibid. Italics in the original.

85. Diary entry dated 7 September 1914; ibid.

86. Diary entry dated 8 September 1914. Tagebuch Rupprecht, BHStA-GH, Nachlaß Kronprinz Rupprecht 699.

87. Diary entry dated 8 September 1914. BHStA-KA, KTB 1914, Nachlaß Krafft von Dellmensingen 145.

88. Diary entry dated 9 September 1914. Tagebuch Rupprecht, BHStA-GH, Nachlaß Rupprecht 699.

89. Ibid.

90. Wenninger diary entry dated 10 September 1914. Schulte, "Neue Dokumente," 172.

91. Diary entry dated 12 August 1914. BHStA-KA, KTB 1914, Nachlaß Krafft von Dellmensingen 145.

92. Wenninger diary entry dated 7 September 1914. Schulte, "Neue Dokumente," 170.

93. Deuringer, *Die Schlacht in Lothringen,* 2:848.

94. Michael S. Neiberg, *Fighting the Great War: A Global History* (Cambridge, MA: Harvard University Press, 2005), 25, puts French casualties at two hundred thousand men and forty-seven hundred officers.

95. *Der Sanitätsdienst im Gefechts- und Schlachtenverlauf im Weltkriege 1914/1918* (Berlin: E. S. Mittler, 1938), 2:342–43, 365.

96. Ibid., 2:421, 436.

97. *Sanitätsbericht über das Deutsche Heer im Weltkriege 1914/1918* (Berlin: E. S. Mittler, 1934), 3:36.

98. WK, 4:524.

99. *Sanitätsdienst im Gefechts- und Schlachtenverlauf im Weltkriege,* 2:31.

100. Martin van Creveld, *Supplying War: Logistics from Wallenstein to Patton* (Cambridge: Cambridge University Press, 1977), 124–30.

101. Tuchman, *Guns of August,* 476.

102. Walter Bloem, *The Advance from Mons 1914* (London: Peter Davies, 1930), 101.

103. WK, 3:195, 227.

104. Ibid., 3:231.

105. Ibid., 3:232.

106. Entry dated 3 September 1914. *Regierte der Kaiser? Kriegstagebücher, Aufzeichnungen und Briefe des Chefs des Marinekabinetts Admiral Georg Alexander von Müller 1914–1918* (Göttingen: Musterschmidt, 1959), 54.

107. WK, 3:236.

108. BA-MA, N 323/9, Nachlaß Boetticher, 5–7; Groß, "There Was a Schlifeffen Plan. Neue Quellen," Hans Ehlert, Michael Epkenhans, and Gerhard P. Groß, eds., *Der Schlieffenplan. Analysen und Dokumente* (Paderborn: Ferdinand Schöningh, 2006), 139–40.

109. WK, 3:241.

110. Spears, *Liaison 1914,* 322.

111. WK, 3:140, 248–49; Hermann von Kuhl, *Der Marnefeldzug 1914* (Berlin: E. S. Mittler, 1921), 124, 126; Louis Koeltz, *Le G.Q.G. allemand et la bataille de la Marne* (Paris: Payot, 1931), 372–73.

112. WK, 3:193.

113. "Meine Erlebnisse u. Erfahrungen als Oberbefehlshaber der 3. Armee im Bewegungskrieg 1914," SHStA, 12693 Personalnachlaß Max Klemens Lothar Freiherr von Hausen (1846–1922) 43a, 117, 135–36, 141, 148.

114. BA-MA, RH 61/50850, Die Tätigkeit der Fliegerverbände der 1. und 2. Armee 2–9 September 1914, 14–15, 18.

115. Tyng, *Campaign of the Marne,* 163.

CHAPTER 8. *Climax: The Ourcq*

1. See chapter 9, AFGG, 2:550ff.

2. Charles F. Horne, ed., *Source Records of the Great War* (USA: National Alumni, 1923), 2:200–03.

3. AFGG, 2:555. Galliéni formally replaced General Victor Michel on 27 August 1914.

4. Joffre to Sixth Army, 1 September 1914. AFGG, 2:529, 589; and 2-2:281.

5. Cited in ibid., 2:614; and 2-2:556.

6. Ibid., 2:557, 576–77.

7. Ibid., 2:571–72, 579; and 2-1:676.

8. Ibid., 2:609.

9. Ibid., 2-2:543.

10. Joffre to army commanders, 2 September 1914. AFGG, 2-2:419–20.

11. Ibid., 2:616; Joseph Galliéni, *Mémoires du général Galliéni: défense de Paris, 25 août 1 septembre 1914* (Paris: Payot, 1920), 95.

12. Ibid., 112; AFGG, 2:621, 623.

13. Robert A. Doughty, *Pyrrhic Victory: French Strategy and Operations in the Great War* (Cambridge, MA, and London: The Belknap Press of Harvard University Press, 2005), 86; also AFGG, 3:14–15.

14. Joffre to Millerand, 3 September 1914. AFGG, 2-2:534–35.

15. Doughty, *Pyrrhic Victory,* 89; Charles J. Huguet, *Britain and the War: A French Indictment* (London: Cassell, 1928), 91. The official history merely mentions the meeting: AFGG, 2:625.

16. B. H. Liddell-Hart, *The Real War, 1914–1918* (Boston and Toronto: Little, Brown, 1930), 90.

17. AFGG, 2:626; Sewell Tyng, *The Campaign of the Marne, 1914* (New York and Toronto: Longmans, Green, 1935), 215.

18. AFGG, 2-2:658–59.

19. Ibid., 2:665; 2-2:705; Joffre, 1:387–88.

20. Ibid., 388.

21. Cited in Edward Spears, *Liaison 1914: A Narrative of the Great Retreat* (London: Eyre & Spottiswoode, 1968), 402.

22. Dated 4 September 1914. AFGG, 2-2:660–61. Also, Joffre to army commanders, 5 September 1914. SHD, 5 N 66.

23. Joffre, 1:390.

24. Joffre to Millerand, 5 September 1914. SHD, 16 N 1674; AFGG, 2-2:768–69. Also Joffre, 1:392.

25. Ibid., 1:393–94; Tyng, *Battle of the Marne,* 223.

26. Spears, *Liaison,* 413–18; Joffre, 1:393–94.

27. BA-MA, RH 61/51061, Die OHL und die Marneschlacht vom 4.–9.9.1914, Stärkenachweisungen Marneschlacht, 9 September 1914.

28. WK, 3:216–17.

29. Ibid., 3:215.

30. Ibid., 3:245–46.

31. Karl von Bülow, *Mein Bericht zur Marneschlacht* (Berlin: August Scherl, 1919), 51.

32. "Meine Erlebnisse u. Erfahrungen als Oberbefehlshaber der 3. Armee im Bewegungskrieg 1914," SHStA, 12693 Personalnachlaß Max Klemens Lothar Freiherr von Hausen (1846–1922) 43a, 153, 162. The passage was excised from Hausen's published memoirs: *Erinnerungen an den Marnefeldzug 1914* (Leipzig: K. F. Koehler, 1920), 182–83.

33. John Horne and Alan Kramer, *German Atrocities, 1914: A History of Denial* (New Haven, CT, and London: Yale University Press, 2001), 74, show that while there were 101 "major incidents" of ten or more civilians killed in Belgium, there were only 28 in France; and while 4,421 Belgian civilians were killed, the figure for France was 725.

34. Bülow, *Bericht zur Marneschlacht,* 50.

35. WK, 4:3–5; Gerhard Tappen, *Bis zur Marne 1914. Beiträge zur Beurteilung der Kriegführung bis zum Abschluß der Marne-Schlacht* (Oldenburg and Berlin: Gerhard Stalling, 1920), 22–23.

36. WK, 3:254.

37. War diary dated 5 September 1914. SHStA, 11356 Generalkommando des XII. Reservekorps 139. Also Hausen, "Meine Erlebnisse," 150–51; Hausen, *Erinnerungen,* 178–80.

38. WK, 4:18, 23, 83, 523.

39. Maréchal Foch, *Mémoires pour server à l'histoire de la guerre de 1914–1918* (Paris: Plon, 1931), 1:90–91; Joffre, 1:405; AFGG, 3:310ff. Also the critical evaluation by Christian Millotat, "Zur ersten Marneschlacht 1914. Der Anteil des Oberbefehlshabers der 3. deutschen Armee, Generaloberst Max Freiherr von Hausen," *Militärgeschichte* 8 (1998): 66–67.

40. WK, 4:29.

41. Hermann von Kuhl, *Der Marnefeldzug 1914* (Berlin: E. S. Mittler, 1921), 132. "The Schlieffen Plan had failed" was his postwar verdict; ibid., 127.

42. Ibid., 67.

43. Eugen Bircher, *Beiträge zur Erforschung der Schlacht an der Marne* (Leipzig: Ernst Bircher, 1922), 1:24–25.

44. AFGG, 2:772; and 3:84–85.

45. Ibid., 3:99–100.

46. Service record from BA-MA, MSg 109, vol. 7.

47. WK, 4:32.

48. Cited in Kuhl, *Marnefeldzug*, 180.

49. Letter dated 5 September 1914. *Wir Kämpfer im Weltkrieg. Selbstzeugnisse deutscher Frontsoldaten,* ed. Wolfgang Foerster and Helmuth Greiner (Berlin: F. W. Peters, 1937), 70.

50. Letter dated 5 September 1914. Ibid., 71–74.

51. Kuhl, *Marnefeldzug,* 182.

52. WK, 4:36.

53. Tyng, *Campaign of the Marne,* 228.

54. BA-MA, RH 61/50850, Die Tätigkeit der Feldfliegerverbände der 1. und 2. Armee 2–9 September 1914, 24.

55. Kluck to Reichsarchiv, 20 December 1925. WK, 4:37.

56. Anthony Clayton, *Paths of Glory: The French Army, 1914–18* (London: Cassel, 2003), 54.

57. Joffre's telephone message to army commanders, 6 September 1914, SHD, 16 N 1674; AFGG, 2-2:889; Joffre, 1:394.

58. Diary entry dated 5 September 1914. Raymond Poincaré, *Au service de la France* (Paris: Plon, 1928), 5:254–55.

59. Diary entry dated 6 September 1914. Huguet, *Britain and the War,* 101.

60. *Field-Marshal Sir Henry Wilson: His Life and Diaries,* ed. C. E. Callwell (London: Cassell, 1927), 1:1777.

61. Georg von der Marwitz, *Weltkriegsbriefe,* ed. Erich von Tschischwitz (Berlin: Steiniger, 1940), 31.

62. Louis Koeltz, *Le G.Q.G. allemand et la bataille de la Marne* (Paris: Payot, 1931), 141–42, 177.

63. WK, 4:53–54, 109, 224.

64. Tappen diary entry dated 6 September 1914. BA-MA, RH 61/51062, Die OHL und die Marne-Schlacht vom 4.–9.9.1914.

65. WK, 4:54, 84; Koeltz, *Le G.Q.G. allemande,* 380–81.

66. See "Die Nachrichtenverbindungen zwischen den Kommandobehörden während des Bewegungskrieges 1914," General Schniewindt 1928. HStA, M 738 Sammlung zur Militärgeschichte 36.

67. Hans Georg Kampe, *Nachrichtentruppe des Heeres und Deutsche Reichspost. Militärisches und staatliches Nachrichtenwesen in Deutschland 1830 bis 1945* (Waldesruh: Dr. Erwin Meißler, 1999), 185–86; BA-MA, RH 61/50850, Die Tätigkeit der Feldfliegerverbände der 1. und 2. Armee 2–9 September 1914, 62ff.

68. Tappen to General Staff historical quartermaster-general, 13 July 1919. BA-MA, RH 61/51060. Also Tappen, *Bis zur Marne 1914,* 24.

69. See AFGG, 3:148ff.

70. BA-MA, RH 61/50850, Die Tätigkeit der Feldfliegerverbände der 1. und 2. Armee 1–9 September 1914, 37–38.

71. Kuhl, *Marnefeldzug,* 202.

72. WK, 4:91.

73. Diary entry dated 7 September 1914. BA-MA, N 324/26, Nachlaß v. Einem.

74. WK, 4:84–85.

75. Diary entry dated 7 September 1914. Moltke, 384.

76. *Der Sanitätsdienst im Gefechts- und Schlachtenverlauf im Weltkriege 1914/1918* (Berlin: E. S. Mittler, 1938), 2:93.

77. Calculations by Second Army's first general staff officer, Lieutenant Colonel Arthur Matthes. WK, 4:221.

78. Cited in Tyng, *Campaign of the Marne,* 249.

79. Ibid., 250.

80. AFGG, 3:266–67.

81. Tyng, *Campaign of the Marne,* 251.

82. BA-MA, RH 61/50661, Kriegserrinerungen des Generalleutnants v. [*sic*] Tappen, 35.

83. HGW-MO, 1:297.

84. Ibid., 1:299.

85. Ibid., 1:309.

86. Ernest W. Hamilton, *The First Seven Divisions: Being a Detailed Account of the Fighting from Mons to Ypres* (New York: E. P. Dutton, 1916), 93–94.

87. John Charteris, *At G.H.Q.* (London: Cassell, 1932), 29.

88. Galliéni, *Mémoires,* 241.

89. Joffre to French and Millerand, 7 September 1914, SHD, 16 N 1674; and Joffre to Galliéni, 7 September 1914, SHD, 5 N 66.

90. BA-MA, RH 61/50850, Die Tätigkeit der Feldfliegerverbände der 1. und 2. Armee 2–9 September 1914, 49.

91. HGW-MO, 1:324.

92. Joffre to French, 8 September 1914, AFGG, 3-2:20; Special Order No. 19, ibid., 22–23. Also Joffre to Galliéni, 8 September 1914, SHD, 16 N 1674; Joffre, 1:411–12.

93. Galliéni to Millerand, 7 September 1914. SHD, 5 N 66.

94. Joffre to Millerand, 8 September 1914. Ibid.

95. Diary entry dated 8 September 1914. Moltke, 384.

96. WK, 3:319–26; Hans von Zwehl, *Maubeuge, Aisne-Verdun. Das VII. Reserve-Korps im Weltkriege von seinem Beginn bis Ende 1916* (Berlin: K. Curtius, 1921), 51ff.; slightly different figures in AFGG, 2:452–77.

97. Cited in *Deutsche Quellen zur Geschichte des Ersten Weltkrieges,* ed. Wolfdieter Bihl (Darmstadt: Wissenschaftliche Buchgesellschaft, 1991), 55; and WK, 4:144.

98. Description in Foch, *Mémoires,* 1:97–98.

99. Joffre to Millerand, 8 September 1914. Joffre, 1:405–06; AFGG, 3-4:846.

100. Artur Baumgarten-Crusius, *Die Marneschlacht insbesondere auf der Front der deutschen dritten Armee* (Leipzig: R. M. Lippold, 1919), 170–71.

101. Hausen, "Meine Erlebnisse," 167–75.

102. WK, 4:91–92.

103. Hausen, "Meine Erlebnisse," 173, 175. There is no mention of this critical decision in Hausen, *Erinnerungen,* 192ff.

104. WK, 4:518.

105. Entry dated 7 September 1914. SHStA, 11356 Generalkommando des XII. Reservekorps 139.

106. Millotat, "Zur ersten Marneschlacht 1914," 69.

107. Hausen, "Meine Erlebnisse," 190; WK, 4:102–03, 171–72; Millotat, "Zur ersten Marneschlacht," 69.

108. Koeltz, *Le G.Q.G. allemand,* 380.

109. Diary entry dated 8 September 1914. BA-MA, RH 61/85, Das Kaiser Alexander-Garde-Grenadier-Regiment Nr. 1 in der Schlacht an der Marne im September 1914.

110. Roland Kleinhenz, "La parcée saxonne sur le front du centre," *Les batailles de la Marne de l'Ourc à Verdun (1914 et 1918)* (Soteca: Éditions, 2004), 156.

111. *Das Marnedrama 1914. Die Kämpfe des Gardekorps und des rechten Flügels der 3. Armee vom 5. bis 8. September,* ed. Thilo von Bose (Oldenburg and Berlin: Gerhard Stalling, 1928), 179.

112. See AFGG, 3:362ff.

113. Hew Strachan, *The First World War* (Oxford: Oxford University Press, 2001), 1:255.

114. Franchet d'Espèrey to Foch, 9:40 PM, 8 September 1914. AFGG, 3-2:129.

115. Ibid., 3:42; Foch, *Mémoires,* 1:121.

116. Poincaré, *Au service de la France,* 5:274.

117. Franz Theodor Poland, *Das Kgl. Sächs. Reserve-Infanterie-Regiment Nr. 103* (Dresden: v. Baensch, 1922), 11–12.

118. Foch's telephone orders, 10:15 AM, 8 September 1914. AFGG, 3-2:123.

119. Eugen Bircher, *Die Krisis in der Marneschlacht. Kämpfe der II. und III. deutschen Armee gegen die 5. und 9. französische Armee am Petit Morin und in den Marais de St. Gond* (Berlin and Leipzig: Ernst Bircher, 1927), 173.

120. Hausen, "Meine Erlebnisse," 198.

121. *Marnedrama 1914. Kämpfe,* 179, 200.

122. Report of 9 September 1914. SHStA, 11250 Sächsischer Militärbevollmächtigter in Berlin 71, Geheimakten A: Verschiedenes.

123. *Das Marne Drama 1914. Der Ausgang der Schlacht,* ed. Thilo von Bose (Berlin and Oldenburg: Gerhard Stalling, 1929), 235; Gotthard Jäschke, "Zum Problem der Marne-Schlacht von 1914," *Historische Zeitschrift* 190 (1960): 344.

124. *Sanitätsbericht über das Deutsche Heer im Weltkriege 1914/1918* (Berlin: E. S. Mittler, 1934), 3:39.

125. Kleinhenz, " La percée saxonne," 163.

126. Julius Paul Köhler, "Hausens großes Beispiel: Seine Bedeutung in den Kämpfen gegen die französische Artilleriefronten während der Marneschlacht 1914," *Sächsische Heimat* 9 (1974): 312–17.

127. *Marne Drama 1914. Ausgang der Schlacht,* 178, 200.

128. This is also the verdict by Kleinhenz, "La percée saxonne," 157.

129. War diary dated 8 September 1914. SHStA, 11356 Generalkommando des XII. Reservekorps 139, 23–24.

130. Alexander von Kluck, *Der Marsch auf Paris und die Marneschlacht 1914* (Berlin: E. S. Mittler, 1920), 118; Gustave de Cornulier-Lucinière, *Le rôle de la cavalerie française à l'aile gauche de la première bataille de la Marne* (Paris: Perrin, 1919); Sewell T. Tyng, "A French Cavalry Raid at the Marne," *The Cavalry Journal* 43 (1934): 19–24; and AFGG, 3:141.

131. Galliéni, *Mémoires,* 162.

132. General Instruction No. 7 dated 7 September 1914. AFGG, 3-1:554; Joffre, 1:413.

133. War diary dated 8 September 1914. BA-MA, RH 61/50850, Die Tätigkeit der Feldfliegerverbände der 1. und 2. Armee 2–9 September 1914, 52.

134. Kluck, *Marsch auf Paris,* 108.

135. WK, 4:200.

136. Galliéni to Maunoury, 8 September 1914. AFGG, 3-2:35.

137. Maunoury telegram to GQG, 6:40 PM, 8 September 1914. Ibid., 3:156.

138. Telephone, Joffre to Maunoury, 8 September 1914, ibid., 3-2:438; Joffre to Millerand, 8 September 1914, SHD, 5 N 66; Joffre, 1:413. Also Barthélemy Palat, *La grande guerre sur le front occidental* (Paris: Chapelot, 1917–29), 6:281.

139. WK, 4:202.
140. Ibid., 4:207.
141. Kuhl, *Marnefeldzug,* 216.
142. Kluck, *Marsch auf Paris,* 121.
143. WK, 4:211.

CHAPTER 9. *Decision: The Marne*

1. Cited in Karl Lange, *Marneschlacht und deutsche Öffentlichkeit 1914–1939. Eine verdrängte Niederlage und ihre Folgen* (Düsseldorf: Bertelsmann Universitätsverlag, 1974), 19. Original in Edward Jenö Egan-Krieger, *Nach 50 Jahren! Die Wahrheit über die Marneschlacht setzt sich durch!* (Bernstein/Burgenland: Selbstverlag, 1965). I am indebted to Annika Mombauer for alerting me to Egan-Krieger's presence at the Marne. He was then a captain. Born in 1886, he died in 1965 after serving in the rank of Generalleutnant in the Luftwaffe in World War II.

2. WK, 4:223ff.

3. Peyton C. March, *The Nation at War* (Garden City, NY: Doubleday, Doran, 1932), 16–17.

4. The only published study of the "Hentsch mission" before the bombing of the Prussian military records at Potsdam in 1945 was by one of the Reichsarchiv staff: Wilhelm Müller-Loebnitz, *Die Sendung des Oberstleutnants Hentsch am 8.–10. September 1914. Auf Grund der Kriegsakten und persönlicher Mitteilungen* (Berlin: E. S. Mittler, 1922).

5. Mutius to Reichsarchiv, 16 March 1923. BA-MA, RH 61/51063, Die OHL und die Marneschlacht vom 4.–9.9.1914. The Reichsarchiv's documentary collection on the Marne is in five folders: RH 61/51060–51064.

6. Hermann von Kuhl, *Der Marnefeldzug, 1914* (Berlin: E. S. Mittler, 1921), 228.

7. Tappen to Reichsarchiv, 10 March 1925. BA-MA, RH 61/51060.

8. The report is in Müller-Loebnitz, *Sendung des Oberstleutnants Hentsch,* 57–59. For a recent analysis, see Hans Plote, "Considérations sur la mission Hentsch," *Les batailles de la Marne de l'Ourcq à Verdun (1914 et 1918)* (Soteca: Éditions, 2004), 89–145.

9. Annika Mombauer, *Helmuth von Moltke and the Origins of the First World War* (Cambridge: Cambridge University Press, 2001), 259; and Mombauer, "The Battle of the Marne: Myths and Reality of Germany's 'Fateful Battle,' " *The Historian* 68 (2006): 756–58.

10. Haeften to Tappen, 24 June 1920. BA-MA, N 56/2 Nachlaß Tappen.

11. Plote, "Considérations sur la mission Hentsch," 110.

12. Hermann Mertz von Quirnheim, *Der Führerwille in Entstehung und Durchführung* (Oldenburg: Gerhard Stalling, 1932), 70.

13. Following from WK, 4:223ff.

14. Major Max von Bauer heard the same from Colonel Tappen that morning. BA-MA, RH 61/51061, "Die Marneschlacht," manuscript dated 1930.

15. BA-MA, RH 61/51061, Major von Rauch to Reichsarchiv, citing Captain König, 25 January 1925; and RH 61, 51064, Wilhelm II to Reichsarchiv, 3 June 1925.

16. All times of arrival and departure are from the log of Hentsch's driver, Ernst von Marx. BA-MA, RH 61/51063, Marx to Reichsarchiv, 24 March 1919.

17. Ibid., 51062, Koeppen's reports to the Reichsarchiv of 23 and 28 February as well as 5 March 1925; and Rauch to Reichsarchiv, 25 January 1925, ibid., 51063.

18. WK, 4:232.

19. Ibid.

20. "Meine Erlebnisse u. Erfahrungen als Oberbefehlshaber der 3. Armee im Bewe-

gungskrieg, 1914," SHStA, 12693 Personalnachlaß Max Klemens Lothar Freiherr von Hausen (1846–1922), 43a, 198.

21. WK, 4:232.

22. Diary entry dated 8 September 1914. *Ein Armeeführer erlebt den Weltkrieg. Persönliche Aufzeichnungen des Generalobersten v. Einem,* ed. Junius Alter (Leipzig: v. Hase & Koehler, 1938), 53.

23. Ibid., 234.

24. Following from WK, 4:235–42.

25. König to Reichsarchiv, 30 March 1925 and 13 January 1926. BA-MA, RH 61/51062.

26. Diary notes dated 11 September 1914. Hans Koeppen, "The Battle of the Marne, 8th and 9th of September, 1914," *The Army Quarterly* 28 (July 1934): 300.

27. König's report to the Reichsarchiv, 8 March 1919. BA-MA, RH 61/51062.

28. Louis Koeltz, *Le G.Q.G. allemand et la bataille de la Marne* (Paris: Payot, 1931), 383.

29. Following from WK, 4:244ff.

30. Moltke, 385.

31. Report 10 AM, 9 September 1914. BA-MA, RH 61/50850, Die Tätigkeit der Feld-fliegerverbände der 1. und 2. Armee 2–9 September 1914, 62.

32. Alexander von Kluck, *Der Marsch auf Paris und die Marneschlacht 1914* (Berlin: E. S. Mittler, 1920), 121; Koeltz, *Le G.Q.G. allemand,* 384. Should read "Dormans."

33. WK, 4:269–70.

34. "Die Nachrichtenverbindungen zwischen den Kommandobehörden während des Bewegungskrieges 1914," General Schniewindt 1928. HStA, M 738 Sammlung zur Militärgeschichte 36.

35. Sewell Tyng, *The Campaign of the Marne, 1914* (New York and Toronto: Longmans, Green, 1935), 279.

36. Lauenstein to his wife, 11 September 1914, BA-MA, RH 61/50676, Der Krieg im Westen 1914–1916; Stein to Reichsarchiv, 3 July 1920, BA-MA, RH 61/51063.

37. Einem to Reichsarchiv, 8 March 1920. BA-MA, N 324/26, Nachlaß v. Einem.

38. Eugen Bircher, *Die Krisis in der Marneschlacht. Kämpfe der II. und III. deutschen Armee gegen die 5. und 9. französische Armee am Petit Morin und in den Marais de St. Gond* (Berlin and Leipzig: Ernst Bircher, 1927), 270–72.

39. Cited in Paul Le Seur, *Aus Meines Lebens Bilder Buch* (Kassel: J. G. Oncken, 1955), 159.

40. Koeppen interview at the Reichsarchiv, 28 August 1920. BA-MA, RH 61/84, Beurteilung der Lage zwischen den Flügeln der 1. und 2. Armee am 9.9.1914.

41. Hentsch's report dated 15 September 1914. WK, 4:256.

42. From ibid., 4:259–65.

43. Kuhl, *Marnefeldzug,* 219–20.

44. WK, 4:253.

45. Ludendorff to Hindenburg, 24 May 1917. BA-MA, RH 61/51062.

46. Marx to Reichsarchiv, 24 March 1919. BA-MA, RH 61/51063. Also WK, 4:266.

47. Kluck, *Marsch auf Paris,* 124–26.

48. Lyncker diary entry dated 9 September 1914. BA-MA, RH 61/948, Der Krieg im Westen 1914–1916.

49. Stein to Reichsarchiv, 6 October 19125. BA-MA, RH 61/51063.

50. Ibid.

51. Diary entry dated 9 September 1914. BA-MA, RH 61/50661, Kriegserinnerungen des Generalleutnants v. [*sic*] Tappen.

52. WK, 4:327–28.

53. Ibid., 4:328.

54. Ibid.

55. Graevenitz to Marchtaler, 11 September 1914. HStA, M 1/2 Berichte des Militär-bevollmächtigten beim Grossen Hauptquartier und des stellv. Militärbevollmächtigten in Berlin, September 1914, vol. 55.

56. Bircher, *Krisis in der Marneschlacht,* 268–69.

57. Diary entry dated 8 September 1914. Tagebuch Rupprecht, BHStA-GH, Nachlaß Kronprinz Rupprecht 699. Also Crown Prince Rupprecht von Bayern, *Mein Kriegstagebuch* (Munich: Deutscher National Verlag, 1923), 1:103.

58. Hans von Zwehl, *Erich v. Falkenhayn, General der Infanterie. Eine biographische Studie* (Berlin: E. S. Mittler, 1926), 66.

59. Wenninger diary dated 7, 10, and 16 September 1914. BHStA-KA, HS 2543, Tage-bücher General von Wenninger.

60. Diary entries dated 9 and 12 September 1914. BA-MA, RH 61/50676, Der Krieg im Westen 1914–1916.

61. Lyncker diary dated 9, 10, and 13 September 1914. Ibid.

62. Overall for 5 September, the French official history lists seventy-five infantry and ten cavalry divisions for Germany and eighty-five infantry and ten cavalry divisions for France. AFGG, 2:811, 818.

63. Ibid., 3:71.

64. Joffre to Millerand, 8 September 1914. SHD, 5 N 66.

65. Tyng, *Campaign of the Marne,* 251.

66. AFGG, 3-1:554.

67. Special Order No. 19. Ibid., 3-2:22–23.

68. Fifth Army Order, 7 September 1914. Ibid., 3:236.

69. M. v. Poseck, *Die Deutsche Kavallerie 1914 in Belgien und Frankreich* (Berlin: E. S. Mit-tler, 1921), 101–02.

70. HGW-MO, 1:337–39.

71. Hew Strachan, *The First World War* (Oxford: Oxford University Press, 2001), 1:260.

72. Cited in Tyng, *Campaign of the Marne,* 333.

73. Ibid., 334; AFGG, 3:288.

74. Christian Mallet, *Impressions and Experiences of a French Trooper, 1914–1915* (New York: E. P. Dutton, 1916), 39.

75. Cited in Strachan, *First World War,* 1:260.

76. Franchet d'Espèrey, 9 September 1914. AFGG, 3-2:528. Also Edward Spears, *Liaison 1914: A Narrative of the Great Retreat* (London: Eyre & Spottiswoode, 1930), 446–47.

77. Instruction particulière No. 20, 9 September 1914. AFGG, 3-2:446. Also Joffre to Millerand, 9 September 1914. SHD, 5 N 66.

78. Joffre to all commanders, 9 September 1914. SHD, 16 N 1674.

79. Langle de Cary to Joffre, 8 September 1914. AFGG, 3-2:87.

80. WK, 4:115–16, 118.

81. Sarrail's General Operations Order No. 32. AFGG, 2-2:790–91.

82. Berthelot to Sarrail, 5 September 1914. Ibid., 2-2:771.

83. Ibid., 3:555.

84. Joffre to Sarrail, 6 September 1914. SHD, 16 N 1674.

85. Joffre to Sarrail, 10 PM, 8 September 1914. AFGG, 3-2:24.

86. Ibid., 2:762–63.

87. Tyng, *Campaign of the Marne,* 304–06; Robert A. Doughty, *Pyrrhic Victory: French Strategy and Operations in the Great War* (Cambridge, MA, and London: The Belknap Press of Harvard University Press, 2005), 95.

88. *Sanitätsbericht über das Deutsche Heer im Weltkriege 1914/1918* (Berlin: E. S. Mittler, 1934), 3:38.

89. See AFGG, 3:610–11, 658.

90. Koeltz, *Le G.Q.G. allemand,* 384.

91. AFGG, 3:648ff.

92. WK, 4:304.

93. HStA, M 33/2 General Kommando XIII. Armee Korps 1914–1918, Kriegstagebuch 28.7.1914–21.1.1915, vol. 884.

94. WK, 4:307.

95. Sarrail to Joffre, 10 September 1914. AFGG, 3-3:65.

96. Joffre to Millerand, 11 September 1914. Ibid., 3-3:426. Also Joffre, 1:420.

97. BA-MA, RH 61/161, Die Fahrten Moltkes, Dommes, Steins und Tappens zur Front am 11., 12., 13. und 14.9.1914, 2.

98. Artur Baumgarten-Crusius, *Die Marneschlacht insbesondere auf der Front der deutschen dritten Armee* (Leipzig: R. M. Lippold, 1919), 170–71, gives 443 officers and 10,402 ranks lost just at the Marne. For casualty figures (killed, missing, wounded, and ill), see *Sanitätsbericht über das Deutsche Heer im Weltkriege 1914/1918* (Berlin: E. S. Mittler, 1934), 3:38.

99. Dresden to Third Army, 18 September 1914. SHStA, 11356 Generalkommando des XII. Reservekorps 273, Ersatz von Mannschaften und Pferden, vol. 1.

100. Moltke, 24; Koeltz, *Le G.Q.G. allemand,* 389.

101. BA-MA, RH 61/161, Die Fahrten Moltkes, Dommes, Steins und Tappens zur Front am 11., 12., 13. und 14.9.1914, 7.

102. Ibid., 5.

103. Ibid., 8.

104. Moltke, 24.

105. BA-MA, RH 61/161, Die Fahrten Moltkes, Donmmes, Steins und Tappenz zur Front am 11., 12., 13. und 14.9.1914, 12.

106. WK, 4:451.

107. Diary entry dated 12 September 1914. BA-MA, RH 61/948, Tagebuch v. Plessen.

108. BA-MA, RH 61/161, Die Fahrten Moltkes, Dommes, Steins und Tappens zur Front am 11., 12., 13. und 14.9.1914, 1–7.

109. Diary entry dated 14 September 1914. BA-MA, RH 61/948, Der Krieg im Westen 1914–1916.

110. WK, 4:483–84.

111. BA-MA, RH 61/50739, Generalleutnant von Stein, der Generalquartiermeister der sechs ersten Kriegswochen, 24. Stein was given command of XIV Reserve Corps.

112. General von Pless diary dated 14 September 1914. BA-MA, RH 61/50676.

113. Moltke, 25.

114. Lange, *Marneschlacht,* 89.

115. Karl von Einem, *Erinnerungen eines Soldaten 1853–1933* (Leipzig: K. F. Koehler, 1933), 176–77.

116. Cited in WK, 4:272.

117. Ibid., 4:284–85.

118. Hausen, "Meine Erlebnisse," 218.

119. WK, 4:283.

120. Ibid., 4:282.

121. Diary entry dated 9 September 1914. RH 61/85, Finck v. Finckenstein, Das Kaiser Alexander Garde-Grenadier Regiment Nr. 1 in der Schlacht an der Marne im September 1914; WK, 4:283.

122. *Das Marnedrama 1914. Der Ausgang der Schlacht,* ed. Thilo von Bose (Oldenburg and Berlin: Gerhard Stalling, 1928), 161, 165.

123. Walter Bloem, *The Advance from Mons, 1914* (London: Peter Davies, 1930), 171.

124. Deputy War Minister Franz von Wandel to all corps commanders, 10 September 1914. HStA, M 1/4 Kriegsministerium, Allg. Armee-Angelegenheiten 1524.

125. Instruction particulière No. 21, 10 September 1914. AFGG, 3-3:18–19. Also Joffre, 1:424.

126. Instruction particulière No. 23, 12 September 1914. AFGG, 3-3:790–91.

127. Maunoury to Joffre, 13 September 1914. Ibid., 3-4:88–89.

128. Franchet d'Espèrey to Joffre, 7 PM, 14 September 1914. Ibid., 3-4:468–69.

129. Foch to Joffre, 14 September 1914. Ibid., 3-4:481.

130. Letter dated 24 October 1914. Archive of the Historial de la Grande Guerre, Château de Péronne.

131. Joffre to Millerand, 17 and 18 September 1914. SHD, 5 N 66; AFGG, 4-1:232, 368.

132. Joffre to Sarrail, 13 September 1914. AFGG, 3-4:14.

133. Ibid., 3-4:59.

134. Foch's General Order of Operations, 13 September 1914. Ibid., 3-4:97–98.

135. Ibid., 3:949, 965.

136. Maréchal Foch, *Mémoires pour server a l'histoire de la guerre de 1914–1918* (Paris: Plon, 1931), 1:143–44.

137. Franchet d'Espèrey to Corps Commanders, 20 September 1914. AFGG, 4-1. *"Durer et tenir."*

138. Joffre to Foch, 21 September 1914. Ibid., 4-1:653.

139. Ibid., 4:7.

140. Reichsarchiv calculation, 1 May 1929. BA-MA, RH 61/50603, Kriegsverluste, Feldstärken, Munitionsverbrauch und Kriegsgefangene im Ersten Weltkrieg. Statistisches Material.

141. Precise figures in AFGG, 3-4:846.

142. Joffre, 1:425.

143. AFGG, 3-4:845. Slightly different figures in ibid., 4-1:554.

EPILOGUE

1. "Taktisch-strategische Aufsätze aus den Jahren 1857 bis 1871," in *Moltkes Militärische Werke,* ed. Großer Generalstab (Berlin: E. S. Mittler, 1900), 2/2:291.

2. Carl von Clausewitz, *On War,* eds. Michael Howard and Peter Paret (Princeton, NJ: Princeton University Press, 1976), 101.

3. Diary entry for 9 September 1914. Marc Bloch, *Memoirs of War, 1914–15* (Ithaca, NY, and London: Cornell University Press, 1980), 87.

4. Hew Strachan, *The First World War* (Oxford: Oxford University Press, 2001), 1:261.

5. See *Der Schlieffenplan: Analysen und Dokumente,* eds. Hans Ehlert, Michael Epkenhans, and Gerhard P. Groß (Paderborn: Ferdinand Schöningh, 2006).

6. Sewell Tyng, *The Campaign of the Marne, 1914* (New York and Toronto: Longmans, Green, 1935), 349.

7. Maréchal Foch, *Mémoires pur server à l'histoire de la guerre de 1914–1918* (Paris: Plon, 1931), 1:144.

8. Clausewitz, *On War,* 76.

9. Diary entry dated 9 September 1914. Moltke, 385.

10. Letter dated 9 September 1914. BHStA-KA, HS 2662 Wenninger.

11. Gabriel Hanotaux, *Histoire illustrée de la guerre de 1914* (Paris: Gounouilhou, 1915–24), 9:104.

12. Gerhard Tappen, *Bis zur Marne. Beiträge zur Beurteilung der Kriegführung bis zum Abschluß der Marne-Schlacht* (Oldenburg: Gerhard Stalling, 1920), 32.

13. Robert T. Foley, "Preparing the German Army for the First World War: The Operational Ideas of Alfred von Schlieffen and Helmuth von Moltke the Younger," *War & Society* 22 (October 2004): 19.

14. Diary entry dated 13 September 1914. BA-MA, RH 61/50676, Der Krieg im Westen 1914–1916.

15. Diary entry dated 1 October 1914. Karl von Einem, *Ein Armeeführer erlebt den Weltkrieg. Persönliche Aufzeichnungen* (Leipzig: v. Hase & Koehler, 1938), 62.

16. Joffre, 1:421.

17. Ibid., 1:370; Robert A. Doughty, *Pyrrhic Victory: French Strategy and Operations in the Great War* (Cambridge, MA, and London: The Belknap Press of Harvard University Press, 2005), 85.

18. Tyng, *Campaign of the Marne,* 189.

19. See AFGG, 3-4:846.

20. Of the active army of 1.6 million, for August it lists 20,253 killed, 78,468 wounded, and 107,794 missing; for September, 18,073 killed, 111,963 wounded, and 83,409 missing. AFGG, 2:825; and 3-4:845.

21. Charles de Gaulle, *France and Her Army* (London and New York: Hutchinson, 1945), 102.

22. *Sanitätsbericht über das Deutsche Heer im Weltkriege 1914/1918* (Berlin: E. S. Mittler, 1938), 3:36.

23. Ibid., 3:39.

24. Ibid., 3:38.

25. BA-MA, RH 61/50775, Die Verluste an Pferden 1914–1918, 2–37.

26. Robert B. Asprey, *The First Battle of the Marne* (Philadelphia and New York: Lippincott, 1962), 100–01.

27. "War Letter by a Socialist Worker," published 10 October 1914. Cited in Bernd Ulrich, *Die Augenzeugen. Deutsche Feldpostbriefe in Kriegs- und Nachkriegszeit 1914–1933* (Essen: Klartext, 1997), 136.

28. Letter dated 17 September 1914. August Messer, "Zur Psychologie des Krieges," *Preussische Jahrbücher* 159 (February 1915): 229. This likely pertains to Karl von Drigalski, professor of medicine at Halle University and a reserve officer serving with the medical corps at the front in 1914. Most authors credit the letter to the famous polar explorer Professor of Geography Erich von Drygalski of Munich University, but his birth date of 1865 would preclude active service at the front in 1914.

29. Letter dated 7 September 1914. *Paroles de poilus: lettres et carnets du front 1914–1918,* eds. Jean-Pierre Guéno and Yves Laplume (Paris: Librio, 1998), 39.

30. Letter dated 27 September 1914. Ibid., 45.

31. Bloch, *Memoirs of War,* 159.

32. Diary entry dated 12 September 1914. Ibid., 152.

33. Cited in *Kriegsbriefe gefallener Studenten,* ed. Philipp Witkop (Munich: Georg Müller, 1928), 59.

34. *Der Sanitätsdienst im Gefechts- und Schlachtenverlauf im Weltkriege 1914/1918* (Berlin: E. S. Mittler, 1938), 2:31, 57 (First Army); 2:93, 120 (Second Army); 2:147–48, 169 (Third Army); 2:208, 229 (Fourth Army); 2:274, 307 (Fifth Army); 2:342, 343 (Sixth Army); and 2:421, 436 (Seventh Army).

35. *Sanitätsbericht über das Deutsche Heer,* 3:27; Holger H. Herwig, *The First World War:*

Germany and Austria-Hungary, 1914–1918 (London: Arnold, 1997), 119. Germany, with a population of 65 million in 1911, had 10,683 suicides. The Kingdom of Württemberg, with a population (2.1 million) roughly equal to that of the German armies, registered 357 suicides. *Statistisches Jahrbuch für das Deutsche Reich 1914* (Berlin: Puttkammer & Mühlbrecht, 1914), 1, 132–33.

36. See Fritz Fischer, *Griff nach der Weltmacht. Die Kriegszielpolitik des kaiserlichen Deutschland 1914/18* (Düsseldorf: Droste, 1961), 113ff.

37. Arnold Rechberg, *Reichsniedergang. Ein Beitrag zu dessen Ursachen aus meinen persönlichen Erinnerungen* (Munich: Musarion, 1919), 21.

38. Diary of Major Hans von Haeften, 18–21 December 1914. BA-MA, MSg 1/1228, Nachlaß v. Alten.

GLOSSARY

Aufmarschplan	German strategic deployment plan
Burg frieden	Literally, "castle truce"; used by Wilhelm II in 1914 to announce an end to domestic strife
Cannae	Battle of the Second Punic War in which Hannibal in 216 BC—in one of the greatest tactical feats in military history—defeated a superior Roman army under Consuls Lucius Aemilius Paullus and Gaius Terentius Varro; model for Alfred von Schlieffen
Casus belli	An occasion for war
Casus foederis	A case within the stipulations of a treaty
Climacteric	A major turning point, or critical stage; a Churchill term
Coup de main	A bold strike; see also *Handstreich*
Coup de théâtre	A theatrical blow
Couverture	French: "covering force"
En avant!	Forward!
Ersatz	Draft replacements
Francs-tireurs	Irregulars; guerrillas; common term for armed civilians
Handstreich	A bold strike; see also *Coup de main*
Hors de combat	"Put out of the fight"; casualties
Kriegsgefahr	Danger of war; state of German premobilization

Landser	German term for common soldier
Landwehr	German reserve; Territorial Army (British); National Guard (American)
Offensive à outrance	All-out offensive; French army doctrine
Poilu	French term for common soldier
La position fortifée	Fortified positions, such as Liège, Namur, Nancy, Verdun
Pantalon rouge	"Red trousers"; worn by French soldiers
Plan de renseignements	French: "deployment plan"
Schlacke	"Cinders"; applied to German troops at the Marne
Schwenkungsflügel	"Pivot wing"; applied to German First, Second, and Third armies
Soixante-quinzes	75s; French 75mm guns
Union sacrée	"Sacred union"; French domestic truce of 1914
Vollmacht	Full power of authority
Westaufmarsch	German strategic deployment plan in the west

INDEX

Langle de Cary, Fernand de: in Alsace-Lorraine, 88; and Ardennes, 146, 149, 150, 151; and Battle of the Marne, 229, 237, 255, 256, 257, 287, 295–96, 297; capture of attack order for, 198; as Fourth Army commander, 62–63; and French war plans, 175; and German buildup in Belgium, 136, 137, 138, 140; and Joffre's reassessment of campaign, 194; Joffre's relationship with, 314; and Moltke's reassessment of campaign, 198; personality and character of, 63; and Sambre-et-Meuse (Charleroi), 160, 161, 164. *See also* Fourth Army, French

Lanrezac, Charles Louis Marie: in Alsace-Lorraine, 88; and Ardennes, 132, 142–45, 150; and British-French relations, 185; as Fifth Army commander, 63, 135; firing of, 195, 314; and French war plans, 174, 175; French's relationship with, 140–41, 176–77; and German buildup in Belgium, 133, 135–37, 138, 140–41; and German invasion of Belgium, 129; Joffre's meetings with, 184–85, 194; and Joffre's reassessment of campaign, 194; Joffre's relationship with, 135, 184–85, 314; and Mons, 153, 155; personal and professional background of, 135; reputation of, 63; and Saint-Quentin battle, 183, 184–85, 187, 188, 189, 192, 195, 218, 221; and Saint-Quentin meeting, 175–77, 194; and Sambre-et-Meuse (Charleroi), 151, 152, 160, 161, 164, 165, 169, 176, 234

Larisch, Alexander von, 164, 231, 258, 261
Lartigue, Raoul de, 241, 248, 253, 294
Lauenstein, Otto von: awards and promotions for, 281; and Battle of the Marne, 252, 275–76; and Charleroi, 151, 152; death of, 281; fitness to command of, 280–81; and German retreat from the Marne, 275–76, 277, 283, 284, 303; health of, 300, 312; and Hentsch tour, 273, 275–76, 277; and Saint-Quentin, 186, 187, 188–89
Le Cateau, Battle of, 177, 182–83, 218, 282
Lefèvre, Jules, 146, 149
Lefèvre, Justinien, 187, 207, 258, 305, 315
Legrand-Girarde, Émile-Edmond, 86, 174, 207, 255, 258, 295, 296, 314
Leman, Gérard Mathieu, 72, 108, 109–10, 111, 112, 113, 117

Leopold (king of Belgium), 71
Lepel, Rudolf von, 247, 250, 263, 264, 265, 277
Levillain, Georges, 203, 314
Lichnowsky, Prince Karl von, 14, 15, 22, 114
Liège (Lüttich): Belgian troops in, 108, 109–10; as Belgium fortress, 71; and Belgium war plans, 71; casualties at, 110, 111, 112, 117; defenses of, 107–8; and deployment of Belgian Army, 72, 73; forts surrounding, 107–8, 109, 112, 116–17; German attack on, 108–17; German ultimatum concerning, 71; and German war plans, 43; history of, 107–8; honors for, 110; Ludendorff's study of, 105, 107; and mobilization in Germany, 51; preparedness of, 72
Lindemann, Karl von, 164, 165
Linsingen, Alexander von, 124, 182, 221, 224, 243, 247, 264, 276
literati, 25, 32–33
Lloyd George, David, 19, 22, 24, 66, 67
Lochow, Ewald von, 153, 154, 182, 221, 248, 263, 290
Longwy, Battle of. *See* Ardennes
Lorraine. *See* Alsace-Lorraine
Louis XIV (king of France), 21, 32, 70, 75, 129
Louvain: and German invasion of Belgium, 126–28
Ludendorff, Erich, 105, 107, 109, 112–13, 114, 115, 117, 217, 283
Ludwig III (king of Bavaria), 82, 99, 205
Luxembourg: and British decision to go to war, 22; and French war plans, 56; and German buildup in Belgium, 138; German invasion of, 22, 108; and German war plans, 34; and mobilization in Germany, 51; as OHL headquarters, 171; Potsdam "war council" discussion about, 14–15
Lyautey, Hubert, 28–29
Lyncker, Moriz von, 121, 170–71, 199, 284, 286, 301, 312

MacDonald, Ramsay, 22
mail, 101–2
Mallet, Christian, 165, 293
Mangin, Charles, 61, 165–66
Margerie, Pierre de, 16, 17
Marlborough, Duke of, 70, 107
Marne: drive to the, 210–24; French operation plan for the, 227–30;

Born in Hamburg, Germany, on 25 September 1941, HOLGER H. HERWIG holds a dual position at the University of Calgary as professor of history and as Canada research chair in the Centre for Military and Strategic Studies. He received his BA (1965) from the University of British Columbia and his MA (1967) and PhD (1971) from the State University of New York at Stony Brook. Dr. Herwig taught at Vanderbilt University in Nashville, Tennessee, from 1971 until 1989. He served as head of the Department of History at Calgary from 1991 until 1996.

Dr. Herwig has published more than a dozen scholarly books, some of which have been translated into Chinese, Czech, German, Polish, Serbo-Croatian, and Spanish, including the prizewinning *The First World War: Germany and Austria-Hungary 1914–1918* and *The Origins of World War I*, with Richard Hamilton.